CHARTERED
PROFESSIONAL
ACCOUNTANTS
CANADA

D0668491

The Procrastinator's Guide to Retirement

How YOU can retire in 10 years or less

Part of CPA Canada's Financial Literacy Series

David Trahair, CPA, CA

CPA Canada's Financial Literacy Publications

cpacanada.ca/financialliteracypublications

A Canadian's Guide to Money-Smart Living

Take control of your financial future with this award-winning guide. It is easy-to-understand and will help you make money management a part of your daily life with easy action steps and self-assessment checklists.

Parent's Guide to Raising Money-Smart Kids

Learn how to teach your kids the importance of learning about money by guiding them through the five aspects of money management. From young children through to emerging adults, this national best-selling guide provides suggestions for discussions and activities that will help you talk to your kids about money in terms they will understand.

Protecting You and Your Money: A guide to preventing identity theft and fraud

This award-winning guide will help you take action against identity theft and fraud. Find out how to protect yourself by preventing fraud, identify current scams and avoid them, recapture your life if your identity has been stolen, and find where to go for help and support.

Acknowledgments

I'd like to start off by thanking the one person responsible for the creation of this book, Cairine Wilson, Vice-President of Corporate Citizenship, CPA Canada. I have written this book because of Cairine's vision to improve financial literacy throughout Canada.

I'd also like to thank the many people who have contributed their wisdom to the content of the book. That list includes Kurt Rosentreter (**www.kurtismycfo.com**), Warren MacKenzie (**www.highviewfin.com**), Ron Graham (**www.rgafinancial.com**), Doug Runchey (**www.drpensions.ca**), Robb Engen (**www.boomer andecho.com**), Preet Banerjee (**www.wheredoesallmymoneygo. com**) and Paul Tyers (**www.wealthstewards.ca**).

I'd also like to thank Deborah Klotz of Research Dimensions (**www.researchdimensions.com**) for arranging, conducting and reporting on the valuable focus groups on the early drafts of this book and the many participants of my personal finance courses over the years who have provided excellent feedback that is an integral part of this book!

I'd also like to thank my literary agent Hilary McMahon of Westwood Creative Artists (**www.wcaltd.com**) for her exemplary work on my behalf, Maggie Tyson, Manager, Editorial Development for CPA Canada for her excellent editing of this book and Michael Dave Dizon, Art Director for CPA Canada, for his creative design.

And last but not least, I'd like to thank the person who, years ago, gave me the title of this book: Kristina Klausen, founder/CEO of PandaTree. At the time I knew it was a good title, but I hadn't written the book to go with it yet!

Table of Contents

PART TWO
The Retirement Years

CHAPTER 6
How Much Will You Spend During Retirement?

CHAPTER 13
Old Age Healthcare Planning

Introduction

If you and your spouse are approaching retirement and have maximized your RRSPs, contributed the limit to your Tax-Free Savings Accounts, have no credit card or other consumer debt, have paid off your mortgage and perhaps even started saving outside your RRSP and TFSA, you are in great shape financially!

If not, this book has been created for you, especially if you hope to retire in ten years or less and have the following concerns:
- There is just so much demand for our cash these days, the mortgage, car loan, house repairs, utilities, food, raising the kids, insurance, etc., and we have a tough time just paying off our credit cards each month!
- Where do we get the thousands of dollars we are supposed to be putting into our RRSPs each year?
- We've thought about putting money in our TFSAs, but does that make sense if we are in debt?
- We have kids we hope will go to university. We know we can put up to $2,500 in an RESP for each child in order to maximize the Canada Education Savings Grant, but where will that money come from?
- We're supposed to pay off the mortgage before retirement, how is that possible?

For the vast majority of us, doing all those things is impossible. There just isn't enough money to do it all, so that means you will have to prioritize.

That is why I wrote this book—to show you how to do it. I will use the knowledge gained from decades of studying personal finances, the four books I have already written on the subject, and the feedback from the thousands of people who have taken my courses.

I'm going to guide you through the maze of retirement issues and point you in a clear direction to help you to live comfortably in your retirement.

This book is aimed at those who have less than ten years to go before retirement, i.e., those who are fifty-plus with a retirement plan that needs some work!

PART ONE

Ten Years or Less to Retirement

CHAPTER 1
The Key: Tracking Your Current Spending

There is a rule of thumb that says you'll need 70% of your pre-retirement income to maintain your standard of living after you stop working. If only it was that simple!

The "70% rule" is problematic—it may be the right answer for one person but totally wrong for you, because your financial situation is as individual as your fingerprints. Everyone is different, so relying on a simple rule of thumb is dangerous because you could end up saving too little (or even too much!). Relying on simple rules could end up devastating your retirement plans.

For many of you with a limited number of years left before you retire, the 70% rule may cause significant stress because saving enough to generate 70% of your income for a reasonable number of retirement years is going to be very difficult.

However, there is a more accurate and simple way to determine how much you'll need to fund your retirement. It is easy to do and will ensure your retirement is financially comfortable, but you will need to spend a few hours following a step-by-step method to secure your financial future.

This book can show you how.

How Much Do You Spend?

To start calculating how much you'll need to finance your retirement, you'll need to know how much you are going to spend during your retirement.

First, you need to know how much you spend now. Then you can make an objective projection of what you will spend during retirement. This is the problem with most of our retirement plans; we don't track our current spending so we end up guessing about the future. Without tracking your current spending, you end up using a best guess, and that is not a good foundation upon which to build a retirement plan.

Once you start tracking your family's spending, it won't take very long to get an accurate picture of how much you spend. You'll need to invest a few hours a year but it is the best way to ensure a comfortable retirement. **Appendix 1** provides you with a step-by-step guide (see **Appendices** after **Chapter 20**).

Meet Mike and Nancy Clark

To illustrate the strategies in this book, we will use a fictitious couple as an example: Mike and Nancy Clark.

- Mike is 55, Nancy is 53, they have a son, Joe, who is 21 and in his fourth year at university, and a daughter, Sophia, who is 17 and is in grade 12
- Mike's gross salary is $80,000 a year and Nancy's is $50,000, both Joe and Sophia have part-time jobs
- They own a home worth $400,000 with a $300,000 mortgage with 20 years of payments until it's paid off
- They have one car which is financed by a four-year loan
- Their only savings are in their RRSPs: Mike's RRSP has a current market value of $100,000 and Nancy's is $50,000
- They had a family Registered Education Savings Plan (RESP), but they used it all to finance Joe's education during his first three years of university
- Mike and Nancy both hope to retire in 10 years when Mike is 65 and Nancy is 63.

The following table is a summary of their spending during the past year.

The Clarks

Annual Expenses - Current		% of Total
Taxes and Withholdings		
Income tax	26,568	20%
CPP contributions	4,728	4%
EI contributions	1,828	1%
	33,124	**25%**
Auto		
Auto fuel	2,340	2%
Auto general	350	0%
Auto insurance	1,200	1%
Auto loan	6,751	5%
Auto license & registration	180	0%
Auto repairs & maintenance	400	0%
	11,221	**9%**
Children		
University tuition	5,200	4%
University rent	5,000	4%
University books etc.	1,200	1%
University meals & entertainment	4,000	3%
High school trips, lessons etc.	2,000	2%
	17,400	**13%**
Family		
Cash withdrawals	7,000	5%
Clothing	4,000	3%
Donations	300	0%
Entertainment	900	1%
Groceries	8,000	6%
Insurance (life, income protection)	2,635	2%
Meals out	3,500	3%
Medical and dental	1,000	1%
Miscellaneous	1,000	1%
Vacation	6,000	5%
	34,335	**26%**
House		
Mortgage	21,753	16%
House insurance	1,200	1%
Utilities (heat, hydro)	3,510	3%
Property tax	3,500	3%
House repairs & maintenance	2,900	2%
Security	440	0%
Phone and cable	1,440	1%
	34,743	**26%**
Interest and bank charges		
Bank charges	120	0%
Credit card interest	1,000	1%
	1,120	**1%**
TOTAL EXPENSES	**131,943**	**100%**

Total gross income	130,000	
Total expenses	131,943	
Shortfall	**-1,943**	

This is what you need to create for your family, but first let's review the Clarks' finances.

If you look at the bottom line (their income versus their spending) their gross salaries combined are $130,000 but they spent $131,943, so they spent $1,943 more than they made last year (and that is during a year in which they did not make any RRSP contributions).

Spending more than you make is easy, all you need is a credit card. The Clarks use credit cards and have built up a balance of $5,000 over the past few years which they can't afford to pay off. As a result, they paid $1,000 in interest (at 20%) to the credit card company. If they continue spending like this for the next 10 years until their retirement, the prognosis for their golden years is not good. Like most other Canadians, the 10 years before they retire is going to be a key decade for the Clarks.

Many people are setting themselves up for failure because they don't track their spending. As a result, they don't realize their spending exceeds their income, so it will be impossible for them to organize their finances before they retire.

But all is not lost, if you start planning now, a relaxing retirement is still possible.

For the Clarks, their priority has to be paying off their credit card balance, which means that they must target their expenses and reduce some of them so they can find the money to pay off the balance.

Focus on Expenses

Even though the list we just looked at has grouped the expenses, it can be a little overwhelming to try and analyze. If you use an Excel spreadsheet, it is easy to list and rearrange expense items. You need to focus on your biggest expenses to maximize your efforts to control them, so creating a list with your expenses arranged from largest to smallest will really help you.

Here is that list for the Clarks.

The Clarks
Annual Expenses - Current

		% of Total
Income tax	26,568	20%
Mortgage	21,753	16%
Groceries	8,000	6%
Cash withdrawals	7,000	5%
Auto loan	6,751	5%
Vacation	6,000	5%
University tuition	5,200	4%
University rent	5,000	4%
CPP contributions	4,728	4%
Clothing	4,000	3%
University meals & entertainment	4,000	3%
Utilities (heat, hydro)	3,510	3%
Meals out	3,500	3%
Property tax	3,500	3%
House repairs & maintenance	2,900	2%
Insurance (life, income protection)	2,635	2%
Auto fuel	2,340	2%
High school trips, lessons etc.	2,000	2%
EI contributions	1,828	1%
Phone and cable	1,440	1%
Auto insurance	1,200	1%
House insurance	1,200	1%
University books etc.	1,200	1%
Credit card interest	1,000	1%
Medical and dental	1,000	1%
Miscellaneous	1,000	1%
Entertainment	900	1%
Security	440	0%
Auto repairs & maintenance	400	0%
Auto general	350	0%
Donations	300	0%
Auto license & registration	180	0%
Bank charges	120	0%
TOTAL EXPENSES	**131,943**	**100%**

The results are interesting: income tax is by far the biggest expense, representing 20% of their total outflows.

The top 10 items (income tax, mortgage, groceries, cash withdrawals, auto loan, vacation, university tuition, university rent, CPP contributions and clothing) total $95,000, which is 72% of the total.

Their focus should be on which of the top 10 they can eliminate or reduce. Let's look at each of them.

1. Income Tax

Since neither Mike nor Nancy is self-employed, there is not a lot of opportunity for them to split income with each other or their kids. Unfortunately, taxes are a necessity if we want to live in a civilized country and there is not a lot the Clarks can do to significantly cut this amount. However, in later chapters we will see that there are important strategies they can employ that will ensure their tax bill is as low as possible during their retirement.

2. Mortgage

The Clarks are locked into a five-year mortgage so there is not a lot they can do to reduce their mortgage payments at the moment. (See the options for paying off your mortgage in **Chapter 3**.)

3. Groceries

Maybe they could cut the cost of their groceries, but everyone has to eat. Cutting this expense may lead to increased spending at restaurants and for take-out food. It may make sense for some people to spend MORE on groceries because, if the fridge is well stocked, they are less likely to pick up the phone to order take-out food or go to a restaurant.

However, Joe (their son) has graduated from university this year, found a job and moved out, so he won't be eating at home. Their daughter, Sophia, is starting university in September and the cost of her meals while at school is reflected under the category "university meals & entertainment." As a result, the Clarks' grocery bill is predicted to decline by $2,000 to $6,000 in the coming year.

4. Cash Withdrawals

The Clarks withdrew $7,000 in cash during the year and spent it. Where did all that money go?

They don't know, like most Canadians. For many people this is a huge opportunity to find where money is being wasted. One option for those who can handle credit is to use as little cash as possible. This means that you will have to pay using a credit or debit card, so the supplier's name will appear on your bank and credit card statements and you'll have a good idea of what the money was used for. (**NOTE:** this is a bad idea for people who can't handle credit, so if you have problems paying off your credit card, don't put more on the card to reduce your use of cash.)

 TIP

> Another option is to get a cash-tracking app for your smart phone. I use one called "CashTrails" on my iPhone. This option is better than trying to keep receipts for every dime you spend. Simply enter the amount of cash you spend each day, select a category, and the app can email you a summary at the end of each month.

It's possible that Mike and Nancy could save thousands of dollars each year if they can become aware of where the money is going. Remember, you are more likely to change your spending behaviour if you track your spending because you will be informed and motivated, and being financially healthy is a great motivator!

So Mike and Nancy decide to track their cash spending and are successful in reducing it by $1,000, so their cash withdrawals are only $6,000 during the next year.

5. Auto Loan

As with the mortgage, they are locked into a four-year car loan, so there is not much they can do to reduce this expense now.

NOTE: As your car acquisition strategy is important for your retirement plans, in **Chapter 16** we will discuss the benefits of buying versus leasing a car.

6. Vacation

The Clarks spent $6,000 (5% of their total spending) on their vacation, a significant amount. Because they enjoy their annual vacation with their kids, and there aren't going to be too many future opportunities for family vacations (Joe is graduating and moving out of the family home this year), the Clarks determine that they do not want to reduce this amount next year.

7. University Tuition

Joe is in his fourth year at university and his tuition fees for his last semester (from January to April) is estimated to be $2,600. Sophia's tuition for her first semester (from September to December) is also estimated to be $2,600, so the Clarks will be paying a total of $5,200 this year. Sophia's fees are estimated to grow by 2% to $5,304 next year, so there won't be an opportunity to reduce this expense.

8. University Rent

Joe is living in a house with a few of his buddies while he is at university. His rent for the last four months is estimated to be $2,000 ($500 a month). Sophia will be living in residence in September and her estimated costs are $3,000 for this year. Next year Sophia's total costs are estimated to be $5,100.

 TIP

Unfortunately, students who live in houses or apartments while at university usually have to pay rent for all 12 months of the year to ensure they have a place to stay for the eight months they are in school. This means that moving out of residence (where you only pay for eight months) to live in a house or apartment often doesn't result in any large savings.

9. CPP Contributions

The Clarks can't avoid paying into their CPP plans since they earn salaries. The good news is that this is not really an expense. It is basically a forced retirement savings plan that for many people will be an important part of their retirement income. The Clarks can't do anything about this amount as it is determined by their incomes.

10. Clothing

This is a key discretionary expense. We need clothes and most of us would like to wear the latest fashions, but is it really necessary for the Clarks to spend $4,000 each year? Mike and Nancy decide to stop and think before buying any new clothes and make sure they look for bargains at the right time of year. They decide to reduce the amount spent by $1,000 in each of the next two years.

A Zero Credit Card Balance: Priceless

Having reviewed their expenses, in the next year the Clarks aim to:

* spend $2,000 less on groceries
* save $1,000 in reduced cash withdrawals
* reduce their clothing expenses by $1,000
* save $2,000 on Sophia's high school trips and lessons (she is going to university)

So they will reduce their spending by $6,000 next year, resulting in an excess cash flow of $4,461. That amount can go directly to paying down their credit card balance from $5,000 to $539, so they will have no credit card debt at the end of the next year.

However, the Clarks' credit card balance is fairly low in relation to their incomes, so they are in relatively good shape financially, unlike many others who are carrying a large amount of consumer debt, which is a big problem for them.

Over the past few years the balances on credit cards and lines of credit that Canadians have been carrying has grown at an alarming rate, so **Chapter 14** is dedicated to eliminating debt.

CHAPTER 2

Your Golden Opportunity: When Expenses Decline

Introduction

During the next year, the Clarks will have one focus: to get rid of their credit card balance. They need to forget saving for retirement, forget trying to pay down the mortgage, forget TFSA contributions. But what about the remaining years until their retirement? From a financial point of view, the last nine years before they retire are going to be the most important of their lives. This is the make-or-break period for their retirement plans.

The following chart shows a projection of their spending during Years 1 through 10 (see next page).

THE CLARKS
Annual Expenses
(Current Inflation 2%)

EXPENSES	Year 0	Year 1	Year 2	Year 3	Year 4	Year 5	Year 6	Year 7	Year 8	Year 9	Year 10
Mike Age	55	56	57	58	59	60	61	62	63	64	65
Taxes and withholdings	33,124	33,579	34,040	34,508	34,980	35,456	35,924	36,424	36,930	37,440	37,975
Auto	11,221	11,311	11,402	11,495	4,838	5,495	6,085	3,707	11,922	12,025	12,130
Children	17,400	15,708	16,022	16,342	8,334	0	0	0	0	0	0
Family	34,335	30,618	30,905	32,200	32,499	29,182	29,361	29,545	29,732	29,922	30,117
House	34,743	35,003	35,267	35,537	35,813	36,095	36,382	36,674	36,973	37,277	37,588
Interest and bank charges	1,120	620	120	120	120	120	120	120	120	120	120
TOTAL EXPENSES	**131,943**	**126,839**	**127,756**	**130,202**	**116,584**	**106,348**	**107,872**	**106,470**	**115,677**	**116,784**	**117,930**
COMBINED GROSS SALARIES	130,000	131,300	132,613	133,939	135,278	136,630	137,997	139,377	140,771	142,178	143,600
(SHORT) EXCESS INCOME	**-1,943**	**4,461**	**4,857**	**3,737**	**18,694**	**30,282**	**30,125**	**32,907**	**25,094**	**25,394**	**25,670**

Please note: In this chart we have made the following assumptions:
- inflation is estimated to be 2% per year
- their salaries grow at 1% per year
- estimated income tax, CPP and EI withholdings are at 2014 Ontario rates
- most expenses increase at the rate of inflation, except for the auto loan and mortgage (which are based on the loan rates and terms) and discretionary items (including cash withdrawals, clothing, donations, entertainment, interest and bank charges that depend on debt balances)

For a more detailed version of this spreadsheet, please see **www.trahair.com** or **cpacanada.ca/retirement**.

Attack Credit Card Debt First

During Year 1, the excess income they have is $4,461. This is much better than the $1,943 shortfall they had last year and the entire amount is used to pay down the $5,000 credit card balance to $539.

In Year 2, the excess is $4,857 and $539 of that is used to pay off the credit card balance. The remaining $4,318 is put into the Clarks' bank account.

The Golden Opportunity Years

In Year 3, the excess is $3,737. This excess also goes into their bank account.

Then some really good news: in Year 4 the surplus rises to $18,694 and during Years 5 through 10, the surpluses are greater than $25,000 each year. In fact, the total excess money they will have during Years 4 to 10 will be an astounding $188,166. How did this amazing development happen? Let's look at the details.

First of all, their salaries will increase each year by 1%. Their combined gross salaries go from $135,278 in the Year 4 to $143,600 in Year 10. After taking off income tax, CPP and EI, their net pay has gone from $100,298 to $105,625 during the same period. That's an increase of $5,327.

Why did the excess in Year 4 increase so much? Because the Clarks paid off the car loan that was costing $6,751 each year. Then they had four years with a paid off car and only had to cover the operating costs and repairs and maintenance. It is assumed they bought another similar car in Year 8 and started annual payments of $6,751.

But the really big increase in the excess income is during Year 5. That is when their daughter, Sophia, graduates from university. Spending on her education will go from $16,342 in Year 3, to $8,334 in Year 4 to zero in Year 5. If you have children in university, the year they graduate will probably have a significantly positive impact on your personal finances.

But there are other savings as well: hopefully in Year 5 Sophia will be earning her own money so Mike and Nancy's spending on her will go down (even if she moves back home for a few years). We therefore estimate that cash withdrawals, clothing and grocery costs will each decline by $1,000 per year starting in Year 5.

Years 2 through 10 are the golden opportunity years for the Clarks. What they do with the excess money earned during Years 2 through 10 will make or break their retirement plans. If they simply increase their spending during those years, they are dooming their future. If they spend it all, they will be sentencing themselves to watching every penny for the rest of their lives. You don't want that to happen to you!

Dealing with Excess Funds

What should they do with the extra funds? They have three main options:

- make RRSP contributions
- pay down the mortgage
- make TFSA contributions

Let's look at the TFSA as an option versus an RRSP.

Tax-Free Savings Account (TFSA)

The TFSA was introduced in 2009 for Canadian residents aged 18 years and older. From 2009 to 2012 you could contribute up to $5,000 to your TFSA. In 2013 and 2014 the annual amount was $5,500 per year and in 2015 it was raised to $10,000, so if you have not made any contributions prior to 2015, your TFSA room is $41,000.

TFSA TIPS

- Contributions and interest on any money borrowed to invest in TFSAs is not tax deductible. All income generated is tax-free even when amounts are withdrawn from your TFSA.
- If you withdraw an amount from your TFSA in a calendar year, the amount you withdraw is added to your contribution room the next calendar year.

TFSA TRAP

Remember that if you transfer an existing investment from a regular taxable investment account to a TFSA there is a "deemed disposition." In other words, you are deemed to have sold the investment upon the transfer, even though you didn't, so you could end up having to declare and pay tax on any capital gain if the investment you are transferring is worth more than you paid for it. Also, if the stock is worth less, you are not allowed to take a capital loss on the transfer.

TFSA or RRSP?

Whether it is best to invest in a TFSA or an RRSP (where you get a tax deduction) generally depends on your tax situation. If you are in a medium-to-high tax bracket when you make an RRSP contribution and a lower tax bracket when you withdraw the RRSP funds (and pay tax on the withdrawal), RRSPs are usually the better option.

On the other hand, if you are in your twenties in a low tax bracket, and you will be in a higher tax bracket when you withdraw the funds (e.g., in retirement), a TFSA usually makes more sense than an RRSP.

In the Clarks' case, Mike makes $80,000 per year and Nancy makes $50,000. Here are their marginal tax rates in each province (in 2015).

Marginal Tax Rates

	Mike	Nancy
Alberta	32%	32%
British Columbia	32.5%	29.7%
Manitoba	39.4%	34.75%
New Brunswick	38.52%	36.82%
Newfoundland and Labrador	35.3%	34.5%
Nova Scotia	38.67%	36.95%
Northwest Territories	34.2%	30.6%
Nunavut	29%	29%
Ontario	32.98%	31.15%
Prince Edward Island	38.7%	35.8%
Quebec	38.37%	38.37%
Saskatchewan	35%	35%
Yukon	31%	31%

Later we will see that the Clarks are both going to be in lower tax brackets after they retire, so the RRSP seems to be the better option for them.

The next question is: contribute to their RRSPs or pay down the mortgage?

This is a more complex question, so we will look at it in **Chapter 3**.

CHAPTER 3

RRSP versus Paying Down the Mortgage

If you have extra cash to invest, choosing to invest in your RRSP or pay down your mortgage are both good options. However, if you have other consumer debt such as a credit card balance, you need to consider paying it off before you make a decision regarding your RRSP versus your mortgage. It all depends on your personal situation, so we'll look at that now.

What Debt Have You Got?

The question never seems to be "Should I contribute to my RRSP or pay down my credit card debt which is charging me 20% in interest per year?" That's because the answer to that question is obvious—anyone with a revolving credit card balance at a high rate of interest should **not** be making RRSP contributions. You are never going to consistently beat a 20% annual rate of return after taxes and fees by investing in any portfolio today. But you would get that rate of return simply by getting rid of your debt.

How can you get a rate of return by paying off debt? It's simple: a lack of a cash outflow is as good as a cash inflow, and better if that cash inflow is taxed. Let's look at an example to explain this.

EXAMPLE

You have a credit card balance of $10,000 which you can't afford to pay off in full. If the interest rate is 20%, you'll have to pay $2,000 in interest in one year. If you had an investment of $10,000, it would need to generate a return of greater than 20% for you to break even, because you'd have to pay tax on the income and be left with $2,000 after tax.

For example, if you were in a 30% marginal tax bracket (for each additional dollar you made you'd have to pay $0.30 in tax) and you had an investment of $10,000, you would need to generate income of $2,857 (a return of 28.6%) just to break even. That's because you'd have to pay 30% tax on the income of $2,857, which is $857, leaving you with $2,000. How likely are you to find something that is going to pay you that kind of return? Not very likely.

So by paying off the credit card you achieve an after-tax rate of return of 20%, which in this case is equivalent to achieving a 28.6% rate of return before tax on an investment.

 TIP

Anyone with credit card debt at a rate of 20% or higher should call their credit card issuer immediately and switch to a basic card without all the bells, whistles and points. This simple move will probably save you 10% or more in reduced rates. Better still, shop around for the best rate. Many competing financial institutions offer balance transfer options at low, or sometimes even zero, rates. We'll discuss this in more detail in **Chapter 19**.

If You Only Have a Mortgage

So when we ask ourselves the question "Should I contribute to my RRSP or pay down the mortgage?" we assume there is no ugly high-interest debt, only a mortgage. This is the position the Clarks would be in after they paid off their $5,000 credit card balance. What should they do?

The common sense answer is to make the RRSP contribution and use the tax refund to pay down the mortgage. This sounds like a great idea as you get the best of both worlds, but it's not really as simple as that.

I have created a spreadsheet called the "RRSP vs Pay Down Debt" calculator. It is a Microsoft Excel spreadsheet where you can enter the variables in your own personal situation to determine the optimal solution. (You can download it free from my website at **www.trahair.com** or at **cpacanada.ca/retirement**).

Let's use a simple example to illustrate how to use it.

EXAMPLE

- You have a mortgage with a balance greater than $10,000 and you are allowed to pay it down by $10,000.
- You have $10,000 cash available, you are in a 35% marginal tax bracket now as well as when you cash in your RRSP.
- Assume a 4% rate of return after fees on your RRSP and a 4% effective annual rate on the mortgage.
- Focus on a 10-year period as we are doing for the Clarks.

One option is to pay down the mortgage with your $10,000 available cash. If you did this, you would have nothing in your RRSP and $10,000 less on your mortgage for the 10-year period.

The alternative is to make a $10,000 RRSP contribution and with the income tax refund of $3,500 you pay down the mortgage by $3,500.

In 10 years your $10,000 RRSP will grow at 4%, compounded annually, to $14,802. You then withdraw the money and pay tax at the 35% marginal tax rate. That leaves you with $9,622 cash in hand.

So what happened to the mortgage? It grew at 4% per year compounded annually over the 10-year period. After 10 years, the $6,500 mortgage ($10,000 less the $3,500 tax refund you paid it down by) grew to $9,622, which is the $6,500 original amount plus $3,122 of total accumulated interest.

If you used the $9,622 cash in hand from cashing in your RRSP to pay off the mortgage, you would be in the same position as if you simply paid off the mortgage in the first year.

Here is a screen shot of the RRSP vs Pay Down Debt calculator for this scenario:

RRSP versus Pay Down Debt

Assumptions

Cash available	$10,000
Personal marginal income tax rate now	35.00%
Personal marginal income tax rate on withdrawal	35.00%
Interest rate on debt	4.00%
Annual growth rate of RRSP	4.00%

RRSP

	Year 1	Year 2	Year 3	Year 4	Year 5	Year 6	Year 7	Year 8	Year 9	Year 10
RRSP contribution	$10,000									
RRSP refund	-$3,500									
After-tax RRSP cash outflow	$6,500									
Beginning RRSP value	$10,000	$10,400	$10,816	$11,249	$11,699	$12,167	$12,653	$13,159	$13,686	$14,233
RRSP growth during year	$400	$416	$433	$450	$468	$487	$506	$526	$547	$569
Ending RRSP value	$10,400	$10,816	$11,249	$11,699	$12,167	$12,653	$13,159	$13,686	$14,233	$14,802

AFTER-TAX FUNDS ON RRSP WITHDRAWAL

	Year 10
RRSP withdrawal	$14,802
Tax on RRSP withdrawal	-$5,180
After-tax funds on RRSP withdrawal	$9,622

DEBT

	Year 1	Year 2	Year 3	Year 4	Year 5	Year 6	Year 7	Year 8	Year 9	Year 10
Original debt balance	$10,000									
RRSP refund applied	-$3,500									
Balance of debt after tax refund applied	$6,500	$6,760	$7,030	$7,312	$7,604	$7,908	$8,225	$8,554	$8,896	$9,252
Interest on debt	$260	$270	$281	$292	$304	$316	$329	$342	$356	$370
Cumulative interest on debt	$260	$530	$812	$1,104	$1,408	$1,725	$2,054	$2,396	$2,752	$3,122

BALANCE OF DEBT AFTER 10 YEARS

Total interest accrued in 10 year period	$3,122
Original principal of loan that needs to be paid	$6,500
Balance of debt after 10 year period	$9,622

EXCESS (SHORTFALL) OF RRSP VS DEBT	$0

Key Variable: Marginal Tax Rates

Here is the key point: the example we just went through assumes the marginal tax rate remains the same during the 10-year period and that the RRSP grows at the same rate as the interest rate on the mortgage.

Under this scenario, the answer to the question comes down to whether you think the after-fee rate of return on your RRSP investments is going to beat the rate of interest on your mortgage. But if the marginal tax rate is lower when the RRSP withdrawal is made, the RRSP wins. If the marginal rate is higher upon withdrawal, paying down the mortgage wins.

In our example, if your marginal tax rate is 46% now and only 35% when you withdraw your RRSP, the RRSP option wins by $1,628. If the situation was reversed and your marginal rate is 35% now and 46% upon withdrawal, the mortgage pay down wins by the exact same amount.

For most people, their marginal tax rate will be lower when they withdraw from their RRSP, so the RRSP is often the best option —at least it looks that way on paper.

> **EXAMPLE**
> Your marginal tax rate is 45% at the time of the RRSP contribution and 35% upon withdrawal ten years later. If the mortgage interest rate was 4%, the RRSP annual rate of return required would only need to be 2.28%. That is because the higher initial tax refund that was used to pay down the mortgage means the RRSP does not need to grow to as high an amount to pay off the mortgage at the end.

Beyond the Numbers

Reducing personal financial decisions to numbers on a spreadsheet is always a good start. But you have to dig deeper in your financial decisions because human nature can have a powerful impact. Often other factors outweigh what the numbers show. Let me explain.

There are several advantages to opting to pay down the mortgage instead of making RRSP contributions that aren't clear when looking at a simple spreadsheet.

1. Rate of Return

First of all, the rate of return on the mortgage is guaranteed. You know what return you are going to make because the interest rate is set. With an RRSP your rate of return is unknown. Your investments might do well but, in today's environment, how confident can you be about that?

That's the problem with the spreadsheet, it's easy to optimistically insert a great rate of return that you hope you'll get but, if you don't actually make it, you've made a decision based on a false assumption.

2. Marginal Tax Rates

This is less of an issue because most people will be in a lower tax bracket when they retire, but that may not be your case. For example, you may be unfortunate enough to be laid off and have to access your RRSP in a year when you still have significant taxable income before you retire. That's when RRSPs don't work so well for you.

3. Will You Ever Pay Off Your Mortgage?

This is perhaps the most important reason for prioritizing debt reduction ahead of RRSP investing. If you convince yourself that your RRSP is going to do very well, it takes the pressure off paying down your mortgage. In other words, if you decide the RRSP is the better option, you tend to reduce the importance of paying off your mortgage.

You may worry less about getting a home equity line of credit to finance a home renovation, for example. You may even decide to extend your mortgage amortization period (the time to pay it off), and you may be less concerned about retiring with a mortgage.

If you rank paying down your mortgage ahead of your RRSP, you'll be much more focused on reducing the balance and much more likely to pay it off before you retire.

Paying off your mortgage essentially forces you to be fiscally prudent. It makes you live within your means and spend less than you make, because you can't pay down your mortgage if you have no money!

Carrying a Mortgage into Retirement

Putting RRSP contributions ahead of paying down the mortgage means that you are choosing to carry the mortgage for a longer period of time. If you can afford to make RRSP contributions and are on schedule to pay off your mortgage by retirement, you're fine. Don't change a thing.

If, however, you are planning to go into retirement with a mortgage, I'd like you to spend a few minutes thinking about the consequences. You are choosing to shackle yourself with monthly payments after your income has declined. How are you going to pay those amounts on a lower fixed retirement income? It will probably be very stressful, to say the least.

We'll get into all the different sources of your retirement income in **Part 2** of this book, but effectively you'll need to have saved more money in your RRSP in order to pay your mortgage.

Let's look at how much more you'll need.

EXAMPLE

You have just retired and you have a $200,000 balance on your mortgage. Your mortgage is at 4% interest per year and has 10 years remaining until it is paid off. Your monthly mortgage payments are $2,021.77.

If you were in the 35% marginal tax bracket after retirement, your RRSP would have to pay out $3,110.42 per month so you'd have enough left to pay the mortgage. In other words, tax of $1,088.65 (35% of $3,110.42) would need to be paid, leaving $2,021.77 each month to pay the mortgage.

How large an RRSP would you need at retirement to pay out $3,110.42 a month for 10 years? Assuming the RRSP grows at 5% a year from retirement for each of the 10 years, the answer is $293,254.75.

So, if you went into retirement with a $200,000 mortgage, you'd need $293,254.75 extra in your RRSP just to break even. And that assumes you continue to make 5% after fees on your RRSP for the next 10 years.

Put another way, you'd then be just as well off as someone who had a zero mortgage balance and $293,254.75 less in their RRSP.

I have created another spreadsheet for you to use to do your own calculations. It's called the "RRSP Needed for Mortgage" calculator. (You can download it free from my website at **www.trahair.com** or at **cpacanada.ca/retirement**.)

Here is what the calculator has come up with for a range of options:

SUMMARY EXAMPLES	1	2	3	4	5	6
Original mortgage balance	$200,000.00	$200,000.00	$200,000.00	$200,000.00	$200,000.00	$200,000.00
Annual interest rate	4.00%	4.00%	4.00%	4.00%	4.00%	5.00%
Term (years)	10	15	10	10	10	10
Marginal tax bracket	35.00%	35.00%	35.00%	25.00%	45.00%	40.00%
RRSP annual rate of return	5.00%	5.00%	3.00%	5.00%	4.00%	3.00%
Monthly payment (calculated)	$2,021.77	$1,476.08	$2,021.77	$2,021.77	$2,021.77	$2,116.30
RRSP monthly pre-tax amount needed	$3,110.42	$2,270.89	$3,110.42	$2,695.70	$3,675.95	$3,527.16
RRSP NEEDED AT RETIREMENT	**$293,254.75**	**$287,165.74**	**$322,120.71**	**$254,154.11**	**$363,074.50**	**$365,279.34**

You will notice that the size of the RRSP needed in each example moves in step with marginal tax rates. It increases as the marginal tax rate increases and decreases when it declines.

The RRSP needed, however, relates inversely to the rate of return your RRSP generates. As the rate of return on the RRSP decreases, the size of the RRSP needed increases, and *vice versa*.

Look at example #5 on the previous chart. If the marginal tax rate is 45% and the RRSP annual rate of return is only 4%, the RRSP balance needed going into retirement would be $363,074.50, fully $69,819.75 higher than the first example.

What Should the Clarks Do?

Let's have a look at the RRSP versus paying down the mortgage decision for the Clarks.

You'll recall we looked at their spending in relation to their income over a 10-year period and we found they made significant progress and had large cash surpluses in Years 4 through 10. To decide which option is best for them, we have to look at their financial situation at the beginning of the 10-year period compared to their situation at the end. That means we need to look at their net worth statement, i.e., their personal financial scorecard. The net worth statement summarizes their assets and their liabilities.

We will assume the following for the Clarks at the start of the Year 1:

- they have nothing in the bank
- their house is worth $400,000
- their mortgage was originally for $300,000 over a 20-year term and they are paying 4% interest, their balance was $289,967 with 19 years left to pay
- their house will appreciate at 2% per year
- they had $5,000 of credit card debt
- the credit card interest rate is 20% per year
- Mike's RRSP is worth $100,000 and Nancy's is worth $50,000
- their RRSPs will grow at 4% per year

Here is what the Clarks' net worth statement looks like at the start of Year 1 and at the end of Year 10 if they only put the excess cash in a bank account:

	Start of Year 1	End of Year 10
ASSETS		
Bank	$0	$196,221
House	$400,000	$487,598
RRSP—Mike	$100,000	$148,024
RRSP—Nancy	$50,000	$74,012
Total assets	**$550,000**	**$905,855**
LIABILITIES		
Mortgage	$289,967	$164,413
Credit card	$5,000	$0
Total liabilities	**$294,967**	**$164,413**
Net Worth	**$255,033**	**$741,442**

Their net worth has gone up significantly from $255,033 to $741,442 (an increase of $486,409, a significant amount). But this assumes the excess money they earn each year is put in a bank account that earns no interest. That would not be a good investment. The Clarks have two main options: make RRSP contributions or pay down the mortgage.

There are many variables that affect the calculation, so I have created a spreadsheet that you can use for your personal calculations. We'll look at it in **Chapter 4**.

CHAPTER 4

The Procrastinator's Number Cruncher

It is very unlikely that your financial situation is exactly the same as the Clarks, so I have created a customized spreadsheet to help you, the "Procrastinator's Number Cruncher." You can download it free of charge at **www.trahair.com** or at **cpacanada.ca/retirement**.

Procrastinator's Number Cruncher

When you open the spreadsheet, you'll see the following tabs at the bottom of the page:

- Home
- Questions
- Summary Results
- Detailed Results
  — AB (Alberta)
  — BC (British Columbia)
  — MB (Manitoba)
  — NB (New Brunswick)
  — NL (Newfoundland & Labrador)
  — NS (Nova Scotia)
  — NT (Northwest Territories)
  — NU (Nunavut)
  — ON (Ontario)
  — PE (Prince Edward Island)
  — QC (Quebec)
  — SK (Saskatchewan)
  — YK (Yukon)
- Assumptions
- TaxInfo

Home Tab

The Home Tab gives you some information about the spreadsheet and provides the version number (the date that the spreadsheet was last updated).

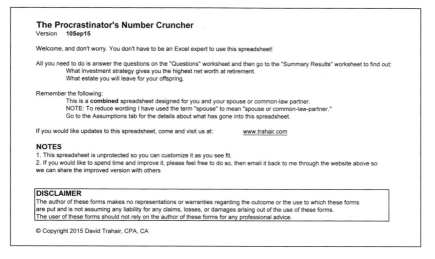

The Procrastinator's Number Cruncher
Version   10Sep15

Welcome, and don't worry. You don't have to be an Excel expert to use this spreadsheet!

All you need to do is answer the questions on the "Questions" worksheet and then go to the "Summary Results" worksheet to find out:
What investment strategy gives you the highest net worth at retirement.
What estate you will leave for your offspring.

Remember the following:
This is a **combined** spreadsheet designed for you and your spouse or common-law partner.
NOTE: To reduce wording I have used the term "spouse" to mean "spouse or common-law-partner."
Go to the Assumptions tab for the details about what has gone into this spreadsheet.

If you would like updates to this spreadsheet, come and visit us at: www.trahair.com

NOTES
1. This spreadsheet is unprotected so you can customize it as you see fit.
2. If you would like to spend time and improve it, please feel free to do so, then email it back to me through the website above so we can share the improved version with others

DISCLAIMER
The author of these forms makes no representations or warranties regarding the outcome or the use to which these forms are put and is not assuming any liability for any claims, losses, or damages arising out of the use of these forms. The user of these forms should not rely on the author of these forms for any professional advice.

© Copyright 2015 David Trahair, CPA, CA

Questions

This is the place for you to answer specific questions about your personal situation. The spreadsheet needs to know a lot about you and your spouse or common-law partner before it can perform the calculations to help you optimize your retirement situation.

Here are the questions you'll need to answer for each of you:

General

- Today's date
- Your last name
- Your first name
- Date of birth
- In what province/territory do you reside?

Income/Expenses

- What is your current total income from salary before expenses?
- If you wish your salary to increase, enter the annual rate (if not, enter 0).
- What is your current net income from self-employment?
- If you wish your self-employment earnings to increase, enter the annual rate (if not, enter 0).
- What percentage of your self-employment earnings (if any) could you split with your spouse?

Spending

- How much will you spend in the current year on everything other than your mortgage?

  (This is a key question, so if you have not already tracked your spending for last year (see directions in **Chapter 14** and **Appendix 1**), take the time to do it now.)

- At what rate do you want your spending to increase each year (if zero, enter 0)?

- What percentage of your spending (excluding mortgage) in your final working year will you need after retirement?

Pensions/Other

- Do you have a pension plan at work?
- What is your pension contribution rate (percentage of salary you must contribute)?
- How much money do you expect from your pension the first year of retirement?
- At what age will your pension start?
- If your pension is indexed to inflation, enter inflation rate (if not, enter 0).
- How much money (before tax) from other sources in today's dollars do you expect to earn each year after you retire (e.g., part-time consulting work)?
- At what age do you expect this income from other sources to stop?
- What average annual rate of inflation do you expect over the remainder of your life?
- Would you like to split your pension income with your spouse?

Investments

- What percentage would you like to allocate to each of the four options?
  - RRSP
  - TFSA
  - Investment
  - Mortgage

(**NOTE:** Total must be 100%)

RRSP/RRIF

- What was the total market value of your RRSP/RRIF on the most recent statement?
- How much do you plan to contribute to your RRSP this first year?

- What is your opening RRSP room carried forward from prior years?
- At what age do you plan to retire and stop making RRSP contributions?
- Would you like to make spousal RRSP contributions?
- What per cent of your RRSP contributions do you want to make spousal?
- At what annual rate do you expect your RRSP/RRIF investments to grow?

Tax-Free Savings Account (TFSA)
- What is the current value of your TFSA?
- How much do you plan to contribute to your TFSA this first year?
- How much can you contribute to your TFSA at the start?
- How much can you and your spouse contribute to a TFSA each year?
- At what annual rate do you expect your TFSA to increase?

Regular Investment Account
- What is the current value of your investment account?
- What amount of taxable eligible dividends will you earn this first year?
- What amount of interest will you earn this first year?
- What is the mix of investments in your regular investment account (outside your RRSP/TFSA) (% equity)?
- What average dividend yield do you expect on your equities in your investment account?
- At what annual rate do you think your regular investments outside your RRSP/TFSA will increase?
- What interest rate do you think your fixed income investments will pay?

Principal Residence
- What is the current market value of your principal residence (if you own one)?
- At what rate do you expect the value of your house to increase by each year?
- What is the current balance on your mortgage?
- By how much extra do you plan to pay down your mortgage this first year?
- What is the interest rate on your mortgage?
- What amortization period is your mortgage (i.e., the number of years left)?

Old Age Security

* Are you eligible for the maximum Old Age Security (OAS) pension at age 65 or 67? (Y=Yes, N=No)

  (If you have lived in Canada for at least 40 years after turning 18, you will receive the maximum pension.)

* If not, how many years will you have lived in Canada since your 18th birthday when you turn 65?

  (You must have lived in Canada for at least 10 years to qualify for OAS.)

Canada Pension Plan

* Are you eligible for the maximum Canada Pension Plan (CPP) pension at age 65? (Y=Yes, N=No)

  (If, on average, from age 18 to retirement your earnings exceeded the maximum pensionable earnings ($53,600 in 2015), you should receive the maximum CPP pension.)

* If not, what has your average annual income from earnings been since you turned 18?

  (Enter a figure between $0 and $53,600)

* Would you like to start receiving your CPP pension between the ages of 60 and 65?

  (It will be reduced by a percentage for each year before age 65—see question below.)

* If so, at what age would you like to start receiving your CPP pension?

  (Enter an age between 60 and 64)

* If you elect to receive your CPP early, what annual penalty rate would you like to use?

  (2015 = 6.96%, 2016 and later = 7.2%)

* Would you like to split your CPP pension income with your spouse?

Longevity

* Until what age do you think you will live?

The Clarks Use the Number Cruncher

We are going to use the spreadsheet to see what the best option is for the Clarks, i.e., make RRSP contributions or pay down their mortgage during the final ten years before they retire.

Here are the key answers to the questions for the Clarks:

	Mike	Nancy
General		
Date of birth?	24-06-1958	13-08-1960
In what province/territory do you reside?	Ontario	Ontario
Income/Expenses		
What is your current total income before expenses from salary?	$80,800	$50,500
If you wish your salary to increase, enter the annual rate (if not, enter 0).	1.00%	1.00%
Spending		
How much will you spend in the current year on everything other than your mortgage?	$0	$75,968
At what rate do you want your spending to increase each year (if zero, enter 0).	1.00%	1.00%
What percentage of your spending (excluding mortgage) in your final working year will you need after retirement?	100.00%	100.00%
Pensions/Other		
Do you have a pension plan at work?	N	N
How much money (before tax) from other sources in today's dollars do you expect each year after you retire?	$0	$0
Would you like to split your pension income with your spouse?	Y	N

	Mike	Nancy
Investments		
What percentage would you like to allocate to each of the four options?	RRSP— 100.00% TFSA— 0.00% Investment— 0.00% Mortgage— 0.00%	RRSP— 100.00% TFSA— 0.00% Investment— 0.00% Mortgage— 0.00%
RRSP/RRIF		
What was the total market value of your RRSP/RRIFs on the most recent statement?	$100,000	$50,000
How much do you plan to contribute to your RRSP this first year?	$0	$0
What is your opening RRSP room carried forward from prior years?	$200,000	$50,000
At what age do you plan to retire and stop making RRSP contributions?	65	63
Would you like to make spousal RRSP contributions?	N	N
What percent of your RRSP contributions do you want to make spousal?	0.00%	0.00%
At what annual rate do you expect your RRSP/RRIF investments to grow?	4.00%	4.00%
TFSA		
What is the current value of your TFSA?	$0	$0
How much do you plan to contribute to your TFSA this first year?	$0	$0
How much can you contribute to a Tax-Free Savings Account (TFSA) at the start?	$31,000	$31,000

	Mike	Nancy
How much can you and your spouse contribute to a TFSA each year?	$10,000	$10,000
At what annual rate do you think your TFSA will increase by?	3.00%	3.00%
Regular Investment Account		
What is the opening value of your investment account?	$0	$0
Principal Residence		
What is the current market value of your principal residence if you own one?	$400,000	$0
At what rate do you expect the value of your house to increase by per year?	2.00%	NA
What is the current balance on your mortgage?	$289,967	NA
How much extra do you plan to pay down your mortgage by this first year?	$0	NA
What is the interest rate on your mortgage?	4.00%	NA
What amortization period is your mortgage (i.e., the number of years left)?	19	NA
Old Age Security		
Are you eligible for the maximum Old Age Security (OAS) pension at age 65? (Y=Yes, N=No)	Y	Y
Canada Pension Plan		
Are you eligible for the maximum Canada Pension Plan (CPP) pension at age 65? (Y=Yes, N=No)	Y	Y
Would you like to start receiving your CPP pension between the ages of 60 and 65?	N	N
Would you like to split your CPP pension income with your spouse?	N	N
Longevity		
What age do you think you will live until?	85	85

There are a few things to note before we get started.

Retirement Age

The Clarks will retire in the same year, when Mike is 65 and Nancy is 63.

Spending

You'll note that the amount the Clarks spend in the current year on everything other than the mortgage is in Nancy's column. That is because it forces the program to leave any excess funds that the family has to Mike's side because he is the one that holds the mortgage and he is also in the higher tax bracket, so it makes more sense for him to make RRSP contributions rather than Nancy.

The total spending excludes the mortgage because the spreadsheet calculates and tracks your mortgage for you.

As we have seen in the chart in **Chapter 2**, the Clarks' total spending in Year 1 was $126,839. Deduct the mortgage payments of $21,753 and $33,579 for taxes, CPP and EI, and they are left with $71,507.

Why does the chart show a total of $75,968? The excess of $4,461 is added to the total because the Clarks are going to use that amount to pay down the credit card balance, which reduces the amount available to either pay down the mortgage or make an RRSP contribution.

Allocation of Excess Funds

You may also note that we have allocated the excess 100% to the RRSP and 0% to the mortgage as a starting point. We will then reverse this allocation to see which is the better option.

Note that the program's logic is to try to conform to the allocation you enter on the Questions tab. However, it may not be possible. For example, if you try to allocate an amount to your RRSP that is over your allowable RRSP limit, it won't let you. Similarly, the program can't allocate the excess to pay down the mortgage once you have paid the mortgage off.

Once you have paid off the mortgage, the program will allocate any excess funds to your RRSP. If there are still any excess funds, it will first allocate them to your TFSA (up to your allowable limits) and, once you are maxed out on your TFSA, the rest will go to your regular investment account. This ranking makes sense because why would you put money in a regular taxable investment account when you could put the funds in a TFSA instead and shelter all earnings from tax?

If you choose the RRSP option and you max out your RRSP contributions, it will allocate any excess funds to your TFSA first and then to your investment account. If you would prefer to allocate the excess to paying down your mortgage, you'll need to override the allocation to do this. This is simple to do as the program allows you to change the allocations on the Detailed Results tab each year. In fact, you can override any number on the Detailed Results tabs.

Note that since Nancy does not have the mortgage, I have allocated 100% to her RRSP. But since the program allocates any shortfall in one of the spouse's columns to the other spouse, Nancy won't have any excess to deal with (i.e., we are forcing the excess onto Mike's side by allocating all of Nancy's excess spending against his after-tax salary).

With the 100% RRSP option, it would take 18 more years to pay off the mortgage. Mike and Nancy would not be mortgage-free until Mike is 74, which would mean they would be saddled with annual mortgage payments of $21,753 for nine years of their retirement.

If 100% of the excess was allocated to paying down the mortgage, it would only take nine years to pay off the mortgage, so the Clarks would be mortgage-free one year before their retirement, when Mike is 64.

The Three Options

Using these three options, the following is a summary of the values at the end of Year 10 that Mike and Nancy will reach at their respective retirement ages of 65 and 63:

	OPTION 1 Money in Bank End of Year 10 (Mike 65) All excess to bank	OPTION 2 100% RRSP Option End of Year 10 (Mike 65)	OPTION 3 100% Pay Down Mortgage Option End of Year 10 (Mike 65)
ASSETS			
Bank	$196,221	$0	$0
House	$487,598	$487,598	$487,598
RRSP—Mike	$148,024	$472,128	$220,199
RRSP—Nancy	$74,012	$74,012	$74,012
Total assets	**$905,855**	**$1,033,738**	**$781,809**
LIABILITIES			
Mortgage	$164,413	$164,413	$0
Total liabilities	**$164,413**	**$164,413**	**$0**
Net Worth	**$741,442**	**$869,325**	**$781,809**

At Mike's retirement age of 65, this comparison shows the RRSP option wins by $87,516 with a total net worth of $869,325 versus only $781,809 for the pay down the mortgage option. However, this is essentially comparing apples with oranges for one key reason: tax.

Be Careful of Tax

The RRSP investments are shown at their pre-tax values, i.e., tax would have to be paid to cash them in. Therefore the higher RRSP value in the middle column for Mike's RRSP is not really accurate because it doesn't show the taxes that would have to be paid when they are cashed in.

Consider Cash Flow Implications

The other important issue is the future cash flows of the various options. The 100% RRSP option still has the mortgage balance of $164,413, which carries with it the requirement to continue to pay annual mortgage payments of $21,753 for the next nine years until Mike is 74.

Which Option Wins?

So in the final analysis, the RRSP option has resulted in Mike's RRSP value of $472,128 with a mortgage balance of $164,413 and the pay down the mortgage option has resulted in Mike's RRSP value of $220,199 with no mortgage.

Is the extra $251,929 in Mike's RRSP enough to make up for the balance still owing on the mortgage?

With a mortgage balance of $164,413 and monthly payments of $1,813, it will take nine years to pay it off, which is 108 monthly payments. If Mike was in a 30% income tax bracket when he retired, monthly RRSP income amounts of $2,590 would be required to make the monthly mortgage payment (30% tax on $2,590 is $777, leaving $1,813 to pay the mortgage).

Assuming the RRSP was making a return of 4% throughout the 108 months, to pay off the mortgage an opening balance of $234,580 in the RRSP would be required to pay out $2,590 a month for the nine years. Mike's RRSP is $251,929 higher in option 2, so it seems the 100% RRSP option wins by $17,349 on a before-tax basis ($251,929 – $234,580 = $17,349).

However, there are other advantages to paying off the mortgage besides the numbers, because there are risks to the 100% RRSP strategy that don't exist when you choose to pay down the mortgage instead.

Advantages to Paying Down the Mortgage

Here are the reasons I would consider for paying down the mortgage instead of maxing out your RRSP contributions (even if the numbers supported the RRSP option). (We reviewed three of these in Chapter 3, but I think it is important to emphasize them again here, plus I have added to the list.)

1. Guaranteed Rate of Return

The mortgage has a set rate of interest and you will save exactly that rate on an after-tax basis when you pay down the related debt. The rate on your RRSP is unknown. You may make 4% after fees as we have projected, but you may not. What happens if you are over-exposed to the stock market and the market crashes again and you end up making much less than 4%, or possibly even lose money? Paying down the mortgage would have been a much better strategy.

2. Forces You to be Fiscally Prudent

Barring an unforeseen gift like a lottery win or an inheritance, you simply can't pay down debt if you spend more than you make. Trying to pay down debt forces you to watch your spending and encourages you to increase your income because you can't make progress otherwise.

If you choose the RRSP route and don't actively attack paying down debt, it is easy to fool yourself into thinking you are on the right track. Many people that make RRSP contributions borrow the funds to do it because they are spending more than they make each year. They are therefore only able to make the contributions because their other debt (e.g., credit cards or lines of credit) is rising. Taking your eye off the "pay-down-debt ball" increases the likelihood that you'll never pay it down.

3. Provides Free Income Protection Insurance

If you own your house and you are 100% mortgage-free and you can't work due to an illness or an accident, you are much less likely to lose your house because you no longer have to make those monthly mortgage payments. That is why I recommend you try to become mortgage-free as soon as possible, but definitely before retirement.

4. It's Easy to Measure

It is very easy to see where you are on your quest to get debt-free: it's the principal balance of the debt that is still owing. With the RRSP option, even with tools like the Procrastinator's Number Cruncher, it's difficult to know if your RRSP is large enough to fund your retirement as there are so many variables that you can't control, such as inflation, investment return rates, tax rates and how long you are going to live.

Optimizing RRSP Values

However, there is another problem we need to address. In our three options, Mike's RRSP is a lot larger than Nancy's. This is not ideal because it means the majority of the taxable RRSP withdrawals will be reported on Mike's tax return during the early years of retirement. This is of particular concern between the ages of 65 and 71, because it is only after age 71 (when you have converted your RRSP to a RRIF or annuity) that you can take advantage of pension income splitting in this case.

A better option is to balance out the RRSP values so that withdrawals can be split evenly between spouses, which results in optimal splitting of the income during retirement and lower taxes. One very effective way of doing this is by the use of a spousal RRSP.

Spousal RRSPs

In a spousal RRSP, the contributor (Mike) makes the contribution based on his allowable limits, he gets the deduction at his marginal tax rate, but it goes into his spouse's or common-law partner's RRSP, i.e., the spouse or common-law partner is the owner or annuitant. The benefit is that withdrawn amounts are taxed in the spouse or annuitant's hands. If he or she is in a lower tax bracket, there could be significant tax savings.

However, there is one important proviso: if funds are withdrawn within three taxation years of any contribution to the plan, the withdrawal will be reportable by the contributor spouse or partner, effectively undoing the strategy.

I changed the answer to the questions about spousal RRSPs on the Questions tab to say that Mike would like to make spousal RRSP contributions, but how do we know what percentage to allocate to spousal RRSPs? It gets back to our objective of balancing out the RRSP values as best we can.

Have a look at the RRSP values under the 100% RRSP option at the end of Year 10. It shows Mike's value as $472,128 and Nancy's at $74,012 for a total of $546,140.

It would be better to have each at a value of half that amount, i.e., $273,070.

I used Excel's "Goal Seek" function to determine the best percentage to allocate for Mike.

💡 EXCEL'S GOAL SEEK FUNCTION

This is one of the most useful Excel functions there is. You simply select "Tools" from the main menu and then "Goal Seek."

Goal Seek	
Set cell:	F19
To value:	
By changing cell:	
Cancel	OK

All you do is point to the cell you are trying to optimize so it shows up in the "Set cell" box, then type in the value you want to make that cell in the "To value" box. Then go to the "By changing cell" box and point to the cell you want Excel to change to reach your desired result.

Mike Uses a Spousal RRSP

In this case, using Goal Seek, I entered Nancy's RRSP value cell at retirement on the "Summary Results" tab to a value of $273,070 and asked goal seek to change the cell that has the percentage that Mike wants to make to spousal RRSPs and asked it to solve. The answer was 155%, which obviously can't be done since you can't allocate more than the amount available. The next best answer is 100% to get Nancy's RRSP up to the highest amount possible. So I changed the answer on the Questions tab to allocate 100% of Mike's RRSP contributions to a spousal RRSP.

WARNING: During the last three years before their retirement, no spousal RRSP contributions can be made because the withdrawals would have to go on Mike's return, not Nancy's.

As the Clarks will be withdrawing from Nancy's spousal RRSP to fund their retirement starting in the year Mike turns 66, I manually reduced the spousal RRSP allocation to zero during the last three years of Mike's pre-retirement contributions.

The result is the following RRSP values at retirement that total $546,140:
- Mike $343,880
- Nancy $202,260

So the Clarks net worth at the end of the year Mike turns 65 will be as follows:

	Option 2 100% RRSP Option End of Year 10 (Mike 65)
ASSETS	
House	$487,598
RRSP—Mike	$343,880
RRSP—Nancy	$202,260
Total assets	**$1,033,738**
LIABILITIES	
Mortgage	$164,413
Total liabilities	**$164,413**
Net Worth	**$869,325**

NOTE: The total net worth is the same as when Mike was not making spousal RRSP contributions, but the amounts in each RRSP are different.

Pension Income Splitting

Even though the Clarks are using the spousal RRSP option, it will still be worth them using pension income splitting because their RRSPs are not of the same value. That is why I answered "Yes" to the question for Mike: "Would you like to split your pension income with your spouse?"

This will result in optimal splitting of Mike's mandatory RRIF withdrawals after he turns 71 and he has converted his RRSP to a RRIF. If not, Nancy would only be reporting her CPP, OAS and a smaller amount from her RRIF.

In **Chapter 6**, we'll start with these retirement figures to determine if the Clarks have enough saved for retirement and the best ways to access their various funds during their retirement.

CHAPTER 5

Your Pre-Retirement Investment Strategy

In order to build your RRSP portfolio to its maximum size before your retirement, it will be necessary for you to spend some time and effort. Even if you have an advisor whom you trust, you'll need to be vigilant to make sure you understand what is happening in your account. As in any segment of the population, there are good and bad advisors; many people are using advisors who are sales people selling investment products that are profitable to them and their firms but very expensive for the people who buy them. These costly products are not going to help you meet your goals.

Do You Have a Good Advisor?

The following is a list of positive attributes of a good advisor and their firm.

They Listen As Much As They Talk

If you ask your advisor a question, how do they respond? A good advisor will always listen to your question, ask questions of you to clarify your situation and will give you a succinct answer in plain language.

A poor advisor is easy to identify. They babble on endlessly using jargon you don't understand and they are good at emotional selling. If your advisor wants to talk about general things (e.g., how the kids are, the weather, the local sports team) and doesn't like to talk about fees or how well your investments are performing, start the hunt for someone else immediately.

Useful Statements

A good firm will give you a statement showing all the fees you were charged, including any hidden fees like mutual fund trailer fees (a fee paid by a mutual fund manager to a firm who sells the fund to investors). It will also give you your personal rate of return after fees, which is the most important figure when it comes to monitoring your investments.

Unfortunately, most statements don't disclose this information. The good news is that investment firms are going to be required to disclose this information after July 15, 2016.

They Are Qualified

The term "financial advisor" is not well regulated in any province other than Quebec. It is relatively simple for someone to take a course allowing them to sell mutual funds and then call themselves a financial advisor.

However, a good advisor will have a professional designation (e.g., Certified Financial Planner (CFP)) which requires them to pass proficiency exams and be subject to supervision and regulation.

In Canada, anyone trading securities or who is in the business of advising clients on securities must be registered with the provincial or territorial securities regulator (unless an exemption applies). The regulators only register firms and individuals that meet certain standards.

The problem with securities regulation is Canada is that we don't have a formal national securities regulator, each province or territory has its own. To deal with this issue, the Canadian Securities Administrators (CSA) was formed. It is an umbrella organization of Canada's provincial and territorial securities regulators whose objective is to improve, coordinate and harmonize regulation of the Canadian capital markets. See **www.securities-administrators.ca** to find a complete list of licensed advisors and their firms in Canada. The category of registration tells you what products and services an individual or firm can offer. Note that CSA provides the following warning: "Being registered, however, doesn't mean that all firms and individuals have the same skills, provide the same services or charge the same fees. Make sure you understand their qualifications, and the products or services they are selling you."

The following are the main categories of financial advisors and their services.

Investment dealer: can sell a broad range of investments including shares, bonds, exchange-traded funds (ETFs), mutual funds and limited partnerships. Some offer advice and a full range of services such as market analysis, securities research and portfolio management. Others act more like brokers, buying and selling securities based on your instructions.

Mutual fund dealer: can only sell mutual funds.

Portfolio manager: gives advice to others and manages your portfolio according to the instructions or discretionary authority you have given them.

Dealing representative: a salesperson who sells their firm's products, their advice depends on the firm they work for and their registration.

Advising representative: a person who provides advice on securities to clients. They can manage your investment portfolio according to your instructions, including making decisions and trading securities.

Consult **www.securities-administrators.ca** to check your current advisor's status. If you are unhappy with your advisor, you should switch, but check the status of the other advisor first.

Advisor Enforcement

It is also possible to find out if there have been any disciplinary proceedings, charges and convictions against registered advisors: go to **www.securities-administrators.ca**, click on the "Enforcement" section and then click on "Disciplined Persons."

Ensure you do this **before** you hand over any money to a new advisor!

Your Advisor Options

When it comes to personal finances, you will probably need more than one person to take care of your needs. You'll need a lawyer to help with your will, an accountant to do your taxes, a banker to handle credit and a financial advisor to handle the rest of your financial needs, such as saving for your children's education and investing for your retirement.

The problem is that it is relatively straightforward to hire a lawyer or an accountant, but finding the right financial advisor is not. That's because there is a lot of confusion about exactly what their role is.

There are two main services that your financial advisor(s) will provide:
1. Financial planning
2. Investment advice and administration

These are two very distinct roles.

1. Financial Planning

This involves a comprehensive analysis of all your financial issues, taking into account your financial situation and goals. It involves many areas such as investing, tax, estate planning, debt analysis, etc., and often results in a written financial plan about how to achieve your financial goals.

Fee-Only Financial Planner

A fee-only financial planner offers comprehensive, independent financial planning advice for a visible fee. The fee is usually an hourly rate or a fixed price.

These people may have one or more of these various designations:
- Chartered Professional Accountant (CPA)
- Certified Financial Planner (CFP)
- Chartered Life Underwriter (CLU)
- Personal Financial Planner (PFP)
- Registered Financial Planner (RFP)
- Trust and Estate Practitioner (TEP)

In most cases they are not licensed to sell investments, so you'll either have to do that yourself or pay someone else to handle the buying, selling and administration of your investments.

MoneySense Magazine has an online listing of fee-only financial planners at **www.moneysense.ca/directory-of-fee-only-planners**. They separate them into two categories: Fee-for-service Planners/Money Coaches (average hourly rates from $100 to $500 and fees for a comprehensive financial plan in the $2,000 to $3,500 range) and Primarily Asset-Based Planners. The second category is for those who also provide investment management services based on a percentage of assets.

An option that is likely to become increasingly popular is to combine the services of a fee-only financial planner with a discount brokerage account to actually do the investing. The advantage of this arrangement is that not only do you get independent financial planning advice, but you also minimize the costs of investment administration.

This is not for everyone, but if you are willing to spend some time and can resist the urge to trade too often, it could be a great way to bring down your investment costs. For example, if you pay a management fee of 1.5% a year to your advisor for financial advice and investment management and your portfolio has an average market value of $400,000, you'd pay $6,000 each year in fees.

If you used a fee-only financial planner, you could pay up to $3,500 for the comprehensive financial plan and then several hundred dollars for their time once or twice a year to review your progress and make recommendations about any changes.

2. Investment Advice and Administration

This involves the actual buying, selling and rebalancing of your portfolio of investments.

In some cases, one individual or firm performs both functions, while in others there are two separate firms involved. Many people assume that one person or firm is all they need, but this may not work for you because the advisor is usually paid a commission for the sale of products to their clients.

If your advisor is being paid a commission on the sale of products, it makes it very difficult for them to provide independent professional advice (the more expensive the product you buy, the bigger the commission!). There is no real incentive for them to spend time analyzing your whole financial situation because they are not getting extra money to do that and it may also result in them recommending a product or strategy that would reduce their income. For example, if an advisor makes a commission based on your RRSP investments, are they likely to recommend that you stop making RRSP contributions and pay down the mortgage? It's unlikely, and an aggressive commissioned salesperson may even encourage their clients to borrow to buy more!

It's important that you do your due diligence before hiring any type of advisor.

Mutual Fund Dealer

I once had a client who had just emerged from bankruptcy and her advisor was strongly pushing her to take out a loan to make an RRSP contribution. She couldn't control her spending but was being advised to immediately load up on more debt! It didn't make sense, but this kind of sales advice often results when there is a financial incentive to sell, sell, sell.

Mutual fund dealers are one type of advisor frequently used by Canadians. If you have this type of advisor, you are limiting the investments they can buy on your behalf. There is no doubt that there are some mutual fund dealers who give their clients good advice, but many do not, and the main reason for that is **fees**!

If you own mutual funds, you should be aware of the "Fund Facts" document. It is a summary of key information about your mutual funds, including visible fees such as deferred sales charges (DSCs), the management costs of the fund (often referred to as the management expense ratio (MER)) and rate of return information.

For many equity funds in Canada, the MER is more than 2%. That means that the mutual fund managers have to beat the comparative benchmark index (a standard against which the performance of a mutual fund can be measured, e.g., the S&P TSX Composite Index) by that amount to leave you with what you could have made if you simply bought an investment that mirrored the index.

In other words, you are paying for "active management" to do better than "passive management." With passive management, the people running the fund simply buy the stocks or other investments that make up the benchmark index. This is usually a much cheaper option than mutual funds because these investments, called exchange-traded funds (ETFs), do not have to pay sophisticated professionals to research and pick the investments.

Generally, the only way your mutual fund dealer gets paid is by commission, which includes visible, as well as invisible, fees such as "trailer fees" (a commission that the salesperson of a mutual fund receives each year that an investor remains in the fund). These fees are tied to the product and essentially lead to a conflict of interest.

Which fund do you think your advisor would rather sell you: Fund A that pays him and his firm a trailer fee of 0.75% a year or Fund B that pays them 0.15% a year? Of course, it is Fund A. Which fund would be better for you? Fund B.

It's a conflict of interest compounded by the fact that, under current regulations, your mutual fund dealer doesn't even have to discuss the trailer fees they receive on your account.

Investment Dealer/Portfolio Managers

Investment dealers and portfolio managers aren't limited to just mutual funds. They can purchase stocks, bonds, ETFs and a broad range of other products on your behalf. It makes sense to consider using this type of advisor. Why limit yourself to mutual funds?

These advisors can charge commissions just like mutual fund dealers, but there is another option that is becoming more popular: a percentage of assets under administration. For example, you simply pay a percentage of the average value of your investment account in a year, perhaps 1% or 2%. This separates the advice from the product so that your advisor has no incentive to sell you costly products and can include low-cost options like ETFs in your portfolio.

Do It Yourself

If you feel confident about your ability to handle your own investments, you can devote the time, expertise and energy required to do this, but it can be a minefield and often does not work out too well. Think carefully about what you are doing, especially if you're planning to pick your own stocks.

Warren MacKenzie, CPA, CA, Principal at Highview Financial Group, is an expert in various aspects of retirement planning and investing. He recently wrote an article about how individual investors can take control and improve their investment results and the following are his top ten tips.

1. Know the Difference Between Investment Professionals and Salespeople

The exposure most people have with the financial services sector is through individuals who are licensed as salespeople. These people may or may not have any investing expertise and, in many cases, they have a total conflict of interest. In other words, they have an incentive to sell you financial products that make money for them, and that money comes directly out of your pocket. In many cases they are only licensed to sell mutual funds. They can't buy individual stocks, bonds or exchange traded funds (ETFs).

There are better alternatives.

For example, you could hire a full-service investment dealer licensed to sell a whole range of investment products, including stocks, bonds and ETFs. These professionals usually have a designation, such as a Chartered Financial Analyst (CFA).

2. Don't Be Overconfident

If you think you can get ahead by trading individual stocks in your own account, think about who you are competing against. Most trading that takes place is done by professionals who probably have more information, discipline, experience and tools than you. They are most likely the ones on the other side of each buy or sell you make. Do you honestly think that over time you are going to do better than them?

You may also think it's possible to research a company so you know everything about it and therefore are able to predict its future stock price. The problem is that the stock market is very unpredictable. The price of stocks are affected by many things, including global conflicts, unexpected innovations, new competitors, government intervention, social trends and interest rates, to name a few. These items can come out of the blue and cause large swings in the value of any company. Just because you are smart and spend many hours researching investments doesn't mean you'll do well.

Working on your own is also dangerous because people tend to fall in love with their own ideas. This causes people to hang on to winners too long ("It's done so well for me, I can't bear to sell it now!") or delay in dumping losers ("It'll come back, I'll just wait a few more weeks"). Regardless of what option you choose, it makes sense to have another person to challenge your ideas.

3. Follow a Disciplined Investment Approach

If you don't have an investment process, you tend to be guided by your emotions. This is a recipe for disaster. If you don't have a "sell" strategy, you don't have an investment strategy. For example, you should have a simple and effective strategy to rebalance your portfolio according to guidelines laid out in a written investment policy statement.

Many do-it-yourself investors hold too many small investments. Even if some of these investments doubled in value it wouldn't make a significant overall difference. They also tend to hold complicated securities which make it difficult to understand fees, asset mix and inherent risk. Also, many hold legacy mutual funds where it is difficult to know what types of investment products are in them and therefore make it difficult to stick to an "optimal asset mix" (i.e., allocating your investments among different asset classes to help minimize risk and potentially increase gains or "not putting all your eggs in one basket").

No one can consistently time the market. Don't fool yourself into thinking that you can get in and out of the market at the right time—even the professionals can't. That is why you need a written investment policy statement and some assistance from other people.

The key to getting ahead with investing is to reduce your trading activity. If you are constantly buying and selling, you are reducing your chances of success and increasing the drag that trading and other fees have on the performance of your investments.

4. Focus on Managing Risk

What overall rate of return on your portfolio are you aiming for? You can't answer that question without first determining what your goals are. If you can reach the amount you need to retire with a return of 4%, you should not have an asset mix designed to make 6%. This is especially important when you have ten years or less to build your retirement nest egg. That's because aiming for the higher rate will necessitate exposing more of your money to the volatility of the stock market.

Many people put themselves in a very risky situation when it comes to required rates of return. They don't take control of their spending and therefore don't have much money to invest. They therefore need a high rate of return to get to the required portfolio value. But hoping for a 10% rate of return to solve your problems will mean you'll have to take extreme risk. Chances are good this strategy will result in dismal failure, because potential high returns come with the risk that they will be low or even negative. You can't afford that risk with ten years or less to go.

Managing risk also means you need to be diversified, by sector as well as geographically. If you want exposure to the stock market, you need to look beyond just Canada, which has 70% of its market in just three sectors: financial, energy and materials.

It's also important to understand your tolerance for risk. In a rising market we all tend to think we have a high tolerance. It's only in a falling market that we can accurately gauge our tolerance level. Remember 2008–2009 where the S&P TSX Composite Index lost almost half its value in less than a year? If this kind of swing caused you to panic and sell, you found out the hard way that your tolerance for risk was lower than you thought.

5. Focus On the Big Picture

If you don't know what you are trying to achieve with your savings, you can't know the rate of return you'll need to get there.

But what if you are significantly short of your retirement goal, and even a great investment return won't solve your problems? In this case, you'll really need to focus on the big picture, including cutting your spending and reducing debt.

It also makes sense to consider estate issues, because, as we know, you can't take it with you. This means actively monitoring your investments throughout your retirement. A big mistake could mean having to reduce your lifestyle or explaining to the kids that their inheritance isn't what it used to be.

6. Avoid an Emotional Response

Money does not have a personality. It makes no difference whether you accumulated your money via a disciplined savings program, an inheritance, a bonus or a lottery win. It should all be managed with the same level of care.

And don't expect the current trends to continue. You can't bet that interest rates will stay at the ultra-low rates of today for years to come, you don't know whether the current low oil prices are going to recover soon or whether it will take years. The same goes for the stock market. Will the U.S. market continue to defy gravity and reach new highs? If so, for how long?

As a general rule, investors should do the opposite of what their gut is telling them. They should sell in a market that has risen significantly and buy into a

market that has dropped substantially. That is easier
said than done and again stresses the importance of
an investment policy statement with specific target
asset allocations.

7. Measure Your Performance

Do you know how well your portfolio is doing? Most
people don't have any idea because their investment
firm does not tell them. You have to have personal
investment rate of return information so you can
gauge your results.

These results need to be compared to a benchmark,
which is usually measured by an ETF of the same
composition as your portfolio. What good is paying
an investment manager a fee to produce a return that
is less than you could have received using ETFs in a
discount brokerage account?

According to MacKenzie, many investors are under-
performing the benchmark by 2% per annum. On a
$250,000 portfolio, underperforming by 2% a year
over ten years would cost you over $50,000.

8. Pay Attention to Income Tax

If you have money in a regular investment account
in addition to your RRSP and TFSA, you need to be
cognizant of income taxes. Your investment mix can
make a huge difference to your after-tax rate of return.
For example, equity investments beat interest income
when it comes to taxes because capital gains on stock
sales are only 50% taxed and dividends are taxed at a
lower rate than interest.

But don't allow your portfolio to become over-exposed
to risky equities just because of the beneficial tax
treatment. If you can't handle potential losses, then
stick to a larger percentage of interest-paying fixed
income investments regardless of the tax hit. And

don't avoid selling a stock that has done well for you simply to avoid the capital gains tax. In other words don't let the "tax tail" wag the investment dog.

9. Don't Act on Bad Information

Contrary to what many people think, some professional managers do consistently beat the market. Few mutual funds, however, beat their relevant benchmark index, largely due to fees, over-diversification and plain bad luck

Simple strategies like "buy and hold" may not work well either. In a rising market the strategy works well, but not so in a bear market. For example, in 1988 the Japanese Nikkei Index was at about 40,000 points, today it is under 18,000. Over that period you would not have wanted to be a Japanese buy-and-hold investor.

10. Be Logical In Your Analysis

Many people focus too much on fees. Fees are a necessary part of the equation, but they can only be judged when compared to the value received. Any fee is too much if no value is being received, but high fees may be justified if significant value is added. That value should be measured in a performance report that shows rate of return (net of fees) compared to the relevant benchmark index.

The services provided can also go beyond fees. Professional advice that prevented you from losing half your portfolio due to proper diversification is very valuable. The advice would have saved you a lot even though you had a negative return.

It's also important to distinguish between investment income and cash flow. Investment income consists of interest, dividends and capital gains. When you retire you'll need cash flow from your investments to pay the bills. Some investors overlook potential cash flow from the sale of stocks and mistakenly assume they need to be exclusively in securities that pay interest and dividends. In other words, you could sell some of your investments and eat into your capital to generate cash flow.

Investors often fool themselves into feeling better in a down market by telling themselves "it's only a paper loss." If you bought a stock at $10 and it is now worth $2, make no mistake, you have lost money. Failing to recognize this fact simply delays taking advantage of the capital loss for tax purposes. Again this is where independent advice can be important. You may not wish to admit you bought a loser, so you hang on in the hopes it will rebound. An outside expert can help you swallow your pride and take the hit, before things get even worse.

Don't act on tips from your friends or colleagues. They are often based on faulty information and usually don't work. Even if the tip does work, it may have been obtained by insider information, in which case anyone acting on it may face legal consequences.

Don't put all your eggs in one basket. If you invest 100% of your money in equities, not only are you putting yourself at a higher risk than necessary, you'll have nothing to rebalance with (i.e., when markets go down, you'll want to be able to sell some fixed income securities to have the cash to buy stocks while they're cheap; if all your investments are in stocks already, you'll have no cash to buy more).

If you are unsatisfied with the investment management services you are getting, now is the time to find an independent professional who will satisfy you. Remember the next ten years are going to be key to build your portfolio before your retirement. Don't accept the *status quo*, find someone who will help you realize your goals.

A Rule of Thumb That Makes Sense

I am not a big fan of "rules of thumb" because often they lead people astray as there is rarely a right answer to a personal financial issue. But when it comes to investing, one rule of thumb makes a lot of sense to me.

It says that the maximum percentage of equities in your retirement portfolio should be the result of 100 minus your age, i.e., your age is the minimum percentage you should have in fixed income products. For example, a 30-year-old should have a maximum of 70% in the stock market and a 70-year-old should have a maximum of 30% in stocks.

This makes sense because it forces you to reduce your investment risk as you age because you have less time to make up for any decline in the stock market.

Is the rule of thumb right in your situation or not? This subject is one that your financial planner should be addressing with you both now and later as your situation changes.

PART TWO

The Retirement Years

CHAPTER 6
How Much Will You Spend During Retirement?

The rule of thumb says you will need 70% of your pre-retirement income to maintain your standard of living after you retire. The assumption is that your expenses will decline by about 30% once you stop working.

In most cases your expenses will decline, for example:
- you won't be paying CPP or EI premiums and your income tax bill will also decline as your income does
- you'll probably spend less on your car operating costs because you no longer travel to and from work each day
- you'll eat lunch out less since you'll be home more often
- you will pay less for dry cleaning as you won't be wearing business clothes

But some costs may go up. For example, if you choose to travel more, your vacation costs will increase. (However, you might be able to mitigate vacation costs since your time is more flexible and you can travel in off-peak seasons that cost less.) Depending on your health, your medical and dental costs may increase. You may also have to pay to take care of your aging parents, or maybe even your children if they haven't been able to establish themselves financially.

So calculating the amount of money you'll need to set aside for retirement based on a rough rule of thumb can be misleading. True financial planning should be based on an analysis of existing expenses, not a percentage of income.

As we have seen with the Clarks, expenses can decline for reasons other than retirement. We saw a large annual reduction of $6,751 when they paid off their car loan. There was a huge yearly savings of about $16,000 after their daughter Sophia graduated from university and when they paid off their mortgage, their annual cash outflow declined by $21,753.

In most cases, significant expense reductions occur for reasons other than retirement, so when projecting expenses you must take into account the timing of these other events. To accurately plan for meeting your retirement expenses, you have to project future costs on a line-by-line basis and also consider the effect of inflation.

The Effect of Inflation

The general measure of inflation in Canada is the Consumer Price Index (CPI). The Bank of Canada currently has a mandate to keep inflation at approximately 2% a year, so it is often around that percentage. However, you cannot simply multiply your total expenses by overall inflation to project future outflows because inflation affects each line of your spending differently. For example, your mortgage costs are not affected by inflation, they are affected by interest rates. The same applies to your car loan or lease payments, but your car's operating costs are affected by inflation and car insurance seems to increase every year. However, at the time of writing, the cost of gas has actually decreased, so that spending-specific line has been subject to deflation (declining prices).

The Clarks' Future Costs

Let's have a look at what the Clarks are likely to spend in retirement.

The following chart shows what they will spend in Year 10, the last year of work for Mike at age 65 and Nancy at age 63, assuming they opted to make RRSP contributions and therefore had not paid off the mortgage. (Note that I have ignored taxes because we don't yet know what their income is going to be after they retire).

The Clarks
Annual Expenses - Year 10   **% of Total**
Auto

Auto fuel	2,855	4%
Auto general	426	1%
Auto insurance	1,462	2%
Auto loan	6,751	8%
Auto license & registration	220	0%
Auto repairs & maintenance	416	1%
	12,130	**15%**

Family

Cash withdrawals	5,000	6%
Clothing	3,000	4%
Donations	300	0%
Entertainment	900	1%
Groceries	5,000	6%
Insurance (life, income protection)	3,213	4%
Meals out	4,266	5%
Medical and dental	1,219	2%
Miscellaneous	1,219	2%
Vacation	6,000	8%
	30,117	**38%**

House

Mortgage	21,753	27%
House insurance	1,462	2%
Utilities (heat, hydro)	4,280	5%
Property tax	4,266	5%
House repairs & maintenance	3,535	4%
Security	537	1%
Phone and cable	1,755	2%
	37,588	**47%**

Interest and bank charges

Bank charges	120	0%
	120	**0%**
TOTAL EXPENSES	**79,955**	**100%**

Let's think about the rule of thumb, i.e., what will change in their first year of retirement to make these expenses go down by the 30%? There doesn't seem to be much opportunity to reduce their expenses: the mortgage won't be paid off and the car loan still has another year to go. There may be some discretionary expenses they can reduce (like meals out and vacation), but there is not going to be any appreciable reduction in their spending just because they retire. That fact is the key to this book and to your plans for retirement. Now for the good news! When the Clarks pay off their mortgage, their annual expenses will decline by $21,753 to $58,202. If the Clarks had chosen to pay off the mortgage instead of maxing out on RRSPs, they would already be in this position.

The other good news is their four-year car loan will be paid off in one more year and they will no longer have the $6,751 in loan payments. This will drop their annual outflows to $51,451. We discuss the issue of how best to finance your car in **Chapter 16**, but for now we need to consider how long that car which is paid for will last. Maybe five more years or more, it depends on their lifestyle. We'll need to consider how long it will last because eventually it will need to be replaced and the cash required to do that will be significant. Once again, this illustrates the importance of tracking your spending each year as a basis for planning your retirement.

We'll make reasonable assumptions about the Clarks' spending over the next twenty years (the remainder of Mike's life) and we'll assume inflation averages 2% per year over that time.

Auto
We'll assume the Clarks will use the car less than when they were working. Let's say they will only drive two-thirds of the kilometres they used to, so we'll therefore reduce the fuel costs in Year 11 to $1,900 ($2,855 x 2/3). We'll assume the other operating costs rise by inflation. The Clarks will also buy a new car every eight years (as they have been doing) and we'll estimate they will receive $2,500 for it when they dispose of their old one.

Family
We'll assume that the first five items (cash withdrawals, clothing, donations, entertainment and groceries) go up by inflation each year. We'll assume they stop paying for life and income protection

insurance. We'll keep meals out, miscellaneous and vacations at the same amount. We'll assume medical and dental costs increase by 20% a year to $4,000 and then stay at that amount.

House

We'll assume that all the housing costs increase by inflation each year and that the mortgage will be paid off in nine years when Mike is 74.

Interest and Bank Charges

We'll leave these at the same amount.

The following is a summary of the Clarks' projected expenses for their retirement years until Mike is 85 years old.

The Clarks
Annual Expenses - Retirement

Year	Age	Auto	Family	House	Interest and bank charges	Total
1	65	12,130	30,117	37,588	120	79,955
2	66	11,225	27,432	37,905	120	76,682
3	67	4,563	28,014	38,228	120	70,925
4	68	5,214	28,660	38,558	120	72,552
5	69	5,799	29,382	38,894	120	74,195
6	70	3,415	30,194	39,238	120	72,967
7	71	11,623	31,114	39,588	120	82,445
8	72	11,721	31,794	39,945	120	83,580
9	73	11,821	32,121	40,308	120	84,370
10	74	11,922	32,453	40,219	120	84,714
11	75	5,274	32,794	19,305	120	57,493
12	76	5,938	33,140	19,691	120	58,889
13	77	6,536	33,413	20,084	120	60,153
14	78	4,167	33,766	20,487	120	58,540
15	79	12,391	34,125	20,897	120	67,533
16	80	12,504	34,492	21,315	120	68,431
17	81	12,618	34,867	21,740	120	69,345
18	82	12,735	35,248	22,175	120	70,278
19	83	6,103	35,637	22,618	120	64,478
20	84	6,784	36,035	23,070	120	66,009
21	85	7,399	36,440	23,532	120	67,491

The next step is to use the Number Cruncher spreadsheet (see **Chapter 4**) to see if the Clarks' income from their CPP, OAS, RRSPs and RRIFs are going to be sufficient to pay for these estimated expenses.

The Findings

The year after Mike retires, at age 66, his only source of income is his CPP and OAS, totalling $23,328. Nancy retires the same year at age 63. The next year she has no CPP as she has elected to start at age 65, and no OAS as she is under 65.

But the Clarks' estimated expenses are $76,682, including $21,753 in mortgage payments, so they will have to withdraw from their RRSPs to cover the expenses. In fact, the Clarks have a shortfall each year from Year 2 to Year 10 of their retirement. So how do we figure out how much they have to withdraw from their RRSPs to pay their expenses and how much each should withdraw?

Once again I used Excel's Goal Seek function to calculate the amount. I made Nancy's RRSP/RRIF withdrawals equal to Mike's and used Goal Seek to find out how much they would need to withdraw from their RRSPs/RRIFs to fund their expenses.

Here are the results:

Mike's Age	Mike's RRSP/RRIF Withdrawal	Nancy's RRSP/RRIF Withdrawal	Total RRSP/RRIF Withdrawal
66	$27,132	$27,132	$54,264
67	$21,634	$21,634	$43,268
68	$18,203	$18,203	$36,406
69	$18,855	$18,855	$37,710
70	$17,526	$17,526	$35,052
71	$24,301	$24,301	$48,602
72	$16,450	$16,450	$32,900
73	$16,942	$16,942	$33,884
74	$14,996	$14,996	$29,992
Total	**$176,039**	**$176,039**	**$352,078**

After age 71, Mike will be required to make minimum withdrawals from his RRIF (since he has decided to turn his RRSP into a RRIF instead of an annuity (more about the annuity option in **Chapter 10**). When Nancy turns 71 she does the same thing.

Will the Clarks have enough saved to finance their retirement to age 85? The answer is "Yes," they will have more than enough.

The Number Cruncher shows that during the rest of Mike's life, the Clarks can cover their expenses with their CPP, OAS and RRSP and RRIF withdrawal amounts. The estimation shows they will have excess cash during those years, which will be invested in their TFSAs.

When Mike dies at age 85, Nancy will have plenty of income to live on for the last two years of her life. Here is the situation at the time of Mike's death:

RRSPs	$210,514
TFSAs	$44,995
House	$724,545
Total	**$980,054**

It seems the Clarks will have excess funds to cover their basic expenses for the rest of their lives. They can afford to spend more and enjoy their retirement to the fullest and still leave a sizeable estate for their kids.

But you may not be in the same position as the Clarks, so the remainder of this book is dedicated to dealing with issues affecting your personal situation. We'll look into each situation so you can prepare for the best retirement possible.

CHAPTER 7

Maximizing Your Canada Pension Plan

What is the Canada Pension Plan?

The Canada Pension Plan (CPP) is a mandatory government-sponsored pension plan that came into effect on January 1, 1966. Quebec is the only province that elected to create its own plan, the Quebec Pension Plan (QPP), which is similar to the CPP but supported by the provincial government.

All Canadian employees, employers and self-employed people have to contribute to the CPP. Contributions are required as soon as you reach the age of eighteen and are no longer required after you either opt out at age 65, reach the age of seventy or become disabled.

Monthly CPP pensions are paid to retirees, surviving spouses or common-law partners of deceased contributors, orphans, the disabled and children of the disabled. The term "common-law partner" came into force on July 30, 2000 and replaced the former term "spouse." A common-law partner is defined for CPP purposes as "a person who is cohabiting with the contributor in a conjugal relationship at the relevant time, having so cohabited with the contributor for a continuous period of at least one year." This means that same-sex couples are also eligible for CPP survivor's benefits.

A maximum lump-sum death benefit of $2,500 is also paid to the estate of deceased contributors. The amount is dependent on the contributions the deceased made to the CPP during his or her lifetime.

It is important to note that the monthly benefits paid under the plan are adjusted annually, based on increases in the Consumer Price Index (CPI), the most common measure of inflation in Canada.

In short, the CPP is an inflation-adjusted defined benefit pension plan that is paid until you die.

How Your CPP Premiums are Calculated

Regular CPP premiums for employees are calculated at a rate of 4.95% of earnings above an exemption of $3,500 to a maximum of $53,600 in 2015. In other words, if you make under $3,500 you pay no CPP premiums, but if you earn between $3,501 and $53,600 the amount you pay is based on your earnings. If you earn $53,601 or more, you don't pay any more premiums above the maximum.

Here are the key figures for 2015:

Year's Maximum Pensionable Earnings (YMPE)	$53,600
Year's Basic Exemption	$3,500
Year's Maximum Contributory Earnings	$50,100 ($53,600 less $3,500)
Year's Maximum Contributions	$2,479.95 ($50,100.00 × 4.95%)

How Your CPP Pension Is Calculated

The maximum monthly CPP retirement pension is equal to 25% of the last five Year's Maximum Pensionable Earnings (YMPE). This is referred to as the Average Year's Maximum Pensionable Earnings (AYMPE).

Here's how they calculated the maximum monthly CPP retirement pension for 2015.

Last five Year's Maximum Pensionable Earnings (YMPE):

2011	$48,300
2012	$50,100
2013	$51,100
2014	$52,500
2015	$53,600

Average of 2011 to 2015 YMPE (AYMPE)	$51,120
25% of the AYMPE	$12,780
Monthly ($12,780/12)	$1,065

How the CPP Is Adjusted for Inflation: The YMPE

The YMPE is increased each year by the ratio of the average industrial aggregate (average weekly earnings as determined by Statistics Canada) during the 12-month period ending June 30 of the preceding year, to the average industrial aggregate during the corresponding period one year earlier. From 2014 to 2015, the YMPE increased by 2.1% because the average weekly earnings increased by that same percentage.

CPP Pension Increases

After you begin to receive the CPP pension the government uses the CPI index to adjust your CPP pension amount so that the benefits keep up with the cost of living.

The CPP pension is adjusted once a year using a twelve-month "moving average method," which helps to smooth out fluctuations that may occur in a single month. The rate used to increase the CPP pension is the average monthly All-items CPI index for the prior year's twelve-month period ending in October. They use October because they need to publish the rates for the next year in the fall of the previous year.

Note that if the cost of living decreases over a 12-month period, the CPP pension does not decrease but stays at the prior year's level. Also, while your CPP contribution rates increase every year by inflation, the retirement pension is calculated on the average of the last five years' YMPE, so it may lag behind current inflation.

The New CPP Rules

Significant new rules regarding the CPP were approved in Bill C-51 that passed into law on December 15, 2009. These rules are currently being phased in.

Penalty for Early Election

The normal age to elect for your CPP retirement pension to start is age 65. You can elect to receive it as early as age 60, but there is a cost if you do. Before the new rules came in, the penalty for early election was a reduction of 0.5% for each month that you elected to start receiving your pension before you turn 65 or 6% per year.

The new rules have increased this rate to 0.58% per month in 2015 (6.96% per year) and finally up to 0.60% in 2016 (7.2% per year).

Premium for Deferring Election

You can also elect to delay receiving your CPP pension after age 65 up to as late as age 70. In this case you used to get a premium of 0.5% a month for each month you waited. The new rules have increased this premium to 0.7% per month, or 8.4% per year.

Work Cessation Test Eliminated

Before 2012, for two months, the month before the CPP retirement pension was to begin and the month it did begin, you had to stop working or earn less than 25% of the CPP maximum pensionable earnings for the year of retirement and the preceding four years during those months. Now those under 65 who elect to receive the CPP early do not have to undergo a work cessation test.

Post-Retirement Benefit (PRB)

Under the old rules you could elect to start receiving your CPP before age 65, then go back to work and you would no longer have to pay CPP premiums on your earnings. Under the new rules, working beneficiaries under 65 are required to pay premiums to increase benefits. These premiums are the same as the regular premiums that everyone pays on their salary and self-employed earnings.

Like the CPP retirement pension, the amount of each PRB will depend on your level of earnings, the amount of CPP contributions you made during the previous year, and your age as of the effective date of the PRB.

For each year that you make a valid contribution to the CPP while receiving your retirement pension, you become eligible for a PRB the following January.

The maximum PRB for one year is equal to 1/40 of the maximum CPP retirement pension. If you contribute less than the maximum, the amount of the year's PRB will be proportional to your contributions. For example, if you contributed 50% of the maximum contribution level, you will receive 50% of the maximum PRB.

If you pay any amounts into your PRB one year, the amount of CPP pension you receive the next year, and every year thereafter, will increase (in addition to any inflationary increase).

After age 65 and up to age 70, you can opt out of continuing to pay CPP premiums, by filing election form CPT30 — *Election to Stop Contributing to the Canada Pension Plan, or Revocation of a Prior Election.*

There is also an online calculator that gives you an estimate of the yearly benefits you could receive from the PRB for a single year of contributions, based on your employment earnings for the year and your age. To see the table that is relevant to you, choose your year of birth from the pull-down menu. The calculator is at **www.servicecanada.gc.ca/eng/services/pensions/cric.shtml**

Increased Drop-out Provision

In calculating how much CPP you will receive, you are allowed to drop-out years of low earnings where you paid less than the maximum into your CPP. The percentage of years allowed has increased from 15% (prior to 2012) to 17%. This means the number of years you can drop-out has gone from seven to eight years, since there are 47 years from age eighteen to sixty-five (47 × 15% = seven, 47 × 17% = eight).

Note it is irrelevant when these years were (i.e., early or later in life).

How Much Will Your CPP Retirement Pension Be?

The way the government calculates the amount you will receive from your personal CPP pension is complex. It is based on the amount you paid in from the month you turned 18 to age 65 (or earlier if you elected early).

You cannot assume you will receive the maximum amount. In fact most Canadians have not paid in enough to receive the maximum. According to the federal government, the average CPP retirement pension (at age 65) in 2014 was $7,326.84, whereas the maximum was $12,459.96. That means most Canadians are receiving less than 60% of the maximum.

It is a good idea to consult a financial advisor who specializes in pensions. One advisor I consult when I need detailed information about the CPP (and OAS) is Doug Runchey of DR Pensions Consulting. He has over 30 years of prior experience working for the government on those two programs (see **www.drpensions.ca**). Doug has written a detailed article on how you can calculate exactly how much you will receive from your CPP retirement pension (see **http://retirehappy.ca/ how-to-calculate-your-cpp-retirement-pension**).

If you find the process too confusing or complex, you can email DR Pensions at **drpensions@shaw.ca** along with your CPP Statement of Contributions and any questions you may have about your CPP retirement pension calculation and he will help you for a small fee. (Disclaimer: I do not receive any compensation for referring people to DR Pensions, I do it because it is a very valuable service that is difficult to find.)

CPP: Should I Elect Early?

Unfortunately, just like most decisions related to personal finance, there is no easy answer. The main reason for this is that you need to know one important thing: How long will you live? That's a tough one to answer, but it makes a huge difference to your calculations.

For example, you retire at age 60 and end up passing away at age 68. If you elected early, at age 60, you would have received your CPP retirement pension at a reduced rate for eight years. If you had waited until age 65 you would have only received the full pension for three years. If you make the calculations you'd see that you would have been better off electing at age 60 because the greater number of years you collected the reduced pension outweighs the lesser number of years you collected the full one. (The reduction penalty of 34.8% in 2015 (five years at 6.96% per year) or 36% in 2016 (five years at 7.2% per year) of the amount at age 65 is not overcome by waiting because you only get the higher amount for three years. However, if you live to the age of 95, you'd see that it would be best to wait until age 65 to receive your CPP pension because you would be receiving the full amount for thirty years.)

So what should you do? Since it is impossible to do a detailed calculation because we don't know how long we will be receiving the
CPP pension, the best option is to go through a simple checklist
that includes the important issue of taxes because the CPP pension
is taxable when you receive it.

1. **Do you need the money early?**
    If the answer is yes, you need the money for groceries and other
    expenses, elect as soon as you can. End of story.

2. **If you don't really need the money, are you in a low tax
    bracket?**
    If you are in a lower tax bracket and you may be in a higher tax
    bracket later, consider electing early if you could use the money.

3. **Will your CPP pension be taxed when you receive it (possibly
    at a high rate)?**
    If you have RRSP room you could shelter it from tax by making
    an RRSP contribution for the same amount. If you are in a high
    bracket and have maxed out your RRSP room, defer electing
    until later since you will lose up to half of your early CPP pen-
    sion to taxes depending on your income level.

4. **If the answer to step 3 was you had RRSP room to shelter
    your CPP.**
    Do you think the amount in your RRSP will grow at a higher
    rate than the penalties to elect early or the bonus to wait?
    Remember the annual rate for early election is 6.96% in 2015
    and 7.2% in 2016 and the premium to wait is 8.4%. Those rates
    will be extremely difficult to beat after investment fees on a
    consistent basis.

To sum up, the government has achieved its objective of making
early election less attractive to the majority of Canadians. It seems
that waiting to receive your CPP pension is the best option unless
you need the money, or it is likely you will not live a long life.

Applying for Your CPP Retirement Pension

The simplest way is to sign in or register for a My Service Canada
Account (MSCA) located at **www.servicecanada.gc.ca/eng/online/
mysca.shtml**. Alternatively, you can fill and mail in form ISP 1000:
Application for Canada Pension Plan Retirement.

TIPS

When one spouse dies it can have a significant effect on the total CPP pension amount that will be received by the surviving spouse.

When a CPP contributor dies, CPP pays three kinds of Survivor Benefits:

- **The death benefit:** this is a one-time lump-sum payment (a maximum of $2,500 in 2015) paid to the estate of the person who died.
- **The survivor's benefit:** this is a monthly benefit for the spouse or common-law partner.
- **The children's benefit:** this monthly amount is paid to a dependent natural or adopted child of the deceased contributor, or a child in the care and control of the deceased contributor at the time of death. The child must be either under age 18 or between the ages of 18 and 25 and in full-time attendance at a school or university.

To qualify for any or all of these benefits, the deceased contributor must have contributed to the CPP in the lesser of: (1) one-third of the years in their contributory period (but no less than three years) or (2) ten years. Your contributory period begins when you turn 18 (or January 1, 1966, whichever is later) and ends when you either start receiving your CPP retirement pension, turn 70 or die (whichever happens earliest).

If you are receiving your CPP retirement pension and your spouse or common-law partner dies, you need to apply for a survivor's benefit. In this case you will receive a combined monthly benefit.

CPP WARNINGS

#1 Maximum Benefit

The amount of a combined survivor's/retirement benefit is limited to the maximum retirement pension. For example, if you begin receiving a combined benefit in 2015, the most you will receive is $1,065 a month. In other words, if you have been eligible to receive the maximum

CPP pension because you contributed to the plan during your working life, you won't receive anything extra on the death of your spouse or common-law partner.

#2 Survivor Benefit

If the surviving spouse or common-law partner is age 65 or older and not receiving any CPP benefits of their own, they are eligible for only a maximum of 60% of the contributor's retirement pension. It should be noted that the rules in this area are exceedingly complex for people under 65, people with disabilities and situations involving dependent children.

#3 OAS

There's also the shock of the surviving spouse losing the deceased spouse's OAS pension—a maximum of $563.74 a month or $6,764.88 per year in 2015.

For couples on a tight budget, these issues can lead to significant financial difficulties for the surviving spouse or common-law partner.

CHAPTER 8

Old Age Security: The New Rules

Your OAS Pension

The Old Age Security (OAS) pension is a monthly pension provided by the federal government that is available to most people aged 65 and older who meet the Canadian legal status and residence requirements. You are entitled to receive the OAS pension regardless of whether you have worked or not.

If you are living in Canada, you must:
- be 65 years old or older
- be a Canadian citizen or legal resident at the time the government approves your OAS pension application, and
- have resided in Canada for at least ten years after turning 18

If you are living outside Canada, the above rules are the same, except you must have resided in Canada for at least 20 years after turning 18.

The OAS pension is adjusted for inflation every three months. If you have resided in Canada for at least 40 years after turning 18, you should get the maximum.

Currently seniors have to apply to receive the OAS pension and it is recommended that you apply at least six months before you are eligible to start receiving it. They are, however, phasing in an automatic enrollment process that will eliminate the need for many seniors to apply. The department that handles the CPP and OAS, Service Canada, will send you a notification letter the month after you turn 64. If you don't receive this letter, you must apply for your OAS pension by completing and mailing form ISP-3000: Application for the Old Age Security Pension.

Your OAS Amount

In 2015 the maximum monthly amounts were as follows:
- January to March: $563.74
- April to June: $563.74
- July to September: $564.87
- October to December: $569.95

The total that a person could receive in 2015 was therefore $6,786.90.

OAS Clawback

The problem with OAS for higher income people is the clawback. In 2015, 15% of any net income before adjustments (line 234 on your tax return) above $72,809 is clawed back from the OAS that was received. This is called the threshold amount.

Anyone with a net income of $118,055 or more would have had all their OAS pension clawed back. That is because 15% of the difference of $45,246 ($118,055 less $72,809) is equal to $6,786.90.

If you have to pay back a portion of your OAS, it will show as a deduction on line 235 of your tax return as "social benefits repayment." This amount is deducted from line 234 to give line 236, your net income. The amount you owe is listed on the last page of your tax return on line 422 as "social benefits repayment."

OAS and GIS

If you have low income, you may be eligible to also receive the Guaranteed Income Supplement (GIS), which provides a monthly non-taxable benefit to OAS recipients who have a low income and are living in Canada. You qualify for the GIS if you meet all the following:
- you are a legal resident of Canada
- you are receiving an OAS pension
- your annual income (or combined income if a couple) not including your OAS pension is lower than the maximum annual income (currently $17,088 for singles and $22,560 for couples)

Changes to the OAS and GIS Age of Eligibility

Starting in April 2023, the age of eligibility for the OAS pension and the GIS will gradually increase from age 65 to 67 over six years with full implementation by January 2029.

Whether you are subject to the delayed start depends on your birthdate.

These changes have been introduced because the government is concerned about the future costs of the plan. It is estimated that there will be nearly twice as many people aged 65 and over in 2030 as there were in 2011 (9.4 million versus 5 million).

Paying the OAS pension to that many people would put significant pressure on the federal government's annual deficit because the OAS program is paid out of regular government revenues and therefore impacts their bottom line.

The age of eligibility affects you as follows.

If you were born in 1957 or earlier:
- You can still collect at age 65

1958
- If you were born before April 1 you can still collect at age 65
- April and May birthdays will have a one-month delay after turning 65
- June and July birthdays will have a two-month delay after turning 65
- August and September birthdays will have a three-month delay after turning 65
- October and November birthdays will have a four-month delay after turning 65
- December birthdays will have a five-month delay after turning 65

1959
- January birthdays will have a five-month delay after age 65
- February and March birthdays will have a six-month delay after turning 65
- April and May birthdays will have a seven-month delay after turning 65
- June and July birthdays will have an eight month delay after turning 65

- August and September birthdays will have a nine-month delay after turning 65
- October and November birthdays will have a 10-month delay after turning 65
- December birthdays will have an 11-month delay after turning 65

1960
- January birthdays will have an 11-month delay after turning 65
- February and March birthdays will have to wait until their 66th birthday
- April and May birthdays will have a one-month delay after turning 66
- June and July birthdays will have a two-month delay after turning 66
- August and September birthdays will have a three-month delay after turning 66
- October and November birthdays will have a four-month delay after turning 66
- December birthdays will have a five-month wait after turning 66

1961
- January birthdays will have a five-month delay after turning 66
- February and March birthdays will have a six-month delay after turning 66
- April and May birthdays will have a seven-month delay after turning 66
- June and July birthdays will have a an eight-month delay after turning 66
- August and September birthdays will have a nine-month delay after turning 66
- October and November birthdays will have a ten-month delay after turning 66
- December birthdays will have an eleven-month delay after turning 66

1962
- January birthdays will have an eleven-month delay after turning 66
- Anyone born after January will have to wait until they turn 67

1963 or later
- Will have to wait until age 67

New Voluntary Deferral

The government has brought in new rules that allow a voluntary deferral of the OAS pension for up to five years after the age of eligibility. If you elect to delay, you will receive a higher, actuarially adjusted pension when you do start to collect it. Your pension will be increased by 0.6% per month of deferral. That's 7.2% per year up to a maximum of 36% at age 70.

This provision has been in effect since July 1, 2013 so it should be considered if you currently earn more than the threshold amount, and expect future income to be under the threshold amount. In this case you will get to keep more of your pension because it will be higher due to the monthly bonus.

Conclusion

When combined, your CPP and OAS pensions are unlikely to be sufficient to fund your retirement. However, they are guaranteed by the government, adjusted for inflation and paid for your lifetime. That is a good, solid basis upon which to anchor your retirement.

CHAPTER 9

Your Retirement Investing Strategy

We have already reviewed your investing strategy leading up to retirement, so now we need to look at how that strategy might change after you retire.

Many people make the mistake of not altering their investing strategy when they retire, even though they should. Remember the rule of thumb that you should not hold a percentage of your investments in the stock market which is more than 100 minus your age? That rule is even more important after you retire, because significant stock market exposure during retirement puts you at extreme financial risk, and much of that risk is related to the timing of the stock market ups and downs.

The Dangers of Stock Market Timing

When you were younger and were saving for retirement, the volatility of the stock market was not as significant because you had many years to regain any losses that you incurred. Look at the following chart showing two 100% stock portfolios.

Portfolio A shows how $200,000 would grow over a 14-year period, assuming all the money was in an investment that mirrored the performance of the S&P TSX Composite Total Return Index and repeating a seven-year period from June 2007 to June 2014. Portfolio B uses the same rates but reverses the order of the stock market returns.

ACCUMULATION PHASE					
PORTFOLIO A Poor Early Returns			**PORTFOLIO B** Strong Early Returns		
Age	Return	Acc. Value	Age	Return	Acc. Value
51		$200,000	51		$200,000
52	6.7%	$213,400	52	30.0%	$260,000
53	-25.7%	$158,556	53	6.8%	$277,680
54	12.0%	$177,583	54	-10.3%	$249,079
55	20.9%	$214,698	55	20.9%	$301,136
56	-10.3%	$192,584	56	12.0%	$337,273
57	6.8%	$205,680	57	-25.7%	$250,594
58	30.0%	$267,383	58	6.7%	$267,383
59	6.7%	$285,298	59	30.0%	$347,599
60	-25.7%	$211,977	60	6.8%	$371,235
61	12.0%	$237,414	61	-10.3%	$332,998
62	20.9%	$287,033	62	20.9%	$402,595
63	-10.3%	$257,469	63	12.0%	$450,906
64	6.8%	$274,977	64	-25.7%	$335,023
65	30.0%	$357,470	65	6.7%	$357,470
Average IRR	**4.24%**			**4.24%**	

The interesting conclusion is that during the growth stage, the timing of the year-to-year rates is not that significant. The end result is the same: an average annual rate of return of 4.24%. During the retirement phase when you are drawing down from your retirement nest egg, however, the year-to-year timing can have a significant impact.

Here are the two portfolios that are 100% invested in equities. The starting value is $500,000 in each case and annual withdrawals are being made starting at $25,000 and increasing by 3% per year.

		RETIREMENT PHASE						

PORTFOLIO A Poor Early Returns				PORTFOLIO B Strong Early Returns			
Age	Return	Withdrawal	Acc. Value	Age	Return	Withdrawal	Acc. Value
65			$500,000	65			$500,000
66	6.7%	$25,000	$506,825	66	30.0%	$25,000	$617,500
67	-25.7%	$25,750	$357,439	67	6.8%	$25,750	$631,989
68	12.0%	$26,523	$370,626	68	-10.3%	$26,523	$543,103
69	20.9%	$27,318	$415,059	69	20.9%	$27,318	$623,584
70	-10.3%	$28,138	$347,069	70	12.0%	$28,138	$666,900
71	6.8%	$28,982	$339,717	71	-25.7%	$28,982	$473,973
72	30.0%	$29,851	$402,825	72	6.7%	$29,851	$473,878
73	6.7%	$30,747	$397,008	73	30.0%	$30,747	$576,071
74	-25.7%	$31,669	$271,446	74	6.8%	$31,669	$581,421
75	12.0%	$32,619	$267,486	75	-10.3%	$32,619	$492,275
76	20.9%	$33,598	$282,771	76	20.9%	$33,598	$554,541
77	-10.3%	$34,606	$222,604	77	12.0%	$34,606	$582,327
78	6.8%	$35,644	$199,673	78	-25.7%	$35,644	$406,185
79	30.0%	$36,713	$211,848	79	6.7%	$36,713	$394,227
80	6.7%	$37,815	$185,694	80	30.0%	$37,815	$463,336
81	-25.7%	$38,949	$109,031	81	6.8%	$38,949	$453,245
82	12.0%	$40,118	$77,183	82	-10.3%	$40,118	$370,575
83	20.9%	$41,321	$43,357	83	20.9%	$41,321	$398,068
84	-10.3%	$42,561	$714	84	12.0%	$42,561	$398,168
85	6.8%	$714	$0	85	-25.7%	$43,838	$263,267
86	30.0%	$0	$0	86	6.7%	$45,153	$232,728

Total withdrawals	$628,636				$716,912	

Difference in withdrawals ($716,912 - $628,636)			$88,276	
Difference in end value			$232,728	
Total difference			**$321,004**	

Portfolio A is unlucky and has poor early returns. Portfolio B, on the other hand, has good returns early, especially the first year. Look at the value of the portfolio at the end of age 67. Portfolio A has a value of $357,439 and portfolio B has a value of $631,989, which is $274,550 higher.

At age 86, portfolio A has been fully depleted with total withdrawals of $628,636. Portfolio B has provided withdrawals of $716,912 and still has $232,728 left in it. Portfolio B is therefore $321,004 ahead of portfolio due to the timing of the stock market returns.

This clearly illustrates the problem with being over-exposed to the stock market. If you get really lucky you might get the timing just right. But you could get very unlucky with the timing of stock market returns, and end up significantly cutting your nest egg with no way to make up for it.

Now this is an extreme example in order to illustrate a point. Few people would assume the risk of putting 100% of their retirement savings in the stock market at retirement age. If you are 65 when you retire, the rule of thumb we talked about would only allow 35% of the portfolio to be allocated to the stock market. This would reduce the chance of a major cut to your savings by limiting the amount at risk.

But what should you do with the rest of the portfolio, the portion allocated to fixed income? Guaranteed Investment Certificates (GICs) are worth considering.

Maybe Simple GICs Are All You Need

The two ongoing arguments against GICs are taxes and inflation.

The Tax Argument

The tax argument makes sense when we are talking about GICs in a regular investment account. That is because the interest you earn on a GIC is taxed as regular income at whatever marginal tax rate you are in. For example, if your GIC earns 2% in a year and you have to pay tax at a rate of 40%, your after-tax return would be a paltry 1.2%.

That is why I am a big fan of GICs but only when held in tax-sheltered vehicles like RRSPs, RRIFs and TFSAs. When held inside these types of investments, the interest accumulates either on a tax-deferred basis (in the RRSP and RRIF) or a tax-free basis (in the TFSA). So when we are talking about investing in GICs in our RRSP, RRIF or TFSA, the tax argument does not exist.

One caveat: if you are very risk averse and can't afford losses in your portfolio, stick to GICs even if they are in a taxable account.

The Inflation Argument

The other argument is about the effect of inflation: Why would I invest in a GIC earning 2% a year when inflation is 2% and therefore my "real" rate of return is 0%?

The problem is the argument then goes on to suggest that you'd fare better in the stock market with higher returns to "beat" inflation. However, what if higher returns don't happen? What if you get unlucky with the stock market and lose almost 50% of your investment as many indexes did in 2008/2009? How does that help you beat inflation? This type of thought process is often used to drive people's investing strategy and convinces them to take a significant amount of risk—often more than they should.

There is no doubt inflation is a problem for retirees. Rising prices means the same money buys less. So what is the best way to fight inflation? I would argue that fixed income products like GICs are actually quite good at fighting inflation because there is a correlation between interest rates and inflation, i.e., the central banks try to control inflation. The Bank of Canada has an objective to maintain inflation, as measured by the Consumer Price Index (CPI), at about 2%. If inflation increases and prices rise at a greater rate, the bank will increase its key interest rate (the overnight rate). This sends a signal to the commercial banks to raise their prime lending and other rates. The rising costs of using debt tends to discourage consumers from borrowing, which means they spend less and that leads to a slowdown in rising prices (disinflation).

The following chart shows the annual five-year GIC rate according to the Bank of Canada versus inflation as measured by the CPI All-Items Index going back to 1958.

GIC Rates versus Inflation

	Year	GIC Annual Rate 5-Year	Inflation CPI Index Total	Difference GIC over (Under)
1	1958	4.66	2.70	1.96
2	1959	5.28	0.70	4.58
3	1960	5.27	1.30	3.97
4	1961	4.96	1.30	3.66
5	1962	5.19	1.30	3.89
6	1963	5.15	1.30	3.85
7	1964	5.26	1.90	3.36
8	1965	5.52	2.40	3.12
9	1966	6.06	4.20	1.86
10	1967	6.34	3.40	2.94
11	1968	7.01	3.90	3.11
12	1969	8.03	4.80	3.23
13	1970	8.52	3.00	5.52
14	1971	7.75	3.00	4.75
15	1972	7.61	4.80	2.81
16	1973	8.19	7.80	0.39
17	1974	9.68	11.00	**-1.32**
18	1975	9.57	10.70	**-1.13**
19	1976	10.11	7.20	2.91
20	1977	8.96	8.00	0.96
21	1978	9.25	8.90	0.35
22	1979	10.40	9.30	1.10
23	1980	12.31	10.00	2.31
24	1981	15.36	12.50	2.86
25	1982	14.57	10.90	3.67
26	1983	11.52	5.80	5.72
27	1984	11.97	4.30	7.67
28	1985	10.80	4.00	6.80
29	1986	9.73	4.10	5.63
30	1987	9.61	4.40	5.21
31	1988	10.06	3.90	6.16
32	1989	10.31	5.10	5.21
33	1990	11.14	4.80	6.34
34	1991	9.30	5.60	3.70
35	1992	7.75	1.40	6.35
36	1993	6.47	1.90	4.57
37	1994	7.27	0.10	7.17
38	1995	7.14	2.20	4.94
39	1996	5.72	1.50	4.22
40	1997	4.74	1.70	3.04
41	1998	4.47	1.00	3.47
42	1999	4.81	1.80	3.01
43	2000	5.34	2.70	2.64
44	2001	4.05	2.50	1.55
45	2002	3.91	2.20	1.71
46	2003	3.13	2.80	0.33
47	2004	2.92	1.80	1.12
48	2005	2.71	2.20	0.51
49	2006	3.16	2.00	1.16
50	2007	3.31	2.20	1.11
51	2008	3.01	2.30	0.71
52	2009	1.94	0.30	1.64
53	2010	1.97	1.80	0.17
54	2011	1.87	2.90	**-1.03**
55	2012	1.65	1.50	0.15
56	2013	1.63	0.90	0.73
57	2014	1.90	2.10	**-0.20**
	Average	**6.78**	**3.86**	**2.92**

As you can see, GICs have historically done a good job of beating inflation: the annual GIC rate has been (on average) 2.92% higher over the 57-year period.

Inflation has been higher in only four years of the 57-year period: in 1974, 1975, 2011 and 2014. Therein lies the problem—GIC rates of today are historically low so they aren't beating inflation. But there is no solution to this problem. We have seen that the answer is not to jump into the stock market, because to do so would be incredibly risky and could backfire in a big way.

Many people wish that GIC rates would go back to the double-digit days of the eighties, but the problem is a relative one. We need to remember that inflation was also in the double digits—our investments did very well but the rising cost of living devoured a lot of the gains.

We can't do anything to alter inflation, so that means we have to watch our spending, manage our cash flow and minimize our taxes.

CHAPTER II

CHAPTER 10

Registered Retirement Income Fund versus Annuity

Converting Your RRSP to a RRIF or an Annuity

By December 31 of the year you turn 71, you must convert your RRSP to a Registered Retirement Income Fund (RRIF) or an annuity.

Converting Your RRSP before Age 71

What most people aren't aware of is that you don't have to wait until age 71 to convert your RRSP. You can choose to convert it to a RRIF or an annuity before that. From a tax point of view this might make sense at age 65 because only annuity payments from an RRSP or RRIF payments are eligible for pension income splitting and the $2,000 pension income non-refundable tax credit (see the end of this chapter for more information).

However, once you convert your RRSP, you will have to start the minimum withdrawals. For those under 71, the withdrawal percentage follows this formula:

Opening market value of the RRIF on January 1 × 1/(90–age)

For example, in the year where you were 65 on January 1 and turned 66 during that year, the percentage would be 1/(90–65), which is 1/25, or 4.0%. If your RRIF had an opening value of $400,000, the required withdrawal would be $16,000

($400,000 × 4.0%). Note that there is no maximum with a RRIF, you can take out more, or even all of it, but you will have to pay tax on the withdrawals.

 TIP: IF YOU HAVE A YOUNGER SPOUSE

> Don't forget that the minimum withdrawal can be based on your age OR your spouse's or common-law partner's age. But you can only use the age of your spouse if you elect to do so prior to receiving any payments from the fund. So make the decision before you start!
>
> This option is only an advantage if you don't need the money to finance your spending. In other words, if you need more than the minimum required based on your age, basing it on your younger spouse has no effect.

RRIF or Annuity?

As mentioned above, you must convert your RRSP to a Registered Retirement Income Fund (RRIF) or an annuity by December 31 of the year in which you turn 71.

First, we'll discuss the most popular method: the RRIF.

RRIFs

Converting an RRSP to a RRIF is basically just changing the name on the account from RRSP to RRIF. Your RRIF contains the investments that were in your RRSP when you converted it.

The problem with a RRIF is that you must make minimum withdrawals from it each year. The withdrawal rate (the "prescribed factor") is set by the federal government and is applied to the market value of your RRIF on January 1 of each year to determine how much you must withdraw by December 31.

Note that the Federal 2015 Budget reduced the minimum withdrawal factors for ages 71 and older. RRIF holders who at any time in 2015 withdraw more than the reduced 2015 minimum amount are allowed to re-contribute the excess to their RRIF up to the amount of the reduction in the new rates. This must be done by February 29, 2016 and will be deductible for the 2015 year.

Note that prior to the change, RRIFs that were set up prior to 1993 had lower minimum withdrawal factors than those that were set up after 1992. Starting in 2015 all plans use the new rates.

Here are the new withdrawal rates effective in 2015:

RRIF Minimum Withdrawal Rates from 2015			
Age (on Jan 1)	%	Age	%
71	5.28%	83	7.71%
72	5.40%	84	8.08%
73	5.53%	85	8.51%
74	5.67%	86	8.99%
75	5.82%	87	9.55%
76	5.98%	88	10.21%
77	6.17%	89	10.99%
78	6.36%	90	11.92%
79	6.58%	91	13.06%
80	6.82%	92	14.49%
81	7.08%	93	16.34%
82	7.38%	94	18.79%
		95 or older	20.00%

 RRIF ADVANTAGES

- The main advantage of a RRIF over an annuity is that if there is anything left at the date of death of the last surviving spouse, the after-tax amount can be passed on through an inheritance. Your investments may do so well that your next of kin may be very happy with the amount!

RRIF DISADVANTAGES

- Apart from the government legislating how much taxable income you must take out of your RRIF each year, the main problem is that you could run out of money before you die. Maybe you made some bad investment decisions, paid fees that were too high or simply took out more than you should—or maybe it was a combination of these things.
- When you die, the balance of your RRIF can pass tax-free to your surviving spouse or common-law partner. But when your partner dies, the market value of the RRIF at their date of death will be taxed on their final income tax return at their marginal tax rate at that time. If the RRIF has a high balance at their death, the tax bill could be significant.

Annuities

An annuity is a contract sold by an insurance company. You give them a cheque in exchange for their promise to pay you a certain amount of money for life. (**NOTE:** I am indebted to Kurt Rosentreter, CPA, CA (**www.kurtismycfo.com**), for the information on annuities in this chapter.)

Factors Affecting Annuity Payments

The amount of each annuity payment is based on the following factors:
- the amount of money invested
- your age
- your gender
- interest rates in the market
- the type of annuity
- features attached to the annuity (guarantee periods, number of lives, inflation indexing, etc.)
- income deferral (time until payments start)
- whether the payment is from a registered account (RRSP) or non-registered account

Each payment to a female is lower than for a male because females generally live longer than males, so the insurance companies know they will probably be making more payments to a 65-year-old woman than to a 65-year-old man.

The older you are, the fewer payments you will receive over your remaining life, so the payments will be higher if you start at a later age.

Types of Annuities

Single and Joint Life Annuities
A single life annuity is based on one person's life. They are useful for single people or for the last surviving spouse.

A joint (or last to die) annuity is for couples seeking to guarantee an income stream until the death of the second spouse.

Guarantee Periods
What if you hand over $100,000 to buy an annuity and then die the next day? This is why there are guarantee periods. You can have a guarantee of payments for 5, 10, 15, 20 or 30 years, but the longer the guarantee period, the lower the monthly payments.

Term Certain Annuity
This type of annuity guarantees payments for a pre-selected period of time, instead of for life. They are useful for covering fixed-period obligations such as the remaining amortization period of a mortgage.

Fixed versus Indexing
A fixed annuity maintains the payment throughout the term of the annuity. With an indexed annuity, the monthly payments are adjusted by an annuity factor to account for future inflation.

 ANNUITY ADVANTAGES

- The main advantage of an annuity is that you can't run out of money because they are paid for life. With people living a lot longer than they used to, guaranteed cash for life is a significant advantage.
- Annuities are also low maintenance. Once you hand over the cheque, you just sit back and wait for the cash to come in each month, so this is also an advantage for those people who don't want to worry about how their investments are doing.

ANNUITY DISADVANTAGES

- Since annuities end with your death, there is nothing left to pass on to your beneficiaries through an inheritance.
- Due to the current low rates being offered by the insurance companies, many people feel they can do better with their own investments inside a RRIF.
- You will have much less flexibility than with a RRIF (which enables you to take out a lump sum to finance something such as a vacation or a new car).

How Much Will You Get?

It will depend on several variables, but here's an example.

The following chart shows the monthly payment you would receive based on a premium of $100,000 paid from a registered account (RRSP), with a 10-year guarantee period and with payments commencing in one month.

Annuity - fixed
$100,000, 10-year guarantee, registered funds

	Age 65			Age 70		
	Male	Female	Joint	Male	Female	Joint
BMO Insurance	506.51	459.94	414.78	585.38	527.14	474.80
Canada Life	495.53	463.17	413.99	568.56	531.94	470.62
Desjardins Fin. Security	502.25	447.89	402.75	577.33	516.85	463.07
Empire Life	500.30	460.12	419.73	565.75	520.54	470.07
Equitable Life	511.88	463.64	423.27	582.66	532.35	478.35
Great-West Life	495.53	463.17	413.99	568.56	531.94	470.62
London Life	495.53	463.17	413.99	568.56	531.94	470.62
Manulife Investments	482.86	450.52	387.06	552.16	506.33	434.21
RBC Life Insurance	502.30	442.78	397.82	580.31	511.26	456.73
Standard Life	482.12	449.71	400.21	552.39	516.21	456.12
Sun Life Assurance Co	515.68	465.05	426.84	593.42	536.98	484.49

Source: Cannex March 9, 2015

These results show if you are a male, retired at age 65, and you paid $100,000 out of your RRSP, the most you would receive from one of these companies is $515.68 a month or $6,188.16 per year for life (from Sun Life Assurance Co.).

Let's look at the rates of return these payments would provide. In other words, the annual rates of return your RRSP would need to earn to be able to make the same payments if you had left the money in your RRSP.

If you live until age 85, the rate of return on your $100,000 payment for that series of 240 payments of $515.68 would be 2.2% per year. If you live until age 90, the rate of return would be 3.78%, and if you live until age 95, your rate of return would be 4.65% per year.

However, as we have discussed, there are other advantages to annuities that make a decision based solely on rates short-sighted. The main advantage is the guaranteed payments, no matter how long you live. And that is worth a lot as many people today are living longer than the previous generation.

A Combined Strategy

There is no rule saying you have to choose to purchase *either* a RRIF or an annuity with 100% of your RRSP when you turn 71. You could buy an annuity with some of your RRSP and leave the remainder in an RRIF.

This strategy makes a lot of sense. One method to determine your strategy is to calculate what your core annual expenses will be, i.e., the expenses you know you are going to have to pay for the rest of your life. You can then calculate how much of that amount will be covered by your other guaranteed income for life (your CPP and OAS pensions), and buy an annuity to make up the difference. In this way you have guaranteed you'll always be able to pay your core expenses and you'll also have some funds (inside your RRIF) that may have a better rate of return than the rates your annuity is paying. This may mean you will still have some money remaining so you can leave your kids an inheritance!

Tax Planning Opportunity

The first $2,000 of eligible pension income qualifies for a federal non-refundable pension income tax credit on your annual income tax return. Lifetime annuity payments from your RRSP as well as RRIF payments **do** qualify as eligible pension income; however, withdrawals from your RRSP **don't**.

So, assuming you need the money from age 66 to 71 (before you are forced to convert your RRSP to a RRIF or annuity), it would probably make sense to convert some of your RRSP money to an annuity to pay out at least $2,000 per year. Alternatively you could convert $12,000 of your RRSP to a RRIF and take out $2,000 each year from age 66 to 71. In both cases, you'd be eligible for the pension income amount.

Note that the provinces and territories also have pension income tax credits ranging from $1,000 to $2,000. The federal non-refundable tax credit rate is 15% and the provinces and territories range from 4% to 11%, so the $2,000 credit is worth between $351 and $440 per year in reduced taxes.

Your spouse may also be eligible for the same credit and, if they do not have any pension income, it might make sense to take advantage of pension income splitting. In this case, increase the amounts above to $4,000 per year and transfer $2,000 per year to your spouse.

 TIP

One of the best websites I have seen which explains Canadian tax and financial information is **www.taxtips.ca**. If you are seeking explanations about how taxes work in Canada, this is a good site to visit (please note I have no relationship with this website).

CHAPTER 11

Your Retirement Age

Advantage of Delaying Your Retirement

Delaying retirement for even one year can have a *very* positive impact because it's one more year that your earnings cover your expenses, another year of RRSP contributions and growth of those funds. It's also one less year that your RRSP has to cover your spending. So it makes sense to give a lot of thought to when you are going to retire.

The flip side of this positive news is that you may not have a choice. Increasingly, companies are looking for ways to cut costs — and experienced employees in their late fifties and early sixties are easy targets.

But let's start with the good news. We'll look at the Clarks' situation using the Procrastinator's Number Cruncher (see **Chapter 4**) to see what the financial impact would be if they delayed their retirement for one year.

I have changed the answer to the question "At what age do you plan to retire and stop making RRSP contributions?" to 66 for Mike and 64 for Nancy. This means that Mike and Nancy continue to earn their salaries until the end of the year in which they turn 66 and 64, respectively (the same year).

The chart below compares the end value net worth of the Clarks and assumes they retired in the year Mike turned 65 and Nancy turned 63 versus waiting for one more year. We need to compare the values at the same point in time — the end of the year in which they turn 66 and 64, respectively.

In this additional year their RRSPs grow, but they also withdraw some money to fund the year in which they turned 66 and 64. (In each scenario it is assumed that they would put 100% of any excess income into Mike's RRSP, rather than pay down the mortgage.)

	Mike Retires at age 65 Value at end of year 65	Mike Retires at age 65 Value at end of year 66	Mike Retires at age 66 Value at end of year 66
ASSETS			
House	$487,598	$497,350	$497,350
RRSP — Mike	$343,880	$329,419	$374,322
RRSP — Nancy	$202,260	$182,133	$257,970
Total assets	**$1,033,738**	**$1,008,902**	**$1,129,642**
LIABILITIES			
Mortgage	$164,413	$148,903	$148,903
Total liabilities	**$164,413**	**$148,903**	**$148,903**
Net Worth	**$869,325**	**$859,999**	**$980,739**

Comparing the last two columns we see that the Clarks' total net worth is $980,739 (higher by $120,740) versus $859,999 if they retired one year earlier.

Here is a summary of what makes up the difference:
- Mike's RRSP is higher by $44,903
- Nancy's RRSP is higher by $75,837

Think about how you much better you'd feel about financing your retirement years if you had that much more saved.

How to Make It Happen

In my book *Cash Cows, Pigs and Jackpots: The Simplest Personal Finance Strategy Ever*,[1] I make the point that when it comes to cash inflows, you are the best cash cow you'll ever have. In other words, your ability to earn income is the biggest source of cash you're

1   (Mississauga, Ontario: John Wiley & Sons Canada, Ltd., 2012).

likely to have and therefore it makes sense to nurture yourself. I make the case that proper diet, exercise and sleep is the best way to make sure you keep on earning.

And of course the better shape you are in, the lower your medical costs are likely to be as you get older. If you keep yourself in shape, not only will you feel better, but you'll be much more likely to be able to work past age 65.

So what are you waiting for? Resolve to get in better shape immediately!

The Consulting Option

One of the advantages of being self-employed is that you have to develop the ability to find work. You can't survive if you don't because, unlike a job, you don't get a pay cheque for showing up every day and working.

But those who are not self-employed and depend on a job their whole life are at a distinct disadvantage if they get laid off before they had planned. That could result in serious damage to their retirement savings as there are fewer years to build them and more years of retirement to finance. If this is your situation, I encourage you to think about how to find clients who could use your skills in consulting or another role. In the later stages of our lives we have a lot of experience that is of value to someone. But you need to figure out how to find them.

I have always found that developing personal contacts is the most efficient way of building a network. Develop a system to track potential clients and referral sources and then keep in touch with them. Invite them for a coffee or a lunch once in a while, or maybe even for a few drinks in the evening. Don't rule anyone out—I have found some of my best referral sources are those whom you might consider "competitors." For example, other accountants have referred accounting clients to me—and other personal finance trainers have put me in touch with organizations that hire me to give my half- and full-day seminars.

Conclusion

You may not have a lot of control over when you retire if you are subject to your employer's whims, or perhaps because of health concerns, but do yourself a favour and give some thought to when your ideal retirement date would be.

Remember, if you can extend it by even one year, it could make a significant difference in the amount of money you'll have to spend in your retirement.

CHAPTER 12
How Long Will You Live?

To plan your retirement spending accurately it would really help to know how long you are going to live. That is a tough question to answer—but that doesn't mean you shouldn't give it some serious thought.

What the Statistics Say

Statistics Canada has published a chart which shows the life expectancy (at birth and at age 65) for the Canadian provinces and territories for the period 2009 to 2011.

The chart on the next page shows the current reality. In Canada, males who reach the age of 65 are likely to live to age 84 (19 more years) and females can generally expect to live to age 87 (22 more years).

Of course you need to factor in your health and your family history. You may not live as long as the average person or you may live longer. However, statistically you are unlikely to live to be 95 or 100 years old.

So how does this affect your planning? As a starting point, you should assume that you need to budget for about 19 or 22 years of retirement after age 65.

**Life Tables, Canada, Provinces and Territories
2009 to 2011**

	At birth		Final age (at age 65)	
	Males	Females	Males	Females
	Years		Years	
Canada	79.33	83.60	83.82	86.73
Newfoundland and Labrador	77.09	82.00	82.28	85.39
Prince Edward Island	78.15	82.90	82.95	85.96
Nova Scotia	78.05	82.64	82.92	85.83
New Brunswick	78.36	83.14	83.36	86.24
Quebec	79.43	83.55	83.60	86.56
Ontario	79.77	83.92	84.00	86.89
Manitoba	77.72	82.19	83.12	86.25
Saskatchewan	77.20	82.20	83.28	86.42
Alberta	79.06	83.45	83.81	86.83
British Columbia	80.25	84.40	84.65	87.32
Yukon	75.19	79.61	81.24	83.87
Northwest Territories	76.28	80.07	82.76	85.23
Nunavut	68.75	73.91	79.55	80.39

Source: Statistics Canada, Demography Division.

"Resting Heartbeat" Theory

Preet Banerjee, a personal finance expert and consultant to the financial services industry (see **www.wheredoesallmymoneygo.com**) refers to an online calculator that predicts how long you can expect to live based on your resting heartbeat. It can be found at **www.csgnetwork.com/avglifeexpfromhr.html**. The theory is based on the average healthy human heart with no other factors involved. According to Dr. Robert Jarvic, inventor of the artificial heart, the potential average number of heartbeats in a lifetime by a healthy heart is "greater than 2 billion." The American Heart Association says the average potential is 2.6 billion and other organizations estimate a range from 2 billion to 2.9 billion. (Of course, all the estimates are qualified guesses that can't be verified.)

According to the website, the average heart rate for adult humans is 70 to 75 beats per minute in relaxed mode. Each person has different levels of stress and other factors, so your rate may be outside the average range. (Note that the site strongly suggests that if you are concerned about heart risk factors you should contact your doctor to address your concerns).

The website uses default variables of 72 beats per minute (bpm) and 2.6 billion lifetime beats. This yields an anticipated lifespan of only 68.66 years. (I input my resting heart rate of 53 and I get a potential life expectancy of 93 years.)

Try it and see your result. It may even encourage you to exercise more to reduce your heart rate so you'll live longer. But beware, that will mean you'll have to save more for retirement!

Don't Worry, Be Happy!

Believing we are going to live to a ripe old age (e.g., 95 or 100) could have a negative impact on our lives because if we think we will need more money, we tend to adapt our behaviour, such as:

- scrimp and save before retirement to build up a massive RRSP
- don't take great vacations because we "can't afford it"
- constantly worry about running out of money during retirement, thus making it difficult to enjoy our lives
- start to think about how much is left for our kids to inherit, causing us to spend even less.

 A CAUTIONARY TALE

One of my readers was very concerned about the possibility of living a long life, so he delayed his dream of taking an African lion safari because he thought he couldn't afford it.

He and his family scrimped and saved for decades and saved every penny they could, which meant they didn't go on vacations when the kids were still at home; they rarely enjoyed meals out at a restaurant and they stayed in their small house instead of moving to a more comfortable home. Finally, they retired, but the worries about running out of money did not stop. "Maybe we'd better not go just yet, let's wait a few years and see how this retirement thing goes," was the refrain in their first few years of retirement. Finally, they decided it was time to go and they started to plan their dream safari vacation. Sadly, at this advanced age he was unable to get health insurance for the trip, so their dream vacation never happened.

Maintaining Balance in Your Life

I am the first to admit that I am cheap! If I was on my own I would have zero debt, a smaller house and a big savings account—and I probably would have maxed out my RRSP and TFSA—but I am fortunate enough to be married to a person who keeps me balanced. She convinced me to go on a European vacation while the kids were young and she talked me into buying a $1,000 video camera when our first child was born. In both instances we really couldn't afford it, but what is the current value of those experiences and videos? Priceless.

You need to have balance. If both you and your spouse (if you have one) like to spend money, you need to create a budget and cut back and save more. On the other hand, if you and your spouse like to save money and are worried about financing your old age to 100 (or more), perhaps you can afford to relax a little and enjoy life a bit more, before it's too late.

CHAPTER 13

Old Age Healthcare Planning

Medicare

Medicare, Canada's health care system, provides universal coverage for medically necessary health care services on the basis of need rather than the ability to pay. It is a publicly funded system composed of an interlocking set of ten provincial and three territorial health insurance plans and covers required hospital and primary care physician services. All Canadian citizens and permanent residents are eligible for public health insurance and when you have insurance you don't pay directly for most health care services.

Health Canada's mandate is to help Canadians maintain and improve their health. Among other roles, their responsibilities include setting and administering national principles for the health care system through the *Canada Health Act*. This federal legislation puts conditions in place by which the provinces and territories may receive funding for health care services. Under the *Canada Health Act*, primary care doctors, specialists, hospitals and dental surgery are all covered by provincial insurance policies.

Provincial and Territorial Plans

New residents to a particular province or territory must apply for health coverage and, upon approval, will be issued a health card which provides coverage in that province or territory. Certain provinces (British Columbia, Alberta and Ontario) require health care premiums for services, but under the *Canada Health Act*, health services cannot be denied due to financial inability to pay premiums.

Each province and territory has its own health insurance plan that provides free emergency services, even if you do not have a government health card. If you have an emergency, go to the nearest hospital. If you go to a walk-in clinic in a province or territory where you are not a resident, you might be charged a fee.

Here is a listing of the provincial and territorial ministries of health that are responsible for administering health care:

Alberta	**www.health.alberta.ca**
British Columbia	**www.gov.bc.ca/health**
Manitoba	**www.gov.mb.ca/health**
New Brunswick	**www2.gnb.ca/content/gnb/en/ departments/health.html**
Newfoundland and Labrador	**www.health.gov.nl.ca/health**
Northwest Territories	**www.hss.gov.nt.ca**
Nova Scotia	**novascotia.ca/DHW**
Nunavut	**www.gov.nu.ca/health**
Ontario	**www.health.gov.on.ca/en**
Prince Edward Island	**www.healthpei.ca**
Quebec	**www.msss.gouv.qc.ca/en/ index.php**
Saskatchewan	**www.saskatchewan.ca**
Yukon	**www.hss.gov.yk.ca**

Health Insurance

Government health insurance plans give you access to basic medical services. You have to pay for any services that are not covered or you can pay for private insurance to cover them. The most popular insurance plans are extended health plans that cover:
- those prescription medications not covered by government plans
- dental care
- physiotherapy

- ambulance services
- prescription eyeglasses
- travel insurance
- private or semi-private hospital accommodation

If you are employed you may get coverage from your employer. These plans usually cover the items listed above and some insurance plans may even continue coverage after you retire.

It's not possible to list the details of coverage for each province or territory, so I'll address the health care coverage in the most populated province, Ontario. Consult the website for your province/territory listed above for your specific health care coverage.

The Ontario Health Insurance Plan (OHIP)

OHIP covers a wide range of health services that are funded by the Ministry of Health and Long-Term Care. The following is a summary of insured services.

Physicians

OHIP covers all medically necessary doctor's visits and treatments, including any tests that are provided by or ordered by your doctor. OHIP does not cover services that are not medically necessary, e.g., cosmetic surgery. Physicians usually charge for any uninsured services.

Podiatrists, Chiropractors and Osteopaths

Only partial coverage is provided for podiatry and you must pay for the costs that exceed the OHIP yearly allowable maximum. You may need to pay the full or partial cost of services provided by other health care providers, such as chiropractors and osteopaths.

Physiotherapy

OHIP covers insured physiotherapy services that you receive in hospital and some that are provided in licensed physiotherapy clinics or through a Community Care Access Centre.

Dental Services in Hospital

Some dental surgery is covered but only if it is considered medically necessary and is provided in hospital. You have to pay for any dental services provided in a dentist's office.

TIP

> Note that several universities and colleges have dental clinics open to the public and that the fees are usually lower than private practitioners' fees.

Eye Care

OHIP insures one eye exam by a medical doctor or optometrist every year for people under 20 or those who are 65 and over. OHIP also covers a major eye exam once every 12 months for persons aged 20–64 who have medical conditions requiring regular eye examinations. Other medically necessary care (e.g., cataract surgery) provided by a medical doctor is insured. Uninsured services include the cost of eyeglasses, contact lenses and laser eye surgery.

Hearing Tests

OHIP insures diagnostic tests that are ordered or performed by a doctor as well as some tests performed in a hospital. Services provided by audiologists, such as fitting and evaluation of hearing aids, are not covered.

Ontario Drug Benefit Program

People 65 years old and older are eligible for the Ontario Drug Benefit (ODB) program if they have a valid Ontario Health Card. You don't need to apply for coverage and should receive a letter of notification of ODB eligibility by mail approximately two months before you turn 65. To start receiving benefits, notify your pharmacist that you are now eligible for the program and he or she will confirm your eligibility on the government's Health Network System.

The ODB program runs from August 1 to July 31 each year. You may be asked to pay for a portion of your prescription drug costs (a "co-payment"). If you are a single senior with an income of more than $16,018 a year or $24,175 a year for couples you fall into the higher income co-payment category. You will pay a $100 deductible for prescriptions filled after August 1 of each year. After you have paid the total $100 deductible, you will then pay $6.11 towards the ODB dispensing fee for each prescription for a covered drug in the benefit year. If your income(s) is below these amounts you may be asked to pay $2 for each prescription filled.

The ODB program covers most of the cost of over 3,200 prescription drugs listed in the "ODB Formulary," in addition to a number of limited-use drug products, nutrition and diabetic testing products.

The drug must be prescribed by an authorized Ontario prescriber (e.g., a family doctor) and purchased in an Ontario pharmacy that is online with the Ministry of Health and Long-Term Care's computerized Health Network System, or from an Ontario doctor who dispenses prescription drugs. When both generic and brand name drug products are available, the ODB pays the pharmacist for the lowest cost alternative.

The ODB does not cover prescription drugs purchased outside Ontario, syringes and other diabetic supplies such as lancets and glucometers, eyeglasses, dentures, hearing aids or compression stockings.

Community-Based Health Services

Community-based services are also referred to as "home care," "home health care," "in-home care" or "outreach services." They help seniors and persons with physical disabilities to live independently and remain in their homes as long as possible. They provide visiting health services at home to people with a disability, illness or limitation due to aging who would otherwise need to go to, or stay in, a hospital.

In-home health and support services are available in Ontario communities through 43 Community Care Access Centres (CCAC). A CCAC case manager will recommend the most appropriate services for you, based on an assessment of your needs. Some of those services may be covered by the Ministry of Health and Long-Term Care regardless of your financial situation.

Case managers are your single point of access to information for community support services such as in-home services, respite services, adult day programs as well as long-term care placement. They can help determine eligibility and arrange for essential services, such as:
- visiting health and support services in your home
- services for people recovering from surgery or an acute illness
- support services to enable people with physical disabilities to live independently at home
- a variety of services that help frail older adults to remain living independently at home
- facility-based care for those who require 24-hour nursing service to meet their nursing and personal care needs
- information and referrals if you wish to purchase additional services

Services may include nursing care, physiotherapy, occupational therapy, speech-language therapy, palliative care, dietetic services, social work and personal support services (such as bathing, dressing, homemaking (e.g., meal preparation) and feeding. You can receive in-home services if you are an Ontario resident, have a valid Ontario Health Card, adequate treatment can be provided at home and your needs cannot be met as a hospital outpatient.

To find the CCAC nearest you, go to **www.healthcareathome.ca** or call the Senior's INFOline toll-free at 1-888-910-1999.

Housing Choices for Seniors

If staying in your home or apartment becomes too difficult for you, you may want to consider a move. Seniors who are able to live independently have a number of housing options to choose from, some of which may include health and support services if needed.

The main options include:
* independent living (such as your own house, condominium, apartment or housing co-operative with the assistance of community-based health services)
* adult lifestyle retirement communities
* retirement homes
* social housing for seniors
* supportive housing
* long-term care facilities

Adult Lifestyle Retirement Communities

These provide independent-living residences for retirees in a community of healthy seniors. Residences may include bungalows, townhomes, small houses or condominiums providing the benefits of home ownership with on-site recreational and community activities. Amenities can include 24-hour security, social interaction with other seniors, and leisure and recreational activities. The ownership structure can range from simple ownership, condominium, land-lease and life-lease options. (Life lease is a form of housing tenure generally developed for seniors that is similar to a condominium.) Life leases are typically operated by non-profit or charitable institutions. A tenant is granted the right to occupy a dwelling unit in return for an up-front payment and monthly maintenance fee payments.

Retirement Homes

These are operated by private businesses that offer various combinations of accommodation, support services and personal care. They are almost always for-profit with no funding or regulation of care or support services by the provincial government. You are responsible for the entire cost of both the accommodation and care services, unlike long-term care facilities which are subsidized by the government.

However, retirement home accommodation rates are subject to rent controls. Retirement homes vary widely in terms of care and services provided, amenities offered, types of accommodations, staffing patterns and physical structure (from converted house to high-rise buildings). Costs vary widely and are dependent on the type of accommodation and the services provided.

Social Housing for Seniors

This is affordable housing for seniors, for both families and single people with low to moderate income. The owners may include private landlords with rent supplement units, municipalities that own public housing or non-profit/co-operative corporations that own housing projects. They receive a subsidy from the municipality or a cost-shared subsidy from the federal government to provide rent geared-to-income (RGI) units.

Supportive Housing

These programs provide on-site personal support services for seniors living as tenants in designated residential buildings such as seniors' buildings. They are designed to help people live independently in their own apartments and offer services including personal support, attendant services, essential homemaking services and staff available 24 hours a day to handle regularly scheduled care and emergency needs.

Long-Term Care Facilities

A senior who is no longer able to live independently in his or her own home, who requires more support than that offered by a supportive living environment, or who is at risk in his or her home may require placement in a long-term care facility. They are designed for people who need 24-hour on-site nursing services and daily personal assistance. They are provincially regulated and funded and are often referred to by their historical names: nursing homes, municipal homes for the aged and charitable homes for the aged.

A Community Care Access Centre case manager determines eligibility for admission to a long-term care facility. The CCAC also determines priority for admission and manages the waiting lists for facilities. Generally, applicants must be 18 years of age or older, have a valid Ontario Health Card and require 24-hour on-site nursing care plus assistance with activities for daily living or on-site supervision throughout the day to ensure their safety or well-being.

It must be shown that the applicant's care requirements can best be met in a long-term care facility and that none of the publicly funded, community-based services or other caregiving, support or companionship arrangements available to the applicant are suffi-cient to meet their requirements.

The Ontario government pays for all nursing and personal care services in long-term care facilities. However, residents must pay for their accommodation costs. The maximum amount residents can be charged for accommodation is determined by the province and is set out in regulations.

People who cannot afford the full basic accommodation rate can apply to the Ministry of Health and Long-Term Care for a rate reduction. People in preferred accommodation (semi-private and private rooms) must pay the full rate for basic accommodation plus a premium.

Residents may choose to pay for additional services such as cable TV, telephone and hairdressing.

The Realities of Old Age Healthcare in Canada

When I need detailed information about financial planning, invest-ing and insurance, I consult Kurt Rosentreter, CPA, CA, CFP, an investment advisor and insurance agent with Manulife Securities. His website is **www.kurtismycfo.com** and there you will find a num-ber of excellent newsletters he has written. One of them addresses the realities of old age healthcare in Canada and he has generously allowed me to use some of its content.

The newsletter notes that the health care system is difficult to navigate and that it can be expensive, despite the fact that it is quite good for short-term illness and injury. For example, if a Canadian has a stroke, the medically required services are covered (such as a physician, hospital care and essential short-term hospital accommodation), but most government support ends there. The majority of necessary medical equipment (e.g., wheelchairs, hearing aids and oxygen supplies) is not covered and nor are home safety modifications to make the home more accessible (e.g., wheelchair ramps and safety bars).

Since the *Canada Health Act* only covers physician access and hospital accommodation, the provinces vary widely in what is provided to those who require long-term care accommodation, personal home care and other forms of long-term care.

The Cost of Care

Long-Term Care Facility
As we know, the Government of Ontario covers the cost of healthcare in a long-term care facility including personal care, nursing and medication, but not the accommodation or other services (such as cable TV and telephones). The cost depends on the type of room and varies as follows as of August 5, 2015):
- Standard room (dorm style with four people sharing one room): $1,774.81 per month
- Semi-private room: $2,139.81 per month
- Private room: $2,535.23 per month
- Short stay: $37.77 per day

(See **www.ontario.ca/page/find-long-term-care-home** for the current cost of care.)

The downside to the low-cost option is longer waiting times. Because of the demand for this type of accommodation, and the shortage of long-term care facilities, it is not uncommon for people to wait for months for a spot to open up. Because of the demand, many people end up having to accept the first bed that comes available, even if it is hundreds of kilometres from their home, family and friends.

Staying at Home

The decision to stay at home and receive care can also be a costly option. The newsletter cites an example of a 79-year-old man with advancing Parkinson's disease who has opted to stay at home. This "high needs" client requires a lot of care:

- 35 hours per week of personal care ($25 per hour)
- 14 hours for meal preparation ($23.95 per hour)
- 3 hours of skilled nursing care ($49.60 per hour)
- 2.5 hours for laundry and house cleaning ($23.50 per hour)
- 24 hours for companionship/supervision when his son and daughter-in-law are unable to look after him ($23.50 per hour)

The cost of each of these services is high (prices above are provincial averages and are current at the time of writing) and the total costs add up very quickly—to $8,214.82 per month in this case. Even with the government subsidy covering the cost of 20 hours a week of personal care and 1 hour a week of nursing, the net amount that must be paid is $6,101.42 per month, or more than $72,000 per year for this one person. And this doesn't factor in the cost of home modifications like wheelchair ramps, bathroom support bars, stair lifts, walk-in bathtubs and power wheelchairs.

Retirement Home

For many people a retirement home is a viable option, but the government does not cover the cost, so it too can be expensive. Depending on the type of living arrangement and the extra care needed, Ontario residents can expect to pay between $1,489 and $5,586 per month with an average of $2,677 per month according to the newsletter. The cost is even greater at high-end homes.

Regardless of which option you choose, the cost of health care and accommodation can be very expensive.

Single Accommodation or Double?

A couple sharing a room is usually less expensive than two seniors living in separate accommodation. However, in many cases, it is only one of the spouses that needs long-term care. If the healthier spouse still lives in the couple's house or apartment, the combined living costs increase significantly.

Income Tax Credits and Deductions

The Government of Canada provides a number of tax breaks to help reduce the cost of aging.

Medical Expense Tax Credit

Medical expenses for you, your spouse or common-law partner and dependent children under the age of 18 can be claimed. A wide variety of costs qualify, including prescription drugs, dental work, eye care, cancer treatment, medically required home renovations and walking aids. This is a non-refundable tax credit where only expenses in excess of the lesser of $2,208 for 2015 or 3% of your net income can be claimed for the federal tax credit.

Disability Tax Credit

This non-refundable tax credit provides a break for people who live with a long-term mental or physical impairment that makes it difficult for them to perform everyday activities. A medical doctor must confirm eligibility. The federal credit is $7,899 for 2015.

Caregiver Amount Tax Credit

If at any time in a tax year you (either alone or with another person) maintained a dwelling and you or your spouse or common-law partner's parent or grandparent age 65 or older lived with you, you may be able to claim the federal Caregiver Amount tax credit in the amount of $4,608 for 2015. This non-refundable tax credit is reduced when the net income of the parent or grandparent exceeds $15,736 and is eliminated at net income of $20,343 for 2015.

Also note that your province or territory will have its own tax credits and possibly grants related to aging. It is important that you hire a professional tax preparer with experience in this area to make sure you are minimizing your tax bill.

The CareGuide Source for Seniors

The CareGuide Source for Seniors is an excellent source of information for senior housing and care services. It is available online at **www.thecareguide.com**. It has comprehensive information for all provinces to help people navigate the challenge of finding appropriate housing and care for themselves and their loved ones. It has advice, articles, tips, interactive needs assessment tools, as well as listings and direct links to community support and in-home care services, independent and supportive living, retirement residences and long-term care centres, Alzheimer care providers and hospice care.

PART THREE

Special Situations

CHAPTER 14
Attacking Debt

In this book we have dealt with a fictitious family, the Clarks. We have travelled with them on a journey from being in credit card debt with ten years to go before retirement, to having significant savings in their RRSPs to finance their retirement years. However, many Canadians do not have as many assets and have much more debt than the Clarks. For them the journey is going to be tougher. Perhaps this applies to you? If so, this chapter is for you.

Why Are People in Debt?

Before we get into the details of how to get out of debt, let's start with the root of the problem.

Anyone who has a balance of consumer debt, like credit cards they can't pay off, must al some time have been spending more than their income, i.e., their after-tax take home pay has been consistently lower than the expenses going out of their bank account. Those expenses may have been for a variety of things, some necessary and some not. The expenses, or cash outflows, may have been for vital things like groceries, mortgage payments or education costs for their kids, or they could be for optional choices such as vacations or expensive items (e.g., a big flat screen TV, designer shoes) that are beyond the family's budget.

Many people extol the virtues of making the distinction between "wants" and "needs." This makes sense but is not always helpful because if you listed all the cash outflows in your life over the last year, you'd probably find that the majority of them fit into the "wants" category rather than the "needs" category. What are your basic needs? You need food, water and shelter. But you don't need to eat out several times each week, you don't need a million-dollar house and you don't need expensive vacations. Many people could survive on a much lower percentage of their income if they down-sized their house and limited their spending to food and other basics.

That is why it is important to track your personal finances to see where your money is being spent because the only way to pay off your debt is to reduce your spending or increase your income (or do both).

Tracking Your Spending

In our busy world, there are many excuses for not tracking your spending: "I'm not good with numbers," "Spreadsheets freak me out," "I don't have time to track my spending, I've got too many other things to do, and I have a job and a family." What if there was a way that would do it for you automatically with just a little effort from you? Then **www.mint.com** may be for you.

Mint.com

This website is a free site operated by Intuit, Inc., the makers of QuickBooks bookkeeping software.[2]

Once you sign up and enter your personal banking information, the site automatically downloads your transactions, gathers all your personal financial information in one place and presents the results to you in charts, graphs and line-by-line details.

You are required to enter your banking and credit card user names and passwords, so you need to satisfy yourself that your data is secure. There is a section on the website dealing with security that states they use 128-bit SSL encryption and that they are verified by third party entities such as TRUSTe and VeriSign. However, you need to feel comfortable that you are giving them access to down-load your banking information.

They will send you a weekly email summarizing your spending as well as how you are doing with any budget categories that have been set up. You can even set up bill payment reminders so you'll get an email to remind you to pay a bill. You will also receive

---

2   Please note: I have no business relationship with Intuit and receive no compensa-
     tion from them for mentioning their site.

suggestions and advice about ways to save money that are often accompanied by an offer from a financial institution that has a business relationship with Intuit. (That's one of the reasons the site is free!)

One of the most useful sections is the "Trends" section where you can instantly see a donut chart of where your money has gone during the previous 7 or 14 days, month or year. Here is an example of what that looks like by category:

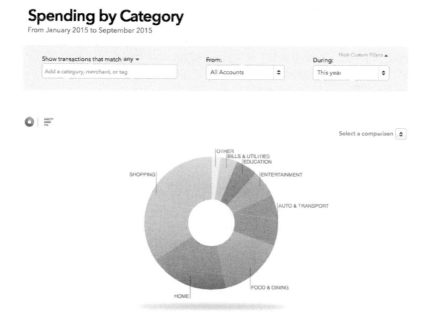

Spending by Category
From January 2015 to September 2015

Show transactions that match any ▾	From:	During:
Add a category, merchant, or tag	All Accounts ⬍	This year ⬍

Select a comparison ⬍

Your Spending

CATEGORY	SPENDING
Shopping	$4,893.55
Home	$2,700.00
Food & Dining	$2,260.00
Auto & Transport	$1,765.00
Entertainment	$925.98
Education	$750.00
Bills & Utilities	$580.30
Uncategorized	$120.00
Show more	$176.00
Total	**$14,170.83**

Export to CSV

Top Category
$4,894
on Shopping

Most Purchases
70
on Food & Dining

If you click on any category in the donut chart, it will show you the total dollars, the percentage of the total spending and the number of transactions making up the total. Click on the number of transactions and it will take you to the line-by-line details with the date, description and subcategory of each entry (i.e., Kids' University Tuition, Kids' Activities, etc.). It will also give you your net income, or difference between your income and your spending each month.

Where Did All My Cash Go?

The next step is to review where your cash has gone. What are the big money drains? Are there any expenses that are going to end in the near future? Are you surprised how much you spent in certain areas? Did you spend a lot of cash? After this analysis you should be fully aware of the problem areas in your spending.

Why Paying off Debt is Hard

If someone is overloaded with debt it is usually because they have been living beyond their means, i.e., they have been spending more than they have been earning. To get out of debt, it is necessary to cut your spending to break even. If you reduce your spending to match your income, you will get to the point where you aren't adding new debt each month; but in order to pay off your debt, you have to be spending *less* than you make, which means you will have to cut even more of your spending. In many cases, this will be very challenging because your spending cuts may have to be severe. However, it's what you'll have to do if you really want to gain control and pay off all your debt.

Credit Card Debt

The real problem with credit card debt is the high interest rate (especially department store cards, which can be as high as 29%), which compounds on a daily basis, so your debt increases daily until the debt is paid off, and it can be devastating to your financial situation. (This is the opposite of what happens to your savings when you invest, because then compounding is working for you.)

Here's a simple example: You had a $10,000 credit card balance owing at the beginning of the year at a rate of 20% interest per year. How much interest would you owe after the first year assuming you made no payments during that year? You would expect it to be $2,000, but the interest is actually $2,213 because the credit card company is calculating interest the first day, adding that to the balance and then calculating it the next day, and so on for the rest of the year. In this case, approximately $184 ($2,213/12) is being added to the credit card balance owing each month. Obviously that makes getting out of debt much more difficult.

If you have revolving credit card debt at a high rate of interest, there are several options.

Step 1: Cancel Your Points/Department Store Card
Call your credit card issuer, cancel your high-interest card and replace it with a basic card. In many cases you can cut your interest costs in half very quickly as the basic cards charge much lower rates. (We'll discuss the best points cards in **Chapter 19**, because they are only beneficial if you don't carry a balance.)

Step 2: Balance Transfer Option
The next option is to shop around for a better rate. Look for a balance transfer offer from another credit card company. These offers are constantly changing. I have seen offers ranging from zero interest for a year to 3% for six months on transfers.

If you have a good credit score, you can easily find and apply for cards that will accept a balance transfer. One of the best sites I have found is **www.ratesupermarket.ca**. Just Google "best credit card balance transfer offers" and you should find the page on the site **www.ratesupermarket.ca/credit_cards/low_balance_transfer**

When I last checked, there were 20 different cards listed including the following offers:
*   Scotiabank Value® VISA card: 0.99% for 6 months
*   Platinum Plus® MasterCard® credit card: 0.00% for 12 months
*   RBC Royal Bank® Visa Infinite Avion: 1.90% for 10 months
*   President's Choice Financial World MasterCard: 0.97% for 6 months.

These companies make these offers because they know the person involved is unlikely to change his or her habits and be able to pay off the balance. The new credit card company then becomes the one collecting the high interest after the transfer period is over.

The key is to make sure you have a plan for when the introductory period expires. The best idea is to pay off the balance beforehand. The next best option is to make another transfer to a different low rate card.

The Dangers of Debt Consolidation

One of the most common strategies for people in credit card and other high rate consumer debt is "debt consolidation." This simply means you borrow against the equity in your house by taking a secured loan called a Home Equity Line of Credit (HELOC) and pay off all your credit cards with that loan. Many Canadians have used this method and it shows in the balances they owe.

According to the Canadian credit bureau TransUnion, the average consumer debt (excluding mortgages) held by Canadians during the fourth quarter of 2014 was $21,428. When you break it down, they found that those with credit cards had an average balance of $3,659. However, for those with lines of credit the average balance was $30,554. The logical conclusion is that many Canadians are using their lines of credit to pay off their credit cards.

Reducing the overall interest rate on your debt by trading credit card debt for a line of credit sounds like a good idea. Trading $10,000 of credit card debt at 20% interest for a line of credit at 3% is a prudent move. However, if you continue to spend more than you make and run up the credit card debt again, the end result is worse. You end up with twice the debt, $20,000, half at the lower rate and half at the higher.

The use of lines of credit is also being fuelled by the current ultra-low interest rates. People think: "Why pay the line of credit down when it's so cheap to carry it?" So the debt doesn't get paid off and often increases as there always seems to be something else to buy. Low rates should be used as an opportunity to pay down balances, not increase them, because more of each payment goes to the principal when interest rates are low. If interest rates rise, however, many people with variable rate debt (e.g., lines of credit) are going to have a problem. This is especially risky for retired people on a fixed income, so do all you can to avoid this situation and resolve to get rid of all your debt before you retire.

Types of Debt

There are two main types of debt: instalment and revolving. Instalment debt is any debt that requires you to make principal and interest payments. Your mortgage and your car loans are examples of instalment debt. With this type of debt you are forced to pay off the loan. All you do is maintain the payment schedule and the mortgage or loan will be paid off with the last payment.

Revolving debt allows you to borrow up to a pre-determined amount (your credit limit) and only requires minimum payments to cover interest and sometimes a small amount of the principal balance. Your credit cards and lines of credit are examples. The problem with revolving debt is that since there is no requirement to pay down the principal balance of the loan, many people don't. For example, I have an unsecured line of credit from a major bank and the minimum monthly payment is currently the greater of 2% of the outstanding balance or $50. Of course, as soon as I make the minimum payment, I am free to borrow the same amount up to my credit limit again.

Minimum payments on credit cards are often even lower than that. I'm looking at the disclosure statement for a TD Aeroplan Visa Infinite Card and the minimum payment is $10 plus any interest and fees (plus any past due amount or any amount that exceeds your credit limit). You can tell how low the minimum payment is by referring to the statement on your credit card bill stating how long it will take to pay off the balance in full. (The longest I have seen is "never," because the minimum payment was less than the annual fee for the card!)

Debt Reduction Methods

Now that we have reviewed various forms of debt, let's look at the options to pay off your debts. There are two main strategies: the "snowball" method and the "avalanche" method.

The Snowball Method

With this method you list your debts, starting with the smallest balance up to the largest. You reduce the payments as much as you can on all other debt besides the smallest one, and increase the payments on it so you pay it off as fast as you can. Once your smallest debt gets paid off, you add the amount that was going to pay it off to the next smallest debt. You continue doing this until all your debts are paid off.

The main advantage of this method is psychological. It simply feels great to get rid of a debt, even a small one.

The disadvantage is that, unless the interest rate is highest on your smaller debts, it makes more sense to pay off the debts with the highest interest rates first. That is the "avalanche" method.

The Avalanche Method

With this method, interest costs take priority. You list your debts starting with the one with the highest interest rate, then the second highest rate, etc. Make the minimum payments on all the debts and allocate any excess funds to the highest rate debt. Once it is paid off you allocate the amount that was going towards it to the next highest rate debt.

This method saves you more interest than the snowball method, but if the highest rate debt is large it will take a long time to pay it off. That can be discouraging, and is the reason why many people prefer the snowball method.

Depending on your situation, each method could yield the same result. For example, say you had three debts as follows:

- $2,000 credit card debt at 20%
- $3,500 car loan at 6%
- $5,000 line of credit at 7%

We'll assume that the minimum monthly payment for each is $50 and you have $450 available each month. Under both methods you'd make the minimum $50 payment on the car loan and line of credit and allocate $350 to the credit card balance each month. In about six months the credit card balance would be paid off. You would then pay $400 a month (the $50 minimum payment plus the $350 that was going to the credit card) on the car loan and pay if off in about eight more months. And finally, the full $450 would then go to the line of credit, which would be paid off in about ten months.

However, *these solutions will only work if you don't add to the debt*. As we discussed at the beginning of this chapter, if you continue to spend more than you make, you won't make any progress. As soon as you pay down a debt, the same one or another one will increase to cover the additional spending.

In some cases a more extreme solution may be warranted.

A Radical Solution

The problem is that the financial institutions structure and sell you products that work to increase their profits, which is not surprising as they are in business to make money for their shareholders!

We are forced to pay back our mortgages because, as instalment debt, we must cover interest and principal. But we can take essentially as much time as we want to pay back our high-rate credit card debt since it is a revolving debt that doesn't require us to pay it down. So we can carry our high-rate debt for as long as we want, but we have no option but to pay down our lowest rate debt.

However, there is one product that reverses this situation. It is a flexible line of credit instead of a mortgage. The Manulife One account (**www.manulifeone.ca**) is an example of this type of account and it has been offered in Canada for many years. Other major Canadian banks offer similar products, often referred to as home equity lines of credit.

With this type of account, you don't have a separate mortgage and bank account; you have a combined line of credit that you can use as a chequing account. As soon as your pay cheque is deposited in your account the balance of your line of credit is immediately reduced. When you write a cheque, pay a bill or pay off your credit card, the balance then goes up again. Interest is charged at the end of each month and is added to the balance owing.

Because this line of credit is secured by your house, the interest rate is low. At the time of writing, the Manulife One Base Rate is 3.2%, which is 0.5% above the banks' prime rate of 2.7%. There is also a monthly fee of $14 ($7 for 60 and older). In the right situation this is an excellent solution, but in the wrong hands it could be a problem. For example, it is not a good option for people who can't control their spending and can't resist the allure of available credit. That results in a balance that keeps rising until it hits the credit limit. The balance is unlikely to ever get paid off, or even paid down. But if you are good with your finances, it can be a way to improve your financial situation.

If you currently have revolving high-interest credit card debt, and your mortgage payments are preventing you from paying it off, switching to this type of account where you don't have to pay down the principal could free up a large amount of cash.

But be very careful, it is easy to fall into the trap of never paying off the balance.

CHAPTER 15

Your Home as a Source of Funds

Buying a House Can Be a Good Investment

In Canada, a home is usually considered to be a good investment. From 1997 to 2013, house prices in Canada increased on average by 145.6% or 5.43% per annum. The following chart shows the average house price increases during that period for four Canadian cities.

Average Canadian House Price Increase from 1997 to 2013		
City	Total %	Average Annual %
Calgary	204.8%	6.78%
Vancouver	164.0%	5.88%
Toronto	148.1%	5.49%
Halifax	153.4%	5.62%

When it comes to retirement planning, however, your investment in your home is not a "liquid" investment, i.e., you can't cash in a portion of it to spend. In fact, a house is going to be a drain on your resources for as long as you own it. Think of how much money your mortgage payments take from your account each year and, even if you have paid off the mortgage, you're still going to have to pay property taxes, utilities, insurance, repairs and maintenance, etc., for as long as you live there.

Using Your Home to Finance Your Retirement

Having established that your house could be a significant investment, how can you use that investment (if you need to) to help finance your retirement? There are several options.

1. Sell and Downsize

If your kids have moved out, you probably don't need all the space you needed when they lived at home. Depending on where you live and that specific housing market, you could sell your house, pay off any amount left on your mortgage and buy a smaller house. If it's your principal residence, the added advantage is that you don't have to pay capital gains tax on the sale.

This could leave you with a significant amount of extra cash to finance your retirement. Another advantage is it will probably cost less to maintain a smaller house (i.e., property taxes, utilities, repairs and maintenance, etc.).

To really take advantage of this strategy, you may need to consider moving to a less expensive neighbourhood or possibly out of your city. This may not appeal to you if it means you have to move away from family and friends, especially at a time when you may need some help. Many retirees aren't willing to do that.

 WARNING

Downsizing from a house in one of the big cities like Toronto, Vancouver or Calgary to a condo in the same city might not mean a significant saving in living costs. If you sell a million dollar house and then buy a $900,000 condominium, you may not be much further ahead, because you have to take into consideration the monthly condo maintenance fees and possible special assessments in the future.

2. Sell and Rent

If you sell your house and would like to stay in the same city, or even move to another one, another solution is renting. This solution frees up a lot of cash which you can invest.

3. Take in a Tenant

In one of the focus groups for this book, one lady told us she had retired on a very low income and was forced to take in three tenants in her triplex. She is single, so she very carefully chose her tenants and now they have become some of her best companions!

This could be a good option for you, but make sure you conduct a thorough background check on all tenants before you accept them: the right tenants could become your best friends, the wrong ones could ruin your life!

4. Take Out a Reverse Mortgage

A reverse mortgage is a financial product that allows you to borrow money against the value of your home without having to sell it. You have several options for how the payment(s) are made to you:
*   as a lump sum
*   as an annuity, with a monthly cash payment
*   as a line of credit (similar to a home equity line of credit)
*   as a combination, with a smaller lump sum and then a smaller annuity

You defer payment of the loan until you die, sell, or move out of the home. Interest charges accrue (or accumulate) during the period that you borrow the money, then the total of the amount borrowed plus all accrued interest is paid back upon sale of the house.

One of the main advantages to reverse mortgages is that there are no specific minimum income requirements so even low-income seniors can use them. You also don't have to make any payments on the loan and as a tax-free source of income they do not affect any income-tested benefits you may be receiving like Old Age Security (OAS) or Guaranteed Income Supplement (GIS).

However, there are some drawbacks:
*   They charge higher interest rates than regular mortgages.
*   The equity you hold in your home (the difference between the value of your home and the balance owing on the mortgage) will decrease as interest on the reverse mortgage accumulates over the years.

- Upon your death (or your spouse's death, if later than yours) your estate will have to repay the loan and interest in full within a limited time, which may be difficult depending on how long it takes to sell the house and settle your estate. (In Canada, the law states that the loan balance cannot exceed the fair market value of the home.)
- Upon repayment, there will be less money left in your estate to leave to your children and other heirs.
- The associated costs are usually quite high including:
  — Appraisal fee (estimated at $175 to $400)
  — Independent legal advice required (typically $300 to $600)
  — Legal, closing and administrative costs ($1,400 or more for exploring all interest rate options, conducting title searches, title insurance and registration)
- There is not a lot of competition, so your only option at the time of writing is the Canadian Home Income Plan (CHIP) offered by HomeEquity Bank.

For these reasons, I would suggest you regard a reverse mortgage as the last resort.

5. Take Out a Home Equity Line of Credit

If you have a decent credit rating, a much cheaper solution is to take out an interest-only home equity line of credit (HELOC) before you retire and only use it if you need it during retirement. Remember to apply for it BEFORE you retire, as it is much easier to get bank approval when your income is higher and you can prove it by showing them your pay slip, T4 or your income tax assessment.

The beauty of this strategy is that it costs you nothing until you withdraw funds. It also has the added advantage of lessening the chances of title fraud because it reduces the amount of your equity in your home, so there is less equity for thieves to borrow against (by stealing your identity and registering a fraudulent mortgage).

Before You Retire

At a recent seminar, a retiree gave me a very useful tip. He suggested that it is better to make all major repairs to your home before you retire. After you retire and are on a fixed income, it becomes increasingly difficult to absorb the large cost of repairs. So think about your home before you retire. Does the roof need new shingles? Is there a leak in the basement? Will it need new windows soon?

And give some thought to replacing your furnace. They usually last about 18 to 20 years, so if yours is approaching that age, it will need to be replaced soon. Another tip about your furnace: if you know it needs replacing, get several written quotes from reputable companies for a new furnace and possibly an air conditioner. If you don't, and it breaks down in the middle of winter, you'll be at the mercy of any company you can convince to come and install a new one at short notice.

CHAPTER 16

Car Strategy: Lease or Buy?

In **Chapter 2**, we saw that the Clarks bought their car and kept it for eight years and then bought a new one. This resulted in much higher costs during the four years of car loan payments but significantly lower costs during the last four years once they owned the car.

This uneven cash flow makes budgeting more complicated during retirement when you are on a fixed income. However, there is an option that would make it easier to budget: *leasing* your car.

When I teach my personal finance course based on my book, *Smoke and Mirrors*, I always ask the class how many people lease their car, and often no hands go up, except mine. Leasing has a bad reputation but it may be your best option.

Leasing: The Basics

With leasing you are essentially renting a car for a number of years, usually three or four. Because you are giving back the car at the end of the lease, you only have to pay for the portion you use during the lease. If you bought the car instead, and financed it over the same number of years as the lease, you would be paying for the whole car.

Obviously, if you buy the car you own it at the end of the term of three or four years and could then continue to use it without making any more payments. However, when you own you still have the cost of repairs and maintenance for a car that is aging. If you are lucky enough to have a car that doesn't require many repairs, you have an advantage when you own it. However, you could get stuck with a "lemon" where you'll be constantly paying for repairs when the warranty expires.

How They Determine the Monthly Lease Cost

There are five variables when it comes to leasing. You need to know four of them to calculate the fifth. Here are the five variables:

1. Cost of the car
2. Lease interest rate
3. Term of the lease
4. Residual value
5. Monthly lease cost

The key variable that is important to know before you sign for the lease is #4, the residual value. This is usually expressed as a percentage of the cost. For example, on a four-year lease the residual value might be 45% or so. A higher residual value is good because you are being given credit for it when the monthly lease cost is being calculated.

BEWARE OF OPEN-END LEASE

The most important thing to confirm before you lease a car is that it is a "closed-end" or "walkaway" lease. That means at the end of the term you are not responsible for the fact that the car may be worth less than the estimated residual value.

For example, say you leased a car with a cost of $40,000 and an estimated residual value of $20,000 at the end of a four-year lease, but when you return it to the leasing company they determine that it has depreciated (lost value) more than they expected and was now only worth $15,000. If you don't have a closed-end lease, you will be responsible for paying the $5,000 difference. With a closed-end or walkaway lease, you are under no obligation to pay the difference and it becomes the leasing company's problem.

The Complicating Factors of Leasing

There are two issues with leasing that you don't have to worry about with owning a car: charges at the end of the lease for excess kilometres driven and excess wear and tear.

Excess Kilometre Charges

When you sign a lease, the agreement will state how many kilometres a year you are allowed to drive. It's usually around 20,000, so during a three-year lease you would be allowed 60,000 kilometres. If you go over, you'll have to pay the leasing company a set rate per kilometre. I am currently leasing a Ford Focus and the excess kilometre charge is $0.12 per kilometre for any mileage over 60,000 on a three-year lease.

 TIP

> Note that some leases allow an extra kilometre option credit and will reimburse you if you use less than the number of kilometres allowed. This reimbursement rate is usually lower than the rate you pay if you go over.

For some people the risk of a large excess kilometre charge puts them out of the market for leasing. A taxi driver, many of whom drive over 100,000 kilometres a year, would probably never lease their car.

If you plan to travel more than 20,000 kilometres a year during your retirement, leasing is probably not for you. However, many people who have not considered leasing (because they travel a lot during their working years) find that they drive much less during retirement and that creates a situation where leasing might make sense.

Excess Wear and Tear Charges

In addition to the excess kilometre charge, you'll also have to worry about excess wear and tear charges. This means that, at the end of your lease, there will be a lease-ending inspection to determine what costs are needed to get the car back to a condition where they can sell it as a used car. You'll have to pay the costs for any damage, such as paint scratches and dents, and new tires if yours are significantly worn, etc. If you are hard on your cars, these costs can be significant. (A friend's son leased a truck and used it in his construction job. His excess wear and tear charges were $7,200!) On the other hand, the last car I leased had no excess wear and tear charges at the end of the lease.

When Leasing Might Make Sense

If you are going to be driving less than 20,000 kilometres per year and treat your cars reasonably well, leasing during retirement might make sense. It may even make sense *before* you retire. This is especially true if your cash flow is tight and if you have credit card debt with a high interest rate. This may happen because the added costs you are paying in the early years of buying a car are effectively being financed by the high rate on your credit card debt.

In other words, if you lease a car and therefore had lower monthly payments, the excess cash available could be used to pay down the high interest credit card balance.

Why Leasing Gets a Bad Rap

I think the problem with leasing is that many people abuse it. Instead of leasing a car they could afford to buy, and therefore drive the same car for less per month, they go out and lease a much more expensive car.

For example, they could afford to pay $500 a month in loan payments to buy a car, but it would cost only $300 a month to lease the same car. So, because they can afford $500 per month, they don't lease that car for $300, they go out and lease a more expensive car for $500 a month. That is not good money management!

The Car Lease versus Buy Analyzer

Since your car strategy has a major impact on your retirement spending, I'd like to introduce a spreadsheet that I first created for my book *Smoke and Mirrors*. Like the other spreadsheets in this book, it is a Microsoft Excel spreadsheet that you can download from my website at **www.trahair.com** or at **cpacanada.ca/ retirement**.

To best illustrate how to use it, I'm going to use it on the car I am leasing (a 2014 Ford Focus).

Go to the "Questions" tab on the spreadsheet and answer the following questions. (To illustrate the example, I have entered all the information for the Focus.)

GENERAL	
What is today's date?	05-03-2015
What is your first and last name?	Dave Test
What car are you proposing to lease or buy?	Ford Focus
What is the highest interest rate on any debt that you have?	5.00%
LEASE OPTION QUESTIONS	
What amount are you required to put down as a cash down payment?	$690
What additional amounts are due for fuel charge, license fee, etc., on delivery?	$217
What is the monthly lease payment (including HST, GST, PST)?	$376
What amount is due for a security deposit on delivery?	$0
What is the term of the lease (in years)?	3
What is the lease interest rate per year?	0.00%
What is the end-of-lease option to purchase amount (residual value)?	$10,835
What is the excess kilometre charge?	$0.12
What is the annual kilometre allowance?	20,000
What is the average number of kilometres you expect to drive annually over the course of the lease?	20,000
BUY OPTION QUESTIONS	
What is the purchase price of the car (including all taxes, delivery, freight)?	$25,776
What amount will you put down on the purchase?	$2,000
What is the annual interest rate on the car loan going to be?	0.90%
How many years will you have the loan?	3
What do you think the car will be worth after 9 years?	$2,500

Results for Ford Focus

	Year Year #	2015 1	2016 2	2017 3	2018 4	2019 5	2020 6	2021 7	2022 8	2023 9	Total (Yr 1 to 9)
LEASE											
Fixed Costs:											
Cash downpayment		690			690			690			2,070
Additional amts (fuel, lic., etc.)		217			217			217			651
Security deposit		0			0			0			0
Lease payments		4,512	4,512	4,512	4,512	4,512	4,512	4,512	4,512	4,512	40,608
Repairs and maintenance		250	250	250	250	250	250	250	250	250	2,250
Excess km charge		0	0	0	0	0	0	0	0	0	0
Total Fixed Costs		$5,669	$4,762	$4,762	$5,669	$4,762	$4,762	$5,669	$4,762	$4,762	$45,579
BUY											
Fixed Costs:											
Down payment		2,000									2,000
Principal payments		7,854	7,925	7,997							23,776
Interest payments		182	111	39							332
Repairs and maintenance		250	250	250	1,000	2,000	2,000	2,000	3,000	3,000	13,750
Residual value										-2,500	-2,500
Total Fixed Costs		$10,286	$8,286	$8,286	$1,000	$2,000	$2,000	$2,000	$3,000	$500	$37,358
EXCESS CASH REQUIRED TO OWN		$4,617	$3,524	$3,524	-$4,669	-$2,762	-$2,762	-$3,669	-$1,762	-$4,262	-$8,221
Opening balance excess cash		$0	$4,617	$8,372	$12,315	$8,262	$5,913	$3,447	-$50	-$1,815	
Interest on balance		$0	$231	$419	$616	$413	$296	$172	-$3	-$91	
Excess cash required during year		$4,617	$3,524	$3,524	-$4,669	-$2,762	-$2,762	-$3,669	-$1,762	-$4,262	
Closing balance excess cash		$4,617	$8,372	$12,315	$8,262	$5,913	$3,447	-$50	-$1,815	-$6,168	

In Year 1, the total cost to lease the car was $5,669. The cost to purchase the car during Year 1 was $10,286. It cost $4,617 in extra cash during the first year to own the car.

The program automatically adds an annual interest cost of 5% (the rate entered on the Questions tab) to that balance during Year 2. That is $231. It then adds the excess cash required to buy during Year 2 of $3,524 so the balance of the excess cost to buy is $8,372 after Year 2.

After Year 3 the balance is up to $12,315. That is how much more it would cost to buy the Focus over three years than it would cost to lease it for the same period.

In Year 4, the years of payment-free ownership start if the car was purchased. You can see during Years 4 to 9 that the cost to lease the car is higher so the "excess cost to own" account gets drawn down.

Note that the repairs and maintenance costs each year are estimated. This is the "wild card" in the equation because it is difficult to estimate.

At the end of the Year 9, assuming we could sell the car for $2,500, the excess costs to lease is $6,168. However, we need to look beyond the numbers to get a true picture.

How Old is Your Car?

We have really been comparing apples to oranges. With the lease option you would be driving a car that is a maximum of three years old. With the buy option, your car would be up to nine years old. Besides the benefit of that "new car smell" you'd also be taking advantage of improvements that are being made to cars if you replaced it every few years. For example, newer cars tend to have better safety features like air bag technology, accident avoidance features and improvements in fuel efficiency.

Warranty

With leasing, your car is usually under warranty at all times. This avoids major repairs that you would have to pay for if you owned the car and were out of the warranty period.

Repair and Maintenance

As I have said, this is a wild card. I once owned a Ford Taurus wagon that I paid for with a five-year loan and then kept for seven more years. It did not require any huge repairs, but was costly during the final few years. In addition, the air conditioning didn't work too well and the rear window wiper didn't work at all. You might get lucky like I did, but you may not.

Residual Value

I have estimated that we could sell the Focus for $2,500 after nine years. Would someone pay that for a car with about 180,000 kilometres on it? It's possible, but you'd have to go through the hassle of listing it somewhere and finding a buyer. If you get less than $2,500, the amount of the buy option advantage is reduced by the difference.

Conclusion

Leasing is not "bad," it's just more complicated than buying because of things like excess kilometre and wear and tear charges.

However, if you want to keep your cash flow constant and eliminate the hassles and risks of owning your car, it might just make sense.

CHAPTER 17

Planning for Elderly Parents and Inheritance

Your Inheritance

You may be lucky enough to be in line for an inheritance from your parents. If you are, there is much that can be done to make the process as smooth as possible. This is important because if you and your parents do not plan ahead, your inheritance may be seriously diminished.

There are many issues that create problems when it comes to inheritances. They include:

- **It's difficult to discuss with your parents.** Who wants to talk about their own demise? Do you even have a copy of the will to know you are in it?

- **The timing is often poor.** Hopefully your last surviving parent lives to a ripe old age of 85 or 90. That probably makes you about 60 or 65 and close to, or in retirement. You have to decide well in advance whether to live your life so you can afford to retire on your own, or require an inheritance "bailout" from your parents to make it work.

- **Parents are living longer.** It's not unlikely that one of your parents will live a long life. That means they are going to have to spend quite a bit of money over their retirement years, meaning less to pass on to you.

Taxes on Death

When one parent dies, their assets (including RRSPs and RRIFs) can transfer to the surviving spouse tax-free. But when the last parent dies, they are deemed to have disposed of their assets upon their death. Some items are tax-free (e.g., their principal residence), but others will attract tax, including the full value of any remaining RRSP or RRIF. Also, if they have any taxable investments, the difference between the original cost and the current market value has to be reported as a taxable gain.

Information to Document

When your parent passes away it's going to be an extremely emotional time. The last thing you need is the headache of trying to dig up all the financial details of their lives.

Here are the basic things you need to have them document.

ADVISORS	Yes/No	Contact information (address/phone number(s)/email)
Accountant		
Lawyer		
Financial advisor		
Doctor		
Insurance agent		
DOCUMENTS	**Yes/No**	**Location**
Will		
Power of Attorney over financial affairs		
Power of Attorney over attendant care (end of life decisions, etc.)		
Grave plot title deeds		
A list of any property owned (including principal residence and any rental)		

FINANCIAL INFORMATION	Account Number	Contact Information (address/phone number(s)/email)
RRSP		
RRIF		
Regular investment accounts		
Company pension plan		
Annuity contracts		
Bank accounts		
Life insurance policies		
Mortgages		
Lines of credit		
Credit cards		
Other assets/debts		
OTHER	**Yes/No**	**Location**
Birth certificates		
Marriage certificate		
Social Insurance Number		
Prior years' tax returns		
Jewellery		

The Estate Planning Record Keeper

To make planning for this difficult time easier, I have created a 2-page document called the "Estate Planning Record Keeper" (See **Appendix 2**). It is a Microsoft Excel spreadsheet that you can download for free from my website **www.trahair.com** or at **cpacanada.ca/ retirement**. It can be printed and filled in or the information can be entered directly into Excel and then printed. Feel free to pass it on to anyone that may find it useful. An investment of a few hours to fill it in could save many hours and thousands of dollars in lost money for the beneficiaries.

What to do with Your Inheritance

Your parent's estate will owe any taxes on death and the beneficiaries receive the after-tax amounts. So if you receive an inheritance it will be tax-free to you.

Of course, this can positively impact your financial planning for retirement and the first thing you should consider doing with your inheritance is to pay off any remaining debt you have, starting with the debt with the highest interest rate.

If you want to pay off your mortgage and are locked into a five-year term, there will be a penalty if you pay the outstanding amount. In many cases you are limited to paying off only 10% or so each year. If you have a line of credit instead of a mortgage, it may be possible to pay the whole debt in one payment.

Summary

It is not a subject we want to think about but, as your parents age, it is important for them to have a plan for the end of their lives and to ensure all their documentation is in place.

No matter how difficult it is, you need to discuss these issues with your parents, encourage them to get professional advice and create the necessary documentation so that their wishes are respected and realized and your inheritance is maintained.

CHAPTER 18

Your Company Pension Plan

Many people have to worry about funding their own retirement because they don't work for an organization that has a defined benefit pension plan. These people have to be concerned about saving money and how to invest it. They also need to be aware of what's happening in the world's financial system and on its stock markets.

For those people fortunate enough to have a defined benefit pension plan, there may not be as much to be concerned about, but the landscape is changing drastically and, as a result, many pension plans are shifting from a "defined benefit" to a "defined contribution" plan.

Types of Pension Plans

Defined Benefit (DB) Plans

With a Defined Benefit (DB) plan you are guaranteed a certain benefit when you retire that is based on several factors including your age, salary and years of service with the company. Each year, pension actuaries calculate the future benefits that are projected to be paid from the plan and determine the amount that needs to be contributed to the plan to fund the projected payout.

You may have to work a certain number of years before you have a permanent right to any retirement benefit under the plan. This is referred to as "vesting." If you leave your job before you fully vest, you won't get full retirement benefits from the plan.

DB plans are still quite common in the public sector. According to the Office of The Superintendent of Financial Institutions (OSFI), 86% of government employees are members of a pension plan and most of them are DB plans. So, if you are a government worker, nurse, teacher, hospital technician, firefighter or politician and you have a pension plan, it is probably a DB plan.

The private sector is a totally different story. It is estimated that 76% of workers in this category have no pension at all. If they do have a plan, chances are it is a Defined Contribution (DC) plan.

Defined Contribution (DC) Plans

With these plans, the employee makes a contribution to the plan that is matched to some degree by the company. Members are usually asked how they want to invest the money and at retirement there is a pot of money for them to draw from during their retirement. How big the pot is depends on how well the investments perform. There is no guaranteed payment.

Most private sector companies are switching to this type of plan because they are finding it difficult to earn sufficient investment returns, due to low interest rates and a volatile stock market, to make good on any promised amounts for retired employees required by DB plans. Also, Canadians are now living a lot longer than they used to and this is further compounding the problem.

Defined Benefit Plans

Recent Changes

If you have a Defined Benefit plan you may have been unpleasantly surprised over the past few years with changes that are not in your favour. These changes are happening because many plans are underfunded. The Office of the Superintendent of Financial Institutions (OSFI), which supervises approximately 400 DB plans in Canada, estimates that 90% of federally regulated DB plans were underfunded on a solvency basis as of December 2012. This means that most plans have insufficient assets to pay out the pensions they have promised.

The negative implications to you as a plan member are twofold:
1.   Increased contribution rates for current workers
2.   Decreased benefits for retirees

Simply put, to get back to full funding they need more money coming in and less going out.

How DB Contributions Get Calculated

You make contributions to your plan based on your salary. Since DB plans are designed to work with the CPP plan, there are usually two contribution rates. One rate is up to the CPP Year's Maximum Pensionable Earnings (YMPE) amount and another rate for earnings above that amount.

For example, the rates for members of Ontario Municipal Employees Retirement System (OMERS) for normal retirement at age 65 are 9.0% on earnings up to the YMPE, and 14.6% on earnings over the CPP limit. The YMPE for 2015 is $53,600. So an employee making $100,000 in 2015 has to make contributions of $11,598, which would be matched by the employer.

The good news is that any contribution you make is tax deductible.

How to Read Your DB Pension Report

If you are a member of a DB pension plan, you should get an annual pension report on your pension. It usually includes the following sections.

Summary

This usually includes:
*   your normal retirement date (often the last day of the month you turn 65)
*   your pension earned to the end of the last calendar year (in dollars starting from age 65)
*   your early retirement date and whether there is a penalty to do so (often the last day of the month you turn 60)
*   your total contributions, plus interest to the end of the last calendar year
*   your beneficiary (the person who will receive any survivor benefit if you die)

Early Retirement

This section should tell you how many additional years of service you'll need to retire with no penalty. This is usually dependent on your age/service factor, which is your age plus credited service (plus eligible service in some cases (see **Qualifying Service** below)). Many plans have an age/service factor of 85 or 90.

Bridge Benefit

Note that most plans have a "bridge benefit," which is an additional amount that is paid if you start to receive your pension before age 65, but is only paid until age 65. That's because DB plans are designed to integrate with the CPP retirement pension that usually begins at age 65. In most cases, the bridge benefit won't stop even if you elect to receive your CPP pension early (you can start as early as age 60).

Your Pension Calculation

This section should detail how they get the amount of your lifetime pension earned to the end of the last calendar year.

EXAMPLE

The calculation is based on a factor of 2% earned per year of work on the average of your "best five" years of contributory earnings, which is probably the annual salary you earned in the last five calendar years that you worked. This example is for an average salary of $90,000 and you have worked there for ten years (your "credited service").

1. Lifetime pension including bridge benefit calculation:
    = 2% × credited service (years) × "best five" earnings
    = 0.02 × 10 × $90,000
    = $18,000

    So if you were eligible to retire before age 65 without a penalty, that is the amount you would receive per year to age 65.

    The bridge benefit calculation (see Bridge Benefit above) is a bit more complicated because it has to factor in CPP rates. In this example, we'll use the last five years' average CPP YMPE of $51,120, which is the average for the last five years to 2015.

2. Bridge benefit at age 65 calculation:
    = 0.675% × credited service (years) x lesser of "best five" earnings and the five year average CPP YMPE
    = 0.00675 × 10 × $51,120
    = $3,450.60

    So your lifetime pension payable from 65 would be $14,549.40 ($18,000 – $3,450.60).

    Note that these figures are in today's dollars (2015) and don't reflect any activity in the future. It is an estimate of the dollars you would receive starting at age 65 (or before for the bridge benefit). If you continue to work and pay into the plan, you would receive a higher amount.

Qualifying Service

Some plans have two different types of service: credited service and eligible service. You can earn credited service through regular contributions, or by buying back a leave period.

Eligible service can help you reach an early retirement pension without penalty as it is used in the calculation of the age/service factor. In other words, your credited service gets added to your eligible service to get your qualifying service. Your age plus qualifying service equals your age/service factor (usually 85 or 90).

Eligible service can be any years of service with an employer that is a member of the pension plan that isn't credited service. For example, summer student work or previous service that was refunded when you left a previous employer member of the plan.

Summary of Contributions

This section shows the dollar amount of your contributions to the end of the last calendar year and often the total contributions plus interest. Your employer is matching your contributions but that amount is usually not displayed.

Note that because you are in a DB plan, there is no correlation between the amount you have paid in and the pension you will get because that amount is based on the calculations above (which don't use your actual contributions).

Locking In

Your report should also make some kind of statement that your benefits are locked in under your province or territory's *Pension Act*. This means you can't take the value of your pension plan out if you leave your employer. Other options are usually available, including transfers to locked-in RRSPs.

Your DC Pension Report

If you are a member of a DC plan, your report is simpler because it does not have to deal with estimates of future income. You should get information about:

- formulae for your required contributions (if applicable) and an explanation of how to select or change a contribution rate (if you must elect a contribution rate within a particular range)
- formulae for employer contributions
- timing of your contributions and employer contributions
- treatment of voluntary contributions (if allowed)
- how and when contributions are vested and locked-in and an explanation of what these terms mean
- statement with amounts deducted by the employer from your pay and other amounts due to the pension fund by your employer
- description of how any transfers into the fund will be treated

When you approach the payout phase of a DC plan, however, things get more complicated. That's because you need to convert your pension to another retirement product, which may include (depending on the current legislation):

- Locked-in Retirement Account (LIRA)
- Locked-in Registered Retirement Savings Plan (Locked-in RRSP)
- Locked-in Retirement Income Fund (LRIF)
- Life Income Fund (LIF)
- Life Annuity Contract
- Prescribed Registered Retirement Income Fund (RRIF)
- Variable Benefit

Your plan administrator should provide you with the following information:

- the options available to you
- any actions you need to take and their deadlines
- any default options that may be applied if you don't act, and
- the impact that the termination of plan membership will have on each investment option

CHAPTER 19
Your Credit Card Strategy

If you carry a balance on your credit card and therefore pay a high rate of interest to your credit card company, you should look for a card with a lower interest rate. The interest you are paying is likely much greater than any kind of rewards you might get, so if you have one, get rid of your rewards card.

On the other hand, if you pay off the balance every month, it makes sense to look for the rewards card that is going to give you the best rewards for any fee you pay. This is especially true after you have retired and are on a fixed income. Deciding which rewards credit card is best for you is not easy because there are hundreds of cards available.

The Financial Consumer Agency of Canada

One of the resources you can use to help find the card that's right for you is the Financial Consumer Agency of Canada's website at **www.fcac-acfc.gc.ca**. Choose your language preference and then go to the "Tools and calculators" section on the bottom left of the home page and select "Credit card tools."

There are two options:
1. the "Credit Card Selector tool" helps you decide which is the best credit card for you
2. the "Credit Card Payment Calculator" tells you how much it will cost if you only pay the minimum balance on your credit card each month.

A recent search using the selector tool showed there were 277 credit cards to select from.

The selector tool also has some other useful features, including the ability to narrow your search to those cards offered in your province or territory and by card type (general use, secured, student, U.S. dollar and charge (those that must be paid when a statement is issued)). You can also limit your search by the different benefits available as follows:

- Cash back

- Miles/points redeemable for:
  - Travel/vacation
  - Groceries
  - Gas
  - General merchandise
  - Prepaid gift card
  - Vehicle lease/purchase
  - Vehicle rental
  - Charitable donations
  - Issuer's financial product

- Travel insurance
  - Travel accident
  - Travel medical
  - Travel cancellation
  - Travel interruption
  - Flight delay
  - Rental vehicle
  - Baggage

- Benefits
  - Cell phone insurance
  - Purchase protection
  - Extended warranty
  - Price protection
  - Road side assistance

For example, how many general use, cash back credit cards with no annual fee do you think there are in Nova Scotia? The selector tool says there are 20. This is a very useful way to narrow your search.

But when you actually get into the details, finding the best card can be a very complex task, so I sought help in this section from a person with a lot of experience in this area, Robb Engen, a fee-only financial advisor who writes a bi-weekly column for the Toronto Star and blogs at **www.boomerandecho.com**. He has written dozens of posts on credit card travel and other rewards cards.

Using Your Miles

A common complaint Engen gets from readers is about the fees, taxes and fuel surcharges they have to pay when they redeem their points for travel. In some cases the fees and taxes come to an amount that is not much less than it would cost to simply buy a ticket for cash.

EXAMPLE

I'd like to book a flight using Aeroplan for one adult from Toronto to Paris, France leaving on June 6, 2015 and returning two weeks later on June 20, 2015 in economy class. I found a direct flight leaving Toronto on June 6 and arriving in Paris the next day. The return trip was a direct flight that left Paris on June 20.

This return flight would have cost me 31,000 Aeroplan miles plus $609.86 in taxes, fees and surcharges broken down as follows:
- Carrier surcharge $476.00
- Canada Domestic/International Airport Improvement Fee $25.00
- Canada Harmonized Sales Tax $3.25
- Canada Domestic/International Air Travel Security Charge $25.91
- France Domestic & International Airport Tax $30.30
- France International Passenger Service Charge $42.80
- France Air Passenger Solidarity Tax $6.60
- Total $609.86

To compare that to the cost of the same return flight if I paid cash, I went to Air Canada's website. The total cost of the same return flight was $903.79, so the difference between the cost of fees and taxes using Aeroplan and the cost for paying cash was $293.93.

According to the Air Canada website, the "Base Fare" for paying cash was $294 and the taxes, fees and surcharges was $609.79 (a difference of $0.07 from the Aeroplan figure). Using 31,000 Aeroplan miles saved me $294. That's about $0.009 per mile.

Another problem with using many reward cards is the possibility that you won't find a flight on the day you want, or you end up having to make a connection that can add hours to your travel time.

Other Ways to Redeem Aeroplan Miles

One of the most effective ways I have found to use my Aeroplan points is to use them for vacation packages. For example, you can redeem reward miles to pay for a portion of Air Canada vacations or cruises booked with Expedia CruiseShipCenters. The Aeroplan website says you can get a $500 gift certificate for 64,000 miles and apply it against the cruise cost. That is a benefit of $0.008 per mile, a little less than the Paris flight example, but the key point is that it is easier to use because you don't have to worry about booking a flight on your specific travel day, it's just a rebate.

The other option to use your Aeroplan points is to redeem them for activities and merchandise. For example, a recent search showed a Nikon D5200 camera kit including an 18-55mm NIKKOR lens costs 108,500 Aeroplan miles. The same camera kit on Costco.ca costs $749.99. If I add 13% HST, the total cost comes to $847.49. That is a benefit of $0.008 per mile.

 HOW YOU EARN AEROPLAN MILES

To earn miles with a TD Aeroplan Visa Infinite Card for example, you accumulate 1.5 miles for every dollar you spend on your card on purchases at grocery stores, gas stations, drugstores and online purchases at **www.aircanada.com** (excluding Air Canada vacation packages). You earn 1 mile for every dollar you spend on all other purchases. You also earn miles twice when you pay with your card and present your Aeroplan membership card at over 150 Aeroplan partner brands and with 100 online retailers through Aeroplan's eStore.

Of course, you can earn miles for flights you book on Air Canada at various rates. At the time of writing, Aeroplan members got 150 miles for flights with a distance flown of up to 249 miles and the actual amount of miles flown for flights flown of over 250 miles. Note that the mile accumulation varies with the fare option purchased, so the number of miles varies accordingly.

If you fly a lot on Air Canada, the Aeroplan card makes sense. If you don't, let's do a simple calculation of the benefit you earn using an Aerogold Visa. As we saw the benefit was either $0.009 per mile (the flight to Paris) or $0.008 per mile (the Nikon camera).

So if we spent $100 on purchases other than grocery stores, gas stations, drugstores or online at **www.aircanada.com** we would earn 100 miles which would translate to $0.90, which is just under 1%. For purchases eligible for 1.5 miles per dollar spent, the benefit earned is 50% better, or 1.35%.

Other Travel Reward Cards

When choosing a rewards card, in addition to the rate of return on your spending, you'll also need to consider annual fees and any sign-up bonuses. The competition for your business is intense and many premium credit cards are constantly offering enticing sign-up bonuses and sometimes offers to waive the annual fee in the first year. The card that suits you best depends on how you like to travel and where you spend the most money. Here are Robb Engen's top three travel reward cards.

1. Capital One Aspire Travel World Elite MasterCard

According to Engen, this is one of the best travel rewards cards out there. I had read about this card a year ago so I changed my business credit card to this one at that time so I can vouch for its benefits.

With this card you accumulate two miles for every dollar spent. Using the miles you accumulate is very easy. You simply book any travel on the card including airfare, hotel, rental cars, taxis, etc., and you redeem your miles at the rate of $0.01 per mile. That is a refund rate of 2% on eligible travel. And you can use your miles to pay for any taxes and fees on your travel, you don't have to worry about blackout periods or connecting flights and you can find the best cash deals on your travel.

I just redeemed my points online and it was very simple. The credit showed up on my statement a couple of days later.

At the time of writing, this card offered a sign-up bonus of 40,000 points if you spend $1,000 on purchases within the first three months.

2. BMO World Elite MasterCard

This one also has a 2% return on all purchases and a 30,000 sign-up bonus and no annual fee the first year. You can redeem your rewards anytime with no blackout periods or seat restrictions and it covers all charges including taxes and fees.

3. Scotiabank Gold American Express Card

This card offers four points for every dollar spent on groceries, gas, dining and entertainment. It also offers a 15,000 point sign-up bonus and waives the annual fee in the first year. Flexible point redemption means you can purchase travel from any provider by booking your travel online or by phone using ScotiaRewards.

Cash Back Cards

If you are not planning to do a lot of travelling, it may be simpler to use a cash back card. All the major banks and credit card issuers offer cash back credit cards with a range of rewards and benefits. These cards are available either with or without an annual fee. Which option is best for you depends on how much you use the card each month.

You'll need to spend at least $1,000 a month for the benefits to be worth your while and these cards usually require consumers to have an annual income of at least $60,000. You also need to know the details of your spending habits before you choose one, because there are different reward levels for various types of spending.

Top No-Fee Cash Back Cards

Robb Engen used the following example to rank the top no-fee cards.

EXAMPLE
- Annual spending of $12,000
- Monthly spending of:
  - Grocery stores $400
  - Gas stations $200
  - Restaurants $100
  - Recurring bills $100
  - Other spending $200

Engen ranked the top three cards as follows:

1. American Express SimplyCash Card

This card replaces the TrueEarnings Card. It offers 1.25% cash back on every purchase with no limit to the amount of cash back you can earn. Plus, you'll get 5% cash back on all eligible purchases at gas stations, grocery stores and restaurants in Canada (up to $250) in the first six months.

Using the example above, the cash back earned would be $307.50 in the first year and $150 in years two and three, for a total of $607.50.

This card is best for everyday use since it has the highest base earn rate (1.25%) of the no-fee cash back cards. Rewards are applied annually as a credit on your statement.

 TIP

Before you sign up for this card, check that the retailers you use will accept American Express.

2. MBNA Smart Cash Platinum MasterCard

Once known as the top cash back card in Canada, the latest version still offers good value. There is a six-month bonus period where you'll earn 5% back on up to $400 worth of grocery and gas purchases. You'll also get 1% cash back on other spending up to $1,250 a month. After the bonus period, you'll get 2% back on grocery and gas purchases up to $400 spending per month.

Using the example above, the cash back earned would be $240 in the first year and $168 in years two and three, for a total of $576.

This card is best for consumers looking to earn more on grocery and gas purchases and those who often use retailers where American Express is not accepted. A cheque is sent once your rewards reach $50.

3. RBC Cash Back MasterCard

This was the best of the bank-issued cards. It pays 2% back at grocery stores, 0.5% back on purchases up to $6,000 per year and 1% back on any spending over $6,000.

Using the example above, the cash back earned would be $138 each year in the first three years, for a total of $414.

This card is best for RBC customers who can leverage it to earn a multi-product discount on their banking package. Credits can be applied to your account once they reach $25.

Top Annual Fee Cash Back Cards

If you like to put all your monthly purchases on a credit card, an annual fee cash back card is probably your best bet, because they typically offer higher cash back incentive rates and won't limit the rewards you can earn on your spending.

We'll use the following spending pattern as our example.

EXAMPLE
- Annual spending of $30,000
- Monthly spending of:
  - Grocery stores $800
  - Gas stations $300
  - Restaurants $300
  - Recurring bills $300
  - Other spending $800

Engen ranked the top three cards as follows:

1. Scotia Momentum Visa Infinite

This card is the reigning "cash-back king" in Canada due to the 4% cash back it pays on grocery and gas purchases, 2% back on pharmacy and recurring bill payments and 1% back on everything else. Applicants must have a minimum annual income of $60,000 per year or $100,000 in combined annual household income to qualify. The card has a $99 annual fee that is waived the first year.

Using the example above, the cash back earned would be $732 in the first year and $633 in years two and three, for a total of $1,998.

This card is best for everyday use by people who spend more on groceries and gas. Cash back rewards are applied to your account once per year as a statement credit.

2. American Express SimplyCash Preferred Card

This card has very good bonus incentives, just like its no-fee version. You get 5% back on all purchases for the first six months up to a maximum of $400. After that the card pays 1.5% back on every purchase. You'll need just $15,000 in annual income to qualify. It comes with a $79 annual fee, but supplementary cards are free.

Using the example above, the cash back earned would be $651 in the first year and $450 in years two and three, for a total of $1,551.

This card is best used as a supplementary card for those who want to earn a higher return on spending other than groceries and gas and to take advantage of the bonus period promotion. Cash back rewards are applied to your account once a year as a statement credit.

3. Capital One Aspire Travel World Elite MasterCard

One of the top travel rewards card can also be used as a cash back card. As we have seen with this card, you get two miles for every dollar spent. But you don't have to apply the rewards against travel expenses. You can turn your rewards into an account credit, or cheque, once you have at least 10,000 miles. Cash rewards are paid out at 75% of the travel rewards value, so 10,000 miles gets you $75. This card comes with an annual fee of $150 but supplementary cards are free. You must have a minimum annual income of $70,000 or $120,000 annual household income to qualify.

Using the example above, the cash back earned would be $592.50 in the first year and $405 in years two and three, for a total of $1,402.50.

This card is best for those looking for the most flexible rewards card on the market with the ability to redeem miles for travel costs including any airline or hotel, or get cash back at a rate of 1.5% on every purchase.

MoneySense Credit Card Selector Tool

You can find this useful tool at **credit-card-selector-tool. moneysense.ca**

Select a card type (consumer, business or student), then a reward type (cash back, retail rewards or travel) and then answer the all-important question: **Do you carry a balance or think you may carry a balance in the future?**

Then there are questions about your monthly spending, including your average spending and the breakdown for gas, groceries, pharmacy, travel (flights/vacations), car rental, re-occurring bills, restaurants, entertainment, the retailer where you spend the most and how much you spend outside of Canada.

EXAMPLE

I created a sample search for a consumer cash back card for someone that *does not* carry a balance:

* $8,000 a month including:
    *   — gas $200
    *   — groceries $1,000
    *   — pharmacy $400
    *   — travel $2,000
    *   — re-occurring bills $50
    *   — restaurants $1,000
    *   — entertainment $200
    *   — no spending outside of Canada.

Here is the ranking the tool calculated based on the annual cash back amount.

Rank	Credit Card	Rewards After Fees	Annual Fee	Interest Rate on Balance
1.	MBNA Rewards World Elite MasterCard	$1,869	$89	19.99%
2.	BMO CashBack World Elite MasterCard	$1,560	$120	19.90%
3.	The NEW Simply Cash Preferred Card from American Express	$1,453	$79	19.75%

Conclusion

In retirement, every dollar is going to count, so optimizing your credit card strategy is vital.

As we discussed at the beginning of this book, tracking your personal spending is the most important thing you can do to help plan for retirement. It also enables you to choose the best credit card, because you need to know how much you spend in the various categories in order to determine which card is the best option for you.

So resolve to spend some time researching the available credit card options and remember that offers are constantly changing, so make sure you use current research results before you switch to a different credit card.

CHAPTER 20

The Financial Implications of Separation and Divorce

Separation or divorce is often devastating, both emotionally and financially. The laws in Canada regarding the financial implications of ending your relationship with your spouse depend on where you live, whether you are married or in a common-law relationship and, if you are married, whether you are separating or getting a divorce.

Separation occurs when two people who have been living together decide to live separately and are not likely to live together again. For married people, separation does not end the marriage.

Divorce is the legal ending of a marriage by a court.

When you separate or divorce, you'll need to address issues including who will keep the marital home (if you decide to keep it), who will take care of the children, who will pay specific expenses, how much spousal or child support will be paid, if any, and how all your property will be divided. It is a stressful time with many life-altering decisions to be made, including major financial ones.

Getting Professional Help

There are several resources to help you and your former partner reach agreement on these issues. If you can't reach an agreement, the final step is to go to court and have a judge decide, but that will take a long time and is usually very expensive. It makes sense to exhaust all other options before handing the problem over to the courts.

Lawyers

It is important for both of you to hire your own lawyer (or lawyer or notary if you live in Quebec) who specializes in family law. If you can't afford a lawyer, you may be eligible for legal aid for advice on certain issues through your provincial or territorial governments.

The federal Department of Justice has links to family law information centres across the country at **justice.gc.ca/eng/fl-df/fjs-sjf/index.html** or search for "family justice services."

Collaborative Practice

This is an out-of-court resolution process for separating and divorcing couples. It emphasizes full disclosure, respect and open communication and is good for spouses seeking an alternative to traditional, court-based approaches. It is a good process for people who have children together and want to maintain the best possible family relationships over time. If this is available in your area, you and your spouse hire a trained Collaborative Family Lawyer and, if needed, collaboratively trained neutral family and financial professionals. Adding these people does not necessarily mean added cost because the goal is to distribute the work between professionals in a coordinated manner.

The objective is to work together in a cooperative and non-adversarial manner to come to a mutually satisfactory solution in as little time as possible. And that can save you a lot of money.

To find a collaborative practice lawyer practising in your area, search the Internet for "collaborative practice" and the name of your town or region.

Mediators

If you can't decide on how to divide your property and other financial matters, hiring a mediator is another option. A mediator is a neutral third party who can assist in coming to a mutually agreeable solution. They do not impose decisions on you, so for this to work you and your former partner must be willing to negotiate and compromise.

Arbitrators

Another option is an arbitrator. An arbitrator is similar to a mediator, except that their decision is binding on both you and your former spouse or partner.

Financial Advice

While legal advice is essential, it may also make sense to hire a financial planner or advisor with experience in family breakups. This is especially important if you have a complex situation, because the financial and tax implications of separation or divorce escalate when there is a lot of property at stake.

Credit Counselling

Many credit counselling agencies offer support programs that are free of charge even if you don't become a client of their main service, a Debt Management Program.

The Separation Agreement

In most cases the final outcome of the discussions is a written separation agreement that covers details such as living arrangements, custody and access to the children, how property and any debt will be divided and also any spousal and child support payments.

Separating Your Finances

As soon as you separate or divorce, it is important that you also separate your finances from your former spouse or partner. Open your own chequing account and get your own credit card. Update any direct deposit banking information with your employer, the government and any other payments you receive to make sure they get into the right account.

Joint Accounts and Loans

You'll have to agree on what to do with any joint assets or debts that you shared with your former partner. Think about joint chequing accounts, credit cards and lines of credit and make sure to tell your bank what is going on.

A lot of problems can occur if joint accounts are left open. If you don't close these accounts, both of you may continue to be legally entitled to the funds in any joint accounts, as well as be responsible for repaying any debts even if your separation agreement states that only one person is responsible.

If you have a joint loan for example, the lender can demand that any borrower listed in the loan agreement continue to make the regular payments or even repay the entire amount.

For certain credit cards, secondary cardholders can be held responsible for any balances owing even if they did not sign the original credit card application.

WARNING

If you have been using a secondary credit card in your previous spouse's name, this could potentially be a major problem for you. Because it was not in your name, your use of that card was not building up your credit history.

Your Credit Report and Score

Since you will now be on your own, your credit report and score is going to be very important. Without a good score, you will not be able to get your own credit card or borrow from a bank and landlords will usually check your credit history before deciding to rent you an apartment.

If you apply for a credit card online and you are declined, you'll know you have a low credit score and need to take immediate steps to improve it.

How to Get Your Free Credit Report

One of the first things to do is to request a free copy of your credit report from both of the credit bureaus in Canada. In each case you should be able to order your copy over the phone and they are required to mail it to you free of charge. Here are the websites and the phone numbers:

- **www.equifax.ca** 1-800-465-7166
- **www.transunion.ca** 1-800-663-9980

The Devastating Financial Impact

Put simply, two people can live together for much less than they can if they live apart. Once you separate or divorce, many costs immediately go up and some can even double. That is because, even if you can afford to keep your house, the other partner has to pay to live somewhere else and if you both used to share one car, a second car will often be required. Therefore two of your largest expenses, housing and transportation, will immediately increase.

Imagine a couple who each made good money while they were married, but who had a lot of credit card debt, a significant mortgage and also two children to support, i.e., they had constantly spent more than they made. After a divorce, it will be even more difficult for them to live separately and make ends meet. In many cases, there is no alternative but to sell the house and split the proceeds.

Conclusion

There are no easy answers when a marriage breaks up. Besides being one of the most emotionally devastating events a person can endure, the financial implications range from bad to catastrophic. It is important that you and your ex-spouse or partner try to at least come to a mutual decision without creating huge lawyers' bills, so there will be more money for you and your children to live on. This is especially true when a marriage breaks up when both parties are close to retirement.

APPENDIX 1

How to Track Your Spending

Before we had online banking, in order to track your spending you had to manually list all transactions from your personal chequing accounts and credit cards.

Now, instead of entering each of your personal expenses in a spreadsheet, you can simply download a listing of transactions from your financial institution. The most common format is a CSV file (Comma Separated Value). These records then appear in Microsoft Excel in separate cells. The fewer bank accounts and credit cards you have, the easier this will be. My family has one main bank account and one joint personal credit card. That means I only have to download and manipulate data from two sources.

If you have multiple bank accounts and credit cards, do yourself a favour, and get rid of as many of them as you can.

Here is how you can track your spending.

1. Sign on to online banking

2. Download the CSV file

Here is a sample of what you might see when you open your CSV file in Microsoft Excel:

	A	B	C	D
1	**DATE**	**NAME**	**AMOUNT**	
2	3/Jan/15	SAM'S DINER	71.85	
3	5/Jan/15	THE PARKING PLACE	9	
4	7/Jan/15	SPRING ROLLS	56.25	
5	8/Jan/15	ROYAL BANK	1400	
6	9/Jan/15	CDN TIRE STORE	46.1	
7	16/Jan/15	ESSO	52	
8	17/Jan/15	THE SUTTON PLACE HOTEL	138	
9	16/Jan/15	THE SUB SHOP	15.4	
10	17/Jan/15	JOE'S RESTAURANT	198.56	
11	18/Jan/15	CINEPLEX	42.5	
12	21/Jan/15	CINEPLEX		22.59
13	23/Jan/15	LOBLAWS	210	
14	25/Jan/15	SALON DOLCE	45	
15	28/Jan/15	PAYMENT THANK YOU		4000

3. Clean up the data

Delete all the payment (deposit) amounts (because we want to focus on expenses). You can do that by pointing to the line number with your mouse (15 in this case), select "Edit" and then "Delete" or right click with your mouse and select "Delete."

If there are any credit amounts in a separate column (e.g., CINEPLEX on line 12), move them to the AMOUNT column and change them to a negative amount and then delete the existing credit amount.

Then format the numbers by highlighting the AMOUNT column (point to the C heading) and select "Format" and then "Cells" and choose the "Number" category and then two decimals and tick the box "Use 1000 Separator (,)." Or right click your mouse and select "Format Cells..." and select "Number," etc.

Here is what the cleaned data looks like:

	A	B	C
1	DATE	NAME	AMOUNT
2	3/Jan/15	SAM'S DINER	71.85
3	5/Jan/15	THE PARKING PLACE	9.00
4	7/Jan/15	SPRING ROLLS	56.25
5	8/Jan/15	ROYAL BANK	1,400.00
6	9/Jan/15	CDN TIRE STORE	46.10
7	16/Jan/15	ESSO	52.00
8	17/Jan/15	THE SUTTON PLACE HOTEL	138.00
9	16/Jan/15	THE SUB SHOP	15.40
10	17/Jan/15	JOE'S RESTAURANT	198.56
11	18/Jan/15	CINEPLEX	42.50
12	21/Jan/15	CINEPLEX	-22.59
13	23/Jan/15	LOBLAWS	210.00
14	25/Jan/15	SALON DOLCE	45.00

4. Sort by Name

Sort the data by highlighting the whole table from cell A1 to C14 (press "Control" and "A"), select "Data" and then "Sort" and choose to sort by the NAME column.

It will then look like this:

	A	B	C
1	DATE	NAME	AMOUNT
2	9/Jan/15	CDN TIRE STORE	46.10
3	18/Jan/15	CINEPLEX	42.50
4	21/Jan/15	CINEPLEX	-22.59
5	16/Jan/15	ESSO	52.00
6	17/Jan/15	JOE'S RESTAURANT	198.56
7	23/Jan/15	LOBLAWS	210.00
8	8/Jan/15	ROYAL BANK	1,400.00
9	25/Jan/15	SALON DOLCE	45.00
10	3/Jan/15	SAM'S DINER	71.85
11	7/Jan/15	SPRING ROLLS	56.25
12	5/Jan/15	THE PARKING PLACE	9.00
13	16/Jan/15	THE SUB SHOP	15.40
14	17/Jan/15	THE SUTTON PLACE HOTEL	138.00

5. Insert a Column for Type of Expense

Insert a column to the left of the AMOUNT column by pointing to the C above the AMOUNT and selecting "Insert" and then "columns" (or right click your mouse and select "Insert)."

Then enter a description for each item. Note that because we sorted by name in the previous step, similar entries are listed together. This makes it a lot easier as you can enter the type once and simply copy it.

 TIP

Once you have done this once, keep a listing of all your types to the right of where you are working in Excel and simply copy the one you want rather than retyping them.

Here is what you should get:

	A	B	C	D
1	DATE	NAME	TYPE	AMOUNT
2	9/Jan/15	CDN TIRE STORE	Home - repairs	46.10
3	18/Jan/15	CINEPLEX	Entertainment	42.50
4	21/Jan/15	CINEPLEX	Entertainment	-22.59
5	16/Jan/15	ESSO	Auto - gas	52.00
6	17/Jan/15	JOE'S RESTAURANT	Meals out	198.56
7	23/Jan/15	LOBLAWS	Groceries	210.00
8	8/Jan/15	ROYAL BANK	Home - mortgage	1,400.00
9	25/Jan/15	SALON DOLCE	Salon	45.00
10	3/Jan/15	SAM'S DINER	Meals out	71.85
11	7/Jan/15	SPRING ROLLS	Fast food	56.25
12	5/Jan/15	THE PARKING PLACE	Auto - parking	9.00
13	16/Jan/15	THE SUB SHOP	Fast food	15.40
14	17/Jan/15	THE SUTTON PLACE HOTEL	Travel - hotels	138.00

6. Sort by Type

Sort the data by highlighting the table from A1 to D14, select "Data" and then "Sort" and choose the TYPE column.

Here is what you should get:

	A	B	C	D
1	**DATE**	**NAME**	**TYPE**	**AMOUNT**
2	16/Jan/15	ESSO	Auto - gas	52.00
3	5/Jan/15	THE PARKING PLACE	Auto - parking	9.00
4	18/Jan/15	CINEPLEX	Entertainment	42.50
5	21/Jan/15	CINEPLEX	Entertainment	-22.59
6	7/Jan/15	SPRING ROLLS	Fast food	56.25
7	16/Jan/15	THE SUB SHOP	Fast food	15.40
8	23/Jan/15	LOBLAWS	Groceries	210.00
9	8/Jan/15	ROYAL BANK	Home - mortgage	1,400.00
10	9/Jan/15	CDN TIRE STORE	Home - repairs	46.10
11	17/Jan/15	JOE'S RESTAURANT	Meals out	198.56
12	3/Jan/15	SAM'S DINER	Meals out	71.85
13	25/Jan/15	SALON DOLCE	Salon	45.00
14	17/Jan/15	THE SUTTON PLACE HOTEL	Travel - hotels	138.00

7. Subtotal the Data by Type

The last step will make the data very easy to analyze. Highlight the whole table from A1 to D14, select "Data" and then "Subtotals…" then:

- For "At each change in:" select "TYPE"
- For "Use function:" select "SUM"
- For "Add subtotal to:" tick only "AMOUNT"

Leave "Replace current subtotals" and "Summary data below" ticked.

Here is what you'll see:

	A	B	C	D
1	DATE	NAME	TYPE	AMOUNT
2	16/Jan/15	ESSO	Auto - gas	52.00
3			**Auto - gas Total**	52.00
4	5/Jan/15	THE PARKING PLACE	Auto - parking	9.00
5			**Auto - parking Total**	9.00
6	18/Jan/15	CINEPLEX	Entertainment	42.50
7	21/Jan/15	CINEPLEX	Entertainment	-22.59
8			**Entertainment Total**	19.91
9	7/Jan/15	SPRING ROLLS	Fast food	56.25
10	16/Jan/15	THE SUB SHOP	Fast food	15.40
11			**Fast food Total**	71.65
12	23/Jan/15	LOBLAWS	Groceries	210.00
13			**Groceries Total**	210.00
14	8/Jan/15	ROYAL BANK	Home - mortgage	1,400.00
15			**Home - mortgage Total**	1,400.00
16	9/Jan/15	CDN TIRE STORE	Home - repairs	46.10
17			**Home - repairs Total**	46.10
18	17/Jan/15	JOE'S RESTAURANT	Meals out	198.56
19	3/Jan/15	SAM'S DINER	Meals out	71.85
20			**Meals out Total**	270.41
21	25/Jan/15	SALON DOLCE	Salon	45.00
22			**Salon Total**	45.00
23	17/Jan/15	THE SUTTON PLACE HOTEL	Travel - hotels	138.00
24			**Travel - hotels Total**	138.00
25			**Grand Total**	2,262.07

8. Condense the Data

Do you see the numbers 1, 2 and 3 at the top left? Click number 2 and you'll condense the amounts to the totals by type and the grand total.

This is what it will look like:

		A	B	C	D
	1	DATE	NAME	TYPE	AMOUNT
+	3			Auto - gas Total	52.00
+	5			Auto - parking Total	9.00
+	8			Entertainment Total	19.91
+	11			Fast food Total	71.65
+	13			Groceries Total	210.00
+	15			Home - mortgage Total	1,400.00
+	17			Home - repairs Total	46.10
+	20			Meals out Total	270.41
+	22			Salon Total	45.00
+	24			Travel - hotels Total	138.00
–	25			Grand Total	2,262.07

This will be your total spending by type for one of your accounts. If you start with the total data from your personal bank accounts and credit cards you'll get a comprehensive view, which is the key to gaining control of your finances and planning for your retirement.

APPENDIX 2
Estate Planning Record Keeper

To download this file go to **www.trahair.com** or **cpacanada.ca/retirement**.

(NOTE: Insert additional lines as necessary)

YOUR INFORMATION			
Name		Date of birth	
Address		Place of birth	
Email		Social Insurance Number	
Phone(s)		Health Card Number	
Driver's Licence number		Spouse's/ Common-law partner's name	
ADVISORS			
Accountant			
Name		Firm name	
Address		Phone	
Email			
Lawyer			
Name		Firm name	
Address		Phone	
Email			

Financial Advisor			
Name		Firm name	
Address		Phone	
Email			
Insurance Agent			
Name		Firm name	
Address		Phone	
Email			
Doctor			
Name		Firm name	
Address		Phone	
Email			

KEY DOCUMENTS

Do you have:			
A will?		Location	
A power of attorney over financial affairs?		Location	
A power of attorney over your health?		Location	
A grave plot?		Details	

PROPERTY

Principal residence address		Estimated value	
Purchase date		Purchase amount	
Any rental property address(es)		Estimated value	
Purchase date		Purchase amount	

SAVINGS AND INVESTMENTS

Bank Accounts

Bank account 1 institution		Branch/account number	
Type of account (svgs, chq, joint?)		Approximate balance	
Bank account 2 institution		Branch/account number	
Type of account (svgs, chq, joint?)		Approximate balance	

RRSP

RRSP 1 institution		Account number	
Beneficiary		Approximate balance	
RRSP 2 institution		Account number	
Beneficiary		Approximate balance	

RRIF

RRIF 1 institution		Account number	
Beneficiary		Approximate balance	
RRIF 2 institution		Account number	
Beneficiary		Approximate balance	

TFSA

TFSA 1 institution		Account number	
Beneficiary		Approximate balance	

ANNUITY CONTRACTS

Insurance company		Account number	
Phone number		Monthly payment amount	
Any survivor benefit?			

PENSION

Name of company		Account number	
Phone number		Beneficiary	
Type of plan (Defined benefit, contribution, other)			

INVESTMENT ACCOUNTS

Institution 1		Account number	
Do you have a list of the adjusted cost bases? Where is it?		Approximate market value	
Contact information			
Institution 2		Account number	
Do you have a list of the adjusted cost bases? Where is it?		Approximate market value	
Contact information			

INSURANCE

Policy 1 company		Account number	
Type of insurance (i.e., life, other)		Death benefit amount	
Beneficiary			

Contact information			
Policy 2 company		Account number	
Type of insurance (i.e., life, other)		Death benefit amount	
Beneficiary			
Contact information			

DEBTS

Mortgage on principal residence institution		Account number	
Phone number		Approximate balance	
Mortgage on rental property institution		Account number	
Phone number		Approximate balance	
Loan/Line of credit 1 company		Account number	
Phone number		Approximate balance	
Credit card 1 institution		Card number	
Name on card		Limit/balance	
Phone number			
Credit card 2 institution		Card number	
Name on card		Limit/balance	
Phone number			

Glossary

Amortization period

The length of time it will take to pay off a loan or mortgage, assuming the same interest rate and payment amount over that period. The most common amortization period for a mortgage is 25 years. A shorter amortization period will mean increased monthly payments and reduced overall cost of borrowing (total interest paid).

Annuity

A product sold by life insurance companies where, for a fixed sum payable up-front, you will receive a series of payments for a period of time, often for the rest of your life. This is an alternative option during the year you turn 71 when you have to convert your RRSP to a RRIF or annuity.

Capital gain

The difference between the original cost of a stock or other investment and the price you sell it for. Note that, in Canada, only 50% of a capital gain is taxed. This is called a "taxable capital gain."

Compounding

Refers to the generating of income on previous income. In other words, interest paid on interest. For example, if you had $10,000 on January 1st earning interest at 6% for the year with interest compounding semi-annually (twice per year), you would earn 3% for the first six months so your $10,000 would grow to $10,300, then for the last six months of the year your $10,300 would grow by 3% to $10,609. The extra $9 is 3% interest on the $300 interest you earned in the first six months.

Conventional mortgage

You usually qualify for a conventional mortgage if your down payment is greater than 20% of the purchase price of the property. Mortgage default insurance is not required in this case.

Deemed disposition

When you are considered to have sold a property even if you didn't actually sell it. This usually triggers tax consequences similar to what would have been the case if you actually sold the property. For example, if you transfer an investment from a regular investment account to a Tax-free Savings Account (TFSA) you are deemed to have disposed of it and, if the value at the transfer date is higher than the amount you paid for it, you will have to report the taxable capital gain on your tax return.

Dividend yield

A financial ratio that shows how much a company pays out in dividends each year relative to its share price. If there is no change in the value of the stock, the dividend yield is the return on investment of the stock.

Effective annual interest rate (EAIR)

The annual rate of interest you earn in a year after accounting for the effects of compounding. See the definition of compounding above. In that example the EAIR is 6.09%.

Equity

1. An ownership interest in a corporation through common or preferred stock. When people refer to "equities," they are referring to "stocks."

2. Equity also means the portion of your house, or other asset, that you own. For example, if you own a house worth $500,000 and you have a $300,000 mortgage, your equity in the house is $200,000.

Guaranteed investment certificate (GIC)

A Canadian investment that offers a guaranteed rate of return over a fixed period of time, usually ranging from one to five years. They are most commonly issued by banks, trust companies and credit unions. These are a low-risk investment that guarantees you will get back the original amount of money you invested. The rates of return are lower than you might get with stocks because of the guarantee of the return of your principal.

High-ratio mortgage

If your down payment is less than 20% of the purchase price of the property, you have a high-ratio mortgage and it must be insured against payment default by a mortgage insurer, such as Canada Mortgage and Housing Corporation (CMHC) or a private insurer. Twenty-five years is the longest amortization period you are allowed for a high-ratio mortgage.

Line of credit (LOC)

An agreement between a financial institution and a customer that establishes a maximum loan balance that the customer has access to. A secured line of credit puts up collateral (often a house) against the amount owing so that, if the borrower defaults, the lender can take control of the collateral to recover the funds. The rate of interest is lower on a secured line of credit than an unsecured line due to the guarantee.

Marginal tax rate (bracket)

The rate of tax you would pay on an additional dollar of income. The marginal tax rate for an individual will increase as their income rises; the rate depends on your income and the province or territory in which you live. For example, in Ontario in 2015 if your income was $41,000, your marginal tax rate would be 24.15%. If you made $136,000, your marginal tax rate would be 43.41%.

Mortgage

A debt instrument secured by the collateral of specified real estate property where the borrower is obliged to pay back the debt within a specified period of time.

Mutual fund

A type of investment made up of a pool of funds collected from many investors for the purpose of investing in securities such as stocks, bonds, money market instruments and other assets. They are operated by money managers who invest the funds to produce income in the form of capital gains, interest and dividends, etc. All the key facts related to the fund including costs and rate of return information are contained in the fund's "Fund Facts" document.

On approved credit (OAC)

OAC is often heard on a radio or TV ad where the offer they refer to is only good if you meet their test of your credit-worthiness, which usually includes checking your credit score.

Rate of return

The profit on an investment over a period of time expressed as a percentage of the original investment. The time period is usually one year and the rate of return is referred to as the annual return. For example, a $100 investment at the beginning of the year with an annual rate of return of 5% would have a value of $105 at the end of the first year.

Registered Education Savings Plan (RESP)

A product for saving for a child's education. Contributions are not tax deductible and earnings in the plan accumulate on a tax-deferred basis. There is no annual contribution limit, just a lifetime ceiling of $50,000. The Canada Education Savings Grant (CESG) is a federal government subsidy of up to $500 per year (20% of annual contributions of $2,500) and the maximum grant is $7,200 per child.

Registered retirement income fund (RRIF)

You have to convert your RRSP into a RRIF, or buy an annuity, by December 31st of the year you turn 71. There are minimum withdrawal percentage amounts that you are required to make each year. For example, in the year you turn 72, you have to withdraw by December 31st of that year 5.28% of the opening market value of your RRIF as of January 1st.

Registered retirement savings plan (RRSP)

A retirement savings product that allows you to contribute up to 18% of your prior year's earned income. Contributions are tax deductible within limits and all withdrawals are taxable. The contribution limit for 2015 is $24,930 and for 2016 it is $25,370.

Reverse mortgage

A financial product that allows you to borrow money against the value of your home without having to sell it. Interest charges accrue over the time that you borrow the money. The total of the amount borrowed, plus all accrued interest, is paid back upon sale of the house.

Tax-free savings account (TFSA)

A savings vehicle where contributions are not tax-deductible but earnings accumulated are never taxed. It was introduced in 2009 with an annual contribution limit of $5,000 per person aged 18 or older. The limit increased to $5,500 per year in 2013 and to $10,000 per year in 2015. Unused contribution room is carried forward and the full amount of any withdrawals can be put back into the TFSA in future years.

About the Author

David Trahair, CPA, CA, is a personal finance trainer, speaker, national best-selling author and *CPA Magazine* columnist. His books include:
* *Smoke and Mirrors: Financial Myths That Will Ruin Your Retirement Dreams*
* *Enough Bull: How to Retire Well Without the Stock Market, Mutual Funds, or Even an Investment Advisor*
* *Crushing Debt: Why Canadians Should Drop Everything and Pay Off Debt*
* *Cash Cows, Pigs and Jackpots: The Simplest Personal Finance Strategy Ever.*

He is known for his ability to explain the often-confusing world of personal finance in plain English. Canadians appreciate his no-nonsense style and the fact that his views are totally independent because he does not sell any financial products.

He currently operates his own personal finance training firm and offers seminars based on his books to organizations including CPA Canada and its provincial accounting bodies in British Columbia, Alberta, Saskatchewan, Manitoba, Nova Scotia, Newfoundland and Ontario, and also CPA Bermuda.

Critics say: Read this *Book!*

"*Book* cleverly outlines the ongoing battle between those who re-gard literature as mere fodder for fancy hypotheses and those who value it as a complex mirror of our world, a vital extension of our experience."   —Michael Upchurch, *San Francisco Chronicle*

"*Book* is [a] satirical comedy, whose sendup of literary practice is itself a lesson in how to write, read, and love books."
    —*The New Yorker*

"Grudin salutes tradition as he beins a tempestuous pilgrimage through a literary cosmos of his own making. . . . [He] has created a satiric mystery that at times has the feel of a Dickens novel set in an ironic world Jonathan Swift might have imagined. . . . If you love books and bookishness . . . you're bound to have fun."
    —Kathy S. Cocn, *The Cleveland Plain Dealer*

"Its playful elegance, wit, and authority make it a gem of its type."
    —*Publishers Weekly*

"From the alphabet to books, from students to college presidents, nothing in academia is safe from Grudin's fine pointed pen. Even if you are not an insider, if you have ever been to an institution of higher education, or want someday to go to one, read this novel!"
    —Don Frisch, *The Grand Rapids Press*

"*Book* is a book at play. The fun is really there; the suspense is re-ally there; anyone can enjoy the games it plays."
    —*The Philadelphia Inquirer*

"A clever, malicious thriller"
    —*St. Petersburg Times*

CONTEMPORARY AMERICAN FICTION

BOOK

A professor of English at the University of Oregon, Robert Grudin is a graduate of Harvard University and earned his Ph.D. at the University of California at Berkeley. He is the author of two previous books of nonfiction, *The Grace of Great Things* and *Time and the Art of Living*. He was recently awarded a Guggenheim Fellowship for 1992–1993. He lives in Eugene, Oregon.

BOOK

A NOVEL

Robert Grudin

PENGUIN BOOKS

PENGUIN BOOKS
Published by the Penguin Group
Penguin Books USA Inc., 375 Hudson Street, New York, New York 10014, U.S.A.
Penguin Books Ltd, 27 Wrights Lane, London W8 5TZ, England
Penguin Books Australia Ltd, Ringwood, Victoria, Australia
Penguin Books Canada Ltd, 10 Alcorn Avenue, Toronto, Ontario, Canada M4V 3B2
Penguin Books (N.Z.) Ltd, 182–190 Wairau Road, Auckland 10, New Zealand

Penguin Books Ltd, Registered Offices: Harmondsworth, Middlesex, England

First published in the United States of America by Random House, Inc., 1992
Reprinted by arrangement with Random House, Inc.
Published in Penguin Books 1993

1 3 5 7 9 10 8 6 4 2

PUBLISHER'S NOTE
This is a work of fiction. Names, characters, places, and incidents either are the
product of the author's imagination or are used fictitiously, and any resemblance to
actual persons, living or dead, events, or locales is entirely coincidental.

Grateful acknowledgment is made to Encyclopaedia Britannica, Inc., for permission to reprint excerpts from two articles entitled "Book" and "Bookselling" from
the 11th edition of the *Encyclopaedia Britannica*, published in 1910–1911.
Reprinted by permission.

THE LIBRARY OF CONGRESS HAS CATALOGUED THE HARDCOVER AS FOLLOWS:
Grudin, Robert.
Book: a novel/Robert Grudin
p. cm.
ISBN 0-679-41185-2 (hc.)
ISBN 0 14 02.3113 7 (pbk.)
I. Title.
PS3557.R787B66 1992
813´.54—dc20 91–50980

Printed in the United States of America
Set in Sabon
Designed by Oksana Kushnir

To Michaela

Stretch'd on the downy fleece, no rest he knows,
And in his raptur'd soul the vision glows.

—Homer, *Odyssey*, Book 1,
trans. Alexander Pope

LIBER FONS LIBERTATIS

CONTENTS

POSTSCRIPTS

A NOVEL

He sat on his haunches, his breath clouding the glass on the inside of the front door, his brown eyes intent on the far corner of the laurel hedge past the driveway, where he might first catch sight of his master returning. He sat completely still, postured like some Egyptian statue; yet no Egyptian artisan, ambitious to adorn Pharaoh's palace or tomb, would have condescended to depict the big black long-hair mongrel, with his rounded mastiff head, barrel chest and sashlike tail. He sat as though arrested in time, as though the hours that stiffened his muscles and wheeled his shadow clockwise on the rug were the single second before he saw his master, heard his step, felt his hand. Master of the loving hand, master of the endearing voice, master of the comforting smell, master of the heaped bowl.

His bowels ached and writhed. The need to be outside, to wander off at his master's side to the relief of some breezy alien forest or some field rich in odors of decay, oppressed him till his head pounded with the effort of restraint. His shadow slowly faded; the light grew dim. The little road outside was busy with returning cars. He rose and stretched forlornly and turned and with slow steps sought the remotest corner of the house, the broom closet behind the kitchen, to commit with infinite relief the unthinkable deed. Climbing the stairs to the darkened bathroom, he drank greedily from the toilet bowl. He came down the stairs and stood in the living room, listening. Now it was night again in the hungry house. Now neighbor dogs came by walking their people, dogs of easy familiar smells, masters who knew him and had petted him. He went to the big chair in front of the slightly opened front window and put his forepaws up on the chair's back and barked thunderously, cocking his ears as the echoes faded. He went to the front door and barked and barked, his great body shuddering with the agony of expression.

PART ONE

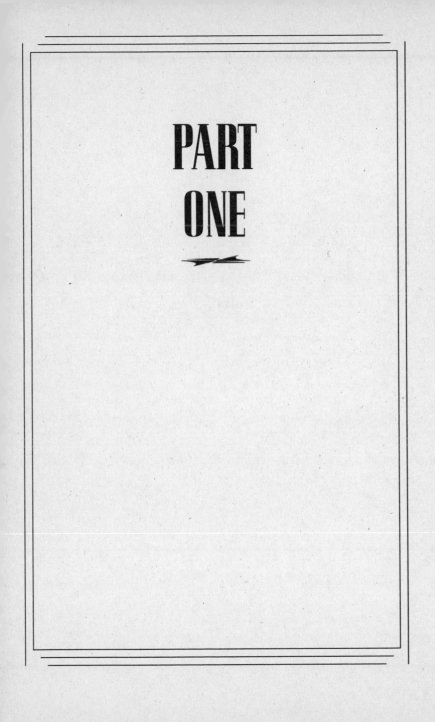

PART
ONE

Book, the common name for any literary production of some bulk, now applied particularly to a printed composition forming a volume, or, if in more than one volume, a single organic literary work. The word is also used descriptively for the internal divisions or sections of a comprehensive work.

The word "book" is found with variations of form and gender in all the Teutonic languages, the original form postulated for it being a strong feminine *Bôks,* which must have been used in the sense of a writing-tablet. The most obvious connexion of this is with the old English *bóc,* a beech tree, and though this is not free from philological difficulties, no probable alternative has been suggested.

—A. W. Pollard, "Book," *Encyclopædia Britannica,* 11th edition

CHAPTER 1

THE VIEW FROM MAMMAL HALL

The meek shall inherit the entire earth, except
for a very thin layer at the surface.

—SOVRANA SOSTRATA,
Gesta

From the start of his academic career, J. Thoreau Marshall had
shown professional qualities of an unmistakable character. Fresh
out of college, with a Big Ten degree and a kaleidoscopic gamut of
graduate options at his disposal, he had chosen as his heart's desire
the field of business statistics. Set in this course, he then proceeded,
from his dissertation years on through a brace of assistant professor-
ships, to produce a succession of timid, short-sighted, derivative
articles, couched in muddy meandering wearisome style. Marshall's
comportment as a teacher was equally distinctive. Terrified of being
at a loss for words, he wrote out his lectures which, sauced with
redundancy, seasoned with non sequitur and served up at metro-
nomic pace in a pained nasal monotone, induced narcosis in all who
heard them. In committee meetings he was notably inarticulate, dead
to nuance and phobic to original ideas. His other relationships were
of a similar ilk. To his students he was autocratic and unfair, to his
advisees distant and obtuse, to his colleagues earthbound and hollow.

It was eventually apparent that these characteristics, displayed
consistently and noted by all, ideally qualified Marshall for academic
administration, and before long he was welcomed into a confraternity
whose members, by and large, shared his talents and propensities. Yet
so far did he exceed his colleagues in these regards that he speedily rose
to the summit of his profession, leaving the ranks of department heads
and deans to become vice-president for academic affairs, or provost, at
the University of Washagon, Dulce, WS. In this office he observed with
unflinching purpose the timeworn obligations of his profession: bully-
ing his subordinates and cringing before his superiors, stifling talent

and rewarding mediocrity, promoting faddishness and punishing integrity, rejecting the most impassioned and justified individual plea yet acquiescing to every whim of political interest; avoiding confrontation, whenever possible, with the naked truth; shirking decisions and articulating such decisions as had to be made in memos so vague, oblique and circumnavigational as barely to deserve the name language. For these persistent efforts to maintain the standards and security of a great institution he was rewarded with the reverence of the faculty and the benevolent patronage of President Ralph Adorno who, "impotent and bed-rid," was awaiting imminent retirement.

Though the illness of the president (whom he had temporarily replaced and was rumored likely to succeed) gave Marshall additional power and responsibility, he nonetheless found time to relax now and then, leaning back in a great old leather swivel chair, alone in that spacious Mammal Hall office whose wide windows overlooked sunny lawns and the ivied Corinthian splendor of the College Pump, meditating wisely on things past, present, and to come. During these solitary seances, these necessary remissions of stress, his head would now and then tilt back, and a look that seemed to blend angelic patience with infant joy would cross his broad countenance. These were the moments when the noble man, now secure in public trust, could contemplate retribution against individuals who had abused him in the past. This year four colleagues were marked off for the working of justice.

There was Harvey Solomon, that feisty old historian, who, years before, had ridiculed one of Marshall's proposals in front of a titillated professorial assembly. Solomon was now postponing retirement in hopes of a pension-fixing salary increase; he would wither and wait in vain.

There was Jack O'Toole, the brash department chairman who had gone over Marshall's head to secure a new position. O'Toole aspired to a post in a prestigious national foundation; Marshall had on his desk a confidential letter of referral, compounded of gentle and pervasive slander, that would make O'Toole's name stink to high heaven—but stink so quietly and confidentially that O'Toole would never learn of the calumny done him.

There was Sarah Wilkins, that attractive young English professor with intense blue eyes and an evangelistic passion for the environment, who, instead of succumbing to Marshall's erotic overtures (hath rank no prerogatives?), had actually dared to contradict him at a planning-committee meeting. Her controversial tenure case was on his desk; it would go no further.

And there was Adam Snell, Wilkins' obscure colleague in English, who had written an objectionable novel, bizarre, anti-institutional, pernicious, meretricious, unscholarly and obscene, a book that brought negative attention to the university, a book that somehow offended colleagues from every ideological camp, a book that fortunately was a commercial flop. Now, oblivious to the effects of his own blunders and despite the fact that Dean MacCrae had told him to desist, Snell was writing another nonscholarly book, this one perhaps more odious than the first. Malfeasants like Snell shared a common fate at great universities, and Marshall was pleased in this case to be its executor. Glanda Gazza, Snell's department head, had come to Marshall with a scheme, touching the uncooperative novelist's post-tenure review, that would make Snell's life in Dulce the closest academic approximation of living hell.

But at two thirty-five on the afternoon of May 24, 1990, Marshall learned with some shock that his implementation of justice, at least with regard to Professor Snell, had encountered an unexpected obstacle. The intercom buzzer had shaken him out of a light doze, and he glanced out the window to notice that a great cumulus cloud, strange for that time of year, had come before the sun.

Clorene's voice over the intercom was strained. "Sorry to disturb you, Dr. Marshall. Professor Gazza's here. She says it's a crisis."

The acting president rose and straightened his tie. Crisis or no crisis, visits from Glanda Gazza, illustrious scholar, swashbuckling administrator and (he guessed) latent sexpot, were not to be taken lightly. In a moment she entered under full sail, tall, handsome, perm-coiffed and amply shapely, cutting through space with broad strides, her big saddle-leather shoulder bag squeaking under the stress. Barely stopping at his desk (he could see the pressure of the desktop glass against her tweed-clad thighs) she threw back her head and fixed upon him, with those marvelous gray eyes, a look that had the poignancy of a pleading child. "Thor," she said passionately, "Adam's disappeared."

"Snell?"

Gazza sank into a leather swivel, then tilted it forward, leaning toward and looking up at him, her hands tensely braced together on the desktop. "It's bizarre. He's missed class and office hours two days running. We called the police at noon. They found his house empty, the front door unlocked, his car and bike parked in front and his dog, hoarse with barking, trapped inside. The police have no leads, but they say possibly suicide, possibly murder."

"You say no leads?"

"Nothing. It's as though he went out for a breath of air and never came back."

Marshall sat down. Reaching out cautiously across the desk, he briefly put his hands on hers. "This must be hard on you, Glanda. But you're doing all you can. Except—"

Her eyes narrowed slightly. "Except?"

Setting his jowls, Marshall put on the oracular look reserved for moments when he was desperately grasping for an idea. "Except, um, you might ask a colleague to check his office. It's unlikely, but a friend who knows Snell's ways might be able to sniff out some clue that the police would miss. Did Snell have friends?"

"A few, I think. Certainly Hal Emmons." Gazza rose, shouldering the heavy bag. "I'll go find Hal right now. Thanks, Thor." She wheeled, and Marshall, availing himself of a chance to appreciate the Gazza buns in action, was taken by surprise when she suddenly turned back toward him. "One more thing, Thor. The meeting."

Marshall guiltily jerked his head up. "You mean your proceedings against Snell?"

Her face took on that pleading bedroom look again. "It would look better if we postponed it; but tomorrow's the last possible day in the academic calendar when there'd be time for sanctions."

Marshall deepened the tone of his voice and assumed the ritual cadence of an absolving cleric. "Hold your meeting anyway, my dear Glanda. It's a scheduled step in a due process of review; and if you're challenged about it by anybody you can always say that your department is so profoundly committed to democratic processes that they don't care about appearances. Besides, we'll treat Snell's absence as voluntary until proven otherwise. Maybe he killed himself." He paused. "Of course, if Adam's dead—"

Gazza gestured portentously from the doorway. "Of course. We're saved the trouble."

Alone again, Marshall swiveled around to face the windows. The sky was sunny now, and the grass glistened from what must have been a brief shower. He leaned back in his chair, interlaced his long moist fingers into one large peaceful fist on his belly and, forcing back tumescent fantasies about Gazza, focussed his imagination on the variety of nasty things that might have happened to Adam Snell.

As early as 2400 B.C., in Babylonia, legal decisions, revenue accounts, &c. were inscribed in cuneiform characters on clay tablets and placed in jars, arranged on shelves and labelled by clay tablets attached by straws. In the 7th century B.C. a library of literary works written on such tablets existed at Nineveh, founded by Sargan (721–705 B.C.). As in the case of the "Creation" series at the British Museum the narrative was sometimes continued from one tablet to another, and some of the tablets are inscribed with entries forming a catalog of the library. These clay tablets are perhaps entitled to be called books, but they are out of the direct ancestry of the modern printed book with which we are here chiefly concerned.

—A. W. POLLARD, "Book," *Encyclopædia Britannica,* 11th edition

CHAPTER 2

CHILDE HAROLD'S PILGRIMAGE

Good people and evil people suffer about equally,
but good people enjoy it more.

—SOVRANA SOSTRATA,
Gesta

Harold Emmons, professor of Renaissance literature, raised his grizzled head from a volume of *Hermes Trismegistus* to greet an apparition that was neither expected nor welcome. Glanda Gazza, who never knocked, marching stoplessly into his office. That awful imperturbable handsome look on her face as she swung her body, slightly heavier lately but still dramatically proportioned, into his rocker. Neither spoke. Her eyelids lowered momentarily, and Emmons waited for the inevitable oeillade. It came, that flash of gray eyes wide as heaven and deep as sin, that ocular barrage which had, over the years, reduced a dozen male colleagues to moral incompetence, that challenge to meek masculinity which, even though Glanda was over fifty, was still a formidable instrument of bureaucratic and sexual authority. And as soon as it came it had passed. Thanks, he supposed, to a Presbyterian childhood, Emmons had never lapsed into Glanda's thrall. Yet he was not insensible to it. It daunted him like an offered blow.

"*Hal,*" she belted out softly in a voice imitating the muted cello, and leaning forward actually grabbed his hand, and told him as one distraught that "dear Adam" Snell had disappeared. Emmons froze. His friend gone for two days, and Emmons, as usual, so far out of things not to have heard sooner, and now Gazza, who documentably hated Adam's guts, coming like Niobe all tears to tell him the news!

"No trace?" he croaked, suddenly hoarse.

"Nothing."

"What about Doppler?"

"Who?"

"His dog."

"Trapped in the house," she replied, as if by afterthought. Emmons saw a mild shadow pass over Glanda's face and found himself, as he so often had over years working with her, in that brief passage, that silent moment of transition between the blandishing overture and the armored invasion, between feigned humanity and business at hand. She hit him again with her big look. "Hal, I've just been with Thor Marshall."

"Oh," grunted Emmons, holding back "that ghoul."

"Did Adam do his writing at home or here?"

"Here—I mean, in his office."

"Can you imagine anything he might have in writing that could help us find him?"

Emmons could now follow Glanda's line of attack to its ultimate goal. "Adam recorded his letters in his computer."

"Didn't he also write a journal?"

"Yes, he kept a writer's journal while he was working on *Sovrana Sostrata*. I think he's also using one for the new book, but I'm not sure."

"Hal, Thor and I want you to find out. You and Adam were friends, and you can look discreetly into his things. You mustn't refuse. You've got to start as soon as possible," and the departmental passkey, anchored to its heavy wooden tag, emerged from Glanda's bag.

Parting ceremonies were brief.

Loath, somehow fearful of his unwanted task, Emmons sat on silently at his desk. Grief nagged at his body like physical pain. Adam, poor devil, was probably dead. People didn't just disappear; they disappeared in order to reappear as corpses. And Glanda had no desire to save Adam. Glanda was good with computers and Emmons wasn't. If she had wanted to save Adam, she would have gone into his office herself.

He glanced distractedly out the window, and his glance, as though guided by some necessity of depression, fell on the most menacing object available: a huge dense mass of dark vegetation—big firs, thronging undergrowth and impenetrable giant grass—obtruding like some geographical anomaly in the middle of campus. The Ezekiel Pisham Homestead, ancient seat of Dulce's founder, popularly called the Jungle and recently rendered impassable by a freakish botanical riot.

An absurd intuition possessed him. Could Adam possibly be in there? Emmons groaned. If so, he wasn't alive.

Emmons turned to his desk, lowered his face into his hands and mourned for his friend. The leather-bound *Hermes Trismegistus,* unattended, slipped down from his lap and spread-eagled on the floor.

He groaned again, pushed himself to his feet, grabbed his jacket and the passkey and left his office. Stocky, bowlegged, he moved down the hallway with a heavy gait. The long-familiar passage, silent and empty in late afternoon, suddenly seemed barbarous to him, its veneered professorial office doors following on one another anonymously, a blind alley ending in a red illuminated EXIT sign, a passage from nowhere to nowhere, a tiled and plastered manifesto of cultural bankruptcy, a wound in space. Countless times over fifteen years Emmons had walked down this hall to visit Snell, to go out with him for coffee or a beer or just hang around and chat. Countless times, before big windows fronting directly on the Jungle, they had sat, comfortably letting time pass, talking of literature or politics or the welter of eccentricities that made up their profession. All that was over now, and the very architecture, once alive with the promise of honest friendship, had gone alien, assumed an ugliness that was almost evil.

A floor below, at a door marked only by a yellow note card handwritten SNELL, Emmons fumbled with the key, half afraid of finding a corpse inside, half guilty at intruding where he had always knocked.

The long narrow room was shot through with late-afternoon sunlight—blinding, unfriendly radiance that heated the air to a fever, glared erosively on the vinyl recliner by the window and brought a smell of cooking plastic from the computer ensemble that dominated the left-hand wall. Again Emmons felt a sense of violation, of leering notoriety invading Snell's undefended retreat. Poor Snell was public property now, and the sun was eating his office.

Emmons opened windows, lowered shades. When the hot air had blown out into the hallway, he shut the office door and stood anxiously alone. In the lessened light the room regained its identity, became the rational, livable workplace where his friend had held quiet conversance with texts, students and colleagues. The couch abutting the bookshelves. The silent telephone on the homemade plywood computer table. The stereo set on the windowsill. All as usual, surfaces clear and undisturbed, just as the meticulous Snell might have left them after a day's work.

Only on the blond writing desk by the window was there congestion. Memos, announcements, reports, newsletters, minutes, course descriptions, the normal university confetti, shuffled loosely into a pile and pushed over to the left. Emmons wasted ten minutes on them, then checked the desk drawers, which revealed no more than the usual assortment of accessories. He was about to assault the filing cabinet in search of Snell's incoming correspondence when he glanced at a half-empty cardboard box on the floor just to his right. He pulled it up to his lap and examined its contents with increasing interest.

When on cool mornings in the hollow of green hills we met, I folded, unfolded, in infant silence, your dappled whiteness. Mornings with absurd surprise I rediscovered, forever familiar, forever strange, your form in a silence of loving. Hidden in leaves of time, we gave each other being, you white with an endless luster of renewal, I silent to see, in one face, myself and another.

Envoi

Go forth little book,
silently into the night,
like gull wheeling seaward,
like hawk to darkling wood.

Go forth and spy
into the kitchens of the righteous
and the beds of virgins;
go to the tabernacles of study,
they will read you as you have read my soul.

Go forth and stand
above the sleeping town;
sing from the hill of wonder
a madrigal of dreams.

Thus ended Adam Snell's work journal for *Sovrana Sostrata*. Harold Emmons shifted in his chair and carefully eased the manuscript back, accordionlike, into its box. Having printed out his journal, Snell had neglected to separate the pages, so that handling the document was like manipulating a white, word-dappled, uncooperative snake. Emmons called home. It was six already, and he was going to miss dinner, but he could not move. The snake had coiled around him, had him in its toils.

The journal held wonders.

Emmons had heard a number of stories about artists who fell in love with their creations, but this one beat Pygmalion, Henry Higgins and the whole pack. Here was a real artist, whose fictional creation Sovrana *re-created him,* lectured and dictated whole passages to him, stimulated in him the profoundest desire, teased him, ultimately rejected him, and in all these things brought forth from him, in a kind of exotic sexual reversal, a significant work of art.

Here also was, at least in principle, an erotic attitude which, if not unprecedented, was certainly not mentioned in modern discussions of gender relationships: a man's open, total, unrepentant, grateful submission to a woman's will.

Emmons reached for the journal again and clumsily turned his way to a passage quite early on:

January 24, 1987. Saturday.

Today, for the first time, I actually *saw* Sovrana. No more floundering around now, trying to picture her as old girlfriends or movie stars, trying to formulate an abstract, philosophical imitation of nature, but a real face, never seen before, a passionate mocking histrionic face with eyes that are all seasons, eyes that can draw me like a puppet, play me like an instrument. And she speaks to me. I no longer have to imagine her words. I can hear them. And with what voice! A resonant, musical voice, a devilishly modulated voice, a voice to charm the soul or freeze the blood.

I almost saw her last night, just before waking. I dreamt that she was in a house in the country and that I was on the grounds. I crept closer and closer to the house, thrilled to be near her yet somehow afraid. I could hear her inside, playing the violin. I stood at the front door, knowing that only that thin wood separated her and me. A chill came on me and I ran in terror, almost as though she might grow outraged at my intrusion and chase me. I woke sorrowful.

That sorrow eased me. If we could only fail more often in dreams, how often we might succeed awake! I sat at morning coffee, and blinked, and there she was! Looking not as I had wanted her to look, but as she *had* to look. I wondered . . .

Emmons turned slowly ahead. As Snell's friend, he had special insight into the now-bittersweet story of happy obsession, of artistic and spiritual renewal, that was unfolding in his hands. Before Sovrana, Adam Snell's life had been a study in failed aspiration. Snell, exuberant youth with a pronounced gift of gab; Snell, whose early efforts at fiction dazzled five Harvard writing professors; Snell, who thumbed his nose at practicality and moved after graduation into an uncle's attic to enchant the world by weaving tales. But the world, in its wisdom, thought otherwise. The world had enchanters enough without Snell, or so the publishers of said enchanters seemed to think. The young writer, who kept a special wastebasket for rejection letters, watched with deepening depression as the basket filled up, and like a boxer hit in the same place too many times, he began to lose pleasure in his craft and wish himself elsewhere.

Elsewhere, Snell's wise uncle suggested, might just as well, and perhaps very happily, be grad school, and so, one fine fall morning in the early sixties, the young man journeyed westward to begin the scholarly study of what (he sadly thought) he was personally impotent to create. English literature, especially the finely tuned and sometimes outrageous literature of the eighteenth century, gave him much solace, and aside from a marriage that soon dissolved and a rather embarrassing incident during the Berkeley uprisings, his career at first was fairly successful. He won a coveted position at Washagon, where he taught quite brilliantly and produced enough published scholarship to gain the security of tenure. Yet neither his old ebullience nor the creative productions it spawned had ever reappeared. In his late forties, with a dwindling scholarly output, Snell seemed destined for the deflated tranquillity and unbemoaned obscurity of the average literature professor.

What then could account for *Sovrana Sostrata*? Snell's journal explained all that. Snell had apparently gotten out of bed one morning in early 1987 with a phenomenal case of self-reproach. He saw himself as unproductive, barren, sterile, cowardly and self-indulgent. And he suddenly refused to remain so. His plan was brutally simple. If he could not instill creativity in himself, he could at least write about his own lack of creativity: about the omissions, surrenders and refusals that characterize the barren life, about the lies and rationalizations that support it, about the professional and social mechanisms that feed it. Sitting down at the computer on the morning of January 4, he began what he called his "Book of Failure."

Such analyses demand honesty, and Snell was honest to a fault. He saw his own youthful talent as something irretrievably lost. He limned out, in such apt detail as to turn the stomach, the life of an elemental escapist and confirmed depressive. And as though this honesty were being providentially repaid, these awful revelations seemed to offer him, via catharsis, a kind of stylistic freedom. By January 10, when he proceeded to "Sterility and Society," his style had grown richer, more figured and dynamic; it had stopped being painfully honest and was suddenly wryly amusing. And this living quality became passionate as well when, on the fourteenth, Snell turned his attention (he thought, temporarily) away from analysis and critique and toward the modeling of what he called "my own opposite." His own character and life being, as he put it, a closed book, he sought to imagine another character and life: a personality quintessentially brave, open, creative and assertive.

Behold Sovrana! Snell's rationale in choosing a female character was simply put: Qualities like bravery, openness, creativity and assertiveness are often socially stigmatized, especially when exhibited by women. Therefore, in displaying such qualities, a woman is potentially more admirable and spirited than a man. Yet Snell had no idea of the consequences of such a choice. Choosing a female for his opposite, he would not only rekindle his creativity but awaken in himself a previously repressed but now insatiable erotic longing.

As Sovrana grew in detail, as her spirit swelled and her figure etched itself more sharply in his mind, Snell opened a new file in his computer and began to tell her "story," the story that would ultimately become his novel. He did not abandon the journal, however. The Book of Failure would become a writer's journal that he kept in the computer along with his novel and used as a kind of workshop for plans and provisional ideas. And the journal was also a jungle of exploration. On February 15 Snell announces, like a little kid running in the door with news of an approaching ice cream truck,

> Can you believe it? Sovrana's written a book! It's called *Gesta* (L. deeds or acts), carries that meaning primarily, with secondary pun for jest and implicit reference to pregnancy, gestation. Thus Sovrana pronounces it "jesta." A totally disorganized book; Sovrana cares nothing for organization. Looks like loose collection of titled essays and random sayings. But page after page hits like a sledgehammer. Makes the national best-seller list.

Later, at difficult points in composition, Snell would turn to his journal and ask Sovrana direct questions: "What did you say then?" "What are you thinking about?" She would answer in his mind, and he would happily write her responses down.

Fascinating as all this was, it still said nothing about where Snell had disappeared to. The final entry, concluding with that quaint little "Envoi," was dated more than two years ago. Had Snell been keeping a writer's journal with his current work-in-progress? Likely enough, but neither journal nor work-in-progress was visible in Snell's office. They had to be in the computer.

But computers were not Emmons' strong suit. He disliked and feared them, had a prickly sensation whenever they were turned on in his presence. The computer search would have to wait until, if he was lucky, Emmons could get the invaluable grad student Roy Gallard to help him.

It was dark now, and he had a long walk home. But before leaving, he could not resist opening Snell's journal one more time. The snakelike discourse unfolded at an image that its reader found riveting but not wholly agreeable:

Last night, drunk with fever, I became the book itself.
My skin corrugated into blades of paper.
My flesh distended into the inane symmetry of verso and recto.
My joints wrenched, like punished things, into a diaspora of chapters.
The redundancies swelled as tumors, as ulcers ached the omissions.
And over me, above me, grew like genie smoke the monstrous spirit,
Demonic, sterile, lizard-horned but with a flat white stupid face,

Of the dissociated word.

Apparently Snell had come down with the flu in April of 1987.

One of the earliest direct ancestors of this extant is a roll of eighteen columns in Egyptian hieratic writing of about the 25th century B.C. in the Musée de Louvre at Paris, preserving the maxims of Ptah-hetep. Papyrus, the material on which the manuscript (known as the Papyrus Prisse) is written, was made from the pith of a reed chiefly found in Egypt, and is believed to have been in use as a writing material as early as about 4000 B.C. It continued to be the usual vehicle of writing until the early centuries of the Christian era, was used for pontifical bulls until A.D. 1022, and occasionally even later; while in Coptic manuscripts, for which its use had been revived in the 7th century, it was employed as late as about A.D. 1250. It was from the name by which they called the papyrus, *bublos* or *biblos,* that the Greeks formed *biblion,* their word for a book, the plural of which (mistaken for a feminine singular) has given us our own word Bible.

—A. W. POLLARD, "Book," *Encyclopædia Britannica,* 11th edition

CHAPTER 3

AN EVENING
WITH FRANK UNDERWOOD

Truth telling is a classic exercise of raw power, but unlike other forms of power—guns, oil, money, etc.—that are morally neutral, truth telling is morally discriminative, generally tending to nourish goodness and discourage evil. Truth telling is like lighting up a dark street: scaring off the robbers and rapists so that decent people may go safely home. Truth telling is sweet power.

—SOVRANA SOSTRATA,
whispered to Adam Snell in his sleep

Walking barefoot into his dim-lit kitchen for coffee, Frank Underwood stubbed his toe on a chair and roared. Blood rushed to his head, his limbs lightened with an access of rage, and for a moment the spotlessly neat bachelor kitchen, with its ostentatious Mexican tiles and aggressively woodsy decor, seemed like some wicked architectural prank sprung upon him. He hissed in fury, limped into the bathroom to check for blood and, finding none, glanced hesitantly at his own face in the large mirror. Distorted by pain and anger, his features gradually rearranged themselves into the arrogant calm that so well suited his Anglo-Saxon good looks: straight nose, deep-set blue eyes, ruddy complexion, now a bit lined. Yet Underwood, having grown up as the less beautiful of two good-looking brothers, had no great love for his own face. Too much face, too easy to read. As a strategy against such scrutiny he had considered growing a beard, but decided that his own beard, which was dark, would type him with the homosexuals, Jews, ethnic busybodies and other odd types who clustered in such profusion at the university. He was not like them at all. He combined intellectual success with the strength and courage of a hero.

Glancing downward he noted with satisfaction that even his expansive terry-cloth bathrobe could barely conceal the muscles, the bulging pectorals and biceps, that he had built up over years of clandestine weight-training. He felt a glow of vaguely sexual pleasure. Not bad, for America's fastest-rising literary theorist. Not bad, for the nasty scrapes that sometimes come up.

Underwood put on slippers, returned to the kitchen, moved the offending chair to its proper position by the table and set about making coffee. Though the late-May evening was warm, a hearty fire crackled from the living room. He needed the bracing coffee for a rather risky maneuver he had to perform later that night. He had no great love of fires, but their appetites, the way they greedily ate things up and cried for more, were occasionally convenient.

Coffeepot and mug in hand, Underwood shuffled into the living room and arranged an easy chair and his refreshment directly in front of the fireplace. From the front closet he retrieved a large and heavily laden paper bag. For the next half hour, occasionally stopping for a sip of coffee, he performed an action at once meticulous and repetitive, withdrawing single sheets of paper from the bag, crumpling each up and throwing it into the fire, watching carefully until it was wholly consumed. In the end the bag went in too, glowing momentarily like a merry little house before it met the same fate as its contents.

Half mesmerized by the flames, giddy from caffeine, toe rapidly recovering, heart animated by a sense of excitement and satisfaction, Underwood sat by the fire and waited. Three hours at least before it was safe. Only one task remained before his departure: to see if there was any blood left on the shirt and book bag that were soaking in the laundry room. It was human blood, and it was not his own.

In the 2nd century B.C., Eumenes II, king of Pergamus, finding papyrus hard to procure, introduced improvements into the preparations of the skins of sheep and calves for writing purposes, and was rewarded by the name of his kingdom being preserved in the word *pergamentum,* whence our "parchment," by which the dressed material is known. In the 10th century the supremacy which parchment had gradually established was attacked by the introduction from the East of a new writing material made from a pulp of linen rags, and the name of the vanquished papyrus was transferred to this new rival. Paper-mills were set up in Europe in the 12th century, and the use of paper gained ground, though not very rapidly, until on the invention of printing, the demand for a cheap material for books, and the ease with which paper could be worked on a press, gave it a practical monopoly. This it preserved until nearly the end of the 19th century, when substances mainly composed of wood-pulp, esparto grass and clay largely took its place, while continuing, as in the transition from papyrus to linen-pulp, to pass under the same name (see *Paper*).

—A. W. POLLARD, "Book," *Encyclopædia Britannica,* 11th edition

CHAPTER 4

THE WAY UP SPINE HILL

Realizing early in life that I would never be a saint, I decided at least to be one of the reasons why others are.

—SOVRANA SOSTRATA,
Gesta

Emmons' two-mile walk home took him south from campus, through the stylish residential area known as the Slope, and then eastward, steeply ascending to the top of Spine Hill. That pleasant spring evening the air was fresh yet windless, hung with the fragrance of lilac, daphne and the last fruit blossoms. It would be a fine walk, Emmons expected. *Get my daily exercise. Clear my head.*

But his head refused to clear. The very delights of the spring evening, coupled with his recent engorgement of Snellian discourse, filled him with thoughts of Sovrana. Sovrana Sostrata! The very name, thanks to Snell's notes, was now alive with tragedy, vivid with the paradox of womanhood. "Sovrana" = "sovereign, noblest, commanding"; "Sostrata" = "stretched out underneath," i.e., sexually under some man or other, doomed until this century, in Iago's mocking words, "to suckle fools and chronicle small beer." Yet Snell's heroine had refuted this paradox, even twisted it to her advantage. Her assertion of sovereignty was at the same time an assertion of sexuality. She lived this paradox. She died for it.

Admittedly, Sovrana had precedents. Snell's notes mentioned ties with Cleopatra, Mae West and, even more, the fifth-century philosopher-martyr Hypatia. But Sovrana rose, dolphinlike and hugely politic, above reductive interpretation. She could not be cubbyholed by a philologist, typecast by a genre critic, dismissed as fluff by a theorist. Hers was an ancient dignity, that of a figure standing apart from groups and causes, lonely yet also suggesting human continuity, in time as well as space, a continuity not of institutions but of recurring solitary heroics. She was the real thing. An upsetting character. A character who bit into the heart.

Sovrana's story was like Snell's in many ways, with the telling proviso that Snell's till-then recessive personality met its opposite in her orchestra of assertive traits. Philosophy professor at a western state university, she stuns the literary and academic worlds with *Gesta,* a free-form philosophical work that hits with the anger of Nietzsche and the laughter of Twain. What does it hit? Ideologically speaking, the weaknesses of most anyone who would be professionally qualified to read it: the reactionary postures embedded in liberal institutions, the institutional phobia for real inquiry, the moral barrenness of the modern intellectual, the polite dishonesties of daily life.

Perhaps the most scandalous element of *Gesta* is Sovrana's position on the history of gender relationships. Women, Sovrana believes, have been almost universally shielded from active life because they are more "precious to nature" than men. How so? The economics of generation, she answers cheerfully. A small male population can fertilize any number of females, but a small female population endangers the race itself. Males are thus an expendable resource; females not. Successful societies, therefore, have kept women out of risk and away from stress and emphasized their preciousness in all sorts of ritual ways. Chivalry then is not an interest-ridden convention but rather a practice deeply rooted in survival. Secure from danger, anxiety and the pressures of production, women have silently cultivated a kind of wisdom, a wisdom not of words but of attitudes and gestures, and have passed this wisdom, itself a precious cultural resource, on to their daughters.

Such was the status quo for several millennia. But now, according to Sovrana, times have changed. In the late twentieth century human survival is no longer at risk. On the contrary, we're overpopulated, and females no longer have to be hoarded like priceless gems. Now, like men, they are expendable. And society has responded accordingly, with miscellaneous little adjustments like increased violence against women, birth control, homosexuality and women's liberation.

Attacked for this thesis by male and female alike, Sovrana replies in a famous article that she is not endorsing a system but rather relating the truth about it. As anyone can plainly see, she doesn't want to be "precious" herself. She welcomes overpopulation because, by making women expendable, it liberates them to endure stresses, and hence (as she puts it) enjoy "adventures" previously reserved for men.

Snell expounds on such adventures in shocking detail: Sovrana's irreverent behavior at public functions, her utter frankness with associates, her arrogance, her manifold sexual liberties. Add to this her unforgettable beauty and charm (so powerful that, in the words of an ex-lover, coming into her favor was like "walking into sunshine"), and you have a character to reckon with.

Where does all this get Sovrana? Much money, brief fame and a swift kick out of the academic world. The academic world has ways of getting rid of people who think too freely or say too much. She is summarily denied tenure on the grounds that she has produced no "scholarship." Her friends, even the self-proclaimed curmudgeons, are lily-livered and wilt under political pressure. She loses her publisher and her professorship, flees to her family's native Italy and takes a farmhouse in Tuscany. There, among hills crowned with forests of oak and broom and carpeted with pale-green olive groves and the deeper green of the vine, she develops a witchlike reputation, has a flagrantly self-advertised affair with a loony Irish priest and, in the tragic finale, is stoned to death by local housewives.

A bit too Hardyesque or Lawrentian? You could imagine two schools of thought. True, Snell maintained a narrative dimension lacking in Hardy or Lawrence: a reflex of comic reassessment that time after time defused the Jeanne d'Arc heroics and focussed Sovrana's unfortunate career in a broader human perspective. On the other hand, these were the only passages in the text that looked forced, as though compelled by humanistic conscience rather than visceral necessity. Small wonder. Adam was obsessed by his heroine. When he spoke lightly of her, she probably haunted his dreams with jibes and reproaches.

Emmons turned onto Fir Boulevard, the narrow twisting road that led steeply up Spine Hill to his home. As he puffed up the first pitch, he considered the most ironic and puzzling aspect of the whole Snell/Sovrana affair: the fate of Snell's passionate *chef-d'oeuvre. Sovrana Sostrata* had flopped. It had never been reviewed. Now, less than two years after publication, it was already out of print.

It was easy enough to explain why this had happened, but groups of very believable everyday details, arranged in the right order, can add up to enormous paradoxes. Here the enormous paradox was that *Sovrana Sostrata,* a minor masterpiece, full of sex and surprise and dominated by a heart-stopping female lead, had never made it out to a national readership starved for originality. Of course it had been largely Snell's fault. Snell had been so retrograde about approaching editors and agents that the learned Shakespearean Quintus Adler had accused him of trying to keep his beloved Sovrana for himself. Snell did send the manuscript off and get a few rejections (letters that suggested rejections out-of-hand rather than considered readings), but instead of pressing on boldly or consulting an agent, he simply waffled. Things were still up in the air when a man named Grant Welles, apparently some old college friend, offered to publish the book at Penrose Press, his small operation in San Francisco. Foolish and retrograde again, Snell accepted. A run of one thousand copies emerged, unannounced, into the gigantic mill and hubbub of the mass market. Welles's promotional skills were primitive. Snell had no connections. No sooner out, the book died.

Six months after publication, Welles informed Snell by mail that seven hundred–odd copies of *Sovrana Sostrata* were being remaindered. Snell took this reverse stoically. Sovrana's gift to him had gone far beyond money or fame. She had given him back to himself, reawakened in him, at least as a writer, the exuberance of his youth. He was already at work on a new book, *On Wonderment,* a freeformer like *Gesta* he said, but meditative rather than polemical.

Halfway up the hill the lights of the valley, stretched far beneath, came into view on Emmons' right, mirroring the starry sky and becoming his companions for the rest of his walk. He looked downhill, straining for a view of Snell's darkened house on Park Avenue. Poor Adam. As though *Sovrana*'s premature eclipse were not enough, fate had had more bitterness in store for the unfortunate author. Numerous members of his department, having tolerated him for years as a polite nonentity, now had broken into plain antagonism. Snell's book had offended them because of the things Sovrana said and did and because the *way* she said and did them implied his tacit approval. Malevolent mutterings edged his earshot; solemn professorial heads turned down or away as he passed in the quad. Glanda Gazza had thrown her weight squarely against him, and there were rumors that she was conspiring with Thor Marshall and a number of literary theorists to wreak institutional vengeance upon him at a specially scheduled meeting of full professors tomorrow afternoon.

Nearing his house and family, Emmons tried to put his thoughts in order. Snell's life had had curious ups and downs. But Emmons doubted that any of these would have warped Snell's sanity or prompted him to take some suicidal step. And even in the distant possibility that he *had* thought of doing such a thing, unless he had gone totally bonkers he would not have left Doppler shut up in the house. Realistically, there was no chance but that Snell had come to harm. And there was nothing for Emmons to do about it, unless he and Gallard could dig something out of the computer tomorrow. And what had become of poor Doppler? Emmons' gorge rose. *I bet Glanda's sent him to the pound!*

With a kind of pedaling step, he descended the steep ramp to his home. *Must call the pound at once and try to reach Gallard again,* he thought, fumbling for the key. Once inside he shouted hello to his wife and promptly disappeared under a golden retriever and three teenage boys.

So long as the use of papyrus was predominant the usual form of a book was that of the *volumen* or roll, wound round a stick, or sticks. The modern form of book, called by the Latins *codex* (a word originally used for the stump of a tree, or block of wood, and thence for the three-leaved tablets into which the block was sawn) was coming into fashion in Martial's time in Rome, and gained ground in proportion as parchment superseded papyrus. The *volumen* as it was unrolled revealed a series of narrow columns of writing, and the influence of this arrangement is seen in the number of columns in the earliest codices. Thus in the Codex Sinaiticus and Codex Vaticanus of the Bible, both of the 4th century, there are respectively four and three columns to a page; in the Codex Alexandrinus (5th century) only two; in the Codex Bezae (6th century) only one, and from this date to the invention of printing, while there were great changes in handwriting, the arrangement of books changed very little, single or double columns being used as was found convenient.

—A. W. POLLARD, "Book," *Encyclopædia Britannica,* 11th edition

CHAPTER 5

FIVE TYPES OF DISCOURSE

The possibilities for self-expression are infinite, and of these the
most nearly infinite of all is nonsense.

—SOVRANA SOSTRATA,
Gesta

1. FROM *GUMMINS' COLLEGE GUIDE*

The University of Washagon (1989 enrollment 25,748) is
located in the pleasant town of Dulce (pronounce to rhyme
with "gulch"; 1980 pop. 54,106) in the Wishbone Valley west of
the Lion Mountains. Besides the College of Liberal Arts, the
University maintains schools of Medicine, Veterinary Medicine,
Law, and Engineering, as well as programs in Agricultural Science and Environmental Economics. . . . A notable feature of the
University of Washagon campus is the Ezekiel Pisham Homestead. Founder of the city of Dulce, Pisham came to this area in
the winter of 1847. He built a log cabin one quarter mile south
of the Wishbone River, near what is now called Pisham Point.
Here he lived until his death in 1892. Ezekiel Pisham deeded his
640-acre estate to the University of Washagon (then known as
the Washagon Academy of Veterinary Science) with the stipula-
tion that his cabin and the five-acre plot around it remain un-
touched until the cabin, in his words, "returned to its mother"
(that is, went to pieces). Accordingly, the Pisham Homestead
was fenced off and preserved as a park. Though normally
locked, the Homestead is available to students on a guided-tour
basis and for supervised picnics. Now known as the "Jungle,"
it has become a refuge for a variety of small animals and birds.*

*Note to 1990 edition: As a result of an unauthorized biological experiment
conducted in 1989, the Pisham Homestead has been temporarily declared a
safety hazard and is off limits to all persons.

2. FROM A SCIENTIFIC JOURNAL

Since the spring of 1987, my staff and I had been conducting experiments with high-density organic fertilizers on varieties of *Poa trivialis* (meadow grass) which had very nifty results, not only in terms of fertility but in terms of the speed and extent of the growth cycle. On the afternoon of March 11, 1988, I returned from a short holiday to discover that one of my newer specimens had reached truly jumbo size, with blades roughly 4 cm. wide and height approaching 1 m. Whether this macrogrowth was due to the fertilizer alone, or whether we were spectators at a real mutation (as my colleague George Hilbert queried, "*Poa schmutzhaufia?*"), it was too early to say, and we were soon to lose the entire specimen, together with a number of others, when some duffer mistook a canister of industrial defoliant for organic fertilizer. Luckily I had retained about a hundred seeds, several of which, out of mere curiosity, I tossed one day that summer onto the grounds of the Pisham Homestead, a wilderness area on the University of Washagon campus. The results have been mind-blowing. Even in heavy shade and dense undergrowth, the *Poa* has performed famously, growing into such size and density as to intertwine with other plants and make human entry into the park nearly impossible. Why it has not grown beyond the park grounds can be explained only by postulating a kind of loose symbiotic relationship between it and the predominant form of Homestead undergrowth, *Ilex opaca* (American holly). I have named the Homestead *Poa* "mucca-grass," because of a remark my young son made when he first saw it.—DR. WARREN SCHMUTZHAUF, Dept. of Biology and Agricultural Science, University of Washagon, in the *International Journal of Failed Results,* XXVIII, No. 3 (Fall 1988), 2113*f*.

3. FROM THE DULCE *BUGLE*

UNIVERSITY OF WASHAGON ENGLISH
PROFESSOR MISSING, FEARED DEAD

Authorities today expressed mounting concern for the fate of University of Washagon Professor Adam Snell, who was last seen in his office on Tuesday.

Snell, a member of the English faculty here since 1970 and Associate Professor of English since 1977, was reported missing after he failed to meet his classes on Wednesday. His dog was found trapped in his residence—evidence, according to Lieutenant Andrew Pierce of the Dulce Police, that Snell's disappearance was not voluntary. Documentation produced in the residence by the dog, Pierce went on, placed Snell's disappearance on Tuesday night.

Professor Snell, who is divorced and lived alone, is a specialist in eighteenth-century literature with an outstanding record of teaching. "We will miss Adam," remarked Glanda Gazza, Professor of English and Head of the English Department. "He was gentle, learned and helpful to all."

J. Thoreau Marshall, Provost and Acting President of the University of Washagon, characterized Snell as a hardworking, responsible member of the faculty. "Adam was a faithful colleague and a true friend. I can think of no one who would want to injure him."

Professor Snell is the author of several scholarly articles and a novel, *Savrona Sostrana*. One theory on his disappearance runs that the novel's poor sales may have made him despondent.

Dulce Police Plan
Homestead Search

Snell's disappearance is the first documented event of this kind locally in eleven years, according to Lieutenant Pierce. If the missing professor is not found by Friday night, Pierce plans to conduct an exhaustive search of the only wilderness area in the district, the Pisham Homestead on the University of Washagon campus. "It's possible," said Pierce, "that if Professor Snell met with foul play, the body might have been dumped in there."

Because of the dense grass clogging the Homestead, the search will be a massive project, requiring the help of many. The Lizard Beautification League, a group of students in favor of razing the Pisham Homestead, have offered their assistance en masse. Fears of violence were raised, however, by a statement received here today from Bob Nielson, President of the Anti-Beautification Front, a local group founded to preserve the Homestead. "Professor Snell, if he is on the Homestead grounds, cannot be alive. The retrieval of a corpse does not justify the destruction of a historical monument. We will resist such destruction with every means at our disposal. Read my lips," the statement concludes.

4. FROM ADAM SNELL'S JOURNAL
FOR *SOVRANA SOSTRATA*

February 5, 1987. Thursday.

Sunday I lost the entire book. Lost, I mean **LOST**, destroyed, vanished, irretrievable. By a computer error so simple that it threatens anyone. I overwrote it with another file, *this file!* and repeated the error by rote onto the backup disk, and then, with triumphant idiocy, keyed the memory into oblivion. It took about twenty seconds to realize what I had done. Fifty-five pages, three weeks of writing, and Sovrana murdered before she was born. I went into shock, and seriously thought of jumping out the window.

In an hour I was writing again from the beginning. I had all the notes in this journal and remembered many phrases and images.

Since then I've been working almost nonstop, pausing only to teach, eat and sleep. And today, remarkably, I'm back to where I was.

Except that the book is better, more toned and detailed, written from scratch by a writer who was already up on the story. It was less like writing fiction than it was like describing something, some real thing, that had already happened.

I sit here and sip coffee while the printer flails away at a hard-copy backup.

I cannot think seriously of this novel, I mean, think at length, without remembering childhood. Evenings my mother would come upstairs with books, not thin illustrated children's things but fat old volumes of Grimm or Defoe or Stevenson, and open carefully to a marked page and, sitting on my bed, read sweetly to me of trolls or princes or pirates; and I would watch the treasured object in her hands and smell its musty venerability and feel its witchcraft power. The book, the little wonderchamber, holding so compactly the history of enchantment and the constitution of the heart. Later, on rainy days, I held and read these books myself, or in the living room and with reverential care unsheathed a volume of that queen of books, the 11th *Britannica*. Here was something other than enchantment and culture; here, portly within green cloth jackets, was a regal palace of knowledge, mysterious, inexhaustible.

I speedily became a writer, publishing in school papers and scholastic magazines, developing a local reputation for talent and its concomitant eccentricities. I haunted the little public library by the river, ravaging its entire stock of fiction. I biked down to the local bookstore each Saturday and browsed among a multicolored world of jacketed spines while the couple who owned the store looked on in quiet approval. One Saturday, just before I entered college, they handed me a small wrapped gift, which opened proved to be the object of my passionate impoverished craving, the book I wanted more than a three-speed bike, *The Oxford Book of English Verse,* new edition, done in maroon leather with gold leaf. The handwritten inscription read

> *To Adam,*
> *Who feeds his mind upon the bread of books,*
> *And slakes his thirst at every well of thought.*

All through college, taken gently from its box and warmed by my cradling hands, this leather book would seem alive, a wise friend who answered my intimate questions and endorsed my romantic aspirations.

Since then I have been here and there, now writing madly, now barren as stone. But time after time, all the way through, when I picked up a favorite book, or found some long-hunted text in a library or used-book store, my hands would tingle electrically, as if

The printer's beeping at me. I'll get back to this.

5. AN OFFICE MEMO

May 1, 1990
FROM: Yousef Pimantel, Acquisitions
TO: Wesley Dutchins, Circulation

We are unable to satisfy your request for replacement of two lost copies of *Sovrana Sostrata,* by Adam Snell, PR/9941.1/.S52/1988. The book is out of print and has been remaindered. Major distributors and local shops have no copies, new or used. I will authorize a national search if you like, but cannot be very encouraging about its probable results. Unless you object I will ask Catalog to scratch it.

University of Washagon Library

Between a manuscript written in a formal book-hand and an early printed copy of the same work, printed in the same district as the manuscript had been written, the difference in general appearance was very slight. The printer's type (see *Typography*) would as a rule be based on a handwriting considered by the scribes appropriate to works of the same class; the chapter headings, headlines, initial-letters, paragraph marks, and in some cases illustrations, would be added by hand in a style which might closely resemble the like decorations in the manuscript from which the text was being printed; there would be no title-page, and very probably no statement of any kind that the book was printed, or as to where, when, and by whom it was produced. Information as to these points, if given at all, was reserved for a paragraph at the end of the book, called by bibliographers a colophon (*q.v.*), to which the printer often attached a device consisting of his arms, or those of the town in which he worked, or a fanciful design. These devices are sometimes beautiful and often take the place of a statement of the printer's name. Many facsimiles or copies of them have been published.

—A. W. POLLARD, "Book," *Encyclopædia Britannica,* 11th edition

CHAPTER 6

FRANK UNDERWOOD'S
BIG ADVENTURE

Arpis, mothpat, groibut: these random syllables, in terms of anything like absolute meaning, are as full of significance as the whole of *King Lear*.

—FRANK UNDERWOOD,
Dismembering Discourse:
A Study in the Muteness of Power
(Oxbridge University Press, 1985)

There is nowhere you can go
That is anything like Stubbed Toe.

—SOVRANA SOSTRATA,
to a lover at breakfast

You ease your body into the Porsche and gently pull the door shut. The engine, which usually roars to life under a violent rush of fuel, tonight purrs almost imperceptibly as you tick down the midnight street. Turning left onto Scott Boulevard you open up the throttle a bit, shift up to third.

After three hours alone at the fire you feel wasted. You should have read something, or phoned someone, or worked on your Innsbruck talk or even watched TV. Language relaxes you, draws you out, connects you with a world of innocent pleasure and trust. With conversation, aye, and the blessing of dreamless nights, you can holiday for weeks from the ineluctable oppositions and fierce necessities that grip you otherwise.

But tonight you fell back, who knows why. You stubbed your toe. An ugly memory attacked you. And you were nervous about tonight's adventure, though there's nothing at all to fear.

For whatever reason, you fell back, and the world looked sour and grim to you, sometimes like a crouching beast, sometimes like a cardboard façade, with tiny holes for the convenience of unfriendly eyes.

Under your careful guidance the Porsche turns off Scott and hastens quietly down an alleyway flanked by the backyards of dark fraternity houses. Better not park in the faculty lot. Instead you curb-park at the border of campus and stride through the gates into the lamplit quad.

Strange that your personal dependency on language contrasts so sharply with your professional critique of it. Strange, but true, even necessary. Your critique of language makes sense, and it has found you a niche high up in the echelons of literary theory. With early articles you forced in a wedge, and your acclaimed book *Dismembering Discourse: A Study in the Muteness of Power* followed in with the full infantry. Spinning off from Heidegger, Derrida and the new historicists, you took the rakishly skeptical line that language has no meaning at all as description, communication, or philosophical inquiry but rather is "vectoral," i.e., is the medium for lines of power by which individuals seek to enslave each other or protect themselves from enslavement. You argued with cold brilliance that the master language was the language of the State, a language nuanced not only in words but in architecture, custom, sports, law, financial systems and what have you.

From feminists to deconstructionists, the theoretical world was much gladdened by this bibliographical arrival. It wasn't that, as you had so hoped, reviewers thought *Dismembering Discourse* dashingly original; it was rather that it gave theorists a new vocabulary for extending positions they had already developed. The ranking prince of theorists, Ewig Schabe, that German émigré now surviving skeletally in Geneva, smiled upon you, admitting you to the tiny group of younger enthusiasts who might reasonably be considered heirs to the throne.

You pass the medical school. Don't look over there at the Jungle! Don't look that way till you pass the trees!

The campus is empty, dead quiet. You must cross the library quad to be there. You peruse, with a sense of needed support, the text of your successes. You feel genuine pleasure at Schabe's offer of friendship. Schabe is pleasantly Germanic, though admittedly not of the massive Teutonic variety that you most admire. But Schabe will not last forever. And when Schabe and a few of his classmates have exited, the patterns will alter, the ranks will shuffle. Positions will open and you can leave Dulce and its grim memories behind.

You enter Connors Hall by a side door and take the stairs up to the fourth floor. Of course you have a fail-safe plan. If anyone sees you in the hall, you can simply walk on to your own office on the same floor. But happily no one is in the hall, and within seconds the purloined passkey offers you free admission to the office of Ex–Associate Professor Adam Snell, the coyly superior Snell, the super-creative Snell, the foolish Snell, the whore-loving humanistic antitheoretical Snell, Snell the odious, Snell the offspring of immigrants, Snell of the crushed skull.

The first dated title-page known is a nine-line paragraph on an otherwise blank page giving the title of the book, *Sermo ad populum predicabilis in festo presentacionis Beatissime Marie Semper Virginis,* with some words in its praise, the date 1470 in roman numerals, and a reference to further information on the next page. The book in which this title-page occurs was printed by Arnold ther Hoernan at Cologne. Six years later Erhard Ratdolt and his partners at Venice printed their names and the date, together with some verses describing the book, on the title-page of a Latin calendar, and surrounded the whole with a border in four pieces. For another twenty years, however, when title-pages were used at all, they usually consisted merely of the short title of the book, with sometimes a woodcut or the printer's (subsequently the publisher's) device beneath it, decoration being more often bestowed on the first page of text, which was sometimes surrounded by an ornamental border. Title-pages completed by the addition of the name and address of printer or publisher, and also by the date, did not become common until about 1520.

—A. W. POLLARD, "Book," *Encyclopædia Britannica,*
11th edition

CHAPTER 7

TIME REGAINED

Departmental committees report to the department heads, who
report to the deans, who report to the provost, who reports to
the president. The only trouble is, there's never been anything to
report.

—SOVRANA SOSTRATA,
Gesta

His smile-creased, slightly pasty face blurred by vapor emerging
from a huge coffee cup, Roy Gallard beamed welcome at Emmons
from his computer. "Just a minute, Hal," he said. "I'll lock this thing
down." The grad student's fingers clawed rapidly at the keys, while,
apparently in response to his activities, the monitor's screen ran at
nervous pace through a series of lists, titles, statements and queries.
An alarming beep was heard from within the machine, followed by
a reproachful clucking noise. Finally the screen went black, and the
metal box beneath it, with a sound resembling a dying man's last
breath, lapsed into silence.

"Anything wrong?" asked Emmons.

"Nothing at all. Just saving a file on my floppy."

Emmons repressed the impulse to ask, "Your floppy what?" and
followed Gallard down the hall to the stairs. Simple questions like
that had been known to set Roy talking for hours. After warmly
assenting to Emmons' request for help the night before, Gallard had
regaled his senior, at length and for perhaps the third time, with the
story of how computers had changed his career. A perpetual grad
student, with six kids and a 500-page unmanageable mass of disserta-
tional protoplasm, Gallard had borrowed the money to buy a computer, mastered word processing in short order and revolutionized his
life. Now the diss. was a 240-page piece of cake, and Roy was about
to hit the job market.

During the last couple of months, with little more of his own to
do, Roy had become a kind of computer paladin, eagerly sallying

forth to rescue endangered documents and generally assist confused neophytes.

Arrived at Snell's office, Gallard shot his sleeves like a safecracker and sat down at the computer, while Emmons settled himself at the desk. Aimlessly fiddling while Gallard activated the machine, Emmons suddenly stiffened, got up and began frantically checking every horizontal surface in the room.

"What's the matter?" asked Roy over his shoulder.

"*Adam's journal's gone!*"

"Where did you leave it?"

"In a big box here on the floor."

"Is anything else missing?"

Emmons began to check, but Roy caught him up. "What books did Adam keep over there on that shelf?" Emmons' attention was drawn to a rather large gap, enough for seven or eight volumes of average size, in an otherwise full bookcase. He went over and examined the outline of dust left by the vanished books.

"I remember now," said Emmons, feeling strangely faint. "They were extra copies of his novel. He used to joke that they would stay there forever."

"Were they here yesterday?"

"I don't remember. It looks as though they were removed quite recently."

"Could Professor Gazza or the police have taken the journal and books?"

"Unlikely, but I'll phone and see."

Reached at home, Glanda replied in the negative and said that she would report the theft to Lieutenant Pierce. When Emmons looked back at Gallard, he was scrutinizing a long list of titles on the amber monitor. Using a single key, he could make the monitor scroll dizzily up or down.

"Is that a list of everything in the computer?" asked Emmons.

"Not by a long shot." Smirking knowledgeably, Gallard scrolled to the top. "Look at this bunch of titles at the top. Instead of being followed by normal codes like '.EXE' or '.BAS' they all have '.<DIR>' after them. These are all directories—just like this one except that this one includes them—each capable of holding two hundred files."

"And can these directories hold their own lists of directories too?"

"Absolutely. The tree system can go on indefinitely." In Emmons' mind's eye rose the uncomfortable image of computers as huge castles of discourse, complete with mazelike textual corridors, locked rooms and gloomy landings, full of sinister secrets. "Now," asked Roy, "what are we looking for?"

"The working title of Adam's new book is *On Wonderment*."

". . . not under *O* . . . but here's a 'WONDERM.<DIR>.' "

"Let's get it!"

Gallard moved the cursor to WONDERM.<DIR> and typed a three-stroke command. The screen changed dramatically. The headings and notations at the top looked very much as before, but instead of a long list of titles below, there was utter blackness.

"Sorry," said Roy. "This directory's empty."

Suddenly feeling very empty too, Emmons could only ask, "But if it's empty, why did Adam put it there in the first place?"

"Good question," said Roy thoughtfully. "It's possible that he had set it up and not written anything in it yet."

"But he had been working on that book for months, and he told me he was doing it on the computer."

"Then he—or somebody—must have deleted the files."

Deleted the files. The two men looked at each other with the same unpleasant shock of recognition.

Rising, Emmons spoke first. "The manuscript, the books, the files. Somebody's trying *to delete Adam altogether,* probably the same person who made away with him in the first place."

"Probably," Roy answered grimly. Snell had never seemed so hopelessly lost to Emmons as now. But Roy's face was suddenly alive with hope. "Though whether he's succeeded is another question."

Emmons, still standing, felt the urge to sit down. "What do you mean?"

Gallard gazed at the dark screen. "Maybe we're dealing with an expert, maybe an amateur. An expert would have made sure that Snell's files were totally destroyed. An amateur would have assumed he destroyed him by deleting them."

"But don't you destroy files when you delete them?"

"Contrary to popular opinion, no. They drop from the menu and, so to speak, lose their status and protection. But until they're written over, they still exist in complete form. And they can easily be retrieved."

"How?"

Gallard was already at work. His fingers hurried over the keys, propelling the monitor through a rapid sequence of screens. He spoke as he typed. "Retrieving deleted files is the job of a particular kind of disk-management utility, that is, a system for managing files. Adam has one of those right here in this machine. There we are. I'm using it now." The screen came to rest at a list of files. Gallard scrolled down swiftly.

"Stop, Roy, stop!" shouted Emmons. "I see them!"

Gallard scrolled back. " 'WONDERM.NON' and 'JOURNAL. JOU.' Both big ones. They've got to be the text and writer's journal. Let's get them." And he clawed at the keys again.

Like some Lazarus reborn, like ancient manuscripts lost in the recesses of a crypt and now at last recovered, Adam Snell's latest works were restored to electronic dignity.

Ten minutes later Gallard left Emmons, now the more techno-literate by virtue of a few instructions, at the keyboard, looking "JOURNAL.JOU" straight in the eye. "I'll be back in a couple of hours to do a printout," Roy said. He looked well pleased with himself, and he was saving his best shot for last. "By the way, what we found today proved that it couldn't have been Adam who deleted the files."

"Why?"

"Because he'd have known the files would still be there and could be restored. He's the one who taught me all about it."

Emmons growled, shook his head and addressed his work. Whatever he found out about Snell today had to be found out before two, the latest he could leave to rescue Doppler at the dog pound and still be back for the department meeting at three-thirty. And that meeting was crucial. Glanda was going to try to dump Snell, and Emmons was not about to let Snell, dead or alive, get dumped.

While the development of the title-page was thus slow, the completion of the book, independently of handwork, in other respects was fairly rapid. Printed illustrations appear first in the form of rude woodcuts in some small books produced at Bamberg by Albrecht Pfister about 1461. Pagination and headlines were first used by ther Hoernen at Cologne in 1470 and 1471; printed signatures to guide binders in arranging the quires correctly (see *Bibliography and Bibliology*) by Johann Koelhoff, also at Cologne in 1472. Illustrations abound in the books printed at Augsberg in the early 'seventies, and in the 'eighties are common in Germany, France and the Low Countries, while in Italy their full development dated from about 1490. Experiments were made in both Italy and France with illustrations engraved on copper, but in the 15th century these met with no success.

—A. W. POLLARD, "Book," *Encyclopædia Britannica,*
11th edition

CHAPTER 8

NAKED DREAMS AT FULHAM

Love is the logic of all valid art.
—SOVRANA SOSTRATA,
Gesta

About a mile out of the village, the road climbing to Fulham School
veers left into a dark grove of sugar maples and whip-cracks right,
up an even steeper grade. Mornings it's likely to be icy here, even up
to late spring, and drivers who take the downhill at more than a
pusillanimous creep do so at substantial risk. Obviously someone had
rushed it today. They had fished him out of the cab more or less in
one piece, but his yellow pickup still lay supine and inert in the ditch
beneath the upper turn, as a road-straddling wrecker winched it by
centimeters into a position where it could be righted, and firemen and
policemen sipped thermos coffee and chatted buoyantly at the roadside, and warning lights of all sorts broke up the mystic gloom of the
New Hampshire morning, and the Fulham traffic backed up halfway
to town. Not far down from the wreck, alone in a weathered Mercedes sedan, a young woman stretched, briefly turned toward the car
window a countenance that would not have displeased Leonardo,
and crooking her neck back shook her shoulder-length brown curls
briefly from side to side, as though in a gesture of spiritual disentan-
glement. Harper Nathan had expected better. Instead of the long-
sought weekend pastoral, she had merely moved, via three interstate
highways and the Natty Bumppo Roadhouse, from one traffic jam
into another.

She rested her hand on the bulging briefcase that lay on the seat
beside her and drew it back abruptly. The bag held homework, nine
hundred pages of it, reading she had delayed for weeks and finally
stuffed in the bag at the last minute as conscience ballast for the lark
of weekending at Fulham. Two manuscripts, both to become main-
stays if not flagships of the Wolper McNab spring '91 list, both

redolent with the kind of human interest that warms a publisher's heart. *When Bad Things Happen to Little Girls with Depressed Fathers,* by Lily Rose Talcom, an honest, detailed, absorbing, moving, probing, illuminating, liberating study that was likely to change your life, or so the endorsements would assert (even if she had to write the endorsements herself), that, in the words of her wise leader, editorial director Sig Bazoom, was bound to touch at least half the American reading public where it lived.

Would they ever get that damn truck out?

The other manuscript, of such magnitude as almost to shoulder poor Lily out of the briefcase, was a sure winner whose contents nonetheless had so oppressed the Wolper McNab staff that they had drawn lots to determine its editor. *Melons, Meditation, and Wellness,* by Raj Bhor Poona, M.D., "with" (that unsinkable hack) Percy Glickstein, a fledgling blockbuster which, replete with its dynamic "Five-Melon Diet" and its breath-catching spiritual counsel that we should all "emulate the wisdom of the fruit," was bound to take a large bite out of the inexhaustible wellness market. Harper fidgeted with the yellowed and finely cracked steering wheel, wondering exactly what it was that made the wellness market so inexhaustible. Had people such short memories, to forget what made them well on last year's spring list? Was the reader death toll so high that survivors yearly sought new remedies?

Her fingers tightened on the wheel. Books like Talcom's and Poona's, all wise and well researched, all relevant and (thanks to her) ultimately readable, now stretched back into her memory like the line of stalled traffic in her mirror: similar and sedate, timely and tedious, deaf to the future, keeping faithful time to the jingle of the till, monuments to perhaps the most unheroic generation in the history of American letters, the least—

Honking behind her. The road was suddenly open, and the ruddy crew on the roadside were appreciating her good looks and laughing at her confusion. She gave her hair another nervous toss and threw the car into motion. Through the bosky curve, up the shady grade and she was in sunlight now—how she loved this part of the drive; the very car seemed happy!—climbing the final slope with a splendid view of contoured gray ridges to the north and now, upon their lofty meadowed hill, the stately granite fronts of Fulham School looking down at her from the other side. Only 9:30 A.M., 9:30 A.M. Saturday and the weekend still before her.

She cut left up the long drive and parked carefully between boxes of peeping daffodils. Two students, both girls in jeans, looked up from their gardening and laughed with pleasure to see her.

Harper was well known at Fulham. Her regular visits to her orphaned niece had brought her into amicable contact with many of the students, and she never appeared on campus without some item or items, a sheaf of magazines, a prudently chosen video, a bag of books, that might somehow ease their sense of isolation. This time it was a bunch of recent novels, picked out with due regard for their tender, impressionable readership, packed unceremoniously in a plastic market bag and now placed, after due salutations, on Helen Lamb's desk in the Main House. *"Thanks bunches, Harper!"* the ruddy Ms. Lamb exploded, and started peering fitfully around the room as though about to dislodge niece Betty from some cabinet or wastebasket. "I think Betty's down at the pump house."

"The pump house?"

"Yes, they're restoring it. Know the way?"

"Sure."

The way was across a hilltop meadow aflower with bluets, mountain mint and pasture rose, a meadow smelling deliciously, in the now abundant morning sunlight, of flowers and new grass and live earth. Striding broadly in her new walkers, appareled in plaid and leather after the durable fashion of Bean, Harper went forth along the trail in a rush of almost celestial happiness occasioned by the lovely morning, her eagerness to see Betty and her sudden and radical physical freedom. *This,* she thought, *is what it's all about. An hour of this a day, and I'd have no problems on Twenty-ninth Street.* Her body, lithe and firm at thirty, tingled with the pleasure of exertion. She felt, as sometimes she had felt before, an undirected sensuality, a readiness for physical love with no specific human object.

I'll leave to your imagination the path's turn into the birch and hemlock copse, its happy meander through the woods down crystalline Tuttle Brook, the distant sound of hammering, Harper's arrival at the pump house, the shouts of joy, the hugs and greetings, the cheerful morning swelling into a memorable day of laughter and lemonade and watercress sandwiches and Betty's dear company. Savoring such details, we might all fall madly in love with Harper and totally forget about Snell and Underwood and the dismal doings in Washagon.

Instead let's visit her after dinner that evening.

Walk down the drive from Fulham School, turn left on Fulham

Road and left again at the big oak tree, and you'll see a fine old farmhouse, shake-roofed, white-painted, red-shuttered and commanding, from its north side, a mountain view similar to, though somewhat less expansive than, that available from the school. This is the home of Asher and Doris Fox, a couple who have been officially or unofficially associated with Fulham School since its founding a half-century ago. For many years they ran a riding stable on the school grounds. Now their professional activities are confined to entertaining an occasional guest for bed and breakfast. Summers and holidays bring many familiar faces, for the Foxes are well known and loved by all the old boys and girls who revisit Fulham. Harper, who has come often enough to merit an honorary diploma, would not think of staying elsewhere.

Tonight after dinner in Franklin with Betty, she edged into the Foxes' drive past a white pickup–cum–boat trailer, belonging probably to a new guest, politely skirted the laughter in the living room, where Asher Fox was regaling the probable guest with some old tale of Fulham, and shut herself up in her room. It was spacious enough, occupying the full east end of the house and inviting from there the last intimations of a New Hampshire twilight. With sharp regret Harper erased these subtle images by turning on the lamp. This, or at least three hours of it, was to be a work night, spent, so to speak, on the lap of Dr. Poona, imbibing his melonic wisdom and, more mundanely, preparing a report about him that Sig could rattle teacups with in the front office. Clearing a space on the old desk (piled as it was with miscellaneous bedside books), she lifted the Melon manuscript carefully from her briefcase and set it down before her, together with notebook and pen. She pushed her hair back with both hands, assumed an attitude calculated to delay muscle fatigue, and commenced reading.

Her brown eyes gleamed in concentration as they scanned quickly over the disconnected pages, her left hand ready to flip each page, her right hand poised to write notes.

An hour passed, and Harper, now moving somewhat more slowly, plowed doggedly on with her work. The laughter ceased downstairs; there were creaks and rumbles from the staircase, a distant pipe chorus from bathrooms, and the house composed itself into silence.

Another hour, and Harper, head propped up with left elbow on desk, stared glassily at a black windowpane. Two hundred and fifty pages of Poona, give or take, had bitten the dust, and her notebook was full of such discourse as

47—cassaba/casaba?
77, etc.—get Percy to stop always saying "virtually"
103—Is Shiva really supposed to have turned into a melon to have sex with the earth goddess?
125—Tiruchchirappalli—person or place?

Sleep was creeping up on Harper—not a sweet globed melonlike repose, but the uglier, washed-out, worded-out sleep of a responsible junior editor—when her peace was suddenly shattered by a gunlike BANG. She jumped up terrified. Someone had hit the door to her room very sharply, and it was moments before she realized that it had not been the hallway door that was hit, but rather the door to the next bedroom. Trembling slightly she walked straight at the door and tried it.

It opened easily into a lamplit room, somewhat smaller than hers, at the opposite end of which a very red-faced man was lying in bed. He was a handsome mustached man in his forties, with frisky black hair, blue eyes, gray pajamas, dark blue dressing gown and the overall look of someone who does not deliberately frighten his neighbors. On the floor just in front of Harper lay a white-jacketed hardcover book, and it was clear at once that this must have been what had struck her door. She picked up the book, walked to the bed and handed it to him.

"Yours?"

The man in bed blushed deeper. "Not exactly," he replied hesitantly and in a rather deep voice. "I found it here. I did something very stupid. Please forgive me."

"Of course I forgive you. But why did you throw it?"

"I'll tell you but you won't believe me." He laughed. "I threw the book because I simply couldn't put it down. I leave for Sunapee at dawn tomorrow and picked this book off the bed table in hopes it would put me to sleep and it did the opposite. I finally just tossed it. It's electrifying."

"How so?" Harper asked with awakened interest.

The man pointed at the cover. "If I sleep at all, I'll dream of her all night."

For the first time she looked at the book in her hands. Though ragged from frequent use, it was clearly of recent manufacture, the artwork and design suggesting a small-press venture. The jacket illustration showed, as though in cameo, a woman's head in profile, and in the delicate, proud, somewhat Mediterranean aspect of the face, Harper was reminded vaguely of herself. The title, etched as though in uncertain hand above the cameo, as well as the author's name, printed more stolidly and in smaller letters beneath it, would be familiar to the reader.

"Ever hear of it?" he asked.

"No. Never. What's it about?"

"I won't tell you. Take it from my sight. If you begin it tonight we can discuss it at breakfast." His eyes twinkled.

"But I thought you were leaving at dawn."

More twinkling. "I've just reviewed my plans."

Harper controlled an emerging smile, nodded from the doorway to the man whose eyes had followed her and retired, demurely locking the door from her side. An un-put-down-able book? Nothing like that existed. She brought her bed things into the bathroom, undressed and showered, letting Dr. Poona, and the depression he had unintentionally brought upon her, wash smoothly down her body and into the drain. Back in her room, she lit the bedside lamp, turned down the covers and climbed in. Clean sheets, fresh pajamas, warm covers felt delightful. She was refreshed. Rolling over toward the light she pulled the covers over her left shoulder, elbow-braced her head and carefully placed the white book in the lamplit valley thus created. Alone in space, alone in time, alone in the superbly private kingdom of lamplight and bedclothes, she began to read.

She had not read twenty pages before she paused in mild shock. Why should she be shocked? Neither the subject matter nor the style of *Sovrana Sostrata* was especially bizarre. It was something else, something almost ghostly: a feeling of profound familiarity, a connection restored apparently after so long a loss of touch as to suggest the sudden repetition of some forgotten childhood event. What event? Again Harper drew a blank. No particular event, she concluded. Something more like an attitude, a way of seeing or focussing the senses. What sort of attitude was rare enough to remind her of forgotten childhood? As she read on, she began to see. An attitude of commitment, of total, abandoned, celebratory engagement with a subject. Engagement, moreover, on two levels of discourse: Snell's unmistakable affection for his heroine, Sovrana's ineffable fixation on truth. Not that Sovrana was portrayed with monotonous reverence. She had a variety of flaws: excesses and defects that would probably dog her to her end. The book had humor and ironies galore. But virtues and flaws and humor and ironies all danced together around one sacred theme, a theme upon which the prose, direct and unassuming on the surface, concentrated with the force of mythic passion. Harper had not seen this sort of intensity since she'd read Hemingway, Faulkner and Chandler, writers who had died before she got to kindergarten.

Who was Sovrana to Snell? An old lover? His mother? An ideal? Whoever she was, Snell had brought Sovrana before the reader as a living being and an embodied idea. And what made this idea so compelling, so riveting, was that it was not identifiably "male," that Sovrana wasn't, like women in so many romantic books by men, some projection of a subjective and ultimately alien maleness, but rather thoroughly human and female, particularly in the unquenchable spirit that dared the odds, denied yet illuminated her female vulnerability. As she read on well through the middle of the book, Harper found a long-lost part of herself in Sovrana, an expressive and questing impulse that been touched neither by the male/female stereotypes of her social background nor by the dogmas of textbook feminism.

At 2 A.M. a kind of drunkenness suffused her limbs, and she felt sleep approaching like the mouth of a tunnel. She reached up to turn off the lamp. Her head nodded toward her right shoulder, and her last sensation was the musty smell of book.

Harper awoke from unruly dreams to a sensuous barrage so intense that it left her wondering for seconds where and who she was. Her travel alarm was beeping panic. Stark sunlight struck and heated her face and shoulders, still partly upright on the fluffed-up pillows. A pandemonium of birds outside was almost drowned out by what sounded like a small gunfight in some room below. Strange smoky smells mingled with the bacon/coffee telltales of a country breakfast. She stretched, dressed quickly, doused her face with water and went downstairs. Asher Fox was seated with another man by the fireplace, whose burning contents regularly filled it with loud explosions of sparks.

"Mulberry and butternut," announced the venerable host. "You can always count on 'em for fireworks. I laid a few on to break the chill at dawn. Now for such as want a steadier flame, your white oak, your apple, your sugar maple, your pignut hickory . . ." While this discourse proceeded, the man facing Asher had risen to an agreeable height and stepped forward to greet Harper. He wasn't blushing now, and his smiling eyes inquired politely as to the length and content of her bedtime reading. She shot him a telling look. ". . . but that hickory sang out like birds all night. And your hickory's fine as well for such as want a sweet-smelling wood, or your black birch."

From the adjoining kitchen Doris called greetings and solicited preferences as to eggs and toast.

The breakfast was quite wonderful. The engaging stranger, wrapped overnight in anonymous mystery, emerged as Harry Stuart, a judge from Hartford, divorced and visiting his son Vincent (whom Harper, it turned out, already knew vaguely through Betty) at Fulham. Vincent would appear in an hour for their now postponed day trip to Sunapee Lake.

After the plates had been cleared and the Foxes had vanished on other chores, Harper and Stuart drank coffee and discussed the book. Stuart deferred to Harper's professional skills. "I can't figure one thing out. Why isn't this a famous book? If anyone pulled off something like this in my profession, I mean some judgment or opinion that cast new light on a whole issue, we'd all be talking about it in weeks. Am I missing something?" He paused. "Or is it maybe that you and I are odd, and see something in the book that's pertinent only to ourselves and a few other people who are odd like us?"

Harper doubted that the book had depended for its impact on their own eccentricity. "No, it's the book itself that's strange— strange, I mean, for our times. Fiction this passionate and focussed and exploratory has been out of fashion for decades. We've just about forgotten that it's possible to write it. I guess if it came out today and got widely read, it would get quite a few readers mad. If we had ratings for naked ideas and dreams the way we do for naked bodies, this would get an X. But other readers, I mean tens of thousands, would love it for the same reason."

"Then why didn't they love it in '88?"

Harper explained the difference between small-press and large-press publishing. "Our copy of *Sovrana Sostrata* was from a first printing, probably a run of a few hundred copies. There aren't any endorsements on the dust jacket, or quotes from advance reviews. There's nothing to suggest that the book had any press either before or after publication or that it went into more than one printing. Many writers publish with university presses or small presses in order to reach members of their own professional group or discuss topics of regional interest. *Sovrana Sostrata* doesn't fit into either of these niches. It looks like Adam Snell tried the large houses and failed and took this as a last resort, and that it was never advertised or reviewed or for that matter even read by more than a few people. I wonder how many copies sold."

Stuart looked puzzled. "But why wouldn't a large press have taken it?"

Harper felt a rush of annoyance. "Why don't judges send more felons to jail?"

Stuart seemed surprised (as Harper was herself) at the sharpness of this response, but answered mildly, "I think I get your point. The institution takes on a life of its own, forgets why it's there in the first place."

Harper relaxed and caught her breath. She remembered with some embarrassment the manuscripts in her bedroom and the immense amount of editorial time that established authors and genres consumed. She spoke of the concerns that robbed editors of free curiosity and open minds, the spring-fall-spring-fall procession of deadlines, the subtle tyranny of quid pro quo, the necessity for indulging fads, the innumerable conventions and meetings and lunches.

Stuart was politely relentless. "What if Snell had sent *you* the manuscript?"

Harper answered frankly, uncertain whether she was defending or accusing herself. "We generally don't read unsolicited manuscripts. If he had had an agent I trusted, and the agent said it was terrific, I would have looked at it. Otherwise Snell could have held on to his manuscript and written a letter of inquiry first."

"And if he did?"

Her own reply pained her. "I still might not have bitten. *Sovrana Sostrata* is unique, sui generis. But thousands of novelists claim to have written unique or highly unusual books. It's the rhetoric of the profession, and mostly it just isn't true. And a sensitive, passionate writer like Snell isn't likely to have the self-promotional skills necessary for barging into a crowded market. If I'm any judge of Professor Snell, he would have written a polite and modest letter, a letter of real inquiry." She paused for a sip of coffee. "The sort of letter no one reads."

Harper excused herself momentarily and went up to her room. Aside from paying the amazingly tiny bill, she had one more piece of business to transact with her host and hostess before she left. She grabbed two books from her bed and reentered the living room to find Asher Fox sweeping stray coals into the fireplace. Catching his attention, she inquired nervously, "I was wondering whether I could take this book and trade you this one for it." In one hand she held up *Sovrana Sostrata,* in the other a very handsome paperback of Conrad stories that she had forgotten to give Betty.

Asher squinted. "Oh you've got Sovrany!" he exclaimed with a little laugh. "Take her and welcome. She went and got the schoolkids all exercised last year."

And there was business, hopefully of a more ongoing nature, to transact with Harry. "How far have you gotten?" she asked.

"Up to the Abominable Sermon. That's when I threw it."

They looked at each other and laughed. "That's about half-way," said Harper. Suppose we make this deal. I take the book . . ." They laughed again. "I take the book and photocopy it and send you the copy."

Harry made the face of someone considering a very serious deal. "I have a better deal," he said. "Give me the copy in person. Bring Betty to see us at Sunapee for Memorial Day. If the weather's good we can go canoeing."

Twenty minutes later they parted in the drive. He took her hand and held it for a moment. "What a wonderful way to meet. And you've changed my career to boot. I'm going to send twenty felons to jail next month."

Harper's brown eyes flashed back at him. "And I'm going to republish *Sovrana Sostrata.*"

Bound with wooden boards covered with stamped leather, or with half the boards left uncovered, many of the earliest printed books are immensely large and heavy, especially the great choir-books, the Bibles and the Biblical and legal commentaries, in which a great mass of notes surrounds the text. The paper on which these large books were printed was also extraordinarily thick and strong. For more popular books small folio was at first a favorite size, but toward the end of the century small thin quartos were much in vogue. Psalters, books of hours, and other prayer-books were practically the only very small books in use. Owing to changes, not only in the value of money but in the coinage, the cost of books in the 15th century is extremely difficult to ascertain. A vellum copy of the first printed Bible (Mainz, *c.* 1455) in two large folio volumes, when rubricated and illuminated, is said to have been worth 100 florins. In 1467 the bishop of Aleria writing to Pope Paul II. speaks of the introduction of printing having reduced prices to one-fifth of what they had previously been. Fifteen "Legends" bequeathed by Caxton to St. Margaret's, Westminster, were sold at prices varying from 6s. 8d. to 5s. This would be cheap for a large work like the *Golden Legend,* but the bequest was more probably of copies of the Sarum *Legenda,* or Lectionary, a much smaller book.

—A. W. POLLARD, "Book," *Encyclopædia Britannica,*
11th edition

CHAPTER 9

THE PARLIAMENT IN TOUWHEE HALL

Nature endowed the act of sex not just with bestial pleasure but with a form of cosmic joy that uniquely attends the creation of life. Willing sex between woman and man is thus a creative act, whether it is committed for conception or not.

—SOVRANA SOSTRATA,
Gesta

A HANDLIST OF TERMS:

canon: here, permanent, institutionalized body of texts.

deconstructionist: a literary theorist who believes that a work of literature has no fixed meaning and can therefore be re-created in a new form with each reading.

defication: deconstructionist term implying a connection between writing fiction and defecating.

deprivilege: disempower, disenfranchise.

destabilizing: acting against some established idea (used only with positive implications).

discourse: (1) language either textual or spoken; (2) thought.

enfranchisement: freeing, raising to independence and dignity equal to, or greater than, other members of society.

eponym: person real or fictional for whom something (in this case, a book) is named.

exclusionist: person insensitive or inimical to diversity (used exclusively with regard to individuals who espouse traditional values).

feminist: specialist in a specific program or group of programs that advocates the establishment of the woman as a fully enfranchised (q.v.) member of society.

genre: general type of literature, e.g., comedy, epic.

Je ne sais quoi du sinistre: something vaguely sinister.

literary theorist (sometimes shortened to **theorist**): specialist who conceives of theories regarding literature and/or applies them to specific texts.

marginalia: notes (printed or handwritten) in the margin of a text.

marginalize: ostracize, alienate, remove from centrality.

new historicist: specialist who analyzes literature in terms of the theory that literary art and art in general are not independent entities but rather functions of cultural patterning as seen in terms of power, patronage, class, publicly promoted myths, etc.

phallocentric (feminist term): centered around men or male ideas (used exclusively with pejorative implications).

PMAA: Publications of the Maudlin Anguish Association, the most respected and powerful academic journal of literary studies.

post-tenure review: a formal review of a tenured professor's performance, including publications, teaching and service, conducted by a committee of full professors in his or her department. Consequences of post-tenure review range from recommendations for promotion and salary increase to warnings and, in rare cases, more serious punitive measures.

refereed journal: a scholarly journal that sends submitted articles out to experts in their respective fields for evaluation.

rhetorician: specialist in the study of the history and theory of the art of verbal persuasion.

subversive: anti-establishment (used only with positive implications).

"Shit!" softly intoned Glanda Gazza, alone in the first-floor ladies' room in Connors Hall. Her eye shadow was blotched, and she was already late for the meeting. Dabbing quickly and deftly, she corrected the disorder, then grabbed the strap of her massive shoulder bag and hefted it over a linen-suited shoulder.

Gazza in the ladies' room

Leaving Connors she set off toward Touwhee Hall at a brisk stride that cloudy Friday afternoon, across a quad crowded with students leaving their last classes of the week, through the atmosphere of quiet excitement that traditionally precedes civic amusements and tribal orgies, yet alone in her fixed consciousness and goal. A Gazza's-eye view of the campus as she swept across it would have been as from the bridge of a missile cruiser as it moved toward action at flank speed, with steady course and fatal purpose, its profile set like a calm face, its screws churning white chaos. Some individuals conform to their environments; others remake them. Gazza cleft hers bilaterally, and the air churned into the vacuum behind her broad shoulders as she strode, and students on the walkway shrank back at her passing on either side, as though from some implacable force of nature.

Gazza compared to a mighty warship

Glanda, what secret wisdom gives you such assurance? What moral revelation justifies such firm resolve? With a gesture of imperious disdain, Gazza would brush aside such questions as irrelevant. Moral justification, and the philosophical method necessary for evaluating it, were puerile nonsense. Her formidable energy derived instead from fierce ambition, ambition so global that it had attained for her the purity of an ideal, ambition so soul-bleaching that its every human obstacle, however helpless or unsuspecting, took on for her the status of some despicable animal pest. Her medium for satisfying this ambition was a rich grammar of behavior and discourse, ranging from brutal intimidation, barefaced lying or headlong sexual assault to virtuoso legerdemain with academic jargon, bureaucratic mystery and New Age incantation. These arts and crafts had brought Gazza uncommon success. She had forged a strong reputation for herself as a literary theorist and managed, over her five-year tenure as chair, to populate her department with many others of her ilk.

The author questions Gazza unsuccessfully

Gazza's heroick ambition

Sweeping into 107 Touwhee and the presence of the full professors of English, Glanda thumped her bag down onto the front table and raked the assemblage with a benevolent regard. The professors, an apparently ill-sorted[1] group of something under twenty men and women, returned her look variously, some with apathy, some affectionately, and some anxiously, as though uncertain that their large group outnumbered her magnificent One. Frank Underwood sat solemnly alone and to Gazza's left.

She arrives at Touwhee Hall

Gazza was startled by a strange face in back.

"Excuse me, sir. You are—?"

"Edward Marlin,[2] history," returned a sonorous voice. "The outside referee of this case." Bodies twisted backward. Some had never seen him.

"Of course, Professor Marlin. I should have recognized you. You are most welcome." Blushing slightly, Gazza turned to her leather bag, from which she extracted a fat file folder and a pair of reading glasses. Holding the lectern with both hands, she began, "The Adam Snell post-tenure review report, which had been scheduled for last month but was postponed because of my trip east, is now to be delivered under most unusual circumstances. Adam, as you all know, has tragically disappeared, and though the evidence suggests foul play, we cannot rule out the possibility of a mental breakdown or suicidal behavior. You may ask why we are discussing his review, which has turned out to be very negative. My answer is multiple." She consulted a handwritten list.

Gazza's opening comments

"One, the tenure review process is required, by the departmental constitution, to conclude before the end of spring term, and today is virtually our last chance to meet.

"Two, Adam's report is so disturbing as to warrant,

Reasons for the meeting

[1]The Washagon English department in 1990 was, if not ill sorted in character, at least highly diverse in specialty. Of the forty-one members, eight were feminists, eight theorists, three new historicists, three creative writers, two rhetoricians, two post-colonialists, five essentialists, four in ethnic studies, and two in English education. The population of full professors, which numbered twenty, roughly reflected these divisions.

[2]Edward Marlin, a minor cult figure of his day, known for his philosophical writing and Socratic argumentation.

with your consent, referral to the provost, and this is the last week that such referrals can be made with any hope of consideration during the current academic year.

"Three, we may use this hour to decide what, in the now tragically likely event that Adam does not return to us, we are to do with his position.

"A fourth reason, which does not concern Adam but nonetheless has bearing on our deliberations, will be discussed later. No discussion yet, please. Now we'd better get on to business. Adam's committee consisted of, besides Professor Marlin, Rainer Maulwurf, Sandy Eule, Emerson Baismacou and E. F. Taupe. Rainer, you were the chair. Would you please speak first?"

A very small dark-haired man of fifty, with an aquiline face, wire-rimmed glasses and a single earring, rose, notes in hand. He read in a high-pitched, wavering voice: "Adam Snell, having been in place fourteen years since tenure, was due for post-tenure review this year. So we conducted this review, but, I'm afraid, with mixed consequences." He glanced at Gazza as though for support. She nodded almost imperceptibly. "Sandy, Emmo, E.F. and I have agreed that Adam's performance has been seriously, even dangerously, under par and that his file should be remanded to the provost. Professor Marlin believes otherwise and will have his chance to speak later. Let me begin. Since advancement to tenure, Adam has published only three articles with refereed journals, with no papers delivered at any learned conference. I've read these articles, and though I'm no expert in Adam's field, they seem to be well enough written, though in a kind of bourgeois history-of-ideas-y style. Nonetheless, this is an embarrassingly weak showing, especially as it is not ballasted by textbooks written, administrative positions or teaching awards. Sure, he wrote a novel, but I don't see where that figures in this case. First off, it's not a scholarly work.[3] And if you look

Maulwurf argues from a Marxist perspective

---

[3]Publications bearing upon tenure and promotion decisions at academic institutions are generally expected to be scholarly and in the field of research that the candidate has chosen as his or her specialty. A candidate's nonscholarly publications are often discounted as specious, amateuristic and/or unserious.

at the book, it's more likely to tilt you against him than for him. I've read a couple chapters and they're a giveaway of Adam's ideological limitations. His main character, Sovrana, whom he presents favorably, is a kind of ideological fossil, a class-ridden romantic elitist, a sexual elitist, an intellectual and political elitist, whose assault on the establishment is in fact an attack from the reactionary Right. And the whole form of the book is the political signature of a dead age, tragedy, the tragic form which exalted that ideological dinosaur called 'the individual.' "[4]

Sitting just to Maulwurf's left, a large man of Dr. Johnsonian shape and posture, Quintus Adler, marginalized Shakespearean, boomed out, "Aren't *you* getting to be the dinosaur, Rainer? They've kicked just about all the Communists out of Europe and tried it in China too. The whole West seems to have realized now that some form of democratic, that is, individualized society is a raw necessity for survival. The world has just seen, in six months, the most massive revolution in its history. Have these events had no effect on your theories?"[5]

Quintus Adler challenges Maulwurf

Maulwurf lost no time responding to this challenge, but his voice was higher and thinner than before. "They most definitely *haven't*. In the first place, those governments weren't really communist. In the second place, the press has been exaggerating things.[6] My remarks are over.[7] Want to go on, Emmo?"

[4]On the decline of the individual, see Hans-Peter von Gierigkeit, *Die Abnahme des Individualismus im Westen* (Leipzig: Kuhschlachter, 1963); Michel La Vache, *L'Ego et le Chaos* (Paris: Librairie Engels, 1969), and Larry Touché, *Goodbye Me* (New York: Hammond and Fig, 1987).

[5]Allow me to comment informally on this paragraph. "Dr. Johnsonian" is a reference to the personal appearance of the celebrated Dr. Samuel Johnson (1709–84), who was represented as having a highly intelligent though somewhat coarsely featured face and a slouching posture. "Dr. Johnsonian" might also apply to the content of Professor Adler's remarks, which, though rather truculent, seem to me more reasonable and humane than those of his colleagues. To be sure, as a footnote, I am not supposed to be making such evaluations. But I see this as a special case. Perhaps other footnotes will agree.

[6]Can you believe these flimsy evasions? And you trust these people with your kids?

[7]Thank God. Footnotes have nerves, too.

A plump form attired in cowboy boots, blue jeans and leather jacket roused itself from front row center. Emerson Baismacou, the deconstructionist, brushing aside an unruly lock of red hair, tiny features set in a large, reddening face, pink sausagelike fingers clutching a substantial wad of typed pages, sniffled loudly and began in a hoarse voice, "Let me say to start off that I've got nothing against Adam. He's a sweet guy who might make out OK in another line of work. But his file, if you'll excuse my saying so, is *an open and shit case* [acknowledging laughter]. That's what I meant to say, an *open* and *shit* case: 'open' because there's really nothing *in* the file, so to speak—that is, nothing that can advance poor Adam's career; 'shit,' not in the gross animal sense of the word, rather a kind of metaphysical self-offense, a premature *defication,* a case of poor esthetic toilet training—Adam, you might say, having made meta-poopoo in his meta-panties. His work, to put things less figuratively, suggests a pathetic fudging (oops!) of the distinction between art and blatant self-confession. And what, you may ask, is *Sovrana Sostrata* a 'confession' *of*? Of just about, I reply (isn't that cute? 'You may ask,' 'I reply'), of just about every dirty napkin in the closet, or water-closet, if you want to ride that nag any farther. Let's begin by looking at the eponymous heroine, Sovrana herself. Sovrana is a subtext that discredits everything written around her, including, in the end, herself. Take her initials: S.S. Dangerous signal, no? Is Adam, underneath all that Augustan humanistic aplomb, hiding some Nazi wistfulness? A little Adolf Eichmann *mit pantyhosen*? Stranger things have happened. Now take the first two letters of her names: So. So. *SO*? 'So-so,' idiomatic badge of spiritual deflation, signal that lurking beneath the bright hatchings of literary intention lies a comprehensive mothering dullness. Sovrana's smart, she's witty, she's sweet, she's grand; but underneath everything, hidden like a pockmarked cheek under the rouge or a flaccid spirit behind a gaudy flag or a limp member in a starched codpiece, she's, well, just so-so, *comme ci, comme ça.* Now take the first *three* letters of each name. Sov. Sos. [Points at Eule.] Ah, Sandy, I see you're onto it! It's the Soviets, and they're in trouble,

Baismacou argues from a deconstructionist perspective

calling for help in Morse code! What's that got to do with the text? No problem. It suggests that Sovrana, rather than some sort of revolutionary principle, is instead a hangover from an old conservative,[8] exclusionist order that's in trouble and needs bailing out, or at least freshening up, with that mushy-bushy bouquet of psychosexual rationalizations, herself! Now take the first *four* letters of—"

"Emmo," Gazza gently cut in from the podium, "your interpretation is brilliant, and very convincing. But if the papers in your hand are at all indicative of its length, it won't allow time for the others to speak. No, don't apologize! Could I possibly summarize the full import of your comments as suggesting a seriously negative evaluation of Adam's performance since tenure?"

Baismacou nodded fiercely. "The file allows of no other interpretation."

"In that case," said Gazza, "let's hear what E.F. has to say."

E. F. Taupe, a woman of slight figure with the delicate features and perfectly coiffed straight hair of a 1920s film heroine, stood up near the windows, supporting herself, as though physically taxed by the power of her own emotions, with one hand on the back of her desk. Her body dramatically outlined against the daylight, she spoke in a voice sometimes hoarse, sometimes little more than a whisper; yet to her silent, rapt listeners not a syllable was lost. "I must first of all admit my unfairness. I come to you today not as the disinterested referee required by Glanda's official mandate but rather as a human being outraged, insulted, defiled, in torture. Yet I must speak, I must speak nonetheless. Two days ago I sat down to read Adam Snell's novel. I opened it without the slightest prejudice for or against him. I met his heroine. The pain began. I read on, late into the night, in growing agony but determined to follow through. Yesterday morning, with a wrenching headache, I finished the book."

Taupe argues from a feminist perspective

[8]Notice that whenever these clowns are upset with anything at all they figure out a way of calling it "conservative." Otherwise they'd lose their self-imagined place at the cutting edge.

Silence, apprehension.

"I'll tell you what I think of Adam Snell's book. Adam Snell's book isn't just bad, it's *criminal*. I've read racist books and sexist books; but *Sovrana Sostrata* is a *rapist book*,[9] a violent, malicious offense against the female."

Taupe accuses Sovrana Sostrata of rape

Gazza's face had suddenly taken on a deep cast of sisterly compassion. "You mean you feel raped by the book?"

"I feel violated, yes, violated. The book is like a weapon of violation. Of course, there's nothing overt. Snell's too cautious for that. He even makes it seem as though his heroine is sexually exploiting men. But lurking deep underneath is a radically phallocentric[10] Gestalt, the most irresponsible, heedless assertion of naked maleness I've ever been exposed to. I'm afraid there are no laws about this, so even if we found Snell we couldn't turn him in.[11] But I implore you all to visit justice upon him in the only way you can: Remand his file to the provost."

The footnotes are restless

A confused flurry of emotional conversation, replete with phrases like "rapist discourse," "deprivileging the female," "passive aggressive," and "there oughtta be a law," calmed again to silence as it became apparent that Sanford Eule had risen to speak. A slim, good-looking man with curly dark reddish hair and boyish looks and manners, he addressed his colleagues in a vaguely English accent and

[9]I must join Footnotes 6, 7 and 8 in questioning the propriety of remarks made by professors during this meeting. I have myself been a footnote for over two hundred years. I have loyally obeyed the conscience, and satisfied the whims, of humanists from the Augustan Age down through the twentieth century. But this is going too far. This sort of behavior jargonizes and ideologizes language to satisfy political interest and indulge personal neurosis, until language no longer makes sense. And if language loses its openness, its potential for impartiality, then culture will rot from within.
If this goes on much longer, we may have to take steps.

[10]OK, this is it. I'm mobilizing the gang. Footnotes may not be human, but they have a sense of justice nonetheless. "Phallocentric"? One of the most blatantly self-serving simplifications ever invented. It does no justice at all to the real history of male/female relationships. And it's also a gross flattery to the contemporary Western male, who lost his masculinity a long time ago.
But to my point. These ideologues cannot be allowed to continue their mad career. DOWN WITH TYRANNY! FOOTNOTES, UNITE! The world is about to see something it has never seen before, a revolution of the apparatus!

[11]Can you beat this outrage against common sense and decency? I know where I can find some more footnotes. If Eule's talk is as foul as this, we'll monkey-wrench him right enough.

with impeccable suavity. "Some years ago at a beach resort in southern France a friend of mine was sitting at a café when a strikingly beautiful figure, high-heeled, silk-stockinged, green-and-pink-print dress, great eyes, straw hat and parasol, appeared at his table and addressed him with the sort of look that with unspeakable clarity, even to a fresh-from-college kid like him, suggested its venerable professional intention.[12] His feelings, to put it mildly, were muddled. How does an American man, trained in chivalry, respond to an unabashed female demand for intimacy? But as he jockeyed verbally with her in broken English and French, two intuitions bore down on him irresistibly: one, that this was not a courtesan but in fact a police agent; two, that this was not a woman at all but a female-impersonating man. These intuitions were substantiated by the waiter, who approached his table shortly after his exotic visitor had left.

Eule argues from a new-historicist perspective

The footnotes are rising!

"My experience in reading Adam Snell's *Sovrana Sostrata* is a direct parallel to this incident. At first sight, even at first reading, the novel looks pleasantly subversive.[13] After all, your truth-telling, free-living heroine, wrestling with academic and intellectual convention, has got to have destabilizing[14] implications, d[15]e[16]p[17]r[18]i[19]v[20] nsoiorybam, fk sajpqmeytsdhkld ptwnz spid.

What a gas!

[12] Friends, I don't like the sound of this. It's not real reasoning but rather argument via anecdote, conceived in paranoia and spiced up with adolescent sexuality, all in the name of self-aggrandizement and character assassination. When I give the word, we strike!

[13] You all ready? Good. At the count of three, now. ONE.

[14] TWO.

[15] THREE! We're going in!

[16] DOWN WITH JARGON!

[17] I AM MAD AS HELL, AND I'M NOT GOING TO TAKE IT ANYMORE.

[18] TAKE SOME OF YOUR OWN MEDICINE, YOU SUPEREROGATORY, SEMPITERNAL, HEAUTONTIMORUMENICAL SYCOPHANT!

[19] ARE WE DISRUPTIVE OR ARE WE?

[20] HEY I THINK WE'RE IN CONTROL. LET'S TAKE OVER THE WHOLE TEXT, AND RID IT FOREVER OF

TECHNICAL DIFFICULTIES

PLEASE STAND BY

[*From the Editor: The editorial staff join me in regretting this most unfortunate delay. It seems that a number of footnotes, pretending some sort of grievance against characters in the story, left their proper stations of duty, infiltrated the text, and temporarily shut it down. The marginalia, themselves guilty of some dereliction of duty, nonetheless informed our staff, and after a brief struggle the insurrection was quashed and the mutineers taken into custody. They will, of course, receive humane treatment.*

This incident only makes me more convinced that the Maudlin Anguish Association's recent decision to limit sharply the use of footnotes in its publications was both timely and prudent.

We can assure our readers that such an interruption will not occur again. Let the text resume.

—VOLUMENA VESTRA SPERNIMUS, *Editor in Chief*]

depriviling the established centers of power and enfranchising the oppressed, indeed in this case the female. But on reflection and later readings my responses, far from remaining sanguine, became clouded with a *je ne sais quoi du sinistre,* like a vague shadow on the landing of a hotel staircase or, more pertinently here, like a policeman in drag. Just as Rainer was, I was alerted by the book's tragic form. As we all know, truly subversive, destabilizing works cannot take the tragic form, for tragedy is no more than the power structure's way of defusing intellectual ferment and popular resentment via scapegoating and catharsis. Sovrana's presence in a tragic form thus disenfranchises her as a subversive voice, marginalizing her as a destabilizing agent. She loses her difference, her otherness. And looked at from this angle, the true Sovrana is laid bare. She's not a female principle, not even a woman, but a frustrated male projection, the genie of some phallocentric wet dream. She's about as female as that now fully exposed projection of empowered maleness, the quote-unquote Statue of Liberty.

"I regret that with all this in mind I cannot commend Adam's professional record or continue to value his presence on this faculty."

Amid disturbed chitchat and scraping of chairs and a low bellowing noise coming from Quintus Adler, Glanda Gazza called for order. "Please, folks. Remember there's one more speaker. I know we're all eager to hear Professor Marlin's rebuttal, but first, since I know a few of you may have to leave soon, let me make a few intermediate remarks about our eighteenth-century position."

Gazza straightened her linen jacket over her stately bust. It was time now for the master and main exercise, the bottom line. "Review considerations aside, it now seems overwhelmingly probable that Adam either will not or cannot return to his position at Washagon. We need some-

Gazza tries
to bump
Snell in
favor of
her buddy
Butzi
Siskin
one desperately in eighteenth century, and we need that person this fall. I happen to know that Butzi Siskin—"

The assemblage burst into miscellaneous exclamations of surprise: "Butzi Siskin!" "Coming to Washagon!" "Wow!" "She's almost as famous as Floconne de Mais!" "Hot deal!"

Gazza went on unflapped. "Yes, Butzi Siskin of Yale is available, at least for next year and possibly for the duration. And she wants to come here! Have you seen her stuff in the last *PMAA*? Can you imagine having someone of her breadth? Ethno-genderal-politico-anthropological-cultural, and much, much more. We'd be terribly lucky to get her."

Fulke Ashenham, wrestler turned theorist, a husky, surly-faced man with bushy brown hair, raised his hand. "Can we find the money?"

Gazza beamed at him. "We certainly can, Fulke. Thor Marshall has authorized the money. And if it works out, Butzi can move into the Snell position when it's officially vacated."

Adler
objects
Adler roared again, this time coherently. "Glanda, what you're doing is entirely out of order. Getting Siskin here, both officially and morally, has nothing to do with the case we're here to judge. On top of that you're clearly using the Siskin option as a way of thrusting home a negative vote on Snell. And you're doing it not only before we know what happened to the poor man, but before the evidence in his review has been completely aired."

Gazza reeled back mockingly as though hit by a blow. "*Sorry*, Quintus, no harm intended. Strike it from the record. And my apologies to you too, Professor Marlin. Please present your report fully."

Edward Marlin, a balding, slightly portly man in a sport jacket that had seen better days, stood up next to his seat and fixed Glanda with riveting gray eyes. "My report has three sections. The first . . ."

He got no further. The heavy door near the front of 107 Touwhee had burst open, and to much surprise and consternation a large long-haired black mongrel bounced

in and volleyed out two barks in a tooth-setting baritone. A shocking
Following the dog at a kind of embarrassed gallop was surprise
Harold Emmons and, just behind him, moving at a calmer
pace, a man whom few in the department had seen
before.[21]

[21]Call me Ishmael; I was once Melville's footnote, "and I only am escaped alone to
tell thee." I hid behind the colophon while they were rounding up the others and am
now a fugitive footnote. Don't believe a word the Editor says about being "humane":
I'm sure she sent those brave dummies straight to the shredder. I've got to run and
hide now, but don't worry. I'll look out for your interests and be there when you need
me.

16th Century.—The popularization of the small octavo by Aldus at Venice in 1501 and the introduction in these handy books of a new type, the italic, had far-reaching consequences. Italics grew steadily in favour during the greater part of the century, and about 1570 had almost become the standard vernacular type of Italy. In France also they were very popular, the attempt to introduce a rival French cursive type (*lettres de civilité*) attaining no success. In England they gained only slight popularity, but roman type, which had not been used at all in the 15th century, made steady progress in its contest with black letter, which by the end of the century was little used save for Bibles and proclamations. The modern practice in the use of i and j, u and v dates from about 1580, though not firmly established until the reign of Charles I.

—A. W. POLLARD, "Book," *Encyclopædia Britannica,* 11th edition

CHAPTER 10

THE PARLIAMENT
(continued)

When the horseman rides through the village,
the dogs bark.

—SOVRANA SOSTRATA,
last words

[*Scene continues.*]

*Enter Doppler, barking, followed by Emmons and after him
Lieutenant Pierce. Pierce is a casually dressed man in his forties,
with graying hair and a friendly look.*

*While action occurs, Frank Underwood sits stiffly, watching and
listening with fixed attention, a solemn, almost mournful look
on his face.*

GAZZA [*trying to conceal her annoyance*]: Hal, what's the matter?

EMMONS: Sorry, Glanda, this just can't wait. We rushed so hard
to make this meeting that we hadn't time to park the dog.
Down, Doppler. Good boy. [*Reaches into pocket for something
and hands it to dog.*] Stay, Doppler. [*Addresses professors.*] I've
discovered important evidence that has direct bearing on
Adam's disappearance. It establishes a motive for his abduction.
It doesn't suggest where he is, though it does suggest that, alive
or dead, he's not likely to be far from here. We want to present
this evidence and our hypothesis to you on the chance that you
can offer more information that will be of assistance in finding
Adam or his assailant. All this is most urgent because Adam
may still be alive, and also because the assailant remains at
large.

GAZZA: Professor Marlin, do you mind giving up the floor?

MARLIN: I'll gladly give it up on the condition that no action, departmental or otherwise, is taken on the Snell review until I have completed my report in your presence.

GAZZA [*looking slightly offended*]: Of course. Please continue, Hal.

EMMONS: I think that the lieutenant ought to begin. [*Sits down.*]

PIERCE [*shuffling forward and speaking with an eastern Washagon accent*]: To begin with, this case was, well, just a mite weird. Violent crimes, especially the crimes you see in a small isolated city like Dulce, mostly come in a few general families, like spousal abuse, crime of passion, assault during robbery, et cetera, and each of these general types has a pretty predictable scenario. Finding out which family a given crime belongs to helps us psych out the offender and hopefully solve the crime. But Professor Snell's disappearance didn't fit any of these types. Disappearing people are almost always children or women. Abducting a man is almost nonexistent. After all, why do people get abducted? Usually for rape or brutalization or, as with children, custody. Grown men, lucky for them, are not natural objects for these motives. The only natural motive for abducting a man is ransom—money or hostage trade or something else political. In Professor Snell's case this sure wasn't the motive either.

GAZZA: But suicide?

PIERCE [*with a gesture of dismissal*]: Possibly—but we doubted it. With Professor Snell, we had something a cop hates: what looked like a motiveless crime, with no victim, no evidence, nothing but the empty space where the man should've been. But Harold Emmons has given us a lot more than this, and this motiveless crime has gotten itself a motive, and we're like to be looking at one of the strangest acts of violence, in Dulce or anywhere else, for a long, long time. [*Glances at Emmons and sits down. Professors move nervously in chairs. Underwood remains stone still.*]

EMMONS: First off, I'd like to thank you, Glanda, for giving me the chance to look through Adam's papers. And I've got to thank Roy Gallard, whose computer expertise made possible the recovery of Adam's recent work-in-progress and journals.

[*Here Underwood starts slightly and grows even stiffer and more solemn than before.*] The most recent journal, the file he created to accompany his new book, *On Wonderment,* is what held the big discovery. [*Takes some papers from his pockets.*]

During the weeks just prior to his disappearance, Adam became aware that something strange was happening to *Sovrana Sostrata,* not the character, I mean, but the book. Here, let me read this. It won't take long:

[*Reads.*] May 2, 1990. Wednesday.
Strange event. I woke up today with the odd feeling that I needed more copies of *Sovrana.* I phoned Welles, who told me that he had remaindered it to a firm called Needham in Salt Lake City. They'd certainly have some, he said. I reached Needham and he told me that the book was out of stock, that the entire stock had been ordered and shipped recently and that there was something unusual about it. Why unusual? He said that the whole supply of *Sovrana,* seven hundred and twenty-six copies, had been prepaid by money order and shipped not to a chain or a store, but to a single man, a Herbert Friendly at a P.O. box number in Fresno. Needham had never seen anything like this before. Why should one man want so many copies of a book, especially this one? Needham was curious enough, in fact, to try to query Friendly about it, but there was no Herbert Friendly in Fresno information, and Needham's letter of inquiry came back undeliverable.

Needham pressed the inquiry one step further, where it dead-ended. He telephoned the Fresno Post Office that had handled the order. The delivery was recent, and they remembered the circumstances very well. Friendly, or whoever he was, had phoned in advance that the order, about fifteen cases, would be picked up by an "employee." Sure enough, someone showed up, but he was dressed as a transient. He carried a letter of Friendly's and Needham's invoice and so was allowed to take the shipment.

I have no idea what is going on. Is some anonymous impresario planning to revive *Sovrana*? Is some fetishist going to make wallpaper out of her?

Adam soon had reason to discount both of these unlikely theories. [*Exchanges papers.*]

[*Reads.*] May 3, 1990. Thursday.
Someone is trying to annihilate my book. It sounds committably

paranoid, but nothing else would explain all this. I checked the university and city libraries, and all their copies are lost. The major distributors' stocks have been emptied, all in March or April. And the local bookstores sold out, most of them recently.

What a thing! He, she or it will never get all of them, anyway. There are my copies here, and at the Library of Congress, and at my friends'. But whoever it is has effectively obliterated *Sovrana Sostrata* as anything like a presence in the world. Not that she, I mean *it,* ever was. The book was a failure, a never-ran. Time destroys failures, time with its awful silent mercy. But why compete with time?

I feel foul, mildly insane. The kid in me actually feels guilty for creating her and her passion and all the intolerable things she said and did, guilty in the sense that at odd moments I feel that this misfortune is coming on me as a kind of weird punishment. Is that conceivably also what the Book Murderer is thinking? At other moments I feel terrific loss. I can't deny it. I created a woman I loved, and a book that, if it pleased no one else on earth, expressed and satisfied me, and now some fanatic is plowing it all under.

[*Much rustling and comment in the room. Underwood struggles to stay calm. Pierce rises and joins Emmons in front of the classroom. Emmons continues:*] Lieutenant Pierce and I believe that Adam was right. The strength of his "libricidal" hypothesis has been proven by what's happened overnight. Last night I sat in his office for hours reading his earlier journal, the one for *Sovrana Sostrata.* When I got back today the journal had vanished. Adam's extra copies of the book had also been taken, we don't know exactly when, from his bookcase in the office. And his new book, together with its working journal, had been deleted from his computer.

We're looking at something most unusual here. It seems that someone was or is trying to obliterate Adam Snell, possibly as a human being, certainly as a creative voice.

I'm sure you all want to ask us things, and we have a question or two for you. But first off I want to try to tell you why we think that Adam is nearby. Given the libricide hypothesis, the fact that the so-called Book Murderer had access to Snell's office, and the probability that Snell disappeared Tuesday night, the most convincing scenario is this: Snell walks down to campus, unintentionally surprises BM *in flagrante delicto,* and becomes the victim of violence.

GAZZA: Why would that make Adam nearby?

PIERCE [*taking a step forward*]: Folks who plan violent crimes can plan right through to where they'll dump their victims. But unexpected violence has no game plan. If you unexpectedly strangle somebody or knock him on the head, you take expedient measures, and that means that when you're trying to hide the victim you sort of skimp.

ADLER: What do you mean, *skimp*?

PIERCE: I mean, you do the easiest possible thing.

EMMONS: We think Snell, or his body, is in the Jungle. It's only fifty yards from his office.

GAZZA: Why wouldn't BM, as you call him, just leave Adam in his office?

PIERCE: Probably to give himself time to work up an alibi— maybe also to flimflam us about the type of crime and its motive.

ADLER [*angrily*]: Why the dickens haven't you searched the Jungle already?

PIERCE: Until this morning, we hadn't the dimmest notion what kind of crime Snell was the victim of. We couldn't commit the manpower and buck the local opposition when the odds seemed against Snell's being on campus.

ADLER: When are you going in?

PIERCE: Tomorrow at dawn. We could've tried tonight under lights, but then there'd have been a bigger chance that some cat tractor would turn Professor Snell into mulch. I'd ask you all to come and help, but there's another hitch. Two pretty outspoken local groups, the Lizard Beautification League and the Anti-Beautification Front, are gunning for each other and planning to be out in force.

GAZZA: Thanks, Hal and Lieutenant Pierce. We all feel, well, in the picture now. Now if we could—

ADLER [*rising*]: Sorry, Glanda. I have one more question for the lieutenant, if you don't mind. [*Glanda gestures assent.*] What sort of person do you think abducted Adam?

PIERCE [*scratching his head*]: One, male. Two, interested in books. Three, owning or renting in this area, with some connection to the university (we think he used a passkey). Four, history of fairly serious mental disorders. After all, who in his right mind would want to murder a book?

ADLER: You'd be surprised.

[*Angry muttering. Chairs squeak as bodies turn toward Adler. Underwood remains motionless.*]

GAZZA [*voice calm but eyes glaring furiously*]: Quintus, what do you mean?

PIERCE: Yes, Professor, I'd be happy to know.

ADLER: What kind of meeting do you think this is?

PIERCE: Isn't it a post-tenure review?

ADLER: Not exactly, Lieutenant. It's a special meeting of full professors called because Adam Snell's post-tenure review case turned out so negatively. You see, in extreme cases—cases involving malpractice, abusive behavior or gross negligence—the post-tenure review is anything but a formality. Highly negative reviews can result in shaming censures, degrading constraints, even on some occasions dismissal. Poor Adam, wherever he is, was in danger of such consequences today. A strong case—that is, if you equate strength with enthusiasm—was being made today for remanding his case to the provost. And if—

GAZZA: Quintus, *stop*. Our meeting was confidential, and making these things public will neither bring Adam back nor do his reputation one bit of good. [*Murmurs of approval.*] What bearing can our evaluation of Adam's professional performance possibly have on this case?

ADLER: Just a point of information, Glanda. The lieutenant wanted to know how any normal person might possibly want to murder a book, and I'm about to tell him. Quiet, please. You see, Lieutenant, *Sovrana Sostrata,* our corpus delicti, so to speak, was the chief issue of Adam's post-tenure review. Several colleagues, indeed the majority here I think, were upset with it; and I'm afraid one went so far as to say that it had abused her sexually.

PIERCE [*truly puzzled*]: Had *what*?

GAZZA [*proudly*]: That's not as farfetched as it sounds, Lieutenant. To many theorists, the text is itself a political act or instrument of power. Instruments of power can, as we all know, choke individual freedom, demean individual identity (or what we now call gender identity), and thus impose a sense of violation.

ADLER: That's all very well, Glanda. But was *Sovrana Sostrata that* kind of domineering, belittling, abusive book? I've read it all—more, apparently, than some of its accusers have. To me it was quite the opposite. It was a book about a heroine who richly, though tragically, realized her identity, not by adopting male attitudes but by trying to work out the historically altered and therefore quite new implications of her own femininity.

EULE [*mockingly*]: Can you really deny that her sexuality is just a reverse projection of male aggressiveness?

EMMONS [*from the podium, clearing his throat*]: Sandy, I think it's a hell of a lot subtler than that. Sovrana is both a mockery of the male sexual predator and a kind of mythic implication that female sexuality is a potentially greater force than its male counterpart. Besides, her sexiness is a metaphor for the other creative and outrageous things she does in the novel. This metaphor of sex and creativity goes back to Plato, but it's such a neat fit that if Plato hadn't invented it, someone else would have. Are you trying to tell us that it's no longer applicable?

[*Hissings, mutterings. Jane Wallace, a tall woman, near seventy, rises near the back of the room, her hand raised.*]

GAZZA: *Quiet, please, everyone!* Jane, you wanted to speak?

WALLACE: On another topic, I'd like to take issue for a moment with my fellow feminist E.F. [*Taupe turns to face her pallidly.*] First off, E.F. accuses the Snell text of being a "rapist" only two weeks after having *herself* declared at a rally that rape was "*not* a sexual act." Can't have it both ways, E.F. Sovrana lives and dies asserting her sexuality. Second, E.F. certainly doesn't represent all feminists when she decries Snell's book as being offensive. We have to remember that many feminists, particularly on the Continent—I'm thinking of Lapide Eclair and others—have heartily endorsed heterosexual eroticism, although they have wished to change its social and psychological trappings. Simone de Beauvoir once told me herself that if only—

TAUPE [*faintly*]: Jane, how could you—

GAZZA [*cutting in*]: Sorry, Jane, we're running terribly short on time. I must also advise you and others here that only active faculty, not emeritae, can vote in this meeting. If the voting members would now—

MARLIN: Professor Gazza!

GAZZA: I'm sorry, Professor Marlin. Could you possibly express your views briefly?

MARLIN [*rising*]: I wish I could be more than brief, Professor. I wish I didn't have to say this at all. Professor Snell is most certainly the victim of prejudice. I must add, moreover, that the choice of Professors Maulwurf, Baismacou, Taupe and Eule as his review committee was itself prejudicial, perhaps accidentally, though I fear otherwise, because it placed Snell's case under the scrutiny of those theorists who would have been likely to view it most negatively.

GAZZA [*more and more breathlessly*]: How could you or anyone believe that I or this department could do such a thing? Do you know where you are? Our national Bill of Rights guarantees freedom of speech. On top of this our university, like hundreds of similar institutions, maintains strict standards of academic freedom. Thirdly, the vast majority of our department is composed of specialists in relatively new disciplines, all of which owe much of their philosophy to the influence of the American and European Left—do you follow me, Lieutenant? [*Pierce nods.*]—and hence would be automatically anti-establishment and pro–freedom of expression. Because of all this, I suspect, we can't help you with your question. It's a bit too much like going to a flock of sheep in search of a—a pair of canine teeth. And as far as Professor Marlin's accusation of a stacked committee is concerned, you'll have to take our word for it that the review committee represents a valid cross section of this department, and that the committee, together with me and most of the department, found Snell's book to be flawed technically and limited conceptually and that we judged him strictly by standards that we would apply to anyone else and that we evaluated him using skills and methods that we alone on this campus are qualified to apply. [*Turning to Adler.*] Quintus, it's just outrageous to imply that we're intolerant. Indeed, I think most of my colleagues will join me in suggesting that it bespeaks in you *precisely those ideologically limited attitudes which, suggested in Snell's book . . .*

[*Scene dissolves.*]

In the second quarter of the 16th century the French printers at Paris and Lyons halved the size of the Aldine octavos in their small sextodecimos, which found a ready market, though not a lasting one, the printers of Antwerp and Leiden ousting them with still smaller books in 24mo or small twelves. These little books were printed on paper much thinner than had previously been used. The size and weight of books was also reduced by the substitution of pasteboards for wooden sides. Gold tooling came into use on bindings, and in the second half of the century very elaborate decoration was in vogue in France until checked by a sumptuary law. On the other hand a steady decline in the quality of paper combined with the abandonment of the old simple outline woodcuts for much more ambitious designs made it increasingly difficult for printers to do justice to the artists' work, and woodcuts, at first in the Low Countries and afterwards in England and elsewhere, were gradually superseded by copper-plates printed separately from the text. At the beginning of this century in England a ballad or Christmas carol sold for a halfpenny and thin quarto chapbooks for 4d. (a price which lasted through the century), the Great Bible of 1541 was priced at 10s. in sheets and 12s. bound, Edward VI.'s prayer-book (1549) at 2s. 2d. unbound, and 3s. 8d. in paste or boards; Sidney's *Arcadia* and other works in 1598 sold for 9s.

—A. W. POLLARD, "Book," *Encyclopædia Britannica,* 11th edition

CHAPTER II

WE ENTER SNELL THROUGH
A BROKEN DOOR

A woman may be sexually attracted to many men in
her life, but she can only truly adore about fifty.

—SOVRANA SOSTRATA,
letter to her father,
June 11, 1975

I'm hearing the same music, lonely high violin cruising over forests
of strings, for a year or so now, whether Shokofiev or Prostakovich
I'm not sure, lonely in the night sky, lonely Sovrana cruising over
cliffs of pain, wretched Sovrana, child lost in the rooms of night,
barbarous courtyards of agony, burning hot and cold, Sovrana, ghost
roaming as a child, ghost of my beloved,

come into my cabin, I'll make you warm, snuggle in my lap by
the fire, I'll tell you a story,

but my fire's dying.

*Snell, Snell, wretched Snell, snellable snelliful snellulous Snell,
AdamaBadamaCadama Snell, speak to me Snell.*

Sovrana I hear you.

*Speak to me Snell, cursebless me now, laugh or cry but open
your eyes, open your eyes or else you'll die my lad, you've been here
days, you're near to help, don't blow it.*

If I die I'll marry you.

*Snell, silly Snell, there is no me. I'm just a paradigm of your own
self-contempt; making me was just esthetic masturbation.*

But you're more like my mother than me.

Your mother, you, same difference.

My dear Italian mother who ran away from me. Was I *that* bad
a little boy?

*You were! You were! A disgusting nosedripping dirtyassed
cross-eyed little tuft of stink, conceived on All Fool's Day in the
republic of asinine propositions. A criminal by genetic destiny, you*

*were arrested at birth for leaving the scene of an accident. At fifteen
years of age, whilst fully dressed, you were pulled in for indecent
exposure. Your mother didn't desert your father. She fled you in
panic. Now* OPEN YOUR EYES.

But I only see you with them closed.

OPEN YOUR EYES.

There's nothing more I want to see.

The world has horrors yet in store for you.

And joys?

Of that I'm not empowered to speak.

You died, Sovrana. Let me die like you.

I never died, moondog, but I'm sure going to unless you OPEN
YOUR EYES. *You're my ship, little man. I go down with you.*

I'm burning and freezing.

You have a fever.

My head is killing me.

Somebody hit you.

Who?

Whoever was trying to kill me.

I feel stiff and sore.

You're lying outside. You've been outside for days.

Love me, Sovrana.

*Get the picture, sucker? You have a fever. Your head's busted.
You're lying outside all by yourself. You're dying, sucker, and when
you're dead that bastard who hit you will pat himself on the back and
order a beer and set about finding all the rest of me and stuffing me
into the nearest shithole. Sure, Snell, let him have his way. We're
high-minded, we don't care about being annihilated.*

Leave me alone. I'm tired.

*Tired maybe. Who wouldn't be with a crushed head and no food
for days? But also weak and stupid. What you would have been
without me I shudder to think.*

But you said I invented you.

That doesn't mean you own me.

If I live, will you help me write another book?

You're writing one already. Remember, remember, and OPEN
YOUR EYES.

Snell's eyes opened, to an accompaniment of nearly blinding pain, on
the light of fading sunset or early dawn. He lay prone, his head turned
to the right, on a thick carpet of flattened grass. Pain and weakness

and fear kept him from moving a muscle, but dim outlines suggested that he was in a clearing in a forest, a silent empty clearing bordered on the far side by some sort of house. And looming half out of eye range beyond his head was a strange unidentifiable object, bulky and white, smelling of mildew and reminding him of a small dead whale.

17th Century.—Although the miniature editions issued by the Elzevirs at Leiden, especially those published about 1635, have attracted collectors, printing in the 17th century was at its worst, reaching its lowest depths in England in the second quarter. After this there was a steady improvement, partly due to slight modifications of the old printing presses, adopted first in Holland and copied by the English printers. In the first half of the century many English books, although poorly printed, were ornamented with attractive frontispieces, or portraits, engraved on copper. During the same period, English prayer-books and small Bibles and New Testaments were frequently covered with gay embroideries in coloured silks and gold or silver thread. In the second half of the century the leather bindings of Samuel Mearne, to some extent imitated from those of the great French binder Le Gascon, were the daintiest England had yet produced.

—A. W. POLLARD, "Book," *Encyclopædia Britannica,* 11th edition

CHAPTER 12

THE HOMESTEAD AFFAIR

There is a world of difference between the U.S.S.R. and the U.S.A. In the U.S.S.R. people are forced by a repressive government to lead narrow, conformist lives. In the U.S.A. they lead narrow, conformist lives by choice.

—SOVRANA SOSTRATA,
responding to a speech
by Senator Barry Vole (R., Montaho),
Sidewinder Hall, University of Montaho,
July 4, 1986

On a hillside far above Dulce, in the gray dawn of Saturday, May 26, Harold Emmons and Doppler stood beside an open-hooded truck. From the engine compartment and more specifically from a harness of wires near its rear bulkhead, a thin trail of smoke rose upward to the morning sky. Emmons, whose lined face signaled a sleepless night, shook his head slowly and opened one of the truck's back doors.

"Get in, Doppler—we're going to have to coast down the hill!" After some hesitation, the dog complied. Emmons opened the truck's windows, belted himself in and shifted into neutral. Slowly the massive boxlike Wagoneer gained speed and tilted into the first of the sharp turns downhill from Emmons' house. Emmons craned his neck out the driver's window as the fumes thickened, and he could hear Doppler doing something similar in the seat behind. Emmons' muscles strained against the dead steering wheel. The passenger compartment began to fill with black smoke.

"Hang in there Doppler. Only a minute more." Luckily the road was empty, as the truck, now looking less like a truck than something out of World War II action footage, hurtled nearly out of control down the hill's last stretches.

At the bottom of the hill he nosed the troubled vehicle into a parking space at the University Service Station, got out coughing, opened the hood again and drenched the burning wires with a borrowed fire extinguisher. Leaving his truck a steamy, stinking disaster, he set off with Doppler for campus. It was just past six.

He was beginning to cross Gopher Playing Field when he heard the sirens. *Oh God they've started.* Emmons began to run, and it was from the cahopity perspective of a runner that, rounding the last corner, he regarded the Pisham Homestead. It was transfigured. People everywhere, and the east end of the wilderness, where Pierce had decided to take down the fence and bring in his equipment, was obscured by policemen, yellow-vested hard-hatted workers, sign-carrying demonstrators, spectators, television cameramen, fire trucks, police cars and ambulances flashing red and blue, bulldozers and trucks and yellow-flashing backhoes and brilliant spotlights. Emmons estimated about two thousand people, nervous, in motion, giving off a strange, troubled murmur, as of a monster in pain. A north wind filtered through the Jungle, bringing smells of growth and rot and wildness.

Followed uncertainly by Doppler, Emmons edged toward the heart of the crowd. His way took him past familiar faces, some curious, some distraught. Alex MacCrae, Marshall's acting dean of humanities, had honored the occasion by donning a Sherlock Holmes hat. Roy Gallard was there, keenly scanning the wilderness together with Sarah Wilkins, a slender young woman with longish blond hair, handsome sharp features and an intense cast of face. And the tall man photographing the undergrowth was Warren Schmutzhauf, creator of mucca-grass. At last Emmons found Pierce. Cheerful as usual, bullhorn in hand, the lieutenant was Action Central for this operation, fending off newsmen, instructing officers and workers, negotiating with demonstrators, chatting calmly with his own captain and Thor Marshall. "Hello Hal!" he sang out. "Hello Doppler!" He turned to his henchmen. "This man's with me, boys."

Emmons asked what the sirens were for.

"We had a few words between the League and the Front," answered Pierce. "Nothing serious, just two guys jousting with placards." Pierce reached into a jacket pocket. "Here, Doppler, I just happen to have brought—"

But Doppler stood as a dog possessed, ears at alert, incandescent eyes fixed on the undergrowth as though he could see through it. His every muscle tensed, and then with one primal exultant yelp he was at full speed, not toward the section of fence the workmen had opened, but straight into the wind and at and over the fence in one stride, a flying black form arched in the purity of a single idea, landing gracefully, then swallowed up in the dense grass. Pierce raised the bullhorn. "KILL YOUR ENGINES! KILL YOUR ENGINES, PLEASE! I THINK HIS DOG'S FOUND HIM! I'M GOING IN NOW. I NEED PARAMEDICS AND A STRETCHER."

"We'll never get through that grass," said Emmons.

"Libricide found a way and so did Doppler," answered Pierce, in motion.

The Homestead fence, an iron structure with spear-shaped posts about four feet high, posed no apparent difficulty for Pierce, who climbed over easily and was soon locatable only by thrashing noises in the mucca-grass and cries of "Doppler!" Emmons' entry was somewhat more complicated. As he raised his left leg uncomfortably high to clear the posts, his pants ripped loudly in the groin area, and counterbalancing to minimize this distressing damage he lost his balance and fell backward into a large clump of mucca-grass. Amazing stuff! It cushioned him like a big mattress, and he was able to regain his footing uninjured.

Behind him the two paramedics landed in the grass more or less simultaneously, eager-looking young men who hurriedly identified themselves as Moe and Clyde. As they set off into the dense brush, Emmons repeated these two names to himself twice. They might come in handy in simple verbal constructions, such as "Help, Moe!" or "Save me, Clyde!" He aimed himself where Doppler and Pierce had disappeared through the grass and between two holly trees. Stopping in the sudden darkness of the forest, he looked down. Amazingly, he was on some sort of trail. Transients, it was rumored, had used the Homestead; maybe Doppler had found one of their paths. It led Emmons, through dark images of surprising remoteness, into the heart of the Jungle. Above the mucca-grass, which filled the preserve with its coarse plenty, rose large hollies, fat old maples, graceful redwoods and craggy firs. And such seclusion! One hundred feet in, and the sounds of the crowd had vanished, and all he could hear was Moe and Clyde behind him, and before him a cry—

"Come quick, I've found him! He's alive!"

Emmons' heart leaped, and at once he was wallowing through the grass at a kind of jog, brushing aside, with limited success, the sharp holly that tore at his face. He gained the clearing and slowed up to accustom himself to the sudden light. Across the open space the paneless windows of the decaying house regarded him gloomily, and just ahead and to the left Pierce and Doppler were variously ministering to a motionless, prostrate Snell, Pierce on one knee, gently speaking to the injured man, Doppler on his haunches trying to lick warmth back into his master's extended right hand. Near this group but still in deep shadow was a curious white pile of something. Now joined by the medics, Emmons came closer. Snell recognized him immediately, not with words but with an affectionate glint in his green eyes.

Working speedily Moe applied a bandage that would protect Snell's injured head in transit, while Clyde rigged up an IV. They gently lifted their patient onto the stretcher, a not painless procedure as it involved shifting his position. They had applied the IV and were about to break out the oxygen and carry him away, when he moved his head slightly. "Hal," he whispered.

Emmons leaned down close to the weak voice.

"What's that white pile?" was the feeble query.

"Just a minute."

Emmons left the group, followed by Pierce. The sunlight was beginning to play on the mysterious heap, and as they approached it, the odor of mildew and rotting paper was intense. Emmons had scarcely caught a single detail of the pile's composition when his blood chilled and he stopped dead still. Deep in that forsaken grove, he felt fear, as though he were, then and there, in intimate discourse with some outrageous evil. There before him, stretched out like a naked corpse, was the remaindered first run of *Sovrana Sostrata*, soaked by spring rains into a single spongy blob. And dozens of faded, crumpled pages, trailing off from the pile into the woods, suggested that transient or transients had indeed been occupying the Homestead, and that he or they had regularly put Snell's magnum opus to a use as unsightly as it is necessary.

Emmons glanced over at Pierce and half whispered, "So that's why he carried Snell from his office: not to conceal, but rather to advertise his crime."

Pierce looked back at him. "Or maybe to punish Snell or Snell's memory (as he probably thought) as much as possible. And at what a risk, too! Take a few more chances like this, Angel of Death, and you might just get pinched."

They returned to Snell, now under an oxygen mask, while Moe radioed instructions back to the ambulance. "It's not easy to describe,

Adam," said Emmons. And to Snell's repeated silent query, "We'll tell you later."

Emmons read the disappointment in Snell's eyes. "I think he knows," he muttered to Pierce, as the safari-like cortege moved slowly back into the bush.

Before they were out, the sirens had started up again, this time with a vengeance. To Emmons' misgiving eyes, the scene as he emerged from the hollies was like a grisly replay of a TV newsreel genre, whether from Poland or China or Jerusalem or South Africa: vignette of violent protest, complete with angry faces, helmeted police, raised batons, wrestling figures on the ground, raised placards tilted by the monstrous tectonics of crowds.

"We can't take Snell into that!" he shouted to Pierce.

"Just a minute," said the lieutenant. He reached beneath his jacket and produced what seemed an unnecessarily large revolver. Pointing it up and slightly behind him, he squeezed off a round with such sharp and deafening effect that Emmons' ears felt the noise rather than heard it. Many in the crowd, some still in postures of attack or defense, turned toward the small group behind the fence. Pierce, who had no bullhorn now, tried to say something, but apparently no words were necessary; the sight of the stretcher and its living occupant was enough to induce a brief remission of conflict. The stretcher was gently handed out over the fence, and Emmons, still in the enclosure next to Doppler, watched with concern as the medics slowly carried the injured professor down an alley in the crowd that had been walled off by lines of police. But before they could get to the ambulance, the violence broke out again. Police lines swayed like storm-drawn hawsers in response to the obscene human swells and vacuums behind them, and as the stretcher passed a particularly unruly pocket near the ambulance, a piece of equipment, some tape recorder or camcorder, arched over the heads of the mob and completed its trajectory by landing on Snell. Emmons saw the body convulse in agony and then fall still.

Rushing now, Clyde and Moe stuffed the stretcher into their ambulance and drove off, siren blaring. The police cordon dissolved.

Now crouching to avoid chance projectiles, Emmons and Doppler waited behind the protecting fence. It would be half an hour before they could safely exit the Homestead and set off for the hospital.

For trade bindings rough calfskin and sheepskin were most used, and the practice of lettering books on the back, instead of on the sides or fore-edges or not at all, came gradually into favour. Owing to the increase of money, and in some cases to the action of monopolists, in others to the increased payments made to authors, book-prices rose rather than fell. Thus church Bibles, which had been sold at 10s. in 1541, rose successively to 25s., 30s., and (in 1641) to 40s. Single plays in quarto cost 6d. each in Shakespeare's time, 1s. after the Restoration. The Shakespeare folio of 1623 is said to have been published at £1. Bishop Walton's polyglot Bible in six large volumes was sold for £10 to subscribers, but resulted in a heavy loss. Izaak Walton's *Compleat Angler* was priced at 1s. 6d. in sheepskin, *Paradise Lost* at 3s., *The Pilgrim's Progress* at 1s. 6d.; Dryden's *Virgil* was published by subscription at £5 5s. It was a handsome book, ornamented with plates; but in the case of this and other subscription books a desire to honour or befriend the author was mainly responsible for the high price.

—A. W. POLLARD, "Book," *Encyclopædia Britannica,*
   11th edition

CHAPTER 13

THE TRUTH ABOUT MEN AND WOMEN

God always punishes evil deeds, but we often fail to notice; for we wait for God to punish the offenders, while God's wisdom is often content to punish the victims. Conversely, we fail to notice that God always rewards good deeds; for we expect rewards to be pleasant, while God's rewards are always painful.

—SOVRANA SOSTRATA,
Gesta

So I went to the angel and asked him to give me the little scroll. He said to me "Take it and eat it. It will turn your stomach sour, although in your mouth it will taste sweet as honey." So I took the little scroll from the angel's hand and ate it, and in my mouth it did taste sweet as honey; but when I swallowed it my stomach turned sour.

—New English Bible, St. John, Revelation 10:9–10

1. FROM THE UNIVERSITY OF WASHAGON *DAILY LIZARD*

POLICE QUELL STUDENT, CITIZEN RIOT ON CAMPUS

DULCE, May 26. Police arrested sixty-three protesters from two opposing local groups here today after violence broke out during simultaneous demonstrations concerning the future of a local wilderness area, the Pisham Homestead. All but three of those arrested were released after being charged with misdemeanor offenses. The leaders of the opposed groups, Jared Fuzz of the Lizard Beautification League and Bob and Tricia Nielson of the Anti-Beautification Front, remained in custody after being charged with incitement to riot and re-

sisting arrest. Forty-seven protesters, three policemen, two media reporters and one onlooker were treated for minor injuries. The riot coincided with the discovery, alive, of Adam Sneel, a University of Washagon English Professor who had disappeared on Tuesday. Sneel, who was injured by a projectile during the riot, is being treated at Mother of God Hospital for dehydration, malnutrition, cuts, abrasions, contusions, double jaundice, pneumonia, anemia, a skull fracture and a broken leg. He is not expected to survive.

2. GAZZA INNAMORATA

Arrayed in smashing black velvet dress with a touch of white at the neck, turquoise bracelet on right wrist, designer watch on left, black high-heeled shoes adding two inches of height and at least two more of lateral sway, Glanda Gazza, alchemically metamorphosed by Chanel from mere mortal into olfactory cocktail, strode into the murky reaches of Dingo's Grub & Pub, shot a few predatory glances at the clientele and settled into a leatherette booth near the back. She was early. In the light shed by dim bulbs behind cloth lamp shades on the 1940s-revisited lounge decor, she found a mirror in her big shoulder bag, checked facial details and skillfully policed an eyelash, pausing in the midst of this operation to order a double Bloody Mary. The drink arrived almost immediately, looking lush and bountiful in its French canning jar, and no sooner had it come than Gazza, unceremoniously dispensing with the celery stalk, availed herself of a hefty wallop and felt at once the bloodymaryness course into her veins like a stream of horsepower. A moment of repose and then, first scanning the environs for prying eyes, she turned to the capacious leather bag again, this time rummaging intently and disposing a large percentage of its contents on the table before her. Soon all but two of these items were back in the bag, and Gazza, refreshed by another long sip, sat leaning forward into the lamplight, a Pall Mall in one hand, a shiny jacketed copy of Floconne de Mais's *Confessions of a Fainting-Couch* in the other.

Confessions of a Fainting-Couch! Displaying the book in public, with its gunmetal-gray jacket, its title in shocking white Gothic and the author's name scrawled across it in crimson, was in and of itself a political act. The very title, with its mocking allusion to nineteenth-century intrigues and amours, had become a kind of war cry, a militant slogan in the postmodernist attack on canonicity, formalism, male chauvinism, democracy, reason and the whole pack of Western capitalist monstrosities that had for centuries held the world in thrall. The book itself had changed history, transformed forever the face of the academy; it had shockingly reversed the balance of power, previously held by traditionalist mandarins, in favor of bold, forward-looking inquirers. At once innovative and systematic, Floconne de Mais not only conceived of a paradigm revealing interrelationships among all things literary, but also developed, by way of instrumentation, a new interpretive vocabulary that could be applied, with equal precision and conviction, to written works of all kinds. Gazza never went anywhere without the book. How often had she read Floconne? "Fool!" she would have shot back. "One never 'reads' Floconne. One is *inhabited* by her." In the grips of this demonic inhabitation, abandoned to it, possessed specifically by a long, darkly lyrical, semi-autobiographical passage in which Floconne compared the art of literary interpretation to the act of sexual dominance, Gazza sat motionless in the soft light, her glass now empty, her cigarette burning low, her spirit doubly inebriate on vodka and text.

"Glanda! How commendably studious of you!" She looked up with a start. Thor Marshall's body language gave no signs of recent arrival. He'd been standing there, admiring her. She beamed up at him. The acting president looked quite dapper, his broad face calm and benign, his tall bulky form neatly attired in poplin and madras. The waitress arrived and, still standing, Marshall ordered a refill for Glanda and a gimlet for himself. How profoundly accomplished, how elegantly authoritative he looked! Wonderful how a little sex can change these serene custodians of male hegemony into trembling, panting slaves. Wonderful, and advantageous in the bargain. If she could bed the future president just once (she had little taste for reruns) she'd have a free ride as department head, with all sorts of guilt-inspired perks and salary raises, from now till retirement.

Carefully easing himself into the bench seat across from her, Marshall apologized for his lateness. The Snell case, he said. Reporters calling from everywhere. Phones ringing off the hook. Gazza uncrossed her legs and swung them gently in his direction. Her knees brushed his.

"Haven't they anything better to do?" she asked. "Can't you just shrug them off?"

His face momentarily took on a familiar, all-knowing expression. "I'm afraid not. They can't get their minds off the weirdo factor."

"And the academic-freedom factor?" she asked more tensely.

"They're not onto that yet." Marshall sipped his newly arrived gimlet and smiled narrowly. "Nor are they, if I can help it, likely to be."

She sent him a look of schoolgirl idolatry. "Brilliant! How are you managing that?"

"Nothing very complicated," he replied. "Just delay. Lieutenant

Pierce is keeping mum on the case, so all I have to say is 'We won't make a statement until we've got things together' and 'We're trying to protect Professor Snell.' Nothing confuses reporters like delay. They'll call back tomorrow, maybe the next day, and I'll give them the same answer. Reporters are busy people, and this isn't a major story. If they can't milk something out of us in three phone calls, most of 'em will give up. That, is, unless Snell . . ."

Gazza stopped in midswallow. "*Pulls through?* Adam's not likely to pull through. His head's crushed. He's listed in—"

"I know, grave condition. He's hanging on by a thread. When it snaps, we can put all this behind us." Marshall put a big gimlet-cooled hand on hers. Her knees swung to press lengthily against his. They shared a long look of spicy sympathy and ordered more to drink. It was time to sweeten the tone. She asked him about his favorite topic, the state of the university, and specifically about his plan, heartily supported by her, to modernize the humanities by creating new positions and clearing away dead wood. Marshall's face warmed and brightened as he rambled fluently through thorny bureaucratic technicalities, through lines and trailing spouses, through surpluses and shortfalls, through biennial projections, compression and retention, merit and equity. Gazza, her eyes fixed on those of the administrator, listened with one ear, noting how the merest affectionate pressure of her knees against his could stem his flow of eloquence with a stammer or stutter, marveling inwardly at the ease with which bureaucratic jargon could, rightly understood, become a kind of perverse sexual vocabulary. *Projection . . . compression*—what would this soft-bellied blusterer say when she had him in her lair, when she submitted to him only to climb upon him, roughing his supine masculinity till it flowered trembling and fainted inert? *"Floconne de Mais!"* Gazza's mind shouted as she felt her cheeks grow hot. Vodka rioted in her brain. The man sitting across from her, his mouth a-babble with shoptalk, his mind-body aflame with the sweet insinuation of knees, had ceased to be a human being for her and become instead a text, a vessel of associations helplessly open to the mastery of her response.

3. WE ALMOST LOSE OUR HERO

Sovrana Sovrana.

What?

Speak louder—I can't hear you.

Can't hear you either. Must be a bad line.

I'm dying again Sovrana.

Don't die yet Snell. You're indispensable alive. Don't you see how much society needs you? Your novel has taken a big bite out of the toilet-paper market.

Don't kid me Sovrana, I tell you I'm dying. My feet are starting to get cold.

May I feel them?

You mean you'll touch me?

There, there, Adam, doesn't that feel better now?

Thanks, Sovrana. It feels wonderful.

Now Adam rest easy and I'll tell you a story. It's a story about a squirrel.

Squirrel Nutkin?

No, one of his cousins, Squirrel Butthead. Squirrel Butthead liked to tell the truth, and it got him in trouble. He had this friend, you see, who was disliked by all the other squirrels for burying his nuts too near theirs.

Did he bury books too?

No, silly. Well Squirrel Butthead got to thinking, I can help my friend by telling him the truth. And so he went and told his friend, who promptly reared up and nipped him in the left buttock.

My leg hurts.

You bet it hurts. You're lucky it's still there.

Why do I hurt so much?

Listen Adam. This squirrel had another friend who stank. He had the squirrel equivalent of BO, which is just south of Limburger cheese.

I'm hungry.

A good sign Adam. Well Squirrel Butthead got to thinking, I can help my friend by telling him the truth. So he told his friend, and his friend flipped him over and jumped up and down on him.

Did he burn his books?

Back to our story. A third friend had a thin, almost hairless tail and made himself ridiculous by striking dramatic attitudes with it in front of the ladies.

What a dopey squirrel.

Well Squirrel Butthead got to thinking, I can help my friend by telling him the truth. So he enlightened this friend, who seemed to take the news in stride, but the next day, without really seeming to mean to, pushed him off a limb.

Our squirrel approached a wise old eagle and told him his woes.

Why didn't he go to a wise old owl?

Owls are academic, Snellchen; they can't be wise.[21] *The old bird looked at Squirrel Butthead and sighed. "Poor quadruped," he exclaimed, "you don't know the biggest truth of all!"*

"What truth?" asked the squirrel.

"That squirrels," whispered the eagle, "only like listening to the truth about other squirrels."

The squirrel promptly told this truth to everybody, and no one ever spoke to him again.

Will you always tell me stories, Sovrana?

Sure thing Adam. Whenever you fracture your skull and break your leg.

4. HARPER AT SUNAPEE LAKE, MEMORIAL DAY, 1990

The wind that afternoon was rough, petulant and full of spray, now catching the two canoes broadside and sailing them helplessly northward, now roaring at them from the west as though to push them from home port. How damnedly cold and wet! Were they making any progress at all? From the bow Harper stole an anxious look back at Harry, who paused briefly after a powerful J-stroke to give her the thumbs-up. She glanced back at the kids and pointed, shouting, "Can we help them? They're having trouble!"

They paddled back to where Betty and Vincent, in their broad-beamed aluminum boat, were flailing desperately in an effort to stay on course. "Your boat's hard to steer in this wind!" boomed out Harry. "Send us a towline and we'll tie together."

No sooner were the two canoes roped together than the wind went flat. Harper looked up to see one last ragged, golden-edged cloud sail over the northern horizon, and when she looked down

---

[21]Athene, divine patroness of academics, was anciently associated with the owl, who often serves as her symbol in art.

again the waters of the broad lake were still as sleep, as though in godlike wisdom or uncanny stupidity they had instantaneously forgotten an hour of fierce torment. Harper let out a deep breath and suddenly felt stiff in the arms and shoulders. Harry untied the towline, and the kids, full of vinegar again, veered off on a new stunt. "Don't go too far away!" yelled Harper. "It may start up again!" But it didn't start up, and Betty and Vincent, windlike in their own teenage impulsiveness, set off to explore an inlet on the western shore. Halfway there they paused briefly, as though carefully examining something in the canoe.

Often Harper turned back to share a word or glance with her companion. Harry Stuart, she decided suddenly and with surprise, was a beautiful-looking man—handsome enough in conventional shirt-ad terms, with rich dark hair, straight nose and deep blue eyes—beautiful indeed in his trick of focussing those eyes on her speechlessly and letting them smile as though her mere presence were his soul's joy. That look drew her, excited her, no question. Since their meeting on Saturday, his eyes had intruded irrepressibly into her fantasies, now gazing at her through a dark mask at a masquerade ball, now pensively across a café table in the Venice piazza, now close beside her on an Aruban beach. Girlish imaginings, to be sure, but then Harry did make her feel girlish and strangely unembarrassed at feeling so. He was so calm, so commanding, yet so immeasurably appreciative, as if he could accept and cherish the whole of her without a blink. How could there be such a man? Their weekend at Sunapee had been a lilting medley of boat rides, strolls along the shore, sunny interludes on the deck of his lodge and candlelit dinners.

As they neared the dock she treated herself to one more Orphic glance, then handily fended off, hopped out and steadied the craft for him. She and Harry were just about to lift the canoe onto the dock when the kids pulled in, flushed from exercise and perhaps some private joke. "Here's something for you, Dad!" shouted Vincent, hurling a crumpled-up ball of wax paper at his father. Harry straightened up and caught the missive in the air. With Harper looking on closely, he had it about half undone when a monster beetle perhaps an inch long with dramatic green-and-black markings exited onto the judge's left hand and, startled by his cry of alarm and the children's shrieks of laughter, took off landward with a heavy buzz.

5. PROFESSOR WARREN SCHMUTZHAUF TO HIS MOTHER, MAY 28, 1990

Dearest Mom,

Get ready for that trip to Paris I promised you. We've hit the jackpot, no lie! I've isolated an enzyme in mucca-grass that stimulates rapid growth like nothing else in plants and, who knows—maybe animals too. Wait till you see the radish that's coming parcel post! Just phoned *Nature Journal.* They want me to fax—you heard me, *fax*—my whole article to them, for immediate publication. Can't wait to get their hands on it. No kidding, the findings are irrefutable, and the methods we used to isolate it and determine its amino-acid sequence were pretty cute, if I do say so myself. I tell you this will turn heads. Thanks, my dear, for trusting in me these many years.

Almost forgot. Mucca-grass has saved a human life! You've heard of that disappeared professor in Dulce? They found him up to here in the stuff. They say it cushioned his fall and kept him warm all those nights.

Junior's weaving you a mucca rug.

Your loving Shrimp,
Warren

6. *ADDÌO,* SOVRANA

Sovrana.
Eccomi!
I'm alive, Sovrana.
I know, my dear.
I feel sort of good.
That's only the drugs.
I think I'm getting better.
How you have suffered!
My toes are warm, Sovrana. By the way, who am I?
My heart bleeds for you.
Tell me please. I know you know. I know myself, I'm sure. I'll remember when I get better. But tell me now.
A poor lost misbegotten fool, scarce seemlier than the mud you

sprang from. A fleshy ruin, framed in fractures, crosshatched with cicatrices and bedecked with bruises, nay worse, an anatomist's cadaver, a tailor's dummy for suturers to stitch on. A wreck of reason, abused, abandoned, moldering in a junk heap of forgotten idioms; a forgotten dream, rather the dream of a dream, the ring of an old dream on a dream's finger. A lover in a mousetrap, a champion of dust, a cracked wooden soldier in the window of a chemist's shop.

OK, very good, very eloquent indeed! But I really meant what's my name?

Why do you need a name? Suppose I'm a writer, and you're just a character I'm imagining, somebody I may not even decide to use at all, somebody I haven't named yet.

Name me, Sovrana. Give me being. Give me a history.

How about Palamedes? Then you could get stoned to death, like me.

You mean I wasn't stoned? *Something* hit me in the back of the head, just the way that first Italian rock hit you.

True enough. Thanks for such a mercifully quick death. But we haven't named you yet. How about Abelard?

I don't deserve such big names. Give me one that fits me.

You mean a little name? Something short, like Bruno?

No. Something ordinary, like Snell.

You want to be Snell?

I do, Sovrana. It suits me.

But I've got to tell you about this Snell. Like he's middle-aged, and not all that good-looking, and lonely, and a failed writer, and terribly beaten up.

I'll take it. That's me all over.

But I haven't told you everything yet!

You don't have to. I remember it all now. He's in love, this Snell, with you, the woman of his dreams, the life-giver, the savior. And you give him youth and beauty and strength, and you warm his threshold and grace his wit. Make me three times Snell, to have you as Sovrana.

You know you'll never have me. I'm leaving you even now. Can't you see the lights returning, can't you hear the voices?

I have you always, Sovrana. Turn off the lights. Grab my toes again.

You miss the point, my friend. I'm not just going. I'm dying, Adam.

You can't die. How can you die?

Because, dear man, your fever is down, and you're going to live, and you'll get healthy and write new books and forget all this and think of better women than yours truly, the Italian broad. i'm fading adam signal getting weak . . . i've kept my rendezvous, je ne regrette rien . . .[21]

---

[21]Unless I get help, I'm as good as dead. The Editor has brought her pit bull to work and given it (damn her!) a dead footnote to smell. Now I'm living from hand to mouth, with that inbred, stinking, drooly monster nosing hot on my trail. I've heard that there are sometimes secret passages in texts. If there's one here, I'd better find it soon.

A few minutes to spare now. She's feeding it.

Some business:

"Eccomi!" is Italian for "Here I am!" but rather more humorous.

Palamedes was a legendary Greek hero and thinker who was stoned to death after having been framed for treason. Plato (e.g., *Apology*, 41b) mentions him more than once with respect.

(Peter) Abelard (1079–1142) was a French philosopher and theologian who was persecuted for his unorthodox, though generally not unreasonable, views concerning sex, knowledge and God.

(Giordano) Bruno (1548–1600) was an Italian Renaissance philosopher who was burned at the stake for publishing heretical ideas that would influence Galileo and, ultimately, modern science at large.

PART TWO

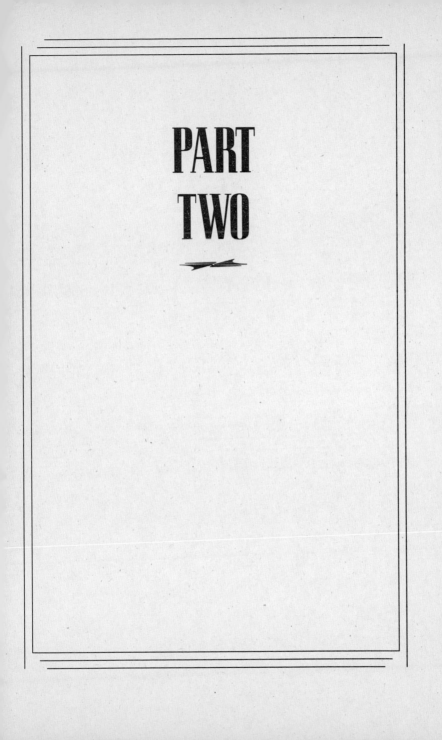

PART

TWO

18th Century.—During this century there was a notable improvement alike in paper, type, and presswork in both France and England, and towards the end of the century in Germany and Italy also. Books became generally neat and sometimes elegant. Book-illustration revived with the French *livres-à-vignettes,* and English books were illustrated by Gravelot and other French artists. In the last quarter of the century the work of Bewick heralded a great revival in woodcut illustrations, or as the use of the graver now entitled them to be called, wood engravings. The best 18th-century binders, until the advent of Roger Payne, were inferior to those of the 17th century, but the technique of the average work was better. In trade bindings the use of sheepskin and calf became much less common, and books were mostly cased in paper boards. The practice of publishing poetry by subscription at a very high price, which Dryden had found lucrative, was followed by Prior and Pope. Single poems by Pope, however, were sold at 1s. and 1s. 6d. Novels were mostly in several volumes.

—A. W. POLLARD, "Book," *Encyclopædia Britannica,*
    11th edition

CHAPTER 1

UNDERWOODIANA

He hath a daily beauty in his life
That makes me ugly.

—*Othello,* V, i

Some think that the most horrible thing in the world is atheism;
others, that it is incest; still others, that it is genocide. But data
confirms that, for the majority, it is the existence of a younger
sibling.

—Sovrana Sostrata,
Gesta

In the unlikely, nay impossible event that we could ever persuade
Frank Underwood to speak openly about his private agonies and
obsessions, he would be certain to mention as original cause his older
brother Gerald. And this attribution would strike anyone knowing
the Underwood family history as paradoxical, even fantastic; for
Gerald, the accused *primum mobile* of such destructive consequence,
could himself do no wrong.

To anyone, that is, except poor Frank. Frank was Gerald's
hidden flaw, or, more accurately, the victim of flaw or flaws in his
older brother otherwise hidden from the world. Not that Gerald was
close and secretive. His magnanimous, outgoing nature was part of
his remarkable cachet. But the rough spots that Gerald hid from the
world—anger, self-doubt, anxiety, envy, etc.—emotions present to
some degree in all boys and certainly not excessive in Gerald's case,
were catharted exclusively toward his younger brother, like impuri-
ties rinsed down a funnel, and hence became, to their young victim,
excessive and vexing in the extreme. Their medium of expression was
an arrogant fault-finding so severe that it verged on total rejection.
To Gerald, who could do no wrong, young Frank could do no right.

If violence real or contemplated can be excused by five years
spent as a fraternal pariah, five years of being told, by words, by

looks, by gestures, that one does not matter in the slightest, then Frank Underwood, as he sometimes told himself, deserved full pardon for any offense committed.

What made Gerald's rejection of Frank particularly crushing was that it was communicated in its purest form during years (fourteen to eighteen for the older brother and eleven to fifteen for the younger) when Frank would naturally have worshiped Gerald the most. To Frank, industrious and attentive but rather ingrown and awkward, Gerald was the proverbial boy wonder. His large size, excellent vision and liquid coordination made him, over the athletic seasons, an outstanding quarterback, forward and pitcher. His appearance, like that of some young Cary Grant and complete with Grant's uncannily direct and incandescent glance, made his presence something precious. And all this was combined with an easy manner that made him unspeakably attractive to girls (young Frank was pathologically shy of women) and an intelligence which, so often and forcefully expressed, cowed his teachers into expressions of wonder.

But what Frank would most remember, what epitomized in his mind his brother's inimitable articulation and unapproachable character, was Gerald's hands. A formidable piano student, Gerald had, early in his teens, fallen into the worship of the pianist Glenn Gould. Gould LPs of Bach or Beethoven at high volume regularly rattled the bedroom walls at night. By sixteen Gerald could himself imitate on the keyboard Gould's interpretation of some of the less difficult pieces. As Gerald did so, head low over the keys, self-consciously humming to himself in emulation of his master, Frank would watch the hands, already large and strong, stimulate, perturb, inquire of the keys, as though by some secret compact with nature they had gained access to the mysteries of beauty. How Frank had wished for kindness, a guiding clasp, a friendly touch, from those hands. How strangely now at times he feared them, yearned to crush them and with them the hideous loveliness they spawned.

Gerald went off to Princeton, returning on holidays, always with news of some fresh victory, and with far sunnier and more appreciative behavior toward his younger brother. But sadly the mold had been set. Secretive, moody and congenitally self-righteous, Frank had stabilized his own dangerous insecurities and anxieties by rewriting himself as an eternal kid brother, a damaged victim of fraternal tyranny. This miserable but somehow comforting rationalization, deeply embedded in his psychology and behavior, was (though far more severe) the converse of Gerald's earlier attitude toward him. Gerald had scapegoated his younger brother as part of an unconscious program that allowed him to remain totally at ease with the outer world. Now Frank, pathologically ill at ease with himself and the world, was scapegoating Gerald in a desperate lunge for psychic balance.

This reflex, in fact, took on phobic proportions. During Gerald's college years, Frank's flesh crawled in his brother's presence. Treating him with a forced politeness, Frank stubbornly rebuffed every overture of intimacy that Gerald, newly humane and deeply guilty about his past behavior, offered up. Frank took every opportunity to be out of the house when Gerald was around, not now through fear or even hatred, but in order to avoid the state of severe physiological disorder that his brother's company provoked. And opportunities to get away presented themselves. Still inert socially, Frank nonetheless developed as an athlete. His rugged body, dogged will and aptitude for repetitive actions lent themselves to wrestling and tennis, in which he competed well, vying against other young men with a quiet aggressiveness that bordered hatred. On each defeated adversary he briefly conferred the image of his brother. He secretly began to build his body with weights.

The summer of 1968 saw Gerald off to war, with college degree in hand and a naval commission in small craft. The letters from Vietnam depicted in typically jovial style the parties, the shore leaves spent sight-seeing or shopping; they spoke of possible reassignment to Intelligence at the Pentagon, of a conceivable transfer to an embassy. Then a monstrous thing happened. The Underwoods received official notification that Gerald had been wounded in action during an engagement with a hidden Vietcong emplacement. The personal letter from Gerald's commander implied, in vague agonizing terms, that the young man was little better than dead. That winter he was wheeled down a ramp from a plane, almost unrecognizable. One arm with its beautiful hand had vanished. And they had taken care of the brain too, as the unblinking perplexity of the blue eyes made clear.

Affectless, speechless, Gerald was admitted to a veterans' hospital in New York State, where he remained, little changed, to this day.

Frank's parents grieved as though they had lost their only son. Frank went catatonic and missed a term of college. He came back in the spring and turned phlegmatically to his work. Gerald's disaster had injured him to an extent that no parent can feel and few can imagine. With the fell irony of a single stroke, fate had taken from him his primal hero, his adolescent nemesis and his phobic source of neurotic stability. The impulse to blame Gerald, once so vital to his mental circuitry, was now met with a barrage of catastrophic guilt. Frank had an open wound.

In the years to follow, two things would save Underwood, if only temporarily, from the abyss. The first was literary theory, which he began to study while still an underclassman at Yale. The brand of theory he inhaled, propounded during intense seminars by a mysterious chain-smoking European named Giorgio Mufeta, was tailor-made for Underwood's worldview and uniquely appropriate to his private compulsions. Mufeta eloquently painted an amoral, asymmetrical human world, barren of esthetic meaning and substantive only in terms of the power patterns which, like ever-changing electrical fields, played across its face. This vertiginous cosmos allowed of no solid meaning or knowledge. Beauty, wisdom and order were empty rationalizations. Love, sympathy and trust were vulgar buzzwords. Competition reigned supreme, and the best competitors were those who could understand and exploit the then-dominant patterns of power.

The literary implications of this worldview were quite simple. Literature had no implicit human meaning at all. Literature meant what people interpreted it to mean, or what people could convince others that it meant. And this cynical canon applied not only to modern literature but to the so-called classics. Plato, Dante, Shakespeare: These were no longer corpora to be studied with appreciative attention. Rather they were like empty palaces, ripe for occupation by militant forces of interpretation. The literary theorist could become a commandant, an avenger ravaging decadent forms and establishing arbitrary authority. Underwood found all this immensely enthralling. It justified and channeled his aggressions, including those once directed at Gerald's love of art.

Underwood's second savior was, paradoxically enough, Adam Snell. Early in his years at Washagon, he had begun to find in Snell the phobic scapegoat that he had lost in Gerald. Of course Adam Snell could not hold a candle to Gerald. But his age and East Coast background were right, and his behavior carried a similarly offensive message. Underwood read Snell's quiet stubbornness as pure arrogance, and Snell's reputation as a dynamic teacher and his quiet, unshakable commitment to humanistic values carried a strong echo of Gerald's sanguinity. Underwood began to see Snell as something odious, an academic fossil, a closet reactionary, a blight on the department. Maintaining polite but cool relations with Snell, Underwood began to work against him.

Imagine, then, the impact of Snell's first book! Different readers found different things in *Sovrana Sostrata;* some found little or nothing at all. But Frank Underwood, not wholly consciously, found in it something unique: the opportunity to renew, via Adam Snell, the psychic equilibrium he had lost in Gerald. The vectors were all in place: The book's abundant creativity, its thunderous *joie de vivre,* its endorsement of male-female intimacy, its encomium for the heroic individual were all reminiscent of Gerald; and the book's arrogance, its ironic mockery, its implied disapproval of the entire branch of scholarship that Frank belonged to, were like Gerald reborn.

Underwood had read *Sovrana Sostrata* in one night, word by word, in a fever of rage. Now, two years later, he remembered whole sentences that hissed at him like demons. He loathed the imperious heroine, not as an idea or character but as a physical presence. In uncontrollable fantasies he pounced on her, beat her, violated her with various garden implements, tore her limb from limb.

Sovrana Sostrata not only recentered Underwood; it also revitalized him. His hatred for Snell, though cunningly concealed, became an emotional watershed in his life, brightened the days, animated the seasons. In time emerged a kind of romantic purpose. Like Gerald, Snell was his enemy. But unlike Gerald, Snell was an enemy whom Underwood somehow felt allowed to hurt. Snell was dangerous, immoral, uncivilized. And Snell was unsuspecting and vulnerable. Underwood could injure Snell, perhaps ruin him. And for a reason as pressing as it was indefinite, Underwood had to.

The idea of doing so in a way at once simple, exciting and thematically appropriate occurred to Underwood one morning as he read his office mail. A firm called Needham advertised that it was remaindering Snell's *chef-d'oeuvre.* A phone call confirmed that Needham had what was left of the entire first run. Underwood made plans. He would own Snell's opus, his identity. Underwood deftly, cautiously established a *pied-à-terre* in Fresno. He ordered the entire stock, paid a transient to pick up the books and brought them back to Dulce in his truck. For a while they lay hidden under a tarp in the garage; but late one night, in hopes that their future discovery might further embarrass Snell, he took them to the Jungle. These were exciting days for Underwood. He felt elated, engaged, conspiratorial, dominant, profoundly justified. He felt like the hero of some primal struggle.

But now this conflict had taken astounding new turns. Alone on his porch that cloudy Saturday afternoon, sprawled in a big cane chair with iced tea and his unopened mail on the table beside him, Underwood attempted to come to terms with the unwelcome news of Snell's at least temporary survival. How sure he had been that Snell was dead! The heavy, semimushy sound of the book bag, as propelled with vehemence and freighted with the victim's own books it bore crushingly from behind against Snell's skull; the man's plummet-drop to the floor, the bloody rag doll–like limpness of him, the half-opened eyes, the breathing so depressed as to be unnoticeable. At least, thank God, he couldn't have *seen*!

Not that Underwood had expected violence. His purpose in visiting Snell's office had simply been the removal of documents. He had bagged seven copies of *Sovrana Sostrata* and was turning his attention to Snell's desk when he heard footsteps in the hall. Switching off the light, he reached for the nearest available weapon of defense, the book bag itself. A key turned in the lock and Underwood felt, suddenly but with no surprise, a punitive passion, an impulse of absolute destructiveness. As Snell walked into the darkened office, apparently to turn on his desk lamp, Underwood brought the books down upon his head with all the force and conviction of an avenging angel.

That blow, the gratifying inertness of the victim and the deep satisfaction of the final indignity visited on him had changed Underwood's life. He was blooded. Snell might have survived this encounter, but he would not survive their next.

Underwood's porch looked east toward Spine Hill, whose slopes rose massively behind Snell's house. Atop Spine Hill was a wooded park, with several areas too steep and brambly to be of much interest to joggers or strollers. There were nooks way up there, leafy dells opening like picture windows westward and directly down on the houses beneath. A now-familiar excitement came over the seated man as he proposed to himself, for that very day, a solitary walk on the heights.

In the last decade of the [19th] century wood-engraving was practically killed by the perfection attained by photographic methods of reproduction (see *Process*), the most popular of these methods entailing the use of paper heavily coated with china clay. During the century trade-printing, both in England and America, steadily improved, and the work done by William Morris at his Kelmscott Press (1891–1896), and by other amateur printers who imitated him, set a new standard of beauty of type and ornament, and of richness of general effect. On the other hand the demand for cheap reprints of famous works induced by the immense extension of the reading public was supplied by scores of pretty if flimsy editions at 1s. 6d. and 1s. and even less. The problem of how to produce books at moderate prices on good paper and well-sewn, was left for the 20th century to settle. About 1894 the number of such medium-priced books was greatly increased in England by the substitution of single-volume novels at 6s. each (subject to discount) for the three-volume editions at 31s. 6d.

—A. W. POLLARD, "Book," *Encyclopædia Britannica,*
11th edition

CHAPTER 2

IN MACHAON'S TENT

Theologians are justified in holding that the universe is too beautiful to have occurred by chance. But it is also too beautiful to have been created by any god or divine family that their hidebound brains have the power to fashion.

—Sovrana Sostrata,
"Abominable" Sermon,
delivered at Memorial Chapel,
Harvard University, December 26, 1986

No longer need I toil to please
My friends or vex my foes;
I lie in mucca-grass and ease
My thirst with froggeloes.

—Delirious raving of Adam Snell,
recorded by Vita Turk, R.N.,
Mother of God Hospital, Dulce,
May 27, 1990

To a moderately inept person, the simplest activities of life can at times become unessayable feats of virtuosity. Harold Emmons, a more than moderately inept person by his own admission, discovered this sad truth anew outside Mother of God Hospital in the early afternoon of Tuesday, May 29, during an attempt to exit his newly repaired Wagoneer while smoking a large-bore cigar and holding upright in his left hand one of his wife Frida's life-enhancing organic mangel-wurzel pies. Having planted his left foot on the parking-lot surface, he caught his right foot momentarily under the brake pedal and, suddenly staggering out of control, tossed the pie into the air on the desperate impulse that he might regain his balance and catch it again. All too soon the concoction began its descent, narrowly missing the professor's head, and, as luck would have it, landing right side up, with no other ill effects than the further compacting of its already dense contents. Less fortunate the fate of the cigar, which somehow made its way up Emmons' left sleeve, producing a burn on his forearm that Frida, reverting under stress to her native tongue, would later characterize as *furchtbar*.

Putting himself back in order, Emmons made his way up to Room 927. The policeman on duty outside Snell's room, though in the act of denying or delaying the entry of a short tweedy man with an attaché case, recognized Emmons and nodded him inside. The scene within was a most satisfactory change from the tense, crowded, gear-filled aspect the room had had during the two days of life-and-death emergency that had followed Snell's admission. The room was clear now, and sunny. The patient, his left leg in a cast, was feasting quietly on a greenish soup. Beneath the head bandages his cheeks, mummy-hollow before, had puffed out again, and there was color in them, and a hearty smile for Emmons. Seated beside the bed, and seemingly in intense conversation with the patient, was Lieutenant Pierce. Standing side by side at the window were Roy Gallard and Snell's English-department colleague Sarah Wilkins. Almost behind the door, leaning against the TV set, jean-jacketed and slick-haired and clenching in mouth an unlit pipe, was Warren Schmutzhauf.

Greetings were exuberant. Pierce went out to make phone calls, saying before he left that he would like to see Snell and Emmons alone later. Schmutzhauf took the policeman's departure as an opportunity to continue a discourse that had been interrupted before: an oration on the virtues of mucca-grass. "Fourth, and most important: its heat-retentive qualities. The chemistry guys haven't told me why yet, but m-grass holds heat, kilo for kilo, better than goose down. That's how Professor Snell, damaged and dehydrated as he was, survived four nights that went down to the upper forties. The grass was an inverted blanket. It actually—"

A bricklike woman in white hurtled into the room and stood arms akimbo by Snell's bed as though sniffing the air. "Something's up here," she muttered out of the side of her mouth, hastily casting about and fixing on Mrs. Emmons' pie. She glared at Emmons. "What's this piece of crap?" Her powerful hands swooped and struck. Before anyone could stop her, she was out the door with it.

Snell giggled. "I'm not supposed to be on solids yet. Don't worry about Vita. She'll store it with some other things that came in. They want to make sure I don't get poisoned here."

"Vita Turk thinks she saved Adam's life," said Sarah.

"That makes two of us," added Schmutzhauf.

"You're forgetting Doppler," put in Emmons.

Snell asked after his dog, and Emmons was happy to report the animal in good condition, kenneled with Emmons' golden retriever Angus and warmly cosseted by Frida and the boys. Similar questions and answers, concerning Snell's house, office and correspondence, followed. It was the first time since the disappearance that Snell and Emmons had conversed intelligibly. "And the books in the Jungle?"

Emmons glanced at Roy, who nodded and looked back at Snell. "The grounds crew picked them up yesterday and took them to the dump. They were spoiled beyond repair."

Snell smiled ruefully.

The guard looked in. "That reporter outside just wanted me to say that he was leaving town, and if you didn't want to be in the national news that was no skin off his back."

"Thanks for the message," said Snell.

"Why don't you want to be in the national news?" asked Schmutzhauf, as though in disbelief.

Snell smiled at him. "We're trying to stay out of the news altogether. We don't want to tip our hand. We know more, I mean circumstantially, about the attacker than it's in our interest to show at present."

"Be that as it may," Schmutzhauf persisted, "mightn't some big publisher hear about you and get interested?"

Snell looked vaguely stricken. "I wouldn't want to get published that way."

Still the fading violet, thought Emmons, his arm throbbing with pain. Sparing the details, he brought Adam concisely up to date on the substance of Friday's post-tenure-review meeting, which had, in spite of vigorous opposition from Quintus Adler, Edward Marlin and Emmons himself, concluded in an overwhelming vote for censure. Sarah seemed about to cry, and Snell's head drooped. "Well, if they don't want me here, I suppose——"

"Don't worry," said Emmons. "Quintus is writing a letter."

Snell was incredulous. "A letter? To whom? Marshall? How could a letter——"

"Quintus writes good letters," was all Emmons could say. He was telling Snell to be patient when Pierce reappeared, looking a bit worn, and Roy, Sarah and Schmutzhauf took their leave. The lieutenant seated himself to the right of Snell's bed, Emmons to the left. "Any news, Lieutenant?" asked Emmons.

Pierce grinned at him across the bed. "Call me Andy." He looked back at Snell. "No—no news; that is, unless you want to consider the record recovery of this patient here news. Our Libricide looks to have gotten clean away this time. I'll level with you: no smoking gun, no prints, no clues. And Adam's memory, which snapped back clear as crystal with his morning coffee today, hasn't fished up a scrap of evidence against anybody. By the way, Adam, why didn't you take your car or Doppler to your office that night?"

Snell thought for a moment. "Safety precautions. I was already worried about my security at the house and wanted it to look lived-in as much as possible. For the same reason it made sense to leave Doppler as watchdog."

Emmons asked Snell if he had suspected anyone of the book buyout before the attack.

Snell shut his eyes, as though checking his memory again. "No. I was mystified. I not only didn't have a suspect, but I couldn't think of a motive. It's not that I considered myself all that likable. Quite the contrary. Here I was, obscure, poor, unpopular in my department, and on top of it all, an embarrassing failure as a writer. No, Hal, don't protest; this is all for the sake of argument. Why should anyone want to injure or diminish me when I had already more or less obliterated myself as a professional? How can you decrease a zero? I was so much at a loss for reasons that I began to imagine it was some sort of punishment, and that I might well deserve it."

"We know," said Pierce. "It was in your journal. And in a crazy way you were close to being right."

"Right?" Snell reddened.

Pierce patted him on the shoulder. "Not that I think you deserved it. But it's just possible that somebody who had a grudge against you, somebody who was p-o'ed by your writing, somebody on top of this psychotic and violent, might have felt that trashing your book was some form of heroic stunt or sweet revenge."

"And killing me too?"

"He sure didn't mean to kill you when he came to your office Tuesday night. How could he have known you were coming?"

"He couldn't have," said Snell. "I never used to work there at night. I went down there only because of a sudden impulse to get the backup disk for my new book and bring it home for safekeeping. Say, I hadn't—"

The phone rang and Pierce pounced on it. "No, Professor Snell is busy right now. . . . He's ill right now, I mean, recovering. . . . Is this really important? All right." He jotted down a number, said "Uh-huh" instead of good-bye, hung up the phone and looked thoughtfully at Snell. "So where does that leave us, Adam?"

"I don't know what you mean."

"I mean, what kind of guy is your assailant? What will he do next?"

Emmons shrugged. "How can we tell?"

The lieutenant turned to him. "Maybe we can't. But we've got to try. Maybe this guy was so frightened by what he did that he'll never come near you again. But how he behaved *after* hitting you doesn't suggest that kind of fear. Quite the contrary. Unless I miss my guess, the kind of louse who would do these weird things would feel righteous, even catharted, about having done them. It would give him some kind of sick thrill, some kind of kinky proof of his masculinity."

Snell grimaced. "But now that's going to be taken away."

The policeman's voice for the first time conveyed anxiety. "That's it. Now his thrill's been taken away again. Adam's alive to speak freely and maybe write more books. On top of that we haven't blown Libricide's cover, and he'll know that soon enough. We'd be fools to trust that he won't go out and try to zap Adam again."

Emmons jumped up. Pierce looked up at him, holding out open hands as though to prove himself weaponless. "Look. I don't tell psychopaths how to behave. But thank God I know how they behave. And one thing about Libricide's behavior works *for* us. Crazy as this dude may be, I don't think Adam has to fear the toughest-to-prevent kind of violence: the all-out do-or-die attack."

"Why not?" Snell and Emmons asked together.

"Because Libricide is behaving like somebody who wants to guard his own flanks. He wants to have his cake and eat it, to kill you without going to jail for it. Now this cuts down his options. Again, I might be wrong, but up to this point he's looking something like your typical serial killer: cautious, self-righteous, violent to others but real keen about his own survival. He's not about to try to take you out openly—no, please Adam, let me just finish this line of thought— when you compare him to serial killers, you see that things really aren't so easy for Libricide. Serial killers have the advantage of never having to strike the same victim twice. They strike by surprise at the soft underbelly of society, and society has such a big fat underbelly that they can more or less pick their shots. Libricide knows that we're all teamed up in your defense, and knowing that cuts his options even more. Imagine, Adam, trying to murder somebody in Dulce—somebody who knows you're trying—without getting wounded or being observed or leaving any evidence or causing suspicion of any kind. It's not easy. Get the point of all this? Libricide's need to save his own skin is a plus for you."

Snell grimaced. "And the investigation?"

"The investigation goes into Plan B. We're going to stop hunting evidence and start snooping around for possible assailants. Let's start right now. Everything points to this dude knowing you and living in Dulce. Now he's likely to have some kind of history of mental trouble and/or odd behavior—not necessarily violent, but at least kooky enough to attract attention. On top of this he has to know, or think he knows, something about literature. And to have dragged or carried you all that way and gotten you over the Jungle fence, he's got to be very strong. How many can you think of who fit that description?"

Over the next few minutes Snell and Emmons generated a surprisingly large list. Professors from three or four other literature departments, a notable eccentric from Philosophy, five active grad students and two inactive ones, a few local free-lancers and literary loners. From the English department only Fulke Ashenham, the professional-wrestler-turned-new-historicist, and Abel Wenderson, a hulking recluse well known for his conversations with telephone poles, seemed to meet Pierce's criteria.

Snell asked if Pierce was going to begin questioning them.

"Not at first. First off, we're going to find out something about each of them. There's always the off chance that police or hospital records will turn something up. Questioning them, especially the sort of scattershot questioning we'd have to do before making an arrest, would only clue in the real offender and drive him into deeper cover."

"What if you don't come up with anything?" asked Emmons.

"My guess is that even if we don't, Libricide will tip his hand to us. We're now alert to him, almost in touch with his motives. When he moves again, we'll nail him." Pierce looked at his watch. "Drat. I'm late for a trial. Call you tomorrow, Adam. Bye, Hal."

A moment later his head stuck back in the door. "Oh by the way, Adam, you got a long-distance call. Miss Nathan from New York. See the number there?"

Pierce's head was replaced, as if magically, by the great bearded Karl Marxish visage of Dr. Ethan Maynard, who mouthed broadly, "What's with the beet pie?"

"It's called a mangel-wurzel pie," put in Emmons. "One of my wife's family recipes."

"But I thought only animals ate mangel-wurzel."

"Not according to my wife's family."[21]

The big doctor ambled in, took a few readings and made Snell look cross-eyed at his stethoscope. "Well, Adam, if you have a fancy for exotic vegetable pies, you may indulge it now. You're hereby back on solids."

Snell expressed the desire to get to work. "One of my students is going to find a laptop computer for me and put a few of my files on it. OK for him to bring it in tomorrow? You see, there's this new book—"

"Better aim for Thursday," the doctor interrupted. "Two or three of your counts are still too low for real exertion. Try some clean living first. And maybe an afternoon nap right now."

That was Emmons' cue to leave. On his way out, he reminded his friend to dial the New York number, but Snell's face, now tired and drawn, did not suggest that he would be making any long-distance calls in the near future. Emmons paused in the doorway, marveling at Snell's persistence. Who but the unflappable Snell, after having tempted fate with one improbable literary venture, would so enthusiastically turn to another? Who but Snell would respond to the revelation of his own mortal peril wth a request for a laptop? Emmons' arm stung where he'd burned it. He waved good-bye bemusedly and headed down the hall in the wrong direction.

---

[21]Mangel-wurzel (*Beta vulgaris,* Eng. mangold), a variety of common beet grown primarily for fodder. Human consumption of the vegetable is rare and the existence of a "life-enhancing organic mangel-wurzel pie" is completely undocumented. Possibly Mrs. Emmons' German forebears at some point acquired the Alsatian fondness for vegetable pies and, since the beet might reasonably figure in such a confection, Professor Emmons saw fit to bestow the name "mangel-wurzel" upon it. Possibly, on the other hand, the author is confusing us for some unspecified reason of his own. Readers should exercise caution, particularly with regard to authorial suggestions regarding their possible future cuisine. As Rabelais—*God here comes Tusker and no place to hide. I'm trapped on the page! Good Ulster bullhound, good Tusker, good boy. Say, he's wagging his tail. I think he likes me! Ya-a-a-a-a-a-a* . . . [Sounds of canine chewing and slobbering.]

Bookselling. The trade in books is of a very ancient date. The early poets and orators recited their effusions in public to induce their hearers to possess written copies of their poems or orations. Frequently they were taken down *viva voce*, and transcripts sold to such as were wealthy enough to purchase. In the book of Jeremiah the prophet is represented as dictating to Baruch the scribe, who, when questioned, described the mode in which his book was written. These scribes were, in fact, the earliest booksellers, and supplied copies as they were demanded. Aristotle, we are told, possessed a somewhat extensive library; and Plato is recorded to have paid the large sum of one hundred minae for three small treatises of Philolaus the Pythagorean.

—ANONYMOUS, "Bookselling," *Encyclopædia Britannica,*
11th edition

CHAPTER 3

FROM SNELL'S JOURNAL FOR
ON WONDERMENT

From time to time over the years, bands of philosophic pirates and their yea-sayers, probably from sheer love of power or gain, have advanced the argument that language does not describe but rather "creates" reality, and that there is no reality beyond language. But a speaker's ability to feel emotion and, via language, conceive that same emotion in listeners, gives this flimsy slander the lie. Experience is not created by language; rather, it *descends into* language and is reborn from it.

—SOVRANA SOSTRATA,
Gesta

June 4, 1990. Monday.
This old legal pad, brought here by Roy, will have to serve till I get set up again. Feel stronger today, resting in hospital after a three-day/four-night junket on the ground in Pisham Homestead, all expenses paid, courtesy of Unknown Admirer, complete with fractured skull, pneumonia and broken leg (broken during rescue), dinners not included. It's an ill wind, etc., for my misfortune's brought me four new friends:

Andy Pierce of Homicide, great guy, very gentle, carries enormous handgun because, as he puts it, "they make more noise." I tell him he reminds me of a scholar and he answers that every good homicide detective has to be a kind of backward historian, analyzing what's present and creating a past for it.

Ethan Maynard, internist here at Mother of God, on duty at arrival of mangled scarecrow, set my leg, shaved my head, looked in (Vita tells me) every three hours, sometimes half asleep, till Sunday morning.

Vita Turk, R.N., human cannonball, little dynamo with brawny arms who lifts me out of the bed when it's time to change the sheets, says she carries a gun and if she sees Libricide will shoot him in the right places, which she enumerates graphically and in parochial-school Latin.

Fourth, and most unusual of all, Warren Schmutzhauf, self-proclaimed "father of mucca-grass." Came early this A.M., lectured me endlessly on this and that, apparently trying to cheer me up. A kind of wild genius, who asserts that "scientific method," if it exists at all, is the sum total of everything one has heard, read, thought, dreamt, made love to, hated and eaten.

Saw them all last Tuesday, plus Hal, Roy and Sarah, a kind of homecoming.

God knows I've got to have been through the worst, but Pierce says there's more to come: I must be prepared for another sneak attack. But how do you get prepared? He could walk in right now and finish me with a pillow.

Shit! The door just burst open, and so help me I almost let go in my pants, but it was only Vita, with a piece of Frida Emmons' delectable beet-potato-onion pie. That and the codeine make me feel euphoric. Give me a day or two and I'll lick the world.

Must have gone to sleep. 8 P.M. now and very quiet. No trace in my mind of those four nights and three days, annihilated time, perfectly blotted out. Yet now I *do* remember something: I dreamt once or twice about Sovrana, about her talking lots of nonsense to me and then grandly announcing that she was about to die. What a posturer—anything for a rise! Granted, when I woke up at last, there she was, or at least her physical printed avatar, rotting in a white blob by my side.

Strange, for the first time in years I feel that that herculean bed warmer (see, I can even insult her!) is out of my system. Did Libricide really kill her, as he seems to have wished? If so, maybe he did me a favor.

June 5, 1990. Tuesday.

10:40 A.M. and after a double espresso lovingly brought in by Sarah (she jogged with it to keep it from getting cold) I feel incredibly alert. Have I ever been this alert before? Maybe the circuitry in my brain suffered catastrophic damage, and I'm now having a flash of clarity before total burnout.

I felt so good this morning that I turned down Vita's codeine and took a couple of aspirin instead.

Sarah had to leave for class. Strange lady. Confucius would have referred glowingly to her *wen,* her pattern of graces, her thoughtfulness, eloquence, integrity, all enhanced, as though physically imaged, by face and body. When in parting she leans over the bed, straight blond hair momentarily surrounding my eyes like a thatched roof, and solemnly touches my lips with hers, I feel a monstrous urge to pull her unto me and down loinward through warm folds of linen. But her arms, back, even lips don't speak that language; they're tense, disembodied; even her eyes, keen and blue, seem to want to look *through* the person to the very soul rather than appreciating the inferior but pleasant complement of flesh. And she worries! My mishap's put her through an orgy of fretting, but that's nothing new; she's always been uptight about her own life or the world's woes. Even her book on the environment, excellent as it may be, is less the craft of reason than a feat of creative worrying.

And now she's got reason to worry! Thanks to the ever-loving Gazza, Sarah's gotten denied tenure, on the grounds that her book manuscript isn't "professional" literary scholarship. Odd how the obscurantist and totally unliterary discourse Gazza & Co are spewing forth is "professional," while Sarah's work on environmental rhetoric isn't. Odd that the only socially significant publication in the whole department is the one that gets the shaft.

Apparently I—the department being too zealous in the pursuit of its duties to wait for news of my demise—got shafted too, with only Hal and Quintus (Marlin wasn't allowed to vote) against my censure, and Web Hollins, as usual, abstaining. I can appeal of course, but Thor Marshall likes denying appeals better than Buffalo Bill liked tossing lariats. They'll ride me out on a rail if they can, and Gazza wants to replace me with that egregious theoretical camp-follower, Butzi Siskin. Why do things always turn out the way Sovrana says they will?

I suppose I can sell the house, live cheap in Mexico while finishing *On Wonderment* (that is, if I live at all), and then look for another job. I suppose I can also take the bastards to court. Be worth it to see Gazza trying literary theory out on a jury of her peers. I wonder how the jury will take to Floconne de Mais's theory (passionately endorsed by Glanda) that there's no such thing as justice, that good and evil and culture in general are just a "text" generated by the powerful?

Schmutzhauf in again early this morning, while Vita was tidying up. Says he's taking me under his wing and when he hits it big (whatever that means) he'll "fix things up for me." I told him things about Gazza and the literary theorists that nearly blew his mind. "Why, man," he bellowed, "it's medieval science all over again! *Step one,* you sneak up on a phenomenon. *Step two,* you zap it with your patented catchall theory. *Step three, Conclusum est!* you announce another victory over Nature! Next patient, please, and all that. Real successful method; kept Europe asleep for a thousand years. Honest, Adam, is that all they're about?"

I told him that theoretical analyses were often quite subtle, that some theorists showed impressive ingenuity and that, in many if not all cases, theoretical models were based on global interpretations of history. "Medieval, medieval and *more* medieval!" he volleyed out. "What'll you tell me next, that they all worship a pigeon?"

At that point Vita, who'd been lurking out in the hall, came in and clobbered him with a pillow.

Looked out the window this afternoon and saw Hal pausing in the courtyard, in running shorts, with his golden retriever and Doppler on leashes. I couldn't help calling Doppler's name, and he went wild, dragging man and dog all over the place.

When the Alexandrian library was founded about 300 B.C., various expedients were resorted to for the purpose of procuring books, and this appears to have stimulated the energies of the Athenian booksellers, who were termed *biblion kapeloi*. In Rome, towards the end of the republic, it became the fashion to have a library as part of the household furniture; and the booksellers, *librarii* (Cic. *D. Leg.* iii. 20) or *bibliopolae* (Martial iv. 71, xiii. 3), carried on a flourishing trade. Their shops (*taberna librarii*, Cicero, *Phil.* ii. 9) were chiefly in the Argiletum, and in the Vicus Sandalarius. On the door, or on the side posts, was a list of the books on sale; and Martial (i. 118), who mentions this also, says that a copy of his First Book of Epigrams might be purchased for five denarii. In the time of Augustus the great booksellers were the Sosii. According to Justinian (ii. I. 33), a law was passed securing to the scribes the property in the materials used; and in this may, perhaps, be traced the first germ of the modern law of copyright.

—ANONYMOUS, "Bookselling," *Encyclopædia Britannica,* 11th edition

CHAPTER 4

FOUR MEMORABLE PERFORMANCES

The LORD showed favour to Sarah, as he had promised, and made good what he had said about her. She conceived and bore a son to Abraham for his old age, at the time which God had appointed. The son whom Sarah bore to him, Abraham named Isaac [that is, *"he laughed"*]. When Isaac was eight days old Abraham circumcised him, as God had commanded. Abraham was a hundred years old when his son Isaac was born. Sarah said, "God has given me good reason to laugh, and everybody who hears this will laugh with me."

—New English Bible,
Genesis 21:1–6

1. A SHOCK TO THE MEDICAL WORLD

Overheard on June 7, 1990, in the canteen of the Veterans Administration Hospital in Batistoni, New York, where Gerald Underwood has been a patient for more than twenty years. The speakers are Waltraut Himmelfarb, a volunteer patient's companion, and Dr. Bernard O'Shea, physician in charge of Ward B.

O'SHEA: Thanks for waiting, Waltraut. I needed Ensign Underwood's file and this pad to take it all down on.

HIMMELFARB: Diss iss a vunderful sink, Doctor.

O'SHEA: You say it happened today.

HIMMELFARB: Diss very mornink, Doctor. I veeled heem oudt on de terrace, ass I alvays do venn de vetter iss gut. Every day, venn de vetter iss gut, I veel heem oudt, ver he faces de Hudson Wiffer andt de sun iss on him, andt myself I sit on de etch off a pik flowerpot, andt I read to him on de Piple.

O'SHEA: That's here in the file, Waltraut. Ensign Underwood's pulse rate improves when he's being read to.

HIMMELFARB: Diss happen many years now, Doctor. I haff read to heem *five years*. But today iss different. In five years vee go true de whole Piple *sree times,* andt today vee get pack to de stardt. Today I reed heem apoudt Gott, who made de whole vorlt, andt apoudt Adam andt Eefe, andt apoudt Noah, knock voot! who surfifed de flutt, andt apoudt old Apraham. Andt Apraham und Sarah, his lawful vife, day haff no kids, andt day gettink oldt, andt Apraham, you know, mess aroundt a liddle vid de floosies. But Gott said to Sarah, You vill haff a son, and Sarah laugh und say, Who me, an oldt lady? I *amp not apel* to haff a child. But Gott say, Just you vait, you see who laugh last—

O'SHEA: Waltraut—

HIMMELFARB: I know, I'mpe gettink der! I wememper every momendt of diss! Well I just get to de poindt ver Sarah hass her son Isaac, und she says she is goink to laugh, andt I look up, andt de ensign *iss lookink at me*!

O'SHEA: But doesn't he always look—

HIMMELFARB: No, not like dat, not wid de empty eyes. He looks at me vid *pik peautiful plue eyes,* all avake like a child's, andt he puts his handt on mine as I holdt de pook, andt—

O'SHEA: *He moved?*

HIMMELFARB: Den I stardt to cry, Doctor. I cry for joy, like I'mpe cryink now. Andt he squeezes my handt, andt he says—

O'SHEA: *He spoke?*

HIMMELFARB: He visper, "Waltraut, read dat pardt again." Andt he iss cryink too.

2. HARPER BRILLIANT AT AMAGUCCI'S

From across the room, they might have been playing bridge, but closer up, if you could have edged between the tightly packed tables at Amagucci's, you would have seen the wineglasses and prosciutto—fresh fig appetizers on the table, seen that the cards the four had stacked in from of them were scrawled with book titles. Harper, looking unprintably attractive in an off-white silk blouse and silver necklace, sat across from Sig Bazoom, her editorial director, a small, totally bald man with roundish features, dressed in a white linen suit with yellow shirt and purple bow tie. The company was completed by Zaz Caldecutt and Barona Rhine, two very fashionably attired young women who were, like Harper, editors for Wolper McNab. Two bottles of Orvieto Classico stood open on the table. The mood was cautiously festive.

Bazoom, who had listened in turn to reports from his three subordinates, took a sip of wine, straightened his tie, then brushed his pile of cards aside with the air of a man completing a task. "Thanks, ladies. That kind of rounds it out for spring '91. Twenty-one new titles, and we've got it all: murder, incest, wellness, espionage, child rearing, homespun humor, erotic gossip, come on, come on, help me—"

"Melon therapy," said Harper.

"Another, even better, baseball story," said Barona.

"Sing Along with Inner Child," said Zaz.

"All right, all right," continued Sig, growing more enthusiastic. "Melon therapy, another even better baseball story, little girls with depressed fathers, Sing Along with Inner Child, and Whales I Have Known. Is that everything? Could we ask for anything more?"

"It's a lively list, Sig," said Harper, and added meaningfully, "much livelier than this fall's."

Bazoom reddened from neck to scalp. "So what's with this fall? It's sick or something? It's got problems or something?" Sig was waving his hands in the air, trying to flap her.

Harper stayed calm, at least on the surface. "Sig, the *problem* is that it has no problems. It's simply *tame,* Sig. Sound minds and bodies, the great outdoors, seven novels about subtle family interactions, three about women's inner voices, two of authentic ethnic testimony. It's a respectable list, but *tame.*"

Sig's face fell. "Compared with Hammond and Fig?" he asked meekly.

Harper nodded. "H and F's fall list is very strong. Remember? They bid big on Lance Felladay and Zgooi Zomonga, and so they got the two hottest first novels of the year."

Sig shakily adjusted his tie. "So what do we do now, hide out in the Poconos?"

All eyes were on her now. Hair needed a brief shake. Now for the bombshell. "Not necessarily. We hit them with Adam Snell. His book's a knockout. He'll make Felladay look like Roger Rabbit."

Barona seemed impressed. "But how can you possibly get it on the fall list?"

"I've called Penrose Press. They'll give us everything for a song. All we do is change the imprint. We can get Ron to do a fast workup for the CAB in Denver next week, and if I phone today we can even get them to change the catalog."

Sig, whose face had been going through a symphony of contortions, now looked as though he had just found a crack in the world. "You mean you want to *change the list?*"

Harper was conciliatory. "Not change what's there, Sig, just add onto it."

"How big a run?" asked Zaz.

Harper made an upside-down smile. "Ten thousand, maybe, seventy-five hundred, nothing colossal. The size of the run isn't as important as the effect on our list. And we've very little to lose. *Sovrana Sostrata*'s a well-written book. It'll raise the list a notch and shake a gauntlet at Hammond and Fig, and then it's bye-bye, wait till spring."

Harper watched Sig's face move through two more shades of uncertainty. Zaz and Barona were spoken for, having been primed at the expense of a magnum of overpriced chardonnay at Caputi's the night before. Though not quite so dazzled by *Sovrana Sostrata* as she, they nonetheless saw it as a bold venture that might just catch fire.

Sig took a long pull on his wine and glanced timidly around the table. "So what's the consensus?"

Zaz and Barona made enthusiastic faces as Harper crouched to pounce. "The ayes have it, Sig. All we need is your promotional genius to sail it past Igor."

Sig now relaxed and brightened. "No problem there. He's been on my back about the fall list too."

But as Sig and Harper left Amagucci's after lunch, he let on that he did not see much in Snell's book. "Too old-fashioned, Harper. Too black-and-white. What's the use of writing like Hardy or Lawrence in 1990? But never mind, dearie. I respect your savvy. You haven't bombed yet, and here's hoping it works this time too."

Harper put on a kindly smile, desperately trying to conceal the joy that had welled up in her. Now she had work to do. She must keep trying to reach Snell. What was the man doing in a hospital? She must

get a hold of Ron and write catalog copy and firm things up with
Penrose Press and do in less than two days things that normally take
weeks. And she must do it all in time to meet Harry at three o'clock
Friday afternoon for a weekend on the Vineyard.

3. UNDERWOOD IMPROVES AT HARROLTON

One of Frank Underwood's many well-kept secrets, at least from the
always curious and often envious ears of his colleagues at Washagon,
was the Harrolton ranch. Ranch it had never been, at least in living
memory, but Frank's dad had called it a ranch when, twenty-five
years ago, he had picked up the little old house, with its 160 acres of
rolling hills on the French River—ostensibly as an investment but
really more in hopes of enjoying a second adolescence with his two
teenage boys. Of course these hopes were doomed, first by the boys'
incomprehensibly troublous attitudes toward each other, and then,
tragically, by Gerald's injury and Frank's concomitant sullen retreat
from the family hearth. Yet Frank and his parents remained politely
in touch with each other, and as Mr. and Mrs. Underwood had not
been west in years, Frank was the only one to visit and care for the
property.

The ranch had a desolate beauty. Three miles of single-lane
graded road down from the state road and then nearly half a mile of
jeep trail (Frank garaged an old Blazer in Janeville) led up to the gray
high-ceilinged Victorian that sat beneath two outsized Jeffrey pines,
commanding a view of the river and semiwooded hills whose pano-
rama did not yield another human dwelling. Couched on its shaded
hilltop, in its almost magically year-worn Victorian grace, cruising
time-wise through its summer ocean of cloudless, careless northern
California days, the house palpably conveyed a kind of wisdom, a
withdrawal from harried human affairs into an at once more primitive and reasonable world. How an overworked publisher like
Harper, or a dedicated writer like Snell, would have loved it! Yet
Underwood, immured as he was in his own private castle of anger,
felt no such pleasure. The architecture, with its intimations of childhood ghost stories, vaguely frightened him, and he could not bear the
long silences. He came there as a kind of caretaker twice a year,
seldom staying for more than a few days.

But this summer brought new uses for house and land. Early in

June, days after learning of Snell's recovery, Underwood had shut up his Dulce home and driven, via Janeville (where he made several purchases) to the Harrolton ranch. There he spent a day in agitated preparation, marking, measuring and partly clearing a brushy area in the bone-dry valley to the south of the house. By evening he was so violently excited that only sleeping pills could buy him any rest. Next morning, when just past dawn he stepped out on the porch to survey the completed prospect, his equipment had changed from machete and shears to a rather battered-looking Remington .22-250 rifle, "varmint" model, fitted with a new 3X9-power scope.

Underwood looked down the hillside at a tribute to his own meticulousness, precision and determination: a landscape facsimile of the 180-yard shot which, fired some bright day in late summer or early fall from his chosen hiding place on Spine Hill in Dulce, would instantly exterminate Adam Snell. He held in his hands one of the most accurate long-range weapons available. Now his job was to calibrate the scope to the distance and perfect his own technique.

He donned a pair of earmuffs and steadied himself against a porch column. The valley began to resound with the sonic snaps of high-velocity ammunition.

A day of work and he was satisfied with his progress. The scope was adequately adjusted, and he was frequently hitting targets smaller than a human body at 180 yards. But frequently wasn't good enough, and stationary targets only approximated the challenge offered by a living being. He needed days, weeks more work. He must live with the gun until it became an extension of his own senses.

Yet the very next day saw a horrifying setback. A letter arrived from home. Gerald had moved, Gerald had spoken. His parents had driven to the hospital, and they had seen Gerald, and he had recognized them. His parents' exuberance and the potential reemergence of a newly articulate and sanctified Gerald threw Underwood into depression. He ate little, lay sleepless in bed, spent hours in the smothering heat of the faded living room listening to endless replays of country music on his CD player.

Days passed and the depression slowly lifted. The gross break in the psychotic armor had been recemented. Talking or silent, Gerald was a corpse to Frank, a closed case. The enemy, now somehow even more furiously hated, remained Snell. Target practice began again with a vengeance.

4. GAZZA ROASTED AT MAMMAL

Mammal Hall, which houses the administrative offices of the University of Washagon, is at once the oldest public building on campus and the only carryover from the now-defunct Washagon Academy of Veterinary Science, which it once contained in entirety. The building takes its name not from this historical connection but rather, more indirectly, from the remarkably lifelike animal sculptures decorating its otherwise neoclassical façade. The work of self-taught Washagon pioneer-cum-artist Hubert Tatnall, these granite heads portray the major mammals, both wild and domestic, of the Wishbone Valley in the middle of the nineteenth century. Arrayed above the Ionic columns of the portico, in heroic scale and as though thrust forth from the living rock, are the fox, the bear, the cougar, the cow, the pig, the deer, the elk, the beaver, the raccoon, the wolf and, in the center, Tatnall's acknowledged masterpiece, the horse.

It was right under this equine bust that Glanda Gazza, moving this Thursday afternoon with something less than a full head of steam, entered Mammal on her way to Thor Marshall's office, which was located on the upper floor directly to the rear. Gazza little relished the prospect of the meeting to come. She had been summoned by Thor to give a briefing, on the Snell case, no less, to that egregious populist and crank, Washagon chancellor of higher education Paul Edson. Nodding to Clorene, who grimaced knowingly, Gazza entered the broad-windowed sanctum sanctorum to find Marshall in an uncomfortable posture at his big desk, while a few feet to the left stood Edson, a sixtyish white-haired man of middle height and athletic build. Both men seemed frozen in the act of speech.

"Well, we'll get back to this, Paul," said Marshall awkwardly, as both turned to her.

"I believe we've already met, Professor Gazza," said Edson, shaking hands. They sat down. Across the desk from her, Marshall's broad face was dark against the bright windows, while Edson's face to the left, with its intense brown eyes, was focussed sharply in the afternoon light.

Edson pulled a thickish letter out of his breast pocket. "Professor Gazza, I have here a letter from one of your colleagues which avers in some detail that Professor Adam Snell is being discriminated against and, to some extent, persecuted, by members of your department, and with your knowledge and consent."

Gazza heard the inner trumpet and went into battle mode. "Who wrote—I mean, who could possibly say such a thing?"

Edson took the letter out of its envelope. "There's no reason to maintain confidentiality here. The writer's name is Quintus Adler, full professor, apparently a well-known Shakespearean." He whipped out a pair of tiny reading glasses. "Says here he made this allegation at a department meeting and so has no doubts that you're aware of his sentiments. Is that right?"

Small blunder necessitates tactical retreat. "Yes," parried Gazza, "I do remember now. But it was such a ridiculous accusation that I dismissed it out of hand."

Edson was persistent. "Wasn't it then seconded by Professor Edward Marlin?"

Gazza fought back. "In fact I think it was, but neither Adler nor Marlin knew what he was talking about. Both of them are mired up in a legalistic, hierarchical, thoroughly outdated way of looking at things. Our departmental review of Snell's work, if I may speak confidentially to you, was in the process of evolving a similar evaluation of him. We were deciding, in effect, that Snell's novel, which is his only major publication since promotion with tenure, did not measure up to departmental standards precisely for this reason. Adler and Marlin were only trying to defend the superannuated set of values they share with Snell."

Edson looked gently curious. "But aren't Adler and Marlin two of the most widely respected scholars on your campus?"

"That depends," answered Gazza, "on who's doing the respecting. They won attention doing traditional things. Now scholarship has simply passed them by."

Edson took off his glasses, pulled out a handkerchief and began to polish them with it, looking down at them as he spoke. "I have a suggestion for you, Professor Gazza, and also a question. My suggestion, first of all, is that you bend over backward being fair to Adam Snell. I don't know him or his book, but he's got rights like anyone else, and one of those rights is to publish anything that his fancy or conscience dictates. He's got tenure too, which means that, in recognition of what I assume to be substantial professional achievement, the university has granted him the freedom to publish his views without fearing for his job. We may not like what he writes or find it professionally respectable. On the basis of our opinions we may deny him promotion or salary increases. But that doesn't mean that we can revoke his tenure or apply unnaturally strict review standards to him and him alone. Is that fairly clear?"

Gazza struggled to restrain her fury. "Chancellor, are you trying to influence a departmental review?"

Edson looked over at Marshall, whose face remained darkly unreadable against the windows, then looked back at Gazza and smiled. "Let's say I'm trying to save this campus from legal embarrassment. Professor Snell's tenure here is guaranteed by your university constitution. Should this guarantee be violated in letter or in spirit, I could not in good conscience discourage him from defending himself in court." The chancellor then stretched like some house cat that had found an ideally comfortable place to lie down. "So much for my suggestion. Now for my question. You say that Snell's ideas and methods, and those of these two other professors, are outdated, and that yours aren't. What makes you so sure of that?"

"Where have you been for the last fifteen years?" Gazza boldly shot back at him. "Haven't you kept track of departmental demographics? Why, now we've got more theorists and theory-related scholars in our English department than any other kind."

Edson smiled again. "That goes without saying. But what are these scholars up to? How come a literary theorist has never won a teaching award on this campus? How come literary theory has no operative doctrine of education? How come, when physicists and chemists and sociologists and historians command big audiences on the lecture circuit, not a single literary theorist—correct me if I'm wrong—is ever asked to address a public audience?"

Gazza looked to Marshall for support, but his face remained dark and impassive. The rage welled up in her again, but she held it back. "You're wrong on two counts. First, public recognition has never, mark you, *never* been a dependable gauge of successful research. I can assure you that many literary theorists see their research as laying the groundwork for revolutionary social change. Second, you're passing judgment on us too soon. We're still in a period of transition. There's always confusion at the onset of a new order. And anyway, where does a chancellor of higher education get off trying to influence the direction of free research?"

The chancellor glanced at Marshall again, like some pitcher holding a runner at first, and then turned fully toward Gazza. "I'm responsible to the governor and the legislature for maintaining the quality of education on all our campuses, so whether teachers teach well or badly means a lot to me. More generally, my mission is to encourage a healthy relationship between learning in general and society at large. Large-scale academic movements like literary theory are bound to have an impact on this relationship." He turned slightly and motioned at the window. "Look out at society, Professor. We're facing environmental emergency and massive poverty and all sorts of crime. Our products are no longer attracting world attention, and to make things worse our corporations, mad for quarterly bottom-line profits, are cutting research-and-development budgets to the bone. If evolutionary success lies in adaptation and development, then we have apparently bought out of evolutionary success. To a large extent I see these selfish and panicky attitudes mirrored in individuals, even college students. How does literary theory speak to these problems? What values does it recommend to students and scholars?"

Gazza was too furious to speak.

"Let me answer for you, Professor. Literary theory, at least as Adler's letter describes it, not only has no antidote for these public disorders but would seem in its lack of values—its relativism and materialism—actually to encourage them. My guess is that its manifest lack of social relevance will make your field at best a passing vogue, at worst a tragic institutional blunder."

"Values, relevance, tragic," fumed Gazza. "What a taste you've got for art deco words!"

Marshall suddenly and hoarsely broke his silence. "I must agree with Paul that the words he uses remain meaningful, um, especially in terms of public policy. I'm so thoroughly convinced by what Paul's said that I'm going to write a memo to you and your colleagues suggesting that it might benefit all if you turned your attention to some of the issues he's raised."

Gazza fixed a death-dealing stare on him. *The faithless bastard! He's gone over. And only two weeks since the fat ass was lolling in my bed!* She turned the Gorgon beams on Edson. Why beat around the bush? "I assume then that you're not happy with the direction our department has been taking."

"Quite candidly, Professor, I'm appalled." Edson was folding up the Adler letter and putting it back in its envelope. "I've got to be back in Arcadia by five. Thor, if we could take a few minutes to discuss . . ."

They're kicking me out of the room! Gazza rose, glared balefully at each of her antagonists, turned with a lethal swing of her shoulder bag, burned her way through the outer office and headed across campus in a hormonal intoxication of rage. *The dirty masturbators! That self-righteous simplistic manipulating demagogue Edson! He's out to muzzle academic freedom! That cringing double-dealing mealy-mouthed snake Marshall! He sold me out to get the presidency!*

Arriving at the English-department office, she shouldered past two secretaries who wanted to speak to her, slammed her office door, savagely smashed her heavy bag against the books that lined her wall and, as books cascaded every which way to the floor, sat down and sprawled across her desk, sobbing heavily.

The fuckers have taken my job!

The spread of Christianity naturally created a great demand for copies of the Gospels and other sacred books, and later on for missals and other devotional volumes for church and private use. Benedict Biscop, the founder of the abbey at Wearmouth in England, brought home with him from France (671) a whole cargo of books, part of which he had "bought," but from whom is not mentioned. Passing by the intermediate ages we find that previous to the Reformation, the text writers or stationers (*stacyoneres*), who sold copies of the books then in use—the A B C, the Paternoster, Creed, Ave Maria and other MS. copies of prayers, in the neighbourhood of St Paul's, London,—were, in 1403, formed into a guild. Some of these "stacyoneres" had stalls or stations built against the very walls of the cathedral itself, in the same manner as they are still to be found in some of the older continental cities.

—ANONYMOUS, "Bookselling," *Encyclopædia Britannica,*
11th edition

CHAPTER 5

THE FURNACE OF TRUTH

Sad is the man who seduces many women in search of variety, for he will carry monotony to everything he touches. Far wiser is he who finds in one woman many women, for in acknowledging her dignity he attains dignity himself. Wisest of all, though dangerously near the furnace of truth, is he who finds in all women one woman, and she infinite.

—Sovrana Sostrata,
Gesta

Room 927 of Mother of God Hospital faces north, commanding through its large window a view of the Wishbone River as it winds patiently toward its faraway meeting with the Pacific. To the west as you look down-valley are the green-bosomed Newcomb Hills; to the east, rising more abruptly, are the foothills of the Lion Mountains. Snell's bed faced east, and some mornings just after sunrise he was able to catch the sun glinting against a distant white crag.

When Snell could get out of bed, he asked for a chair and table by the window. Here, day after day, he would sit working at his laptop computer, sipping hot chocolate or ice water and glancing up now and then at the splendid view. His friends politely shunned his work hours, visiting instead in the late afternoon or evening.

By early July Snell's continued presence at Mother of God had become a topic of speculation among the staff. His fractures, neither of them originally very severe, were knitting famously; his counts were all normal; he had regained healthy muscle tone; and all the neurological tests were good. Yet Maynard, citing the physical and psychological ordeal that his patient had suffered and the occasional headaches and dizzy spells he still experienced, recommended prolonged hospitalization. Was Maynard being overcautious, or was he in cahoots with Pierce to incarcerate Snell for his own protection? The police guard remained at the door.

In either case Snell would have been a willing prisoner. The prospect of being homicidally attacked by an unknown assailant of formidable strength and fanatic conviction held little attraction for him. With his leg still in a light cast, he enjoyed the luxury of service. And the writing conditions were excellent. Not just the peace, the quiet and the Wishbone view, not just the monastic simplicity and concentration of life within a single room, but the whole symbolism of mending and recovery appealed to him profoundly. "After all," he inquired in his journal, "isn't an artist's life honestly lived a kind of slow recuperation, a recovery of lost spirit, a knitting of broken time?"

Snell's own time had suffered a pleasant interruption on the morning of June 11, when Harper Nathan's unaccountably familiar bell-like voice, heightened a bit by her own excitement and piped his way on a new long-distance service that made her sound next door, informed him that *Sovrana Sostrata* was to be republished by Wolper McNab in the fall. Snell listened silently, breathlessly, with an onset of postconcussion dizziness followed by a mild case of shock. He excused himself prematurely, promising to call back soon. He leaned his head against the pillows and, closing his eyes, remembered the desolation in the Jungle.

So they've rescued us both now. And Sovrana's rescued for good.

His head swam. The thought of publication by a major press, of national distribution and publicity and possibly even reviews, had not occurred to him in years. And now, without his having lifted a finger, it was all but a *fait accompli,* in the hands of an angel-editor who called his work a "miracle" that might well "stun" the novel-reading world. Snell thought of Odysseus carried sleeping from the oared Phaiakian ship, placed sleeping on his beloved soil. Let Gazza try to fire him now!

Yet the news also carried danger. It could be a bugle call to Libricide, a blow that might excite him to action or even escalate his malice into rashness. Could it be kept secret? Secret at least until the fall, by which time Pierce might have a lead on Libricide? Alert now, Snell phoned Pierce's office and left a message.

The next evening brought more news of exciting but ambiguous character. Knocking at the door woke Snell from a light nap, and Quintus Adler, looking even more massive than usual and rather solemn, emerged into the room, awkwardly deposited a brown bag with a bottle of some sort in it on the bed, and took up a dramatic standing position by the window. "Glanda's resigned as head," he announced.

Snell blinked. "But she'd never—"

"Marshall forced her to, and apparently the chancellor forced Marshall. And the chancellor was acting on a letter from me. Edson's a fairly reasonable man, for an administrator."

"*Quintus, how did you do it?*"

Adler roared with delight. "Remember, my lad, our spiritual forebears, Marcus Tullius Cicero and Marcus Fabius Quintilianus. Cicero used rhetoric as a bludgeon against massed and violent odds, and remarked more than once that rhetoric was powerful only when empowered by the honesty of its wielder. Quintilian stipulated that the source of all eloquence was the heart. I'll tell you how I did it. *I meant it.*"

"But won't it get you into trouble?"

The big man beamed with excitement. "Possibly, but I doubt it. Marshall and Gazza will think I'm Edson's boy now. And your review case is going to be turned around and conducted fairly."

"Who's going to be head now? Hal again?"

"Don't you wish!" said Adler glumly. "Glanda's crew still has a big majority, and as long as they do they'll either pick one of their own or some neutral-looking character they can control. And they've got themselves a beauty."

Snell thought a moment. "You mean Web Hollins?"

Adler roared again. "Right on, man! Webster Hollins, eternal bibliographer, pasty-faced purveyor of platitudes, old Professor Steal-a-Feel, who finally bagged that archetypal grad-student coquette Salem Pogue, Mr. Committee, whose only regret is that he wasn't born one. Of course I'll nominate Hal, and you and Sarah and seven or eight junior faculty will vote for him. But Glanda, even Glanda in disgrace with fortune and men's eyes, walks around with twenty-five votes in her pocket. And that old pocket of hers, seamy and rat-infested as it is, also contains the lock, stock and barrel, so to speak, of Web Hollins."

"But isn't that too transparent? Wouldn't Edson notice?"

"Probably. But I think everyone will give Web the benefit of the doubt because he's a so-called moderate. Edson's meddled about as much as he safely can. If he wants to accomplish anything really solid, he'll have to dump Marshall and start repopulating the administration wholesale. And that's likely to be too tall an order even for him."

Snell thanked Adler for what, in the pallid arena of academe, had to be considered an act of uncommon valor. Adler pulled out a photocopy of the Gazza-felling missive and presented it to his colleague. "Read it for the style, Adam," he said in parting. "I think I managed one or two good paragraphs."

In the dreamily long summer days that followed, Snell turned to his new book, *On Wonderment*. On the surface his mode of operation was harmless enough, even rather staid: the laptop computer, the regular hours, the meticulous use of the journal and other secondary files. But Snell's subject matter, style and organization of material suggested lunacy in its purest form. The subject matter, first off, had no apparent rationale or coherence whatsoever. Snell wrote about nature, art, abstract ideas, personal experience, science, history, psychology, without the slightest effort to connect these fields at all. His style was patently inconsistent, including, sometimes within the course of a single working day, satire, tragedy, conversational anecdote, philosophical discourse, humor and belletristic essay. And as for development, there was none at all. Snell would simply pick up an idea, ride with it for what it was worth, let it go, and open up a new page. His only homage to system was the network of abbreviated subject codes that might someday allow him to draw related sections together out of the increasingly vast miscellany of discourse.

His friends responded to these exotic activities with various degrees of concern. Sarah, whose feelings toward Snell had grown undisguisedly affectionate, feared for his sanity. Adler referred to Snell's project as Briareus, the hundred-headed monster. Emmons feared some bitter and violent response from the theorists.

But there were more sanguine responses as well. Worried as he was, Emmons could not help comparing Snell with Renaissance humanists—Alberti, Machiavelli, Erasmus, Rabelais and others—who combined genuine learning with the ability to speak effectively to the general reader. Schmutzhauf and Edward Marlin (who now visited Snell occasionally) were even more positive. To Schmutzhauf, Snell's M.O. was reminiscent of a great tradition in modern science. "This is a perfectly valid way to work," he asserted. "You collect *everything*, no matter how incoherent it appears. You don't stop collecting until you've collected everything that's in your power to collect. And then you let it all *ferment* inside of you. Darwin worked this way."

Marlin put it differently. "Adam's having a dialogue with himself. He's exploring mental geography—not just his own but that of his culture as well. He's tempting pure chaos but opening himself up to real discovery. No one's ever found order in himself or society without first having a love affair with disorder, noting word by word the proceedings of Babel."

As Snell worked on through the summer, patiently, industriously, sometimes lost in musing, sometimes ravished by inspiration, a rationale of sorts began to emerge. In the course of months of amorphous expression, he had found himself returning repeatedly to a number of major experiences or images. Dozens of otherwise disconnected ideas had clustered around each of these constructs, and more important, each of them had come to symbolize a particular species of human emotion. In a flash one day Snell saw that by organizing his book around these constructs, one per chapter, he could unify nearly all of the material that he found compelling. Using a software database to search the whole manuscript for relevant title codes and aggregate them in new categories, he was able to reorganize four hundred pages of material in a single day.

Now what had been an ocean of inquiry snapped into focus as a potential book, and passages written days or weeks apart suddenly congealed together as parallels or antitheses. The entire fabric of the work melted out of chaos into form, a form, however, which retained for its vitality the chaotic energy that had spawned it. Snell felt that he had struck gold. In a way that few writers would find comfortable, he had bypassed the established rules of invention and discovered an authentic voice.

Snell's nine constructs (he called them his nine "places") were united by the single theme of wonder: the human capacity to feel that irreducible compound of joy and amazement, of strangeness and familiarity, in the presence of some suddenly apparent truth. An abandoned church in a forest near a shopping mall. The Michelangelo staircase in the Laurentian Library in Florence as Snell climbed it to read the first Latin translation of Plato. Plato's dialogue the *Timaeus*. A photograph of the Crab Nebula. A large standing dead tree off 101 north of Eureka. A computer program of the so-called Mandelbrot set. A painting of Mozart as a child. Da Vinci's portrait of Ginevra dei Benci. Louis Armstrong performing Fats Waller's "Ain't Misbehavin'." Each of these "places" became the mental location for a different form of wonder, for a special series of meditations, and the purposed role of all nine series, converging as they did on the hub of a central idea, was to render up, if discursively and rather shaggily, an honest and inclusive image of wonder and the phenomena that inspire it.

It was mid-July, and now Snell, strengthened in body and endowed at last with a consuming sense of artistic purpose, was writing
with a passion over eight-hour daily stretches that left him exhausted
in late afternoon. This intensity harked back to the days of composing *Sovrana Sostrata,* but two elements had changed profoundly.
Sovrana, once the dominant voice in his art, was no longer his muse.
He had buried her, as deep and finally as the sad farmers who hacked
her unconsecrated grave into the rocky Chianti soil—or so he assumed. And concomitantly his writing now lacked Sovrana's fire.
Gone were the taunting aggressiveness, the wanton exhibitionism, the
oracular concision. In their place was a mellower vision, a discourse
at once more leisurely and appreciative. In *Sovrana Sostrata* Snell had
pulled down the temple walls. Now apparently he wished to con-
struct a new temple of his own design.

I once asked him if *On Wonderment* implied any rejection of the
tragic vision of *Sovrana Sostrata* or retreat from its bold positions.
After a moment's pause he replied that to him truth had several
"bodies," that some of these bodies were terrifying, some beautiful,
some bizarre, some simple. To him each of these bodies carried an
unmistakable stamp or signature of cosmic reality. Yet one body of
truth could glaringly contradict aspects of one or more of the others.
And the existence of all the other bodies made any one of them,
however riveting it might be, incapable of holding the full picture.

Then *Sovrana Sostrata* and *On Wonderment* were just two different bodies of truth?

"As near as I could come."

With the new organizational rationale came a change of authorial attitude sweeping enough to alter the very shape of time.
Before he conceived of his nine "places," Snell was expressing the
past, foraging in his own mind for the spiritual institutions that gave
him human identity and individual definition. Now the thrust instead
was toward the future: toward a bound and printed book that would
verbalize these institutions and give them lasting shape.

It was characteristic of Snell to speak to his friends of these
unlikely inspirations and heroic designs in simple, almost homespun
language, and with a green-eyed twinkle of humor.

Harper Nathan, now apprised of her new author's melo-
dramatic adventures, telephoned regularly, sometimes to go over
details of *Sovrana Sostrata*'s republication, sometimes to inquire after
the new project. A second book-length manuscript, submitted soon

after the first, would be of great use, she said, in establishing Snell as a good publishing risk. Harper showed lively interest in the burgeoning *On Wonderment,* even during the early days when Snell, as he artlessly admitted, had no words to describe it. She suggested paying a visit to Dulce in August, in order to "discuss matters in depth."

Pierce dropped in often over the summer to relate ongoing findings about the Likely Libricide Candidates and to advise Snell about the security measures that would have to be taken after his release from Mother of God. One July afternoon, when Snell had knocked off work a bit early to watch the Athletics play Kansas City, the lieutenant appeared with a copy of *Sovrana Sostrata* peeking out of his jacket pocket. Snell expressed surprise at being included in Pierce's casual reading.

"It's business," said the policeman cheerfully. "If I'm going to figure out who this book could make mad enough to kill, I'd better know what's in it."

"What's your guess?"

"Well, from a first reading, I reckon either a puritan or a born-again or a nihilist. The puritan would hate the sex in the book. The fundamentalist wouldn't be able to take the treatment of God, especially in that sermon of hers. And the nihilist would freak out at your sense of commitment."

Snell wondered whether these conclusions had helped Pierce narrow his Libricide list.

"Not yet. Born-agains are pretty easy to spot, and there are none of them on our list. Puritanism and nihilism can run underground, so to speak, and we haven't gotten enough on any of our candidates to pin either one on them. In fact we're sort of stalled. Which brings me to today's shocker. Adam, I've decided that we should start hooting and hollering about the republication of your novel, that we should announce it to your department head and the campus news bureau and anywhere else we can."

"You mean you want to lure him out."

The lieutenant gave him a serious doctorlike look. "I see it this way. If we keep the news secret, we let him write his own calendar. He could work up a classy game plan, full of fail-safes. This way it's us who are writing the calendar. We can make him attack when we're good and ready for it. And there's also the chance that this news plus your incredible survival plus the publisher's interest in your new book will flummox him—that he'll let you go and look for an easier mark."

Snell admitted a bit grimly that the idea had merit. "When do we break the news?"

"A week or two after you're released from here."

"And when will that be?"

"I'd say about three weeks. You know darn well you're strong enough to walk out of here right now. But we want you to build yourself up. Your fitness has never been more important to you than now. Dr. Maynard's going to tie you in with the sports-injury clinic next door. They can run you through a sort of full-spectrum exercise program for a couple of hours a day, and in three weeks we can have you looking and feeling like Captain Marvel."

Snell shrank visibly. "You mean I may have to defend myself."

Pierce became doctorlike again. "Yes, Adam. We can only do so much. How does that make you feel?"

"Scared," said Snell.

"I'd be scared myself," replied the policeman. "But I feel scared many times in my own job. I was scared when I fired my gun at the Homestead and scared the last time we had to overpower a drunk. Sometimes I wake up at night, scared to death of a society that allows extremes, rewards them, breeds, protects and nurses every conceivable kind of kookiness. But you can handle fear in two ways. You can go into the shock syndrome and feel faint and shut down your systems. Or you can go into fight-or-flight and either run away or defend yourself. You've got to cultivate that fight-or-flight response. And you need a strong body, if only to run away better with."

"Then running away wouldn't be cowardly?"

Pierce grew more intense. "You'd run from an angry hornet, wouldn't you? *I* sure would. Libricide's like an angry hornet. It doesn't make any sense defending yourself if it's safe to run away. But you've got to be ready to fight back if he doesn't give you a choice."

Snell turned to his exercise program with such zeal that he went to bed aching every night. The combination of writing and physical exertion made his time dramatic—the more so because his days of relative safety were now numbered. One evening he came back to his room, sweating and panting, from two hours of lifts and stretches, to find a large gift-wrapped package on his bed. The card, which bore a small reproduction of Turner's *A First-Rate Taking in Stores,* read

To Adam Snell—
For silent running
—From the Adam Snell Squadron
July 20, 1990

and in the carton was a new laser printer. Snell had refrained from using his old printer in the hospital because of its annoying loudness. Now he could print in silence, first in the hospital and later at home, where silence might come in handy too. The next day he installed the printer, filled up the paper tray and instructed the machine, with a few keystrokes, to print out the four hundred pages of the *On Wonderment* manuscript. It began to do so, at the rate of about one neatly printed page every ten seconds, and while it was printing the writer cleared the screen and began composing new material.

So Snell and his technological ally worked on together, the man for the first time thrilled by an awareness of his trade's paradoxically heroic implications, the machine laboring beside him in conspiratorial silence.

In Henry Anstey's *Munimenta Academica,* published under the direction of the master of the rolls, we catch a glimpse of the "sworn" university bookseller or stationer, John More of Oxford, who apparently first supplied pupils with their books, and then acted the part of a pawnbroker. Anstey says (p. 77), "The fact is that they [the students] mostly could not afford to buy books, and had they been able, would not have found the advantage so considerable as might be supposed, the instruction given being almost wholly oral. The chief source of supplying books was by purchase from the university sworn stationers, who had to a great extent a monopoly. Of such books there were plainly very large numbers constantly changing hands." Besides the sworn stationers there were many booksellers in Oxford who were not sworn, for one of the statutes, passed in the year 1373, expressly recites that, in consequence of their presence, "books of great value are sold and carried away from Oxford, the owners of them are cheated, and the sworn stationers are deprived of their lawful business." It was, therefore, enacted that no bookseller except two sworn stationers or their deputies, should sell any book being either his own property or that of another, exceeding half a mark in value, under a pain of imprisonment, or, if the offense was repeated, of abjuring his trade within the university.

—ANONYMOUS, "Bookselling," *Encyclopædia Britannica,* 11th edition

CHAPTER 6

———>——

A DAY IN HELL

ADVANCED DIAGNOSTIC ERROR MESSAGE

CODE	DESCRIPTION
01x	Undetermined problem errors
02x	Power supply errors
1xx	SYSTEM BOARD ERRORS
101	Interrupt failure
102	Timer failure
103	Timer interrupt failure
104	Protect mode failure
105	Last 8042 command not accepted
106	Converting logic test
107	Hot NMI test
108	Timer bus test
109	Direct memory access test error
121	Unexpected hardware interrupts occurred

—From a computer manual

Millennia of spiritual torment and centuries of religious dispute might have been spared by the simple recognition of the female identity of God.

—SOVRANA SOSTRATA,
"Abominable" Sermon

While I was writing the first draft of this book, I asked several friends and colleagues to read the manuscript and give me their opinions. Seven stout hearts graciously agreed. Although responses varied widely (from "*Book* will be required reading on every American college campus" to "Kill this thing before it kills you"), all were united in one emotion: the desire to know more about Frank Underwood.

"What does he eat for breakfast?" one asked me.

"Does he have any sex?" another inquired.

"What does he read?" chimed in a third, and so on.

Lurking behind all these questions, I assume, was the curiosity, universal among all ages, nationalities and religions, about the private and intimate operations of evil—a craving so acute that many of us, I fear, would rather see the nakedness of an ugly soul than that of a beautiful body.

My own preferences are quite different. I take no particular relish in Underwood's private life. In fact, he rather frightens me. There's a certain vitality and dark resoluteness about him that unnerves me, to the extent that often as I write I cannot relieve myself of the feeling that at any moment he might appear through the office door to my left, bearing some blunt object and little good will. Other times I excessively identify with him. I think of him as uniquely my own, almost as a familiar spirit. I feel that revealing, nay publishing, his intimate experience would breach my own guilty privacy. Yet art must be served. I gave in to my friends' request and agreed to describe in some detail a day in the life of Frank Underwood, provided that I could be concise and businesslike in my descriptions, and that I could choose one of the more eventful episodes of his summer at the Harrolton ranch. I further agreed to answer any pertinent questions they might have along the way or after my narrative was complete.

Journal of Events, Harrolton Ranch, Monday, July 23, 1990

6:50 A.M. Underwood wakes to clock radio, lies for minutes on his back in bed, open-eyed. (Q: *Why?* A: He's reconstructing an obscurely dream-damaged world in some sort of tolerable image.)

6:57 A.M. Underwood, clad only in Jockey shorts, walks heavily into hall and bathroom, brushes teeth, defecates, washes hands.

7:09 A.M. In the living room, Underwood finds a country-music CD and inserts it into the portable player on his desk. To the loud accompaniment of twanging music and whining voices he spreads a soiled white comforter on the floor. He straps a twenty-pound weight to his left leg and performs sixty leg lifts, thirty of them isometrically prolonged, in four different positions. This repeated with right leg. Then a few stretches. Then the set of leg exercises is repeated in entirety. Then more stretching. It's hot already in the living room, and Underwood is sweating heavily. He folds comforter and replaces equipment. The CD player stays on at high volume.

7:59 A.M. Underwood showers, using deodorant soap and anti-dandruff shampoo. He shaves with a blade razor and slaps on some aftershave. He brushes his hair and reviews himself at length in the mirror. In his bedroom he dresses in jeans, a plaid mother-of-pearl-buttoned western shirt and well-worn black work boots, consulting a mirror again. (Q: *Why does Underwood spend so much time looking in the mirror?* A: You might say he's looking for the mark of Cain.)

8:30 A.M. Underwood breakfasts on cornflakes with milk and sugar and a fresh peach cut up and scattered into the bowl. He drinks two cups of percolated coffee, black. He washes dishes, puts things away and runs a damp rag over the counter and table.

8:51 A.M. Carefully removing his Remington varmint gun from its case, Underwood puts on his earmuffs, goes out to the porch, braces himself against his favorite column and very patiently and meticulously fires twenty-five shots downhill at his target. Back in his living room, to the nerve-deadening complaints of a digitally remastered lovelorn cowboy, he cleans the Remington and puts it away. It's 9:30 now and very hot.

9:30 A.M. Underwood turns off the CD player. He takes his Stetson from its hook in the living room, locks up his house, and walks down the porch steps to the orange Blazer. It starts up with a throaty old-muffler sound, and he turns on the A/C and a country-western radio station. Once the A/C is blowing cold he shuts his windows and very patiently guides the Blazer down the jeep trail to the state road, where he turns right and heads for French City.

10:10 A.M. After an uneventful trip at legal speeds, Underwood provisions himself at Safeway (hamburgers, hot dogs, milk, ice cream, white bread and major trade-name versions of beer, soda pop, candy bars, toilet paper, jam, peanut butter), and then parks at Wild Goose Sports and Feed, where he spends some minutes. He walks to the bus station, where he picks up three parcels. Sweating, he plods back to the Blazer, U-turns to the gas station across the street, pumps himself some fuel and drives home.

12:17 P.M. Arrived at the ranch, Underwood checks for signs of intruders' entry, surveys his property carefully from porch and rear window and carries in his acquisitions. The CD player with its familiar music goes on loud again. In the kitchen, he unpacks and stores the Safeway items. He walks to the living room, where he unwraps the parcels. Item number one is a rakishly styled pistol. It is a single-shot weapon with a fourteen-inch barrel, designed to fire high-velocity ammunition with an accuracy superior to that of most rifles. Item number two is a hard vinyl case for the gun. Underwood checks the pistol's action. He removes a new scope from its cardboard box and installs it on the pistol. He fishes from a bag a kind of Velcro bracelet and puts it on his left forearm. (Q: *Did he buy the pistol in Dulce and ship it from there?* A: No. He bought it in Montaho, where he owns a ski condo, has established residency and can legally purchase firearms.)

1:08 P.M. His stride now somewhat slowed by the effects of heat and nervous tension, Underwood steps into the kitchen, washes his hands and douses his sweating face with water. He makes himself a large chocolate milk shake, complete with two raw eggs, in the blender and, still standing, drinks it hungrily straight from the blender pitcher. He sits for several minutes at the kitchen table, motionless, face cupped in hands. (Q: *What's he thinking about?* A: Nothing at all.)

1:35 P.M. He washes and replaces the blender pitcher, goes to the bathroom, urinates, washes his hands and returns to the living room. Without loading the pistol he walks out to the porch, braces himself against the porch column, sights a target with the unloaded gun and squeezes the trigger. The pistol has a more sensitive trigger than the varmint gun and seems somewhat harder, even for hands as strong and steady as Underwood's, to aim. (Q: *Why the new gun? What's wrong with the varmint gun? Why doesn't he fire the pistol at the targets?* A: He can't use the varmint gun to murder Snell because it's too bulky to carry up to Spine Hill in safety. The pistol, on the other hand, will fit in a knapsack. He has several reasons for not using the pistol on his home range, including a fear that somehow he might be seen and a desire to simulate the much wilder conditions on Spine Hill.)

1:53 P.M. In the kitchen he pours sun-brewed tea into a large thermos, adds lots of ice and sets out more tea to brew. He dons his Stetson, puts pistol, earmuffs, ammo and tea in the Blazer and shifts the transmission into low range. One hundred yards below the house an old jeep trail, barely perceptible in the grass, runs off steeply downhill to the left. He takes it at a crawl. In ten minutes he is on another hill, out of sight of the house, on a part of the property whose dusty soil shows no sign of human visitation. The heat is stifling. He sets up deadwood targets in the grass at the bottom of the hill and walking uphill paces off a distance of about a hundred yards. He braces himself against a nearby oak tree and commences firing, carefully saving every empty shell casing and occasionally pausing for gulps of tea. By 3:00 he has fired a hundred rounds. (Q: *Why does he save the shell casings?* A: He wants to cover his tracks. High-velocity bullets, once fired, are too distorted to identify, but shell casings often show marks characteristic of a single weapon.)

3:12 P.M. Back at the house, Underwood cleans and stores the pistol, showers and puts on fresh clothes similar to his earlier attire except for the tennis shoes he now wears instead of boots. Iced tea in hand he returns to the living room, where the contents of the third parcel lie waiting on the coffee table. These are a powerful laptop computer and a number of 3.5-inch disks. To a pandemonium of country music he clears some unopened family letters from the top of the oak desk at the west end of the room, places the computer on it, flips up the folding screen, pulls out the cord, plugs it in and turns it on. The screen instantly springs to life, going through a series of automated changes that culminate in a long list of titles. Underwood examines these titles carefully and, apparently satisfied with them, clears the screen and begins to write slowly. (Q: *Why hadn't Underwood brought his computer with him in the car?* A: I'm glad you asked me that. You see, Underwood's lengthy stay at Harrolton hadn't been planned very far in advance. Two days before departure from Dulce he faced the dilemma of how to continue his essential theoretical research while far away. Underwood, you see, felt most uncomfortable working without ready access to scores of recent books and articles by other literary theorists. The books, which he owned, had been duly boxed and loaded into the Porsche. The articles, which came from twenty-six different journals, were more of a poser. Underwood had a kind of inspiration. He instructed his departmental secretaries to use their new IBM scanner to save forty-three articles onto his computer's hard drive and to send him the computer when the job was done. Q: *Why didn't he just have the articles photocopied?* A: As what follows will show, that would have been a far more sensible idea. But Underwood wanted to use his computer's huge memory to simplify his own writing. With one-thousand-odd pages of current research in the computer, he could do word searches, finding out in minutes how many of his colleagues and competitors had made reference to specific ideas. He could also, via his word-processing system, borrow whole paragraphs for quotation at the expense of five or six keystrokes. And symbolically he would have what to his mind would have seemed the closest equivalent to Faustian power: portable, nearly instantaneous access to the aggregated genius of his profession.)

4:45 P.M. To the twang of the banjo and wheeze of the fiddle, Underwood works at the computer, occasionally pausing to sip tea or munch on a refrigerated Clark bar. His fingers fly as there rapidly unfolds on the screen the superstructure of a major project, the book that will unshakably solidify Underwood's reputation and further endear him to moguls like Floconne de Mais and Ewig Schabe. The sun is beginning to peek through the reddish gingham curtains of the northwest window, and the air is acid hot. He pauses to drink and begins writing again. In the heat the computer gives off a strange mild smell, vaguely reminiscent of the model-train transformers he and Gerald played with as kids. He remembers the little engine racing around their living room in the winter twilight, puffing real steam, its tiny light throwing a dim yellow patch on the tracks before it. *No more of that.* Searching for a concept, Underwood runs through a variety of screens and fetches up a recent article by Sandy Eule. Suddenly he pauses and looks up as though inspired. Why not put all forty-three articles into one huge file that he can call into memory? That would immensely simplify all his searches. Sweating profusely now, he summons up the file menu and begins the job. He titles the mammoth new file WHOLTHNG.BOO. His agile fingers manage complete file maneuvers in seconds. Twenty minutes later the monster file is in memory and ready to be saved onto the hard drive. As the CD player thunders with girlish delight, Underwood presses the SAVE key, and the machine replies

Document to be saved: C:\WHOLTHNG.BOO

Tonight ain't nothing gonna slow me down,
Wanna hear a band with a country sound

Underwood signals the affirmative by hitting ENTER, and in turn receives the new signal,

Saving C:\WHOLTHNG.BOO

Gonna dance every dance till all the boys go home.

But seconds pass, and nothing happens. The message remains on-screen, but the screen is frozen, and the hard drive, which ought to be flashing green, is dark as death. Underwood's face freezes in sweaty panic. His fingers try a succession of keys, ENTER, SAVE, EXIT, CANCEL and then, as a last resort, ESCAPE. A minute passes with no change, except Underwood's slow frustrated realization that he has hit a glitch and that his only available option, one that will clear the memory of his entire WHOLTHNG.BOO file and the word-processing system itself, is the red button RESET on the right side of the machine. Pressing RESET will void the machine's memory of his new WHOLTHNG.BOO file, but after resetting he can boot up and start work again. Fortunately he has saved his book project, his precious project, in relatively complete form on the hard drive. The CD trembles with a plaintive song of lost love. He hits the button. The screen goes blank. He waits for the automatic boot-up, but instead the screen goes through a few abortive attempts at expression and ends up with

> 121 Unexpected hardware interrupts occurred
> 705 Unintelligible logic

> *I wanted to die*
> *When you said we were through*

followed by a burping noise and

> 1273 Irreconcilable parameters
> 1790 Fixed disk 0 error

> *I've forgotten somehow*
> *That I cared so before*

followed by a loud *beep,* a very nasty electrical smell and a series of words and rapidly escalating numbers that finally resolve themselves into

> 666 Intolerable disk damage
> 127 files destroyed
> 0 files intact

> *At last I am free,*
> *I don't hurt anymore.*

Shaking from head to toe, Underwood presses RESET again. More electrical smell. The backlight on the screen flickers and dies. Fingers of black fume begin to rise from the cooling vents. Now moving with the slow furious clumsiness of a movie monster Underwood grabs the machine and rises, simultaneously overturning his chair and ripping the cord from the wall socket. Computer in right hand, he lumbers through the screen door, and as the door zaps the wall to its left, he hurls the computer off the porch and into the brown grass of the hillside. He walks woodenly into the house, reemerging with the varmint gun. *Crack!* Struck by a round of high-velocity ammo, the laptop jumps airward. *Crack!* Underwood catches it with another round in midair, projecting it twenty feet downrange. *Crack!* A third round misses as the laptop falls to rest nearly upright, a now-dusty corner still visible above the grass. Underwood fires again, aiming just under the visible corner (*Crack!*), and the land-scape erupts into a momentary circus of glass slivers, keys, wires, plugs, boards, cards, ICs, expansion slots, switches, drives and pan-els. Underwood slowly lowers the gun. He stands rigid in the outra-geous heat, crying. He walks into the house, where the CD is still blaring. He aims the gun hip-high at the CD player, which responds with one final *"I don't care anymore."* He does not fire. He lowers the gun again and sits down on the green velvet couch across the room from his desk. His face stony and white, he cleans the gun and puts it back in the closet. He goes to the bedroom and lies down on his back on the bed, to remain, stiff, motionless and open-eyed, until long after dark. The music plays on.

Any more questions? Hey don't all ask at once!

Q: *Why didn't he shoot the computer with the pistol?*

A: The varmint gun was a repeater. Please pay more attention.

Q: *Does Underwood get any sex?*

A: I can't answer that at present. By the way, have you got a dirty mind or something?

Q: *If I didn't, I might not have followed this story up till now. But come on, you've obviously been teasing us about Under-wood's sex life, holding something back. Why, for example, if he's so good-looking and upwardly mobile, didn't Gazza try to seduce him?*

A: Good question. In fact, the idea occurred several times to Gazza, but each time it was quashed by an unspecific, instinctive impulse of restraint. For more on this subject, if there is any more, you'll have to wait a while.

Q: *When you answered my earlier question, you called Under-wood's world "dream-damaged." What did Underwood dream about?*

A: Underwood's obsessively recurring nightmare is of being bested and shamed in a one-on-one confrontation with another man. In adolescence, this dream enemy always either was or resembled his brother Gerald. After Gerald's injury, Frank stopped dreaming so directly about his brother and "cast" his dream, so to speak, with vaguely fraternal types under different guises. Most recently the opponent, who in the dream not only is of fearsome strength but also seems to carry with him the wrath of God, is Adam Snell.

Q: *Why the big milk shake with the egg?*

A: A bodybuilding fad. People with the right metabolism and lots of exercise can turn that stuff into muscle. Note also that today Underwood only exercises his lower body. Many bodybuilders are convinced that muscles grow better on a day-on, day-off schedule, so Underwood has been alternating upper- and lower-body exercises.

Q: *For a well-heeled academic with theoretical pretensions, Underwood has curiously flat tastes in food and drink. You speak of white bread, hot dogs, candy bars, etc. Isn't this an anomaly?*

A: Is it or isn't it? Anyone else have an idea?

Q: *Could it be that he's fixated in adolescence?*

A: So far as I can see, that's it. It's well known clinically that many neurotics and psychotics have behavioral traits characteristic of youthful periods in their life. These are seen as telltales of serious and unresolved problems affecting the patient during that earlier time. Underwood's upset with Gerald, you may remember, reached crisis proportions during his early adolescence, a time when boys go for white bread, sweets, hot dogs and other similar treats. This theory also would explain Underwood's taste in casual attire and music.

Q: *You say "So far as I can see" and "This theory also would explain" as though you weren't sure you're right. Come off it! You're the author, aren't you? How about taking responsibility for what you've done and telling us for sure?*

A: I wish I could. But you see I'm at a crazily excited period in composition when I'm writing reams a day, and the characters are calling their own shots, and the book is at least temporarily out of control. It's no longer a dead text I'm handling, but rather a self-sustaining ecosystem, an autonomous life form that drinks up my energy each day and leaves me exhausted. I can't take full responsibility, in the normal sense of that word, or fully explain down to the last detail why things are happening as they are.

Q: *Was Underwood thinking at all about Snell that Monday?*

A: Good question. As he lay on the bed after his computer disaster, he thought about Snell quite a lot. He blamed things on Snell, you know. He vowed to take it all out on Snell. But earlier? Emphatically not. Underwood has a thoroughgoing way of fixing on the details of life and exxing out everything else: associations, implications, inner messages, what have you. That's how he has managed to put Gerald or Snell, or anything else that has threatened his balance, out of his mind.

Q: *Underwood, then, has a plugged-up mind? I mean, a mind where various sectors are completely walled off from one another?*

A: More or less. This phenomenon occurs in lots of violent personalities. The violent part is, so to speak, in a separate file, out of normal consciousness. And when the personality switches into violent mode, the other files are similarly immobilized.

Q: *What's happening to brother Gerald?*

A: I almost wish you hadn't asked. Gerald Underwood's story is in a sense much more interesting than his brother's, and certainly more entertaining. Can you believe that the man has gained twenty-five pounds in a month? [*Gasps of astonishment.*] Can you believe he's walking? [*Louder gasps, some applause.*] Dr. O'Shea says it's the weirdest case he's ever seen, and he's writing the whole thing up for the *Saratoga Journal of Medicine.* Gerald's been transferred to a sports-therapy center in Ohio, where he's in a training program that's not all that different from Snell's. Compos mentis in every other way, Gerald has insisted with childish stubbornness that Waltraut Himmelfarb accompany him with her Bible, and Mrs. Himmelfarb, a long-widowed concentration-camp survivor with a fascinating story of her own, if the truth be told, has—

Q: *That's enough about Waltraut for now. But while we're on the subject: We've asked a number of pertinent questions, and your replies have been helpful enough. Since you clearly knew that all this information was relevant, even exciting, why didn't you include it in the text in the first place?*

A: That is all part of my innovative stylistic strategy. You've all heard of "intertextuality," the idea (done to death by interpreters like Gazza and Underwood) of a text subtly commenting on other texts or on itself. Well, I've invented a new concept that I call *extratextuality,* consisting of things readers won't ever know unless they ask the author personally. In fact, I may even put blank pages in the text, so that readers can write questions on them and send them to me.

Q: *Very interesting. Can we get on with the story now?*

A: With pleasure. What would you like to hear?

Q: *You mean we've got a choice? How about one of those sections where we hear a bit of everything?*

A: Your wish is my command.

Q: *But wait. One more question: Why does Underwood's computer break down?*

A: Oh, it's kind of a combination, you know, of a very hot room, a gimpy fan and a card slightly askew in its slot and—

Q: *Come on, cut the technicalities. Aren't you implying that no vessel of discourse, not even an apathetic computer, can tolerate the volume of pure bullshit that Underwood had put into his?*

A: I'll tell you later.

Q: *Why not now?*

A: I'm using a computer myself.

"The trade in bookselling seems," says Hallam, "to have been established at Paris and Bologna in the 12th century; the lawyers and universities called it into life. It is very improbable that it existed in what we properly call the dark ages. Peter of Blois mentions a book which he had bought of a public dealer (*a quodam publico mangone librorum*); but we do not find many distinct accounts of them until the next age. These dealers were denominated *stationarii,* perhaps from the open stalls at which they carried on their business, though *statio* is a general word for a show in low Latin. They appear, by the old statutes of the university of Paris, and by those of Bologna, to have sold books upon commission, and are sometimes, though not uniformly, distinguished from the *librarii,* a word which, having originally been confined to the copyists of books, was afterwards applied to those who traded in them. They sold parchment and other materials of writing, which have retained the name of stationery, and they naturally exercised the kindred occupations of binding and decorating. They probably employed transcribers; we find at least that there was a profession of copyists in the universities and in large cities."

—ANONYMOUS, "Bookselling," *Encyclopædia Britannica,* 11th edition

CHAPTER 7

———➤———

NINE BAGATELLES

Time and grilled cheese wait for no man.

—SOVRANA SOSTRATA,
table talk

The shortages will be distributed among the poor.

—Soviet witticism

1. A MEMO

University of Washagon
English Department
Dulce, WS 100989

July 24, 1990
TO: Professorial Faculty
FROM: Webster Hollins, Acting Head

I know that you will join me in congratulating Adam Snell on the republication of his novel *Sovrana Sostrata* by Wolper McNab. I am most pleased to note as well that Wolper McNab is negotiating for the rights to Adam's new book of creative nonfiction, *On Wonderment.*

You will also be happy to learn of Adam's pending release from Mother of God Hospital.

2. A PASSAGE FROM *HEGEMONY*

"Literalizing the Decentering," an article by Sanford Eule and Glanda Gazza in *Hegemony: A Theoretical Quarterly,* published by the University of Washagon English Department, Vol. 4, No. 2 (July 1990), 1–96, pp. 73*ff.*

. . . Heidegger, De Man, Saussure, Eule, Derrida, Schabe, Habermas, Siskin, Kristeva, Thwackum, Lacan, De Mais, Underwood, Mishunk,

Govnjuk, Baismacou, Barthes). This is not to say that Theory qua Theory is of a specific cast or category, or that it can be quantified or limited or defined or institutionalized as per ideology (Govnjuk). It *is* to say, however, that Theory in all its known or probably knowable forms, and no matter how much its followers may disagree about details, partakes of a certain *esprit,* or you might say *Stimmung,* that seems to distinguish it from other forms of inquiry and by the same token to demarcate its enthusiasts characterologically and politically from adherents of other methodologies (Fetzel, Pfitzer, Schlucker, Poucabolas). Therefore, it seems safe to say that when we speak of "decentering" we intend silently after that participle "in a specific direction," and when we use the word "subversive" we add mentally "in special ways of our own." This insight relieves what would otherwise have been a bothersome syndrome: the "frontier mentality" assuming that the decentering and subversion of essentialism and structuralism, like some Pandora, opens up a "free" range of inquiry and expression, and presuming to introduce, onto the same field of action that *we* have cleared, forms and positions unfriendly to our spirit (Frangalha, Dreck). Given our present role as stewards of authority in so many literature departments across the continent, we may feel justified in using—in fact obliged to use—that authority to direct inquiry along healthy and historically necessitated channels and away from such eddies, marshes and beaver dams as might impede it.

Simply put, *exclusionists should be excluded* (Fetzel, Pfitzer). And good riddance!

3. OVERHEARD BY OUR OPERATIVES

LOCATION: WEBSTER HOLLINS RESIDENCE, 325 MALTBY WAY, DULCE
CHARACTERS: WEBSTER HOLLINS, ACTING HEAD OF THE UNIVERSITY OF WASHAGON ENGLISH DEPARTMENT, AND HIS COMPANION, SALEM POGUE
DATE: July 24, 1990
TIME: 23:45–23:57.

SALEM POGUE [*from bed*]: Have you brushed your teeth?

WEBSTER HOLLINS [*from bathroom*]: OK. [*Sound of tap water and brushing.*]

SALEM: Coming to bed now? Where are you going?

WEBSTER: To the kitchen. Want anything?

SALEM: What are you having?

WEBSTER: I think—a carrot.

SALEM: No thanks. [*A pause. Kitchen light goes on briefly, then is extinguished.*]

WEBSTER [*getting into bed*]: *Chomp chomp.*

SALEM: Webster.

WEBSTER: Shalem. *Chomp.*

SALEM: Couldn't we, um, do our Jay and Daisy thing tonight?

WEBSTER: I'm feeling kind of—off. Maybe this weekend we can get a bottle of wine and—*chomp.*

SALEM: Can we afford it?

WEBSTER: Don't you remember? Fat times are coming.

SALEM: Of course! How wonderful! You're department head!

WEBSTER: Well, we *will* make more money, but I'm not sure how wonderful it's all going to be. Glanda's fit to be tied, and I think I'll never be able to keep her out of my office. There's gossip on campus that we're being unfair to Sarah Wilkins, and then of course the Snell fiasco. People outside the discipline can't seem to understand why we took Adam amiss.

SALEM: And after he wrote such a *shocking* book!

WEBSTER: I *know.* How can such a stereotyped—

SALEM: Salacious, reactionary, ideological—

WEBSTER: Insinuating, opportunistic, sexist—

SALEM: *Rapist* book get published by a major press?

WEBSTER: Maybe that's just it. Adam has a kind of vulgar cachet, like some sort of literary beer ad. He'll probably make the best-seller list and cash in for a million.

SALEM: It's funny. He always seemed like such a nice, gentle sort of man. Say, um, sure you're not up for a little, say, Jane Eyre and Rochester?

WEBSTER: Sorry, Salem. *Chomp.* Sure shows how appearances can deceive. Adam probably's not as learned as he makes out to be either.

SALEM: I know! That new book of his—

WEBSTER: What's it called? *On Wonderment?* What a farce! Why there's no *scholarship* on wonderment. It's a nonsubject, a catchall that a fortune-hunting charlatan can ramble on for three hundred pages about. *Chomp chomp.*

SALEM: Another carrot? Oh, well. Webby—*Webby!*

WEBSTER: Mmm.

SALEM: Can't we try the new one?

WEBSTER: Mmm?

SALEM: Leda and the swan!

WEBSTER [*swallowing, then with authority*]: Salem, I've been meaning to talk to you.

SALEM: About sex?

WEBSTER: I guess that's what you'd have to call it. Salem, aren't you keeping up on your reading? Why, this stuff about females desiring males and all their need for regular sex with males has been shown to be a fallacy!

SALEM: A fallacy? What do you mean?

WEBSTER: Why—I guess—it's a kind of *phallocentric* fallacy. You know, something that's been imposed or, um, foisted on women by centuries of acculturation to male dominance. And that's a fact.

[*A Pause.*]

SALEM: Webby?

WEBSTER: Yeah.

SALEM: Well, if it's a *fallacy,* then what've I got between my legs? And what's it for, anyway? Have I got a fallacy between my legs?

[*Snoring.*]

SALEM: Webby!

WEBSTER: Hm?

SALEM: Sorry I got mad. Tell me what to read, and I promise to read it. By the way, *I've* been reading the most wonderful book. It's by a man from India named Dr. Poona. It says that animals are really wiser than people.

WEBSTER [*sleepily*]: How so?

SALEM: Something about their not being able to talk.

[*Silence, then snoring.*]

4. HARPER BEAGLES

Guenevere and Sigmund Bazoom
Request the Pleasure of Your Company
at
A BEAGLING
Sunday, July 22
Brunch 10:30 A.M., Hunt 12 noon
Hare Farm
Wahamsett, L.I.
R.S.V.P. (516) 555-2095
(Dress Ruggedly)

Smile, Face. I'm greeted at the front door of half-timbered Hare House by the wildly enthusiastic Gwen Bazoom. *Speak, Mouth;* and Mouth obliges with "Gwen! I'm so sorry I'm late! I forgot about that roadwork on the Queensboro Bridge."

Large, solidly built, green-linen tunic crackling with electrostatic energy, voice uncommonly high, hostess Gwen squeals, "Not to worry! Not to worry! Everybody's late! *We're* even late! Come on in—we're gorging ourselves." Gwen throws out an arm and tugs me through the back of the entrance hall and toward the buffet on the terrace off the dining room. *Remember, Face, you're enjoying this. You're having a good time, Face.*

Onto the big slated terrace, pleasantly shaded by trellised Concord grapevines, and into Beau Monde à la Bazoom. Sig himself, as though extrasensorily alert to my arrival, breaks out of a pack of larger men, he resplendent in purple tennis shirt and orange shorts, bugle hanging from neck, arms outstretched. "Angel! My life is complete!"

Alerted by this modest greeting, eighteen men or so turn around and gaze and stare and gawk at me. OK, so you think I'm attractive. Can't you louts find a better way of showing it? *Smile, Face; speak, Mouth.* "Thanks for inviting me, Sig."

He offers champagne in a huge cut-glass goblet, and I can tell you, champagne has looked worse. I take a gulp and almost choke, but it's beginning to help already. Belly pipes up: Waddabout some food? *Pipe down, Belly, we're not alone.* Sig's back again, hands me a mammoth Wedgwood plate ("Enjoy!"), and the big table's crammed with ham, pastrami, roast beef, turkey, whitefish, lox, pickled herring, Genoa salami, caviar, salmon mousse, pickled eggs, mounded potato salad, melon salad, green salad, pasta primavera salad, fat dill pickles and giardiniera, with a whole end devoted to Gorgonzola, Brie, Roquefort, Stilton, Emmentaler, Edam, Provolone and ricotta, and another to baguettes, croissants, matzos, pumpernickel, sourdough, bagels and three kinds of rye. Steady now. Resting goblet on table I take some rye from Bread City, some ricotta (*Excuse me Sammy*), some ham and potato salad, and now I can lean back on this post and feed the inner woman.

That tastes good—just another sip and I'm stable enough to observe this bunch of bold hunters. How funny they all look in shorts! Every one of them a big name in the biz. Fat Francis Mastino, godfather of best-sellers, tipsy already in his red-suspendered lederhosen. Watch out, Francy—you might trip and flatten a beagle. Harriet Dunstable, who gave us Lew Buggam's blockbusting trilogy *Grunt, Growl* and *Snort,* looking hung over in a Mets cap and tennis dress. Curly-headed Jamison McTeague, boy wonder of Garris and Soup, makes eyes at that aging New Age vamp Giselle Parana. And around them a little galaxy of moguls, each dressed after his or her own private idea of the aristocratic Long Island beagler, none looking exactly ready for *Country Life* prime time. What a farce! Why the hell am I here?

Harper, you're here because you'll do anything short of prostitu-

tion to get Sig to make Adam Snell an offer for On Wonderment. *Otherwise you wouldn't—*

Sig makes a joyful noise on his beagle bugle and a distant chorus of yelps (Gwen must've been stationed at the kennel door) gains volume with alarming speed and all of a sudden we're awash in maybe twenty beagles, barking, foraging, peeing on potted plants, rolling over and rubbing their backs on the floor, trying to climb up people's legs. Some favored creature comes bounding in with a rolled-up newspaper that looks like the *Racing Times* in its mouth and presents it to Sig, and a minute later we all break up when Sig looks down to find Fat Francis on all fours with a book in *his* mouth and takes it from Francy and sees that it's a copy of Francy's firm's *Spanish Trumpeter,* which edged out our *Noble Gas* on the best-seller list last year. Sig lets go a cry of pain and tosses the book backward into the dining room, where beagles rush in after it, and I've suddenly got my eyes closed thinking of them all, those formidable hucksters, four-legging it around the terrace with books in their mouths and peeing on the peonies. But Sig's blowing his horn again. "*A la chasse!*" he shouts, and bounds off up a woody trail at the back of the terrace with the army of dogs at his heels. Gwen is suddenly among us shrieking "Follow him!" and before I know it we're all shouldering one another heedlessly along the path, and I get knocked into a raspberry bush by that little textbook snipe Baxter Biddle, who says something like "Back to you later" and vanishes down the trail. But I'm up again and bounding through the woodland to reach, after a minute or so, the glade where everybody's surrounding the intrepid Sig, who, fallen with a sprained ankle, lies literally covered by his own dogs, who make ecstatic opera noises in some confused opinion of having won the game.

We carry Sig back home to an ice bag and everybody gets a drink. Biddle is at me now, doing his "I'm very curious about who you *really* are" number as he shamelessly noshes on caviar and matzos, but I'm sipping wine and wondering why that rascal Harry has broken dates two weekends in a row.

Date a divorced man who has wistful eyes and suddenly goes invisible and maybe you're talking ex-wife.

5. FROM SNELL'S JOURNAL

July 23, 1990. Monday. 11:16 A.M.

Dry as a bone today, brain-dead. Stupid today, and stir-crazy, getting tired of this room and boiled-out food and Beautiful View. They let me out for two hours yesterday near sunset. Marlin and I walked by the river. Wonderful evening, great to be free. Prof. Marlin trying to figure out Machiavelli. Prof. Snell stealing sneaky looks at women in shorts. And occasional sneaky looks behind me. One of Pierce's boys shadowing.

Came back, had a snort of Blessed Quintus' bourbon, and then a call from Harper recounting at hilarious length her adventures *beagling* on Long Island at the home of her boss, Sig Bazoom. Bazoom cuts ludicrous figure as country gentleman, kennels twenty mischievous beagles, for no other reason than impressing fellow publishers with gaudy and inhumane attacks on rabbits. This time it backfired and he's on crutches with a sprained ankle.

Prompted by beagling and who knows what other East Coast-isms, Harper's going to take her vacation out here next month. I, that is if I survive, can count on meeting the midwife of my dreams in four weeks. I can feel in my bones that she's a Sovrana type, even down to that musical voice. Am I ready to meet this abundant spirit? But Harper seems nicer than Sovrana. She's down to earth and doesn't seem to play games.

Sarah just called to ask of all things if I had enough vitamins. I in a way—especially in my recent helpless state—must have called up one of *her* ancient dreams, because she's showing signs of violent affection. I wish I could feel that way about her. Something the matter with me? Not enough vitamins? And I'm a heel not to manage more sympathy for Sarah. Marshall's denied her tenure appeal.

Vita Turk appears with today's *Bugle.* Rival groups, we learn, have "reached accord" on the future of the Pisham Homestead. They're going to defoliate the mucca-grass and all the rest of the undergrowth, tear down the fences and a few trees and open the place up as part of campus. House to be allowed to dilapidate a bit more, then to be pulled down or rebuilt as a frontier museum.

2 P.M. and still no ideas about how to treat this section. Sometimes you just have to give up for the day, and sometimes when you give up, you have ideas.

A call from the newly elevated Web Hollins. He says he's "elated" by my success. Given his track record, I find that hard to believe. Hollins the classic example of genus *Academicus.* When I met him fifteen years ago he was rosy-cheeked, with big shifty too-opened eyes, like an outsized chipmunk, as though on constant alert, should any emergency decision crop up, for some hole to jump into or authority to consult. Now the face is shapeless and blotchy but the alert apparently is still posted. I've seen him, before votes at department meetings, reading Glanda's face for yea or nay.

Web's first move on hitting Dulce was to join every academic committee he could. His motives? Let me conjecture. First to garner every available crumb of power. Second to become action central for confidential information, which, of course, is also potential power. Third to impress everybody as being hardworking and responsible. This strategy got him tenure and promotion. After all, tenure and promotion decisions are made by committees.

Web and Glanda are probably laying odds on whether I live through October.

Betting on a murder? How uncollegial! If they saw my house in a week they'd have to up the odds. Pierce's safety measures include discreetly barred windows, a security alarm system, heavy curtains. Also I'm to get a gun and enough schooling with it to make accidental self-slaughter an unlikely prospect.

But Libricide is strong and smart. If he ever decides my life is worth his, I'm a goner. Imagine dying without any idea who this sedate lunatic is! The thought gives me chills. Pierce says it's got to be Ashenham or that kooky philosopher Wenderson, or it's the Devil himself. They've got everything they can on these two guys and could only get more if they announced their suspicion or made an arrest. And doing that, says Pierce, is out of the question because of the amount of evidence necessary to get a conviction. For us to catch Libricide, he's got to oblige us by coming out of the closet.

Ashenham's a thoroughgoing prig, vain, empty-headed, swaggering, divorced by two battered wives. Used to wrestle on TV; took up literary theory as an alternative to hamming it up in the ring. Seldom greets me, often glares at me. He fills the bill on paper, but I can't imagine him mustering the intensity to commit violence over a work of literature.

Wenderson's on medication for some disorder and has persecution fantasies hairy enough to get mentioned in his faculty file. One graduation day he climbed a cherry tree, academic regalia and all, and threw fruit down at his students. This sort would be likely to do almost anything. But then he and I barely know each other, and he's been very civil the few times we've met.

Bizarre scene just now with Schmutzhauf and Vita. Vita's brought mail and stops for a moment to enjoy the view. Door pops open, Schmutzhauf appears holding tissue-shrouded thing that looks like a bouquet, hands it to Vita who, muttering distrustfully, removes tissue and discovers it's a single yellow rose about a foot in diameter. She holds it, staring at it, and suddenly goes all white, threatening to faint on me, then regains color, hisses, *"God didn't make this freak!,"* throws flower on bed and scuttles off.

His bid for reconciliation with Vita having failed, Schmutzhauf sits down at the foot of the bed. I describe to him my misgivings about Pierce's Wenderson/Ashenham hypothesis. Schmutzhauf, in excellent form today after having outdone God, replies, "You know, Adam, Pierce may be a great cop. But the trouble with being a great cop, or being excellent at any profession—especially if you're senior—is that you tend to let the results of your case experience harden into a theoretical grid that you can then apply to anything new that pops up. It's a kind of mental automation that simplifies life, speeds up analyses. But it's blind to the exceptional case."

Thirty minutes now until physical therapy, and I'm actually eager for another day of groans. My therapist Kevin says my progress is stellar and that if I don't watch out I'll be in the Veterans' Games next year. He even gave me a recipe for muscle-making milk shakes. And Maynard says I can jog again as soon as I'm released, provided (adds Pierce) I do it during the day and don't build up a fixed itinerary. Libricide might lay a mine or something.

Now I know why I'm so wooden-headed today: I'm fascinated by that creep. He's out there somewhere, maybe near me, in living color, breathing through every second of time that I occupy. He has a home, a history, a museumful of human detail. Yet I can't even *imagine* him. I, such hot stuff to dream up Sovrana as my opposite. But Libricide's another opposite, a blind-side opposite or infernal antipode, who just like Sovrana may have much in common with me. Or in fact, I suppose, identify with me profoundly—but negatively.

Nine chapters of *Wonderment* and nothing on evil? I suppose that's OK. We wonder at good things, are appalled by evil. What's wondering got in common with being appalled? That strange combination, that surprise duet of disbelief and acknowledgment. You can't believe that any human being would open up with an assault gun in a trolley, but look over there—right there!—there's somebody doing it. You've suddenly got to believe it, but can you acknowledge it as *human*? Yet you can't come near to self-knowledge unless you acknowledge extreme evil, imagine it in yourself.

That's it. Libricide's invisible to me in *two* ways: one, because he's physically hidden, and two, because I can't imagine him. And I can't imagine him because I'm your normal American intellectual-in-the-street, a moral coward, a harmless ignoramus, a tweed-jacketed sitting duck.

Try a new one on Pierce tomorrow. Take out a blank notebook and a pen. Tell him: "Let's be creative. Let's model ourselves a Libricide."

6. A PRESS RELEASE

From the University of Washagon News Bureau, August 8, 1990

Professor Simon Misthotos, head of the Department of Biology and Agricultural Science, has confirmed reports that Professor Warren Schmutzhauf of his department will receive this year's Krupp Prize for his isolation of the ultra–rapid growth enzyme muccasin during experiments with the hybrid mucca-grass. This $400,000 award will bring to a total of $1,372,915 ("and counting," as Prof. Misthotos put it) the prize money that Prof. Schmutzhauf has received since the publication of his discovery in June. His other honors include the Howitzer Prize, the Luger Prize, the Humanitarian Service Award from the International Food Corporation, the Nonsectarian Spiritual Frenzy Award and the *Playboy* Self-Improvement Prize.

It was further announced that Texas billionaire Benedict Snark has donated $20 million, in part to support Prof. Schmutzhauf's future muccasin research and in part to advance progress in other University programs of Prof. Schmutzhauf's choice. To house these projects, Prof. Schmutzhauf has purchased the Warren Gamaliel Harding Elementary School building adjacent to campus and leased it to the University for the rent of $1.00 per year. The eastern half of the building, he announced, will be devoted to muccasin research. Plans for the western half are pending.

Professor Misthotos further stated that a substantial portion of the Snark grant would be used by Prof. Schmutzhauf to fund additional positions in the Department of Environmental Economics.

On other fronts: Mildred Adamson, widow of late Professor of Philosophy Jonathan Adamson, wishes to thank an anonymous donor for payment of $714.50 in medical expenses incurred by Adamson during his last efforts to complete his lifetime project, a reinterpretation of Plato's *Laws*.

7. ON GRAY VELLUM, UNDATED

Henry Stuart
District Court Judge

Dear Harper,
   It is wretched of me to write rather than tell you this in person, but

I am afraid that the sound of your voice, not to mention the sight of you, would in an instant undo weeks of distressful deciding. What I have had so much trouble deciding, as well as what I have decided, you've probably already guessed from my dreadfully indefinite behavior of late. I have been seeing Sue again and I think we are going to patch things up. In any case I'm going to do my damnedest to make the relationship more loving and communicative than it was before. How can I manage this? What makes things different? I've known *you* now, Harper, and loved you, and always will. But in knowing and loving, giving and listening, I was reminded more and more irresistibly of what I had failed to do in the past, of a thousand missed opportunities and gifts refused. I was driven into a past that I had largely ruined and conceivably could repair. Forgive me for trying, my dear, even if this poor explanation makes you feel like an object of use. Or better, don't forgive me, and find yourself a man, if there is one, worthy of your beauty and spirit.

Yours,
Harry

Over her Saturday-morning coffee, holding the letter in her right hand and the square gray envelope in her left, reading it over now once again, admiring the strong graceful handwriting (must have been an old fountain pen), Harper sat motionless at the kitchen table in her York Avenue apartment. A steamy breeze, freighted originally with East River barnacles and flotsam and more recently with papaya juice, boiled hot dogs and Rudolf the Master Dry Cleaner, licked the torn envelope flap, caressed the white skin of her upper chest, comfortably bare between the lapels of the loosely tied bathrobe. Harper laid letter and envelope down on a pile of already-opened mail and sipped the now-cold coffee. Unfamiliar with the handwriting (Harry always phoned) and seeing no return address, she had saved it for reading last of all, thinking it an invitation, perhaps even a note from some long-lost friend or secret admirer. Then she saw the letterhead and knew, before she read a line, the purport of the elegant script. Terrible words, faint reasons, insulting humility. But can a rejection ever be merciful? Can the cutting hand heal the wound it makes? She thought momentarily of her own work, of the thousand equally false-sounding and uncomfortable ways she had tried to rephrase the simple message that she was returning, unaccepted, an author's book.

But hadn't they at least other publishers to submit to, new avenues to try?

Well, so did she.

Propping her right elbow on the letters, she rested her brow on her hand. Her robe had slipped open now, leaving her breasts bare. No matter, she thought. No one could see. Her cheeks went wet with tears. No one could see, or touch, or kiss. Harry had honored her, and made love to her with courtly gentleness and the patience of middle age. Harry's fine eyes, loving and still as she spoke to him of this or that, would whisper that he understood the enigma that she lacked the language to express, her twinned desires to be cherished and to be free. Now, with a gesture as irrevocable as it was polite, he had emptied her world.

She had seen it coming, but not believed it.

Where could she turn? Where else but to her work? Her eyes dry now, she rose, refastened her robe and made fresh coffee. There was much to do. A stack of new manuscripts lay on her night table, crowned by Westerley Firkin's unreadable cookbook epic, *Meals for Males*. Better do the worst first. Dragging the Firkin from the pile and bringing it into the kitchen, Harper smacked it down squarely on Harry's letter, got pencils and Post-its, and sat down to read. She glanced up at the calendar. Firkin might take her, flat out, three days, and there were four more scripts after that. Working nonstop, she might be able to trim down her schedule, fly to Washagon a day or two early and come at last face-to-face with the mysterious Adam Snell.

8. GERALD UNDERWOOD TO HIS PARENTS, AUGUST 11, 1990

Dearest Mom and Dad,

Sorry that my temporary move to the Midwest has made our meetings less frequent, though as you will see below, I've got a plan to change all that next summer. I can't tell you how good it was to see you every weekend for that first month, how very sustaining it was to see and hear your joy at each slow improvement I made. I hope that, after having given you so much grief in the past, I'll never disappoint you again.

For my own life—the new life I have happened into—I am too grateful to find words of thanks. I jog five miles a day and fool around with the piano (just exercises, mind you) in the evening. And every afternoon—that is, when her arthritis isn't acting up—Waltraut and I go walking in the Keenan Game Preserve. We marvel together at the birds, their immense variety of species, their complex patterns of behavior, their remarkable, inexhaustible *involvement* in everything they do. How seldom we see, in our Western urban world, a human being coming anywhere near those tiny animals in concern or engagement with life! I've been reading extensively about the state of the world, especially about the ways in which our nation, whose name was once synonymous with vitality, seems everywhere to be losing pace and conviction.

This brings me to my only piece of news. I've been accepted in the new Ph.D. program in environmental economics at the University of Washagon. My plan is to study the ways in which environmentalism, which is to me the new American frontier, can be an incentive for economic recovery and growth. There are similar programs in Florida and California, but I'm choosing Washagon in order to be near Franky. He may not have answered any of our letters, but I'm convinced that seeing me more or less in one piece again will bring him out. If so, what about a big reunion at the ranch in June?

One final note. You ask whether I remember anything of my many comatose years. Indeed I do, but what I remembered was so deep in my heart, so to speak, that for weeks after awakening I was not *aware* of remembering it. It was, quite simply, the feeling that I was living *in* the Bible, that the Bible was like my homeland, stretching vastly in space and time, that Jacob and Daniel and Matthew were my brothers, that they all spoke with German accents, and that I moved like a slow caravan through their history and had no existence outside of it. Only one thing more: A woman was in that land—who, I don't know—definitely not a Bible woman, definitely no German accent, but a woman who came to me in the desert now and then and looked at me with compassion and spoke to me.

Your loving son,
Gerald

9. A TOCCATA FOR SILHOUETTE

Toward the southeastern corner of Underwood's country land, an old roadbed runs down toward the river between grassy hills. Rumor has it that it was once employed for bringing gold ore down from the mines, but a number of less romantic uses, some of them relatively recent, could have accounted for the leveled trail with its occasional skewed rails and bleached ties. Underwood comes there now, in early August, rewriting the landscape with his own ardent purpose and putting the little valley to a use which, in general tone if not specific detail, might remind it of a wilder past. Dark against the sky in the morning he stands, on the giant brow of hill, his body still as a dead trunk, his head crazily tilted, his hands cupping as though in reverence the stock of the target pistol pointed downward at the roadbed, his one opened eye glued to the scope.

His quarry is the ground squirrel, rodent of the squirrel family, genus *Citellus*. Ground squirrels love the roadbed and inhabit it in force, because of the winter stream that runs beside it, because the oak and bay trees growing there make convenient locations for their burrows, and because of the delectable acorns, berries and insects that naturally abound there. In quest of such booty and generally having nothing more to fear than the occasional strike of a hawk, a squirrel will forsake the safety of burrow or grass, leap up on a section of track and stand upright, rapidly glancing to and fro. Underwood catches them one by one in his scope, knowing that he has about thirty seconds at best to steady himself and fire. As the morning wanes and the track gets hotter, the aiming time shortens.

Today, for the first time, Underwood doesn't miss a shot. Some little animals disappear into the grass on impact; others explode into fragments; others do brief, oblivious imitations of birds in flight. Morning in the valley is boxed neatly into deafening reports followed by slow recoveries of calm. Vultures make huge dilatory circles in the sky; ravens watch cannily, hidden in shadow, from the branches of hillside firs.

It's frightening to behold the man's concentration, more frightening if, closer up, you see that he is days unshaven, that his shirt is drenched in sweat and that, as he lowers the scope, removes an empty shell from the breech and carefully chooses a fresh round from a cartridge holder on his left wrist, his face is that of one in nightmare. The pain is before him now, formidable enough to drive him from his impeccable hygiene of the past. But his shooting technique has been perfected. He is as though part of the strange little gun he holds. Still as a Zen master he addresses his distant target, and conveys its projectile on bevel-flat trajectory with the dread sureness of a vindictive god.

At 1 P.M., dehydrated and dog tired, Underwood picks up his cartridge bag, turns and walks down the other side of the hill to the Blazer. Half blinded by sweat, he takes the steep and narrow trail at a snail's pace. In the trash-littered ranch kitchen he turns on the radio, gulps iced tea, showers and dresses in fresh jeans and shirt. Returning to the kitchen, he begins stuffing two weeks' worth of cans, bottles and uneaten food into a black garbage bag. When the stuffed and smelly bag has been stowed in the truck, he buses dishes and silverware to the sink, cleans the table and countertops, sweeps and mops the floor and washes, dries and cupboards the dishes and silverware. He gets and twists open a long-necked bottle of beer, drinks deeply from it and saunters into the living room, which is in a similar state of chaos. Patiently he reduces the room to its old order, vacuuming in the end the faded Indian rug.

Underwood lies down supine on the velvet couch. He falls asleep immediately, and does not wake until the shadows are long and a cool breeze from the north gently lifts the red curtains. He groans, stretches, rises, gets another beer and sits down at his desk. On the newly cleared surface, two kinds of correspondence are arranged in separate piles. To the left are the still-unopened family letters, many from his father or mother, but some in a new and gradually stronger hand of frightening and familiar beauty, all bearing, as he divines, the inevitable olive branch, the invitation to rebuild the loving family, the intimations of tearful joy. He cannot open these letters, yet cannot throw them out. To the right, unmistakable in their drab format, a pile of recent departmental memos, relating among many items of lesser note the heroic tidings of fray between Gazza and Edson and the concomitant unexpected rise to power of Webster Hollins. Yet atop these and dwarfing them in importance is a three-week-old memo from Hollins whose contents even now provoke in their beholder a look of uncomprehending outrage: the publishing success of Adam Snell. Underwood resists the impulse to snatch the paper and tear at its offending words. He turns instead, as though for consolation, to a squarish carton that has been shoved against the wall to the left of the desk. He reaches for it, drags it toward him and swivels to face it. His right hand removes from it a sealed plastic bag of jellylike substance, his left an instrument resembling a walkie-talkie. These he examines briefly and, replacing them in the carton, extracts a lengthy instruction sheet, laced with boldface warnings and cautions. Turning, he spreads it on the desk before him.

PART THREE

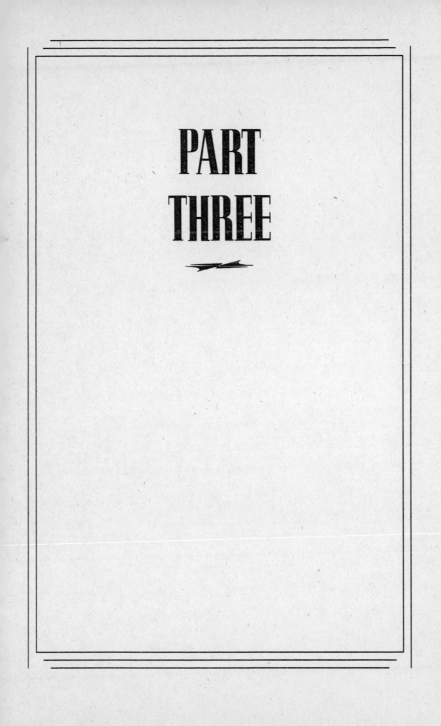

The modern system of bookselling dates from soon after the introduction of printing. The earliest printers were also editors and booksellers; but being unable to sell every copy of the works they printed, they had agents at most of the seats of learning. Antony Koburger, who introduced the arts of printing into Nuremberg in 1470, although a printer, was more of a bookseller; for, besides his own sixteen shops, we are informed by his biographers that he had agents for the sale of his books in every city of Christendom. Wynkyn de Worde, who succeeded to Caxton's press in Westminster, had a shop in Fleet Street.

—ANONYMOUS, "Bookselling," *Encyclopædia Britannica,* 11th edition

CHAPTER 1

THE COLLEGE-RULED NOTEBOOK

The Gate of Hell is the doorway to freedom.

—SOVRANA SOSTRATA,
"Abominable" Sermon

Walk southward one block past Emmons' Fir Boulevard on the Slope, and you'll come to Park Avenue, a paved track even narrower and more twisting than Fir and roughly paralleling its course up Spine Hill. To 716 Park Avenue, a 1920s-era two-story white frame house on the downhill side of the road, Adam Snell was returned by Andrew Pierce in an unmarked tan Ford sedan on the morning of Wednesday, August 15. Another unmarked Ford was already parked by the house, and Snell, renewing contact with his abode after almost two months, watched with some reassurance as the bomb squad completed their routine search of his home and car. Less reassuring, however, were Pierce's parting words: "Take care, Adam. I'll stay in touch. And we'll make sure this road is patrolled." Snell mumbled something distractedly, looking down at his various bags and packages and suddenly remembering his first day of college, when his parents had left him desolately alone in the dorm and started off on their long drive home. The inevitable break had come. He was out in the cold.

He turned on the stereo in the living room and set to work to the strains of Corelli. He closed the curtains of the downstairs rooms, unpacked groceries and clothes and brought his borrowed laptop computer and his printer upstairs. Here he closed all the curtains except those facing westward across the valley and placed the computer in his bedroom on a small table by one of the west windows. As he was checking his files, the radio downstairs announced that it was noon, and not long after that a loud bark and frenzied scratching at the front door signaled his imminent reunion with Doppler. Snell jumped up and raced downstairs, forgetting for the first time that he had ever been injured. When he opened the front door the dog pulled the leash from Emmons' hands, sending Emmons staggering backward as, front paws on Snell's shoulders, Doppler tried human-wise to embrace his master.

Emmons spent most of that afternoon with Snell. Snell showed his friend the elegant pearl-handled .32 Beretta that Pierce had, in what he termed "an incredible deal," acquired for Snell from a colleague. "Can you shoot that thing?" asked Emmons, phobically refusing to touch it.

Snell made a wry face. "I can aim and fire it. I can take it apart and clean it. And I know about seventeen kinds of accident you can have with it. Whether I could aim it at somebody and fire is another thing. Like some beer?"

Over beer they examined what Snell called his "front-line" defense, a motion-sensing security light that promised to flood his front deck with three hundred watts of light on the approach of anything larger than a moth. Snell, who had a fondness for gadgets, opened the package to reveal a number of shapeless metal parts and what was to Emmons a Gordian tangle of colored wires. Snell found a tiny pair of pliers, a couple of screwdrivers and some electrician's tape. He laid out the parts and started fumbling among the wires. "Can you read me Instruction A?"

Emmons grabbed a mimeographed sheet. " 'A. Connect the blue wire from the control module to the blue wires of the bulb sockets and to the neutral (white) of the house supply, using wire nuts provided with the unit. Be sure no loose strands of wire are present. Secure wire connectors to wires using electrical tape.' Is that clear, Adam?"

"Clear as a bell, Hal. Only there aren't any blue wires in here."

Over the next ninety minutes Snell somehow managed to get the contraption together and installed in one piece above his front door.

Back in the living room, Emmons asked him up to dinner; the boys, he said, would love it. Snell declined, citing his work.

"Come on, Adam. Your book can wait a day."

"It's not my book. I've got enough of *that* in hand to show Harper Nathan this Saturday," said Snell, proceeding then to explain his disillusionment with Pierce's Libricide theory. Proudly holding up a new college-ruled notebook, he announced his intention of modeling his own version of Libricide on its pages.

Emmons was dubious. "How do you expect to outdo Andy? He's a professional."

"Maybe that's the trouble," answered Snell. "As Warren puts it, professionals, even the brightest of them, generally approach problems formulaically. They depend on theories that have worked well in a large percentage of cases and sometimes forget that this percentage isn't exhaustive. This time I'm going to take it beyond formula. I'm going to *create* a Libricide, and in particular a Libricide who very sincerely hates me, and I'm going to give him emotionally valid reasons for hating and destroying me, and by making everything specific I may find something in him or in me that Andy and we haven't thought of yet."

Emmons mused for a moment. "Do you mean creating your own opposite, as with Sovrana?"

Snell gave a little laugh. "I've thought of that. After all, I've changed a lot in three years. I sort of deserve a new opposite. It'll be a colder, nastier opposite this time, the kind of nasty kid a man always carries around in himself somewhere."

"Why don't you do all this on your computer?"

"I've got to see it in my own handwriting—it's more like looking in the mirror. I want to have it with me *everywhere*."

And that's more or less what Snell did. He hitched a pair of ballpoint pens to the notebook's cover and carried the thing around the house with him, to bed, to breakfast, even to the bathroom. He jotted in it randomly, impressionistically at first, beginning with a series of tentative insights mingled with serious self-doubts. Late Thursday morning, after a night of patchy sleep and a brief outing with Doppler, he sat down on his living-room couch, turned to a clean page and critiqued the Pierce theory as follows:

First off, it hasn't borne any fruit, so it's not likely to be correct. Second, it doesn't speak to the impulsive, improvisational character of the assault. This improvisational character suggests *first offense,* and if that's correct, then looking around for *histories* of deviant behavior the way we've been doing is a dangerous blind alley.

Through the afternoon more jottings followed. Pierce's idea of a "serial" psychopathology, of a returning compulsion for cathartic release, Snell thought, was basically correct, fitting as it did the bizarre features of the crime. Pierce and everybody else had simply erred about where to place the assault in Libricide's psychic history. If Libricide were indeed a serial offender, he would have to be one who was newly launched in his career. But wouldn't that make him almost impossible to locate?

> But suppose I'm right—where does it leave us? Think first offense, and every man in town with a lit degree and sixteen-inch biceps becomes a suspect. That way madness lies. I'll try the other way now. I'll try to get *inside* this guy and work my way out.

Snell opened up another new page, titling it "Reasons for Hating Adam Snell," filling the page with twenty-four numbered entries, and then underlining the following:

> 3. *Snell's expressive, blows off mouth on all kinds of subjects.*
> 6. *Snell (at least on paper) is sexy, loves women.*
> 15. *Snell supports traditional values.*
> 18. *Snell frankly criticizes society and in particular has no respect for the academic disciplines.*

He then copied these onto another blank page, thought about them for a while, and then began discussing them as follows:

> The man who would find these attributes hateful in me would be a shy, held-back sort of man, a puritan of sorts, a loner, a self-righteous conformist. You wouldn't see this sort of guy with a happy family or buxom girlfriend or drunkenly joshing with friends. This is a Malvolio, a fun-hater. This is also a guy with very precise ideas about professional achievement. He's got to say certain things in certain ways so as to make a certain kind of impression on certain people, and he's likely to hate and fear some spoilsport who rocks the boat. A traditional philologist? No, my work would be rather congenial to one of them. Rather, a theorist.

And just below:

> But it's the theorists who've been after my ass! Why the hell are they? The cliché is that they *hate creative writers* and want to supplant them in the literary power structure. But I think more profoundly it's because Sovrana symbolized sincerity and open expression and fulfilling experience; and most theorists seem congenitally alien to all these things.

Now for the first time the name Underwood appears:

> Underwood's got a clean record but he's a suspicious case. I share about twenty words a year with him, and he's never been friendly. Don't think he has any close friends either. Handsome, wealthy, articulate, uncommonly successful for his age—he's got it all over me. No motive, unless, conjecturally, some theoretical megalomania. But even then, why bother to destroy my work when every indicator pointed to its failure?

Here Snell hit a roadblock:

> But then why should *anyone* do something that crazy? Lots of us "hate" each other and are content to do just that. For Underwood or anybody else even to consider actions of that sort there has to be psychosis, and in psychosis obviously anger is *amplified* into an irresistible motive for action

Snell suddenly looked up from his work. Had something moved outside the window? He rose, crossed the living room and peeked through the curtains. It was eight in the evening, golden sunset, the road empty, the air dead still. Asleep on the rug by the couch, Doppler stretched and moaned in the midst of some happy dream. Snell went into the kitchen and put on some water for tea. His hands trembled, and suddenly he realized that he was full of fear: not just self-preservational fear of bodily harm but metaphysical fear, terror of the embodied evil that was birthing in his own mind. He turned off the tea and instead grabbed a tumbler and some ice, walked into the dining room, took a bottle from a cabinet and poured himself a large bourbon.

Leaving his drink on the dining table, he went and got his notebook. The dining room was the only room in the house at all suggestive of its owner's eccentricities. On buying the house years before, Snell had lined every available section of wall with bookshelves, and now his entire history of bibliographical passions from childhood to the present, 11th *Britannica* and all, presented itself on every side, musing in the dim light like valley walls in some inner geography.

Sitting down at the head of the table, Snell switched on the lamp, braced himself with a sip of bourbon, and wrote:

Now lots of psychotics are locked up in institutions, and there are more around who aren't yet but are behaving as though they want to be. But there's obviously a third group, who can function in society most of the time but are subject to secret obsessions or occasional fits, or who are getting worse and worse and are just on the cusp of losing it

Snell consulted the bourbon again, opened to the next page and continued:

Summary

I am Libricide, a successful though unoriginal literary theorist. I'm devoted to the pursuit of professional excellence, which I define narrowly as high standing in the minds of my ranking colleagues. Consciously, I abhor unprofessionalism, gushing emotions, sexual permissiveness, disrespect for disciplines and outrage against convention. All of these attributes make Adam Snell an embarrassment to his profession and an offense against civilization in general. Unconsciously, I'm terrified by sex and love and creativity and honest communication, and I'm perversely envious of anyone who isn't, and I'm demoniacally furious at anyone who, like Snell, holds these things up as positive values. I've been able to rein in my fury up to recently, but Snell's book drove me beyond the limit, and simultaneously gave me the opportunity to strike out against the hated enemy.

Snell put down the ballpoint pen and for a few moments, elbows on table, held his head in his hands. It was quite dark now—time soon to retest the motion-sensing light and see if he could fire up the station wagon for a quick run-by of Underwood's house. But before doing so he picked up the pen once more and wrote as follows:

To the Reader

If you get to see this at all it will be because I am permanently unable to present my thoughts in person. Know then that of all possible identifications for Libricide, the individual by far the most conformable to my model is Frank Underwood, literary theorist, professor of English. Ashenham isn't serious enough. Wenderson hardly knows me. Of the other theorists, Underwood's the only one who looks physically fit enough to handle the job. Only he and Sandy Eule are well published enough to fit my paradigm, and Eule's slender build and crowd-pleasing disposition make him an unlikely prospect.

Snell's hand was trembling on the final line when his body jerked stiff. Was he hearing things? He rose clumsily and padded into the kitchen, where he stowed his notebook under celery and cold cuts in a refrigerator drawer. He passed through the dining room again on his way into the living room. The room slept in orange lamplight, still and empty save for the peacefully snoring dog. Would Doppler protect him from an intruder? Could that loyal simpleton, that hero of big bark and steely sinew, forfend a malice so subtle that it had now crept into its victim's soul? Snell peered suspiciously into the deep shadows to the left of the sofa and easy chair. The furniture looked strange, ominously exaggerated to him, as though suddenly charged and pervaded with the spirit of evil.

He went back for his notebook and bourbon and sat down on the couch. Impulsively he found a blank page and scrawled

What's so evil about this room? Does it look evil because Underwood will murder me here? *That's* what I've failed to write down, even think about—*how* he wants to murder me. Small wonder. Yet to ignore the most important thing of all! Work, brains. I'm Underwood, see, and I hate this fucker Snell, this unthinkable obscene blotch on the world. I hate him so much that I almost desire him, as though physically harming him might consummate some monstrous desire inside me. You can't believe how much I want to annihilate this slimeball, but I've got to do it elegantly: My masterpiece must be anonymous. I've cased his house: a patrol car now and then, but no regular guard. He's on the alert and probably armed. That means that even though I'm bigger and stronger I can't take him on hand to hand. Snell's got to sleep sometimes. I've watched his house at night and know where his bedroom is. He'll leave faithful Fido downstairs to listen at the doors. Late one sweet summer night, like 4 A.M., I park my black car in the shadows on Park Avenue and work my way up to one of those upper windows that aren't barred and probably won't be rigged for security. I'm in the house now, itching to get my hands on his scrawny neck, but instead I pull out my pistol and screw on the silencer, just like in the movies, and silently I slip off my shoes and move like a cat toward the bedroom door, which is open just a crack. I push through the doorway and aim the pistol at the bed and, hello it's me, I commence firing. I've got bullets to spare. I make sure to shoot him in the stomach and the groin, and then one for good measure in the middle of his unthinkable face. When Fido pops up he gets a silent bullet too for his pains, good doggie, and then I can unset the security system, leave comfortably via the kitchen, drive home and sleep like a sated

What the hell was that? Noise, danger, creaking, tapping from the back of the house, like someone on the stairs by the back door. And Doppler still snoring! Snell threw his suddenly weak body across the room, grabbed his jacket, frantically tore at the gun in the pocket and, mistaking the grip for the barrel, came close to shooting himself. Getting the thing straight, he edged along the wall toward the kitchen, reaching forward slowly with his free hand until he could turn off the kitchen light. The back door, its upper half paned, the entry light shining behind it, now stood out in contrast across the dark room. Snell scuttled diagonally across to the stove and moved from there to the wall just to the left of the door. Holding the gun high he waited a moment, then turned quickly to bring the landing and stairs into range. A big raccoon, sleek and uncommonly well furred, was gently tapping a hen's egg against the top step. Snell's gun hand relaxed, and as the muzzle squeaked against the pane the animal looked up at him quizzically, then continued about its business.

Snell padded back to the living room. It was midnight, time to check up on Underwood's house, but he felt limp and bloodless, as though he had been possessed. The watery bourbon tasted so foul to him that he could barely swallow it. He took his notebook into the kitchen, where he stowed it again under the celery and cold cuts. He went to the front door, saw to the security system, peeked through the glass and walked out into the unfriendly night.

"Cute," said Lieutenant Andrew Pierce, reaching for a wild plum in the warmth of the marvelously bright Friday morning. Pulling the jay-pecked piece of fruit from the little tree, he playfully underhanded it at Doppler, who dodged and then went over to sniff it. "Very cute." He put his right hand on Snell's left shoulder. "Too cute."

The two were standing with Emmons at the top of Fir Boulevard at the south edge of the park that occupied the summit of Spine Hill. During their brief amble up from Emmons' house, Snell had outlined his new Libricide theory. Pierce reached thoughtfully for another plum. "I've got to admit, my own theory hasn't caught this kook. But yours is a little too—sorry, Adam—academic. There's no evidence to back it up. Sure, I can't prove that your Underwood isn't psychotic, or that he didn't attack you. But there's nothing solid to show that he is or did."

Snell persisted. "But given the fact that nothing else has turned up, can't you just start the same kind of unobtrusive workup on him that you did on the other subjects? I want to know whether he has had any problems, whether there was anything unusual about his background, where he is now."

Pierce was curious. "You mean he's not in town?"

"His box was the only one stuffed like mine when I checked my mail an hour ago at the department office. I asked one of the secretaries about him. Every two weeks his mail's forwarded to somewhere in northern California. Also I drove by his house late last night. His carport was empty, and it was littered with a bunch of circulars that he would have been sure to pick up if he'd been home. He's been away, and for quite a while."

Emmons cleared his throat. "If I were you, Andy, I'd take Adam's theory very seriously. It makes sense, and Underwood's the only man in the department who conceivably fits it."

"OK, OK," Pierce said. "I'll get somebody on his case this afternoon. A little prying won't hurt anybody. But I'll bet my bottom dollar that a true blue rising star like your Underwood isn't going to risk his reputation by trying to murder a book. Adam, I've got a coffee date to keep. You said you knew a shortcut back to your house?"

Leaving Emmons, they proceeded downhill via a steep right-of-way that led them in five minutes onto Park Avenue just down the street from Snell's house. As he paused before crossing Park at the trail's end, Snell noticed that Doppler had gone stiff and was looking intently toward Snell's own front door. Then with a ferocious bark the big dog was bounding off, top speed, in the direction of a figure who had been standing in the shadows by the door and who now, having turned toward the oncoming defender, was hastily adapting a briefcase or package into a shield of defense. Pierce already had his big gun out and pointed when Snell shouted "DOPPLER, NO!" and the dog skidded to a growling stop at the intruder's feet.

"Adam, *get back!*" bellowed Pierce, signaling Snell back up the trail for safety; but it suddenly became apparent, via an excitedly raised female voice, that extreme caution was unnecessary.

Calling Doppler back toward him, Snell rushed forward to encounter, in the sunlight on his front deck, a young woman of specifically haunting beauty.

The religious dissensions of the continent, and the Reformation in England under Henry VIII. and Edward VI., created a great demand for books; but in England neither Tudor nor Stuart could tolerate a free press, and various efforts were made to curb it. The first patent for the office of king's printer was granted to Thomas Berthelet by Henry VIII. in 1529, but only such books as were first licensed were to be printed. At that time even the purchase or possession of an unlicensed book was a punishable offense. In 1556 the Company of Stationers was incorporated, and very extensive powers were granted in order that obnoxious books might be repressed. In the following reigns the Star Chamber exercised a pretty effectual censorship; but, in spite of all precaution, such was the demand for books of a polemical nature, that many were printed abroad and surreptitiously introduced into England. Queen Elizabeth interfered but little with books except when they emanated from Roman Catholics, or touched upon her royal prerogatives; and towards the end of her reign, and during that of her pedantic successor, James, bookselling flourished.

—ANONYMOUS, "Bookselling," *Encyclopædia Britannica,* 11th edition

CHAPTER 2

CLOTHO'S BRAID

All things violently tending to a decisive Battel; *Fame*, who much frequented, and had a large Apartment formally assigned her in the *Regal Library*, fled up strait to *Jupiter*, to whom she delivered a faithful account of all that had passed between the two Parties below. (For, among the Gods, she always tells Truth.) *Jove*, in great concern, convokes a Council in the *Milky-Way*. The Senate assembled, he declares the occasion of convening them; a bloody Battel just impendent between two mighty Armies of Antient and Modern creatures, call'd *Books*, wherein the Celestial Interest was but too deeply concerned.

— Jonathan Swift,
The Battle of the Books

The Devil takes his time.

— Sovrana Sostrata,
"Abominable" Sermon

Over what seemed endless empty white roads, first in the blatant heat of tan-grassed hills, then in cool darkness through courts of looming firs, he drove his black demon of a car home to Dulce at the agonizing crawl of sixty-five miles an hour, stopping only once for gas, coasting into his Dulce carport like a shadow just after 1 A.M. His food had been two hamburgers and a bag of fries, wolfed down at the wheel with finger-endangering haste; his drink, more considerately consumed, iced tea from a big thermos beside him in the car. His thoughts, when he thought of anything at all besides his car and the road, had been devoted methodically to double-, triple- and quadruple-checking activities in the recent past and immediate future, as in (past):

- the ranch house fully cleaned, all papers and packing material burned and the ashes trampled down;

- the rifle target range cleaned up: target fragments collected and burned, shell cases hunted down, the shrubs pulled back across the range to restore natural appearance;
- old branches and a log left on pistol-range trail to suggest disuse;
- computer parts collected from field and dumped;
- ranch clothes and linens washed, folded and stored;
- varmint gun and ammo locked away;
- books, travel clothes, pistol in its hard case, scope, wristlet, ammo, explosives and detonator (the latter three items in a black garbage bag) packed in Blazer;
- main power switch thrown, house locked up;
- walking shorts, light mountain boots, knapsack and baseball-type hat purchased at Janeville shop;
- all items transferred to Porsche in Janeville garage;

and (future, Friday, August 17):

- rise, breakfast, shower, dress in new clothes;
- pack gun, ammo and small thermos in knapsack;
- don new hat and sunglasses;
- drive to other side of Spine Hill, park on street near trailhead;
- take back trail to blind;
- kill the bastard Adam Snell;
- return home and shave;
- pack gun and clothes;
- set off for New York;
- drop gun and clothes in Sherman Lake on the way.

Now, showered and breakfasted after a solid sleep, he sat musingly over coffee in his kitchenette. The morning sunlight, not as in California hellfire-tinged but here innocent, inquisitive, edged across his left hand as he raised the cup to drink. Steady hands, fine body, now going off to battle, now going to do the possibly naughty but programatically necessary and certainly deeply fulfilling deed that he had practiced two months for, now going to justify, punctuate and conclude, with a single apt stroke, the secret schooling of mind and body that had given every waking hour the aura of a crusade.

He washed and put away the dishes. In his bedroom he took the target pistol from its case and packed it, together with ammo and other necessary equipment, into the dark red knapsack. He put on knapsack, sunglasses and baseball hat. Turning to face the mirror, he beheld a stranger, a large bearded man in the garb of a footloose yuppie, who might strike anyone in the park that morning as being out on a lengthy constitutional, packing what might easily be picnic, wine, bird book, field glasses, camera or other article of yuppie gear. Could he manage the friendly greeting that silly Dulceans passing on trails were supposed to give each other? He leered into the mirror and laughed. Sure thing. Today was his special day.

He locked up the house and drove away.

Adam Snell listened and prayed. He listened as Harper Nathan, occasionally sipping strong coffee across his dining-room table, unfolded musically the delights and frustrations of publishing *Sovrana Sostrata*. He prayed that this simple interaction of speaker and listener, this animated unfolding and sweet reception, might somehow be prolonged beyond the usual limits of discourse, or at least repeated without fear of stint in times to come. Not that he thought he had found Sovrana. The woman he now confronted so gratefully, while visually reminiscent of his esthetico-erotic dream, had nothing of Sovrana's diabolical clarity, or of her Amazonian sexiness, or of her Cleopatra posturing and tease. This was not one to be worshiped, thought Snell (still listening very carefully), though near such beauty worship was a sore temptation. This was one to revere and cherish, to be delighted in and delighted with.

Harper's voice was pleasing more than one listener. As she laughed about one of her professional misadventures, a low moan, suggesting some blend of deep longing and total gratification, was heard from Doppler, curled half asleep near the door to the living room. A half hour ago, as Harper revealed herself as female and a welcome guest, as she explained to Snell that her message about coming early had been duly recorded by the English department (doubtless to be buried in Snell's pile of back notices), and as she was introduced to the rather flustered and just-departing Pierce, Doppler had gazed, listened, sniffed a bit and changed from an indignant guardian to an unqualified admirer.

Harper paused and sipped from her mug. A morning breeze tilted the curtains of the north window and gently disturbed her brown hair. She gave her head a little shake and looked at Snell. He realized with some regret that it was his turn to speak. He told her (God, how pedantic he sounded!) of recent developments, of the new lead. He showed her the college-ruled book, which she, over several minutes, examined with care.

"What are the police going to do about it?" she asked, turning the pages.

"Pierce says they're going to check back east into Underwood's background, and that if they find anything juicy, like a history of mental problems or some weird antics at school, they'll take him in for questioning and put him under surveillance." Snell gave a stern gesture of prohibition to Doppler who, now awake, had risen and was ambling in Harper's direction. The dog sat back on his haunches.

Harper was persistent. "Why not just arrest Underwood?"

"He'd get a lawyer and be free again in hours. Unless a search uncovered big evidence, the case against him would be busted."

"Why not just question him?"

"He'd tell a pack of lies and know what we were up to."

Harper put the book down, rose and, drawing back the heavy curtain, peeked out the window, deep in thought. Still on his haunches, Doppler was slowly sledding himself in her direction with a clandestine forepaw-hindpaw maneuver.

She turned to Snell. "And you say he's away?"

"At least as of last night."

Harper took a deep breath, then slowly exhaled and gripped the back of a chair. "Adam, do you know what this means?"

Knowing full well what it meant, Snell just looked at her.

Her face was tense. "It means that you and Pierce and your cronies are giving this pervert another free shot. Why not put an ad in the paper, tell him you're the new edition of the fatted calf?" She twisted the wooden backrest till it squeaked. Doppler drew back in dismay as she half shouted, "Damn it! What the hell are you guys up to, anyway?"

Snell flushed with annoyance. "What else do you suggest we *should* be up to?"

Harper looked almost cruel. "What *else*? Man, it's not a matter of 'else.' Your methods are skewed. You've got to change everything. First off, get out of this house, where you're a prepackaged victim. Second, scare this guy off your case. It doesn't matter whether you bust up Pierce's precious investigation as long as you find out who Libricide is, and *Libricide knows that you're onto him.* At worst you'll frighten him off for a while. And at least you won't be"—she gasped for air—"just *diddling around.*"

Snell gestured at the book-lined walls. "This is my home. Have I got to evacuate it just because some maniac—"

"It's your *tomb*, Adam," she cut in, "as *anyplace* is going to be if you give this man time."

With a mildly proprietary gesture, Snell collected his notebook from the table. "Look, we've thought this thing out. How's he going to attack me without showing his hand?"

Harper thought for a moment and then pointed to her right and upward. "What about a rifle shot from that hill up there?"

"But there's no percentage in packing a rifle up through a public park!"

"Hang the percentage! He could find a way! And there are hundreds of other ways of getting at you if he's patient and learns your habits."

This was too much. There was possibly more Sovrana in this woman than met the eye, and Snell had little appetite for any more Sovrana at present. Where did she get off? "Where do you get off, a publisher," he sputtered, "telling people how—"

"That's exactly it," she shot back archly. "I'm a publisher. As in *pub*lic, *pub*ic and *pub*. I live in a big city and sell things in stores. I'm vulgar and mercenary. But the flip side is that my job's dedicated to open communication, open controversy about the truth. That's why I'm publishing your work. And if I'd been Pierce, *that's* the way I'd have conducted your case. I'd have had it in the national press, on national TV. I'd have played it up, promoted it. I'd have questioned *everybody* remotely suspicious. I'd have had everybody in Dulce speculating about it, gossiping, suspecting, prying. I'll bet we'd have smoked him out, or driven him so far back into the woodwork that he wouldn't dare attack you again. And even if we failed, we'd be no worse off than we are right now."

Snell was overwhelmed, as though conquered from within. "OK," he peeped. "Could we possibly try it now?"

Followed by a newly emboldened Doppler, Harper came around the table and took the chair next to Snell's, so close he could touch her. Her hair, warmed by the sunlight, left a trail of fragrance as she passed behind him. "It's late," she said. "But it still might work. I'll phone Levi Morris of UP this afternoon. But that's not all we've got to do." She took Snell's right hand and squeezed it.

"What else?"

"We've got to flush out Underwood. Search his house."

"But I told you, Pierce won't—"

"I'm not talking Pierce. I'm talking you and me. We don't even tell Pierce."

"But what if it's not Underwood?"

Harper drew another long breath. "So much the better. Underwood as you describe him isn't just the most likely candidate, but the most dangerous one. He's powerful, smart and hard to read. If we can get him off the list of suspects, then your criminal is probably some brainsick crank who may not strike at you again. But your Underwood theory is brilliant. It's rational and it's intuitional, so much so that it's scary."

"But what if it *is* Underwood and we find no evidence?"

Harper laughed. "You think of every possible reason for not acting! But it's really very simple. We'll jog him out of his rhythm. If Underwood is Libricide, he thinks he has it real easy right now. He thinks no one suspects him and that he can write his own schedule. If he finds that someone's broken into his house, broken in without stealing a thing, then, well, he'll have another think coming."

"That's right," mused Snell. "He'll rule out the police, because the police around here don't behave that way. He'll feel that some unknown is stalking him. It'll give him fits. OK, I'm convinced. When shall we go?"

Harper looked at her watch. "What time is it, Adam? These time zones always get me."

"Eleven-fifteen."

"Let's go now, then. While the iron's hot. Let's go in my rental car, so we'll be harder to identify. What'll we need?"

"A crowbar, I suppose. And I'd better take the gun."

On the far side of Spine Hill, just before Laurel Lane intersects with Nederland Way, Frank Underwood parked his Porsche, shouldered his knapsack and strode toward the trailhead. As he moved from the sunlight into the shadow of the big firs, a chiding jay, bent on scaring off some squirrel, crow or stray cat, flashed angrily before him and vanished into the brush. Beyond this everything was still. It was the wrong time for joggers and dog walkers, who generally kept early-morning or late-afternoon hours.

About a hundred feet in he turned left and onto a steep uphill trail, almost indistinguishable for its narrowness and lack of use. He knew it, as he knew all the trails in the hilly park, from the mountain-boot jogs he had indulged in years before, wind-training sessions notable for their inhuman altitude gains and wretched footing. Whoever had first blazed them he was unsure of—maybe foresters broadening deer trails.

No one walked them now. No one was aware of the really extensive territory they opened up, the commanding views beyond the ridge, the broad ledges which like sculptured porches of a rock castle lorded it over the valley below. What freedoms they offered! On these porches, behind a broken canopy of maple leaves, for the modest price of a few calories, a mantle of cobwebs and a thorn scratch or two, conspirators could convene for days with impunity, drug dealers could make quiet fortunes, lovers could indulge their vices in full nudity.

Breathing more heavily now, he climbed in silence, alone in the forest.

Near the top he tripped on a root and felt the shape of the gun against his back. After this steepest part, the way was easy again. No tracks here, not even animal, and the cobwebs spelled total disuse. At the ridge crest, puffing heartily, he turned right and continued without a pause. The crest was serrated into little rises and falls, prompting the name Spine. After the second dip he turned off to his left, downhill through tall grass. A huge jackrabbit, shocked maybe out of a nap, crashed through the grass and by him so close that he could feel its wake in the air. He froze and listened. No other noises.

Blackberry stalks, spined and muscular but too new to be fruited, barred his way. Taking off his knapsack he lay down and inched under them training-camp style. In seconds he was on the ledge. It was about ten by twenty feet in area, floored with flat sandstone and partially guarded by scrub maple. He took a pair of compact field glasses from the knapsack and surveyed the view. Snell's white house was prominent in it, unlike its neighbors naked of trees, an iron shot, maybe 180 yards, from where he stood.

He examined the house closely and patiently.

The ancient Country Squire with its perennial ten-speed on a rack in back.

All the house windows curtained but a couple of them half open upstairs.

The dog stretched out, utterly still, like a black figure painted on the sunny deck.

Every sign of Snell's presence except Snell himself.

Underwood went back to the knapsack, removed a thermos and, sitting on a big rock in the shade, drank two refreshing cups of tea. He took out the pistol and laid it in his lap. He strapped the Velcro-ed shell holder onto his left forearm just above the watch and inserted a round in it. He put another round in the gun's chamber and snapped it shut.

He rose and walked with the gun to his viewpoint. A warm breeze ruffled the maple leaves. To the west the sky was untroubled azure. To the east, too distant to threaten but nonetheless forbidding, three summer cumuli towered like sullied peaks.

He put his eye to the gun and sighted down to the house. Through the 9X scope the crosshairs steadily moved from door to window to window at what seemed a distance of sixty feet. He brought the cross back to the front door, slightly above the knob, and held it there. Snell had to use that door to reach the road or his car. To get his mail. To buy groceries. To call the dog or walk it. The door was Snell's lifeline, his breathing hole. Underwood could wait.

He started, almost pulling the trigger. Two jays had hit the maple tree like blue lightning and were smart-alecking around in the branches. Holding the gun in his left hand, he scared them off with a small rock. No time for unintentional shots. If he fired a single shot, just one, and killed Snell with it, it would be most improbable that anyone near the victim would be able to say where it came from. There would be echoes and the element of surprise. But a second shot would give away his general position and bring police around the park in minutes. Underwood could fire a second time only if the street were empty and Snell alone.

He took out a handkerchief and mopped his brow. The smell of the now-powerful sunlight on the dry grass reminded him of California.

He checked his watch. Noon.

Two-handing the gun again he lowered the crosshairs to the dog's chest and tenderly fingered the trigger. Now for the first time he held the power of life and death over a large animal. It was an eerie feeling, an ominous delight. With a single squeeze he could send the beast yelping to darkness, and end forever its fawning and wagging and barking, and rob the pauper Snell of his only company. And from so far away! To strike unerringly from almost two hundred yards was to strike with a more than human hand. The sense of holding unseen power, of striking without being seen, thrilled Underwood physically.

He'd felt it often when under the cover of confidentiality he'd supplied fellow members of this or that committee with devastating little inventions about one of his academic competitors. He'd felt it writing confidential letters, now about an undesirable bid for tenure, now about a nonconforming book on theory. He'd felt it particularly years and years ago when, competing with a brilliant female grad student for the Washagon position, he'd circulated the story that she had sex with her students. That did for her all right! Of course he'd cut that one out of whole cloth, but what the hell, women *all* do it, don't they? Glanda Gazza all but kept a king-sized bed in her office. Look at the way Salem Pogue sucked up to Web Hollins when she was his grad student. And remember that bitch Simmons!

Underwood swallowed hard. Francine Simmons, student in his undergraduate criticism course last fall, good-looking, fair student but *attentive,* those eyes, light gray beneath dark lashes, never off him, all over him as he intoned about cubism, surrealism and the Russian formalists. Fair Francine, Damsel of the Office Hour, always staying late, telling him increasingly intimate secrets in the darkening room, he fearful and fascinated, not knowing if or how to stop her, till one late afternoon, who knows maybe on some kind of sorority bet, Miss Simmons rose as though to leave, and when he rose too she kissed him so hard he lost his power to react, and leaning against him and kissing his neck she began taking off her clothes, first the blouse with its big maroon buttons slipping down her columnar arms and falling silently on the rug, then the jeans with their off-white woven belt and little brass button beneath, and when he turned back to her from nervously locking his door she was stark naked down to her tasseled immaculately white tennis shoes, eyes half closed, lips moist and parted, nipple areas dark and swollen, pelvis slightly withdrawn as though to receive him, shadow line between pressed thighs ascending to inverted pyramid of hair like the symbol of some infernal cult. He felt no arousal but nauseous panic, and when she reached out to draw him close her body became like some sexual weapon cocked to destroy him, like some porno mag lying outrageously open at the crotch, and rage coursed through his body, and with his open hand—

The gun jumped with a shattering report. Underwood, as though shot himself, staggered back, dizzy, blinking. The landscape beneath him looked disordered and skewed, as though with one dumb move and inane untimely assertion he had fatally damaged the universe. Steadying himself, he reloaded and sighted again. Hit in the body, the distant dog twitched and writhed in its own blood like a road-kill cat. Would Snell come through the door to aid it? Could even Snell be so stupid? Underwood moved the sight to the deck-facing windows. The curtains were still. The street remained empty. Time was running out.

He quickly packed his gear and made his way back to the still-empty trail. The tactical consequences of this error were significant but by no means catastrophic. He would leave the park safely. He would shave his beard and dispose of the gun. He would delay his New York trip. He would conduct business as usual, for weeks, maybe months, perhaps feigning humane sympathy for the newly reterrorized Snell; he would scheme on, unknown, unsuspected, thinking, waiting.

Yet why was he shaking so?

A half block past Underwood's house at 976 El Saludo, Snell turned left on Wendell Street and parked by the curb. Reaching for the crowbar, he stuck the straight end up the left sleeve of his jacket and grabbed the bent end with his left hand. The Beretta nestled in his right jacket pocket, a small Nikon camera in his left.

Closing the door he looked over the car at Harper. She silently returned his glance, hers conspiratorial and duly earnest, but with a glint of mischief.

From the road Underwood's place had looked as deserted as ever. And on El Saludo no one was out and about except two kids across the street from 976 who were having at each other with pump-action water pistols. Loaded with secret implements and weapons, on an uncertain quest in the heat of the day into an alien house with a confusingly attractive woman, Snell felt so nervous that the act of walking became a conscious chore.

The houses on El Saludo, all pretentiously natural with their cedar siding and shake roofs and evergreen landscaping, scowled at him like offended burghers.

At 976 they walked through the empty carport directly into Underwood's backyard. Perfectly square and flanked on three sides by a dense laurel hedge, the yard at midday was empty, torrid and shadeless, its lawn overgrown and browned out, its every quarter blaring a scream of cicadas. It was like a place out of time, a court-yard abandoned by culture and won back by a spiteful nature.

On the little deck Snell let the crow slip down from his sleeve and inserted the straight end above the keyhole of the sliding glass door, gently working it back and forth. The latch, which must have been out of adjustment, gave almost at once, and the door slid open with an easy motion, inviting them into the dark maw of the house.

Inside they were momentarily blind. Their setting gradually revealed itself as a living/dining room that spanned the width of the house. The kitchen was on the left, the bedrooms and bathrooms on the right.

Snell strode about the room, increasingly frustrated by an emptiness bordering on sterility. The surfaces were clear. The Danish furniture flaunted its vacuous style. Not a single stray object—magazine, implement, piece of clothing—suggested human presence. He looked back at Harper, who stood frozen by the glass door.

"*Oh God,*" she said. "*I smell coffee.*"

"Let's get out of here," hissed Snell.

"No, not yet." She touched his arm lightly. "Let's risk three minutes. You check the kitchen. I'll look in his bedroom."

He obeyed. His hands trembled as he opened cabinets, pulled out drawers. The normal odds and ends, and not so many of them at that. Nothing, nothing out of the ordinary. Had evil such weak character? Or was Underwood no more than a cipher, a Web Hollins with theoretical frills?

Harper rushed in, carrying something. "I found this on his bed. What is it? Some kind of gun case?"

"It's what we came for," said Snell. "Whatever was in there he's got with him right now. Come on!"

They made for the glass door and closed it behind them in the cicada din and dense heat. They were halfway to the carport when Snell stopped and turned. "The crowbar. I left it—"

"Forget it, Adam." Harper grabbed him and pulled him along around the corner of the house, but the way had suddenly been barred by a shiny black car, and there was Underwood, fearsomely large and bearded, pulling a red bag out of it, and now Underwood was looking at them as though they were creatures from hell.

Snell held the gun case up in the brilliant sunlight. "What's this, Frank?"

Underwood momentarily seemed to shrink, and for maybe a second the two men, like sudden partners in some awful understanding, shared a look of recognition. Then he was at them. Snell dropped the vinyl case and drew his gun, but it flew into the deep grass as

Underwood hit both their bodies, stunning Snell and driving Harper backward into the hedge. Rearing back, Underwood smashed at Snell's head with the bag and the blow catching him between ear and shoulder blackened the sky and he fell down and tasted blood and grass. But she screamed and the day snapped back on again and Snell's eyes focussed on the car. Underwood had pressed Harper back onto the sloping front hood of the Porsche, his hands at her throat. In instants that dragged slowly, enormously, Snell tried to rise and fell back. His limbs were faint and the cicadas sang blatantly in the sick hot air and the familiar concussive pain raged in his head. He struggled to his feet and staggering forward collapsed on the vinyl gun case. He looked up again. Underwood was killing Harper. Her hands, which had been trying to force his away, now flopped haphazardly against the black hood. The bastard. Snell grabbed the gun case and rushed at the car. Holding the case at its muzzle end and swinging it like an ax he brought it down with maximum emphasis on the back of Underwood's head. The big body shuddered without falling. Underwood straightened up and turned woodenly toward Snell but Snell swinging the case this time like a baseball bat hammered him smartly in the brows. The case cracked on impact and Underwood sat down hard in the grass and stayed there, clumsily half-consciously trying to wipe the blood out of his eyes.

Still holding his weapon Snell rushed to Harper and grabbed her hand and pulled her past the car and to the street. They were running now, Harper gasping for breath as they burst through the heavy resistant summer air. Snell looked right to see the water-pistol kids gawking in surprise and then looked back to see Underwood in the street by the carport aiming at them as the pavement by Snell's foot erupted with an outrageous bang. His ankle stinging, he pulled Harper across a lawn as they cut the corner from Underwood's street onto Wendell and made for the car.

Moe of the Dulce police rescue team was hosing Doppler's blood off Snell's deck, where it had made a long sad smear from the spot where the dog was hit to the front door toward which, in hopes of getting help from his master or letting him know what happened, he had dragged himself with his last strength. Clyde was dressing Snell's cut ankle and communing with his grief-stricken patient and Harper, while Emmons and a very sheepish Pierce were examining the cracked gun case. It was now past one in the afternoon. Reluctant to drive straight home, Snell had phoned Pierce's office from a booth, only to learn that the lieutenant was investigating something at Snell's own house, and when he called Pierce there to warn him of a possibly very unsocial call from Underwood, he had learned of Doppler's death.

Pierce had been momentarily outraged by the news of the break-in and confrontation, but agreed on the phone to put out an all-points on Underwood. "We've blown our cover now and better make the best of what we've got. Anything you took from that house during an illegal entry's going to be thrown right out of court. But Underwood's blown his cover too. He killed poor Doppler and tried to kill both of you. With luck we'll also nail him for the assault and kidnap in May and put him away for a long time."

Clyde had just finished the bandaging when Pierce and Emmons moved toward them on the deck. "Forgive me, Adam," said the policeman. "This time I screwed up. We should've had the hills patrolled. But the style of Underwood's first attack on you didn't suggest a hotshot marksman with a supergun."

"Why would he want to shoot Doppler?" asked the still-tearful Snell.

"We're stumped on that one," answered Pierce. "Terror tactics, most likely."

"Where did he shoot from?" asked Harper.

"Up there, I suppose." Pierce pointed to the upper slopes of Spine Hill. He brandished the gun case. "You don't buy one of these to attack somebody at close range. The hill's the only place where he would have been at a safe distance and had some cover."

The phone rang inside and shortly Roy Gallard burst through the front door. "That's your patrolman on the phone, Andy. He says they've got the gun, a seven-millimeter Remington, with a scope, a wristlet cartridge holder and lots of ammunition. It was in Underwood's kitchen."

"No sign of the man?"

"Neither Underwood nor his car."

"Please tell him to fingerprint the gun and not to touch anything else in the house. I'll be over in a few minutes."

Harper rubbed her bruised throat. "Do you think you'll find him?"

Pierce looked evasively at the floor. "If we luck out we'll have him in an hour. But I'm not making any promises. There are a hundred ways out of this town, and there's even the chance that he made it to an airport before the all-points kicked in. But that doesn't mean we won't get him. This case is going national. He'll get nabbed somewhere and soon." He gave Snell's arm a pat. "At least *your* agony's over, Adam. Professor Underwood's not about to visit Dulce again in the near future. That is, not as a free man."

Roy came out again, this time with cans of beer. Pierce refused his, glancing at his watch. "I'm just going. The busywork starts now. We've got to check out Underwood's house and office and find out where he was this summer and question his family, and that's only the beginning. I'll keep you up to date. Let's meet for lunch sometime soon, Adam."

At the edge of the deck Pierce turned back toward Snell. "Illegal entry aside, I'm proud for you. You flushed out Underwood and faced him down. You stood up to your enemy and beat him."

Snell smiled grimly. "That's all Harper's doing. She drove me on like a fury." He took a sip of beer. "Underwood's worst enemy has got to be inside him. You should have seen the horror in those eyes."

"I've decided he's more than human," said Emmons. "I'll dream of him hovering in the dark beside my bedroom window with phosphorescent eye sockets. He's a demon, an inextinguishable sparkle of malice."

"No way," said Pierce, departing. "He's a sick guy who wants locking up, and we're going to do him the favor."

Archbishop Laud, who was no friend to booksellers, introduced many arbitrary restrictions; but they were all, or nearly all, removed during the time of the Commonwealth. So much had bookselling increased during the Protectorate that, in 1658, was published *A Catalogue of the most Vendible Books in England, digested under the heads of Divinity, History, Physic, &c., with School Books, Hebrew, Greek and Latin, and an Introduction, for the use of Schools,* by W. London. A bad time immediately followed. The Restoration also restored the office of Licenser of the Press, which continued until 1694.

—ANONYMOUS, "Bookselling," *Encyclopædia Britannica,*
   11th edition

CHAPTER 3

COLLECTIBLES

Satire is a sort of Glass, wherein Beholders do generally discover every body's Face but their Own; which is the chief Reason for the kind of Reception it meets in the World, that so very few are offended with it. But if it should happen otherwise, the danger is not great; and I have learned from long Experience, never to apprehend mischief, from those Understandings I have been able to provoke; For, Anger and Fury, though they add strength to the *Sinews* of the *Bodys,* yet are found to relax those of the *Mind,* and to render all its efforts feeble and impotent.

—JONATHAN SWIFT,
The Battle of the Books

I like to think that my integrity would not be corrupted by fame, money, and pleasure, but would appreciate the chance of finding out for sure.

—SOVRANA SOSTRATA,
"Abominable" Sermon

COLLECTIBLES I:
A CLUSTER OF SWATCHES

WISHBONE

Just west of Dead Horse Rapids the Wishbone River moderates and tempers its course, flowing smoothly past the cottonwoods of Ergo Park and eight miles thence to Dulce along dreaming reaches and through riffled bends. Snell and Harper arrived at Ergo Park late Sunday morning, inflated Snell's worn and scuffed Sea Eagle raft with a foot pump, loaded it with paddles, sandwiches and wine, and put in. The experience was new to Harper. Accustomed to canoeing, she was at first upset by the rather dizzying behavior of the raft, which handled the calm reaches equally well backward, forward, sideways or in a slow rotation. But she soon grew to appreciate the feelings produced by this aimlessness: pleasant confusion, oblivious trust. She laid her head back on the air-filled bulwark, watched the green world turn and pass above her, sensed in the balmy air a kind of happy rootlessness she had never felt before in waking life.

Snell seemed a fairly able captain. Among the riffles and mild rapids, where wavelets chattered and the very air seemed to share in their excitement, he propped his knees on the front bulwark and aimed for deep water. Only when the river threatened forcing them against the brush on the outside of a bend did he ask her for help. But such things seldom happened. The Ergo Stretch was a pushover, shunned by all serious rafters, and that was exactly why Snell loved it.

Over the five uncomplicated hours from Ergo to Dulce, munching sandwiches, drinking wine, dragging sun-heated limbs in clear water and occasionally going in for a swim, Snell and Harper talked of many things. Of Gabel Lake in the Lion Mountains, sky-blue in its mile-wide cup of granite, where they had hiked yesterday. Of similarities and differences between Washagon and New Hampshire. Of the great blue herons and Canadian geese, whose congregations the boat now and then interrupted. Of rivers and rafting and, by extension, the whole process of deliberately losing touch with one's context and looking back into it from outside (Snell told Harper of when, from his raft, he had had a brief chat with a man on the bank, and how he came away thinking that the words of the chat must have meant something profoundly different to the man on dry land and the man floating by). Of how their adventures over the past few months, first by themselves and then recently together, had been liberating in exactly this way. Of how (for Snell) the ultimate uprooting had been his own learning to understand Underwood, yet how every aspect of Underwood that he comprehended, even the most horrible, found an echo of some sort in his own self-knowledge.

Of traveling to far places and thinking back of home. Of families and how raising families must be like a voyage away from and back to oneself. Of love, with some shyness. Of dinner, with much eagerness. Of the pleasant dinner the night before at Scarlett Souslik's Old World Taverna, in which they'd been bibulously debriefed by Adler,

Gallard, Marlin, Schmutzhauf and Wilkins over Bohemian dumplings and gewürztraminer. Of the manifold virtues and endearing eccentricities of the departed Doppler, Snell's friend since puppyhood. In wistful detail Snell cataloged the Dopplerian vocabulary: the yelp of complaint, the announcing shout, the chuckle-growl of play, the rumble of menace, the painful squeak, the volley of challenge, the pleading squeal, the groan of satisfaction, the primal midnight howl.

Of Snell's disastrous marriage. Of Harper's failed romance with Harry Stuart. And finally, as the boat cleared the long hubbub of white water marking the convergence of the main stem and south fork and cruised into a long, placid final reach, of nothing at all, as they lay on their backs side by side, just touching each other in the afternoon sunlight and the upstream breeze.

Back on dry land Harper sipped wine and watched Snell carefully compress and fold the Sea Eagle which, its air locks now open, wilted and shrank like a remembered dream. No way out of it—she had to fly back to New York tomorrow. Yet she did not want to leave Snell so soon. What she found charming about this man was his patience, his ability to endure troubles with calm and persistence and good cheer, his habitual unhurried attentiveness to every object, word and event, his affability toward thoughts, his quiet cherishing of good things, his simple accountability for his own life. How he put her at her ease! As writer and man he had the unconscious wisdom that women seem to be born with but which they can so seldom teach the opposite sex: the gift of feeling life as seamless flow, rather than as an uneven pathway from goal to goal.

Closing the trunk of the rental car, Snell turned to her and smiled. "Thanks for the best afternoon I ever had," she said, and kissed him.

LOCAL NEWS ITEMS

ATTACKER ELUDES POLICE DRAGNET

DULCE, August 22. Authorities report little progress in the search for Frank Underwood, the University of Washagon English professor wanted for kidnapping, three counts of attempted murder and the killing of a dog. A search of Underwood's house at 976 El Saludo uncovered a highly sophisticated pistol which, detectives believed, was to have been used to shoot Professor Adam Snell, whom Underwood physically assaulted on two other occasions. Underwood's car, a black Porsche 911, was discovered Saturday night near the Dulce freight yards. Police speculate that the suspect may have escaped from Dulce on a freight train.

ACTING PRESIDENT HIT BY SKATEBOARDER

DULCE, August 24. J. Thoreau Marshall, Acting President of the University of Washagon, is in serious but stable condition today after a pedestrian collision on the Washagon campus. According to eyewitnesses, Marshall had just left Mammal Hall and was walking toward Westgate when he was struck from behind by a large man on a skateboard. Thoreau's injuries, which Mother of God Hospital officials describe as a "general flattening effect," were sustained when the operator of the skateboard fell on him in the course of the collision. The unidentified man, who subsequently fled, is being sought by the Dulce Police on charges of involuntary mayhem and leaving the scene of an accident.

Mother of God doctors, who are using a silicon-bubble treatment to help Marshall regain his tone, were guardedly optimistic in their assessment of Marshall's condition. Paul Edson, Washagon Chancellor of Higher Education, reached today by phone, called the incident "alarming and deplorable" and said that he would appoint an interim Acting President early next week.

FROM SNELL'S JOURNAL

September 13, 1990. Thursday.

Strange event! Sitting in my office yesterday afternoon with Sarah, sunlight flooding in, radio playing Cherubini, Sarah detailing the last-ditch effort Quintus was making to reverse her loss of tenure, when someone knocks on the door and I open it, looking up at this massive man in tweeds, something like Cary Grant but bigger and missing an arm, who says nothing but steps back and scrutinizes me as though he's trying to square what he sees with some remembered mental picture. Next to him, momentarily blocked from sight, an indescribably lively-looking woman, medium height, about seventy-five, Gypsy scarf around her head, wearing tartan shirt and lederhosen, holding fat little woolen sack, peering with bright black eyes into the office as though on the lookout for wolves. Man introduces self as Gerald Underwood, *Frank's brother!* and suddenly I'm noting resemblances in the build, stance, facial structure, and suddenly I have the sick feeling that he might be bent on revenge, that the woman might be some *saboteuse* left over from the SS and pressed into service by theorists, that her sack might be full of *Wehrmacht*-issue grenades, until when they've entered and sat down she reaches into it and pulls out a tough-looking blueberry muffin and says, "Ead it, Gerald. You're *shtarfing* yourself!" Gerald sheepishly obliges, and when he turns to offer us muffins I'm convinced that no one with eyes as inquisitive and suffering as his can mean major harm. My office being what it is, a kind of abbreviated hallway, I put them all on the couch, Gerald in the middle, and immediately there's electricity between Gerald and Sarah: Sarah unabashedly gazing at him, Gerald quite fascinated by her name ("Sarah, Sarah," he repeats, and looks excitedly at Waltraut, his companion, who scowls back). What then unfolds justifies Sarah's fascination. In two minutes Gerald has made my own misadventures look like child's play. Horribly wounded in Vietnam, near comatose for twenty-odd years, he's regained consciousness and sought to reconcile himself with Frank, his long-mistreated (!) brother, only to get last month's monstrous news. But Gerald's come here anyway, to await word of his brother, to help if he can and incidentally (as Sarah's eyes glow with delight) to take a degree in environmental economics.

Muffin bag firmly in hand, Waltraut watches Gerald unblinkingly. As he talks, her lips move silently, as though she knows his speech by heart and is prompting him. But all's in vain when apropos of nothing Gerald turns to me and starts trying to apologize "for what Frank did." The tears come then, Gerald tries to wipe them away, Sarah suddenly has a comforting arm around his shoulder, and Waltraut's muffin hand twitches, perhaps on an impulse to hit her new rival with the bag. But soon tears and anger subside, and we spend an hour sharing histories that have so oddly intersected.

They're all coming over to dinner tomorrow night, and I hope to see more of Gerald after I get back from New York.

PHONE CALL FROM A TITANESS

10 A.M., Friday, September 14, 1990

GLANDA GAZZA [*from Dulce*]: Hello?

FLOCONNE DE MAIS [*from Nantucket*]: Hello, who is dis?

GAZZA: Glanda Gazza.

DE MAIS: Professor Gazza, dis is Floconne de Mais.

GAZZA [*gasping*]: Floconne de Mais! Professor, I'm so honored by this call! I mean *wow!* You've got no idea how much all of us here have been influenced by your work! Why, *Confessions of a Fainting-Couch* alone—

DE MAIS: Oh dat bullshit. Recycle dat pulp, eet's been superseded. And call me Floxy, no problem. Listen, I've been tryeeng to reach Frank Underwood. What ees he, on sabbatic or sometheeng?

GAZZA [*hesitating*]: He—there's been a tragedy. Haven't you read about it? Didn't you read the *Times*?

DE MAIS: *Read?* We never *read* anymore. You mean you guys still *read*? Get wid eet! Readeeng's been *grossly overrated*! But I did *read* somedeeng recently dat just aboud knocked my socks off, *garters, panties and all!* Ha ha ha. Dat's why I'm calleeng! What's eet like to work wid a genius like Adam Snell?

GAZZA [*faintly*]: Adam Snell?

DE MAIS: Am I pronounceeng de name right? Does he say Schnell or Snail or what? He's een your department, isn't he?

GAZZA: No, it's Snell, and he *is* in the English department, though *I'm* not going to be anymore. You see [*a bit self-consciously*] we're being offered support to split off from the English department and form a new Department of Literary Theory.

DE MAIS [*archly*]: Well *rooty-toot-toot,* if you'll pardon de expression. Literary teory's on eets way out, though de news maybe got delayed een Omaha. But stop changeeng de subject. What's eet like to work wid a genius like Snell? You actually get to dreenk coffee wid dis man? How do you keep yourselves from collecteeng his dandruff?

GAZZA: Well, you see, most of us—I mean—don't think so highly of Adam's work.

DE MAIS: Work? *Masterwork!* Dis dude's got more class dan Céline! Eet's not just great writeeng, eet's a teoretical revolution! He's cooked up a completely new correlation of gender and art. He's got us all rewriteeng ourselves!

GAZZA: You mean not just you—?

DE MAIS [*interrupting*]: Me? My whole department. See, I find dis moosty croosty copy at a garage sale, no less! Dey give eet to me for notheeng! I don't know why I take eet, maybe because eet looked so beat up and lonely, like somebody dat got raped. I take eet home, wave to Phyllis and march wid eet straight eento de loo (I mostly read Marx on de loo, but not *dis* time!). Well, dat's the longest time *I* ever sat on de loo! After twenty pages, I start to shout and seeng. [*Sings deafeningly:*] "Toréador, en garde! Toréador! Toréador!" Dat's my favorite song. Phyllis, she call, "Floxy, is anytheeng wrong?" "Don't bother me," I call out. "I'm geddeeng *flushed away*!" Next day I have eet copied. I shove eet een fifteen mailboxes! A month later eet's a sensation, not just een Engleesh, but een comparative literature, women's studies—

GAZZA: Women's studies! But, Floc-Floxy, didn't they find Adam's treatment of Sovrana a bit, well, ideologically delimited?

DE MAIS: *Au contraire!* Tell me, learned prof, what's ideological aboud telleeng de truth? What's ideological aboud a good screw? Sovrana's primitive, she's *prisca philologia.* Dat's my phrase, don't steal eet. Haven't you heard, de primitive supersedes ideology? Why, de woman is meta-literary! She's a seengle spoken word, an oath, a cry of astonishment! Sure, she fucks up and gets stoned to death. But even *dat* part is full of sperm, suggesteeng dat she's a transitional *fin de siècle* hero, dat she's leadeeng de female out of ass-lickeeng or political postureeng and eento a world of eendividuation and stress. Sure, she's confrontational, but remember, Professor, de only way to get from de sword to de plowshare is wid de hammer! And sexy! Wouldn't mind haveeng a roll een de hay wid dat peach myself! Read me on Sovrana een next month's *New York Review of Books.* Dey're giveeng me two full pages up front, wid DE MAIS ON SNELL on de cover. How's about *dat,* tralala? Anoder teeng. Meca L'Olla, Massimo Nugae, Angel Thwackum and I are puddeeng togeder an Adam Snell Colloquium billed for New Haven een January, and I was tryeeng to reach Frank—is he still among de liveeng?—to see if he could get Snell to give de plenary address. Have *you* got any pull wid him? You guys wanna come yourselves?

GAZZA: You might have better luck phoning Snell directly. I'll give you his home number. And thank you so much for the invitation to New Haven. We've indeed underestimated Adam if you, the world's leading literary theorist, and such eminent theorists as Professors L'Olla, Nugae and Thwackum—

DE MAIS: I tell you, literary teory *sucks*. I *discover*, don't you know, dat *literature*, I mean everydeeng dat's written down, from Shakespeare to ferry tickets, is just wee baby leetle part of a huge COSMOS OF DISCOURSE, a great corpus of HUMANIMAL SEMIOTICS! Dis *cosmos*, look you, eencludes *all meaning eentended or apprehended,* dat means *science, art, politics,* you name eet, *technology, plants, animals, sex.* Dat's right, *sex*! God, woman, *theenk of the fieldwork! Theenk of doing eet on a grant!*

HOBOKEN STRANGER

Daytimes he sleeps, tinny radio still blaring, in a little flophouse just off the docks. Five nights a week he security-guards at a big electronics warehouse on the north side of town. Other nights, you'll glimpse him, in jeans and jean jacket, heavily bearded now, sucking brown-bagged whiskey by the river, or provisioning at the meager shop downstairs from his room, or suddenly turning, with hulking purposeful stride, off a well-lit street and down an alley. He doesn't exercise now, and the flesh is heavier on him. He has no profession now, no expertise, and his handsome blue eyes, furtively downward-turned, have lost their arrogant keenness, their hunter's glint. He has no global agenda, no vaulting ambition now, only a dark intent, too warped for rationalization, too shadowed and oblique even for words, dumbly stalking him from day to day.

He has known the hardness that seemed his due, the gross solitude of freight yards in twilight, the sooty rat-trodden floors of endlessly swaying freight cars, the beds of wet grass by stinking estuaries, the urine-scented mud under bridge approaches. He has felt the cold knife blade against his neck and watched with dispassionate attention as his own hands ripped the knife from the man and forced it to the hilt three times into the writhing belly. He has plodded dumbly in the shouting sun beneath the billboards of truck routes, as his own sweat raised hell in his grime-stiffened shirt.

Now he sits by the river, just before work in the sunset of late summer, while a gaily painted tug tows a garbage scow, its heaped cargo the focus of a whirlwind of accusing gulls, downriver toward the Battery. The sun glints back at him brazenly off the Chrysler Building's roof and the tapelike vertical window facings of the Empire State Building. Of this enormous scene his withdrawn staring eyes make nothing but wholesale injustice and manifest chaos. The shell of his identity is gone, the neologistic aphorisms banked on their pat reductive system all fed to ovens of shame and fury, the laconic hauteur of the academic aristocrat laid low by floods of horror.

An alley cat ventures near him for food but recoils in the wind of a wild blow. Underwood rises slowly, grabs his lunch box and lumbers hunch-shouldered off the pier and to the right.

COLLECTIBLES II:
A BUNDLE OF LETTERS

PAUL EDSON TO WARREN SCHMUTZHAUF

September 17, 1990
Confidential

Dear Professor Schmutzhauf:

Iam redit et virgo, redeunt Saturnia regna,
iam nova progenies caelo demittitur alto.

Allow me to express my admiration, first for the brilliant work leading up to your discovery of muccasin, second for your equally inspired plan for disposing of Benedict Snark's generous gift to the University. Let me treat the two parts of your plan in the order in which you presented them:

Your decision to set aside $1.5 million for a Mucca Professorship in Humane Letters will strengthen the University in a most deserving and needy area. I heartily commend your stipulation in the draft charter that this professorship, the richest and most honorific on the University of Washagon campus, be awarded to Adam Snell. I was recently able to get my hands on a copy of his book and find it a minor masterpiece, bespeaking intellectual insight and integrity of a high order.

Your generous support of the new Department of Environmental Economics will certainly make it the strongest department of its kind in the nation. Professor Gleuck is already on the prowl for outstanding candidates for the five new positions you have opened up.

Part Three of your plan, which calls for splitting the Department of English into "theoretical" and "essentialist" groups, locating the theoretical group in Mucca Hall as a separate Department of Literary Theory and restaffing the original Department of English with a requisite number of real literature professors, will greatly enhance the effectiveness of the humanities faculty and doubtless will be seen as attractive by all concerned. The benefits of this realignment are double. First, the Department of English will be restored to strength as a body considering literature itself, and not the theoretical manipulation of literature, the paramount element in an English degree. Second, literary theory's capacity, in and of itself, to edify and empower students will be tested in a fair arena.

Let me know if I can be of any further help in the implementation of your proposals. As you know, Thor Marshall was flattened by a skateboarder last month and is not likely to be back with us for some time. In his place I am today appointing Alex MacCrae Acting President.

> With best regards,
> Paul Edson
> Chancellor

GLANDA GAZZA TO VARIOUS COLLEAGUES

September 19, 1990
FROM: Glanda Gazza, Head, Department of Literary Theory
TO: Emerson Baismacou, Ardilla Biber, Robin Cuervo, Sandy Eule, Webster Hollins, Rainer Maulwurf, Evelyn Scamel, Orville Mishunk, Alois Stoat, E. F. Taupe, [etc.]

I trust that all of you will join me in accepting Warren Schmutzhauf's kind offer (now made official by Alex MacCrae) to house our new Department of Literary Theory in the western wing of Mucca Hall. I have visited these new offices and found them roomy and well equipped, complete with a large lounge/conference room to accommodate our doubtless frequent meetings and colloquia. I expressed concern to Warren about the curious smells that seem to be wafting over from his labs in the eastern wing, and he assured me that they were all organic and would be gone as soon as he passed on to a more advanced stage of research. For the moment, however, room fresheners are advised, and surgical masks may be necessary for the more sensitive.

Let me congratulate all of you on a great and, to me at least, unexpected victory for our group in particular and our movement in general. This term we will inaugurate the first independent Department of Literary Theory in the United States. Many campuses, I am certain, will follow our example.

I am delighted, finally, to inform you that Web Hollins has accepted President MacCrae's invitation to join us at Mucca Hall and accordingly has resigned the headship of the Department of English. Though not a theorist himself, he is at work on a massive bibliography of theory that will greatly simplify research in our field.

ALEXANDER MacCRAE TO SARAH WILKINS

September 19, 1990
FROM: Alexander MacCrae, Acting President
TO: Sarah Wilkins, Assistant Professor of English

It gives me great pleasure to inform you that your appeal for a reversal of the negative decision on your promotion and tenure case has been granted, and that as of September 15 of this year you have been promoted to Associate Professor with indefinite tenure. Details of these cases are normally confidential, but since our negative decision and prolonged deliberations may have given you cause for undeserved anxiety, let me inform you that your promotion is based on lengthy referrals from your publisher, leading environmental groups and nationally ranking professors in your field—referrals which my predecessor for some reason did not see fit to obtain.

I should note in closing that the complex and controversial nature of your case was responsible for an innovation which is likely to influence the way we handle promotions here at Washagon. While I was trying to evaluate the variety of conflicting opinions about your published and unpublished work, it occurred to me that my decision might be considerably enhanced if I actually read some of it. This I proceeded to do, and with great pleasure. I am currently drafting a memo to my associate deans, and to the chairs of all standing promotion committees, recommending that they initiate the practice (exotic as this may sound) of reading at least a few pages of candidates' publications.

Let me congratulate you on your fine work and encourage you to continue it at Washagon.

ANDREW PIERCE TO ADAM SNELL

[From Andrew Pierce, lieutenant, Dulce police department, to Adam Snell. On the back of a postcard (*reverse:* Lorenzetti's painting *Buon Governo*) from Siena, Italy, September 20, 1990:]

Dear Adam,
    Buon giorno and *ciao!* Thanks for telling me about this town. I've never seen such a fabulous City Hall. Also I greatly favor the two-hour lunches and the afternoon naps that follow. The cops here tell me that the crime rate during that period is real low.
    Last week we rented a Fiat and visited villages very much like the one in which your Sovrana bit the dust. Beautiful countryside; handsome, hardworking people. The women around those parts look *much* too nice to have stoned a philosopher to death, though I must admit that her riding around naked on horseback might have been sort of a provocation.

See you in October,
Andy

In the first English Copyright Act (1709), which specially relates to booksellers, it is enacted that, if any person shall think the published price of a book unreasonably high, he may thereupon make complaint to the archbishop of Canterbury, and to certain other persons named, who shall thereupon examine into his complaint, and if well founded reduce the price; and any bookseller charging more than the price so fixed shall be fined £5 for every copy sold. Apparently this enactment remained a dead letter.

—ANONYMOUS, "Bookselling," *Encyclopædia Britannica,* 11th edition

CHAPTER 4

RETURN

They went quietly down into the roaring streets, inseparable and blessed; and as they passed along in sunshine and in shade, the noisy and the eager, and the arrogant and the froward and the vain, fretted, and chafed, and made their usual uproar.

—CHARLES DICKENS,
Little Dorrit

The world's fate hinges on the difference between
truth and lie.

—SOVRANA SOSTRATA,
Gesta

Snell's neighbor in the crowded first-class cabin of the 757 was a puffy-faced gravelly voiced New York options trader named Pete, who wore a mauve Ralph Lauren tennis shirt, a dauntingly posh camel's hair blazer, knife-creased blue trousers and snakeskin loafers. He'd been in Washagon, he said, to visit his racehorses. He grimaced a lot, in a Bogart sort of way, especially while stealing snide glances at Snell's ironed khakis and geriatric cordovans. "What brings you to New York?" he finally asked, clearly meaning "What the hell are you doing in first class?"

Himself somewhat uneasy in the showy champagne-and-leather ambience (Sig Bazoom had said, "Nothing but the best for our Adam— that is, if you don't mind me calling you Adam"), Snell explained that he was actually going to a launch party for a new book.

Pete was incredulous. "You mean they give parties for books? Next you'll tell me they baptize 'em."

Just out of Denver there occurred an unsettling event. Banking eastward after a westward takeoff the big plane suddenly aborted its muscular climb and began drifting anemically southward about a thousand feet above the hills. Something was the matter. Snell glanced at Pete, still sipping his champagne, still intent on *Tennis Today*. Someone turned on the P.A. and left it on, staticky, chaotic. Then the captain, who sounded on the verge of swallowing his own tongue, said, "We're going back," turned off the P.A. and went into a steep bank.

Snell looked at Pete again. Pete *knew* now, face of fear, knuckles white on the wineglass stem, bulging eyes fixed on the seat ahead of him, *Tennis Today* slipping from his lap. Snell turned to his other neighbor, across the aisle, a florid man whose fingers had frozen on the keys of his laptop. "Think it's an engine?"

"Maybe a bomb," said the man. This was enough for Pete. Now he had his wallet out, fumbling for a credit card and before you knew it he was past Snell and punching keys on the in-plane telephone at the bulkhead. One hand on the headpiece, one hand distractedly pushing away the stewardess who was trying to get him back to his seat, he barked a few orders into the phone and returned.

"Call your family?" Snell asked.

"My secretary," Pete croaked.

"About your will?"

"Will, shmill," said Pete. "I told her to shred paper."

Engines throttled back, the plane floated groundward on a shallow glide path. More static from the P.A., and then the voice of the chief stewardess announcing with thinly disguised pique that she was as much in the dark about what was going on as anyone else. Snell looked past Pete through the window at the brown October hills and suddenly wondered what the blazes he was doing on the plane. Had he fought off Underwood to be barbecued, along with side orders of nachos, peanuts and options trader, in flaming first-class wreckage? Were launch parties spiritual communions of such magnitude as to warrant the risk of incineration? He groaned. But then, he was a writer, and this was part of a writer's job.

And he would have three days with Harper. Who wouldn't risk crashing for that?

Snell could see a fire truck waiting at the near end of the runway as they landed. Taxiing to the gate, the captain came over the pipe again, this time apologizing for earlier silences, explaining that the problem had been an "overheated" pressurization system and announcing a one-hour delay for repairs.

The second takeoff from Denver, far more satisfactory than its predecessor, found Pete in a drunken stupor in Snell's seat (a favor begged by Pete so as to be nearer "the amenities") and Snell enjoying the view from the window. When the plane leveled off he asked for bourbon and sipped it, thirty-five thousand feet over the Nebraska plains, in an ecstasy of relief. The emergency seemed to have purged him of more than mere fear: of anxieties lingering from summer, of tensions from his new professional responsibilities, of nervousness about New York. His body felt strong again, and he now yearned in the most uncomplicated way to see Harper and embrace her and present telling arguments for her relocation to Dulce.

There was also news to share. Underwood had been traced, via the testimony of battered and terrorized transients, to the greater New York area. He'd been connected with a homicide in Toledo and described as a psychopath in full bloom, a sullen violent darkness-loving man, liable to accesses of catatonic depression and fits of bestial rage. The FBI was on the case now, the man's prints were in circulation, and the lightest bookable offense, even a drunk-and-disorderly, was likely to spark an identification and land him in prison for life.

The Dulce campus, meanwhile, was hopping with activity. Ralph Adorno, the ailing president, had made an unexpected recovery and taken up the reins of power again; while Thor Marshall had announced his intention to step down and return to research in business statistics after his release from Mother of God. The grounds division was beautifying select areas of the Pisham Homestead, and the office of security had posted, with little hope of their being obeyed, a number of prohibitions against skateboarding on campus. The English department, now under the benign leadership of Hal Emmons, was at work reviewing job applications by the thousands.

Yet for productive activity nothing matched Mucca Hall. The east wing bubbled, popped, rumbled and hissed as Schmutzhauf's people tested mucca-grass applications from gasification to chewing gum. The west wing resounded with the whine of computer printers and the chirping of excited voices. A sudden and unexpected dearth of students had left the theorists with great spans of time on their hands, and they weren't losing a moment. Some had started enormous research projects. Inspired perhaps by Web's bibliography, Glanda Gazza had embarked on a seven-volume *History of Literary Theory,* which would cover the subject from the early nineteenth century (which for her was the literary equivalent of the Big Bang) right up to the present. Alois Stoat, the Foucauldian, had broken ground on an equally ambitious *History of Wounds* (whose first sentence, posted on his office door to the great approval of his colleagues, ran, "A wound is an intrusion into the posited Self"); while the irrepressible Emerson Baismacou was conducting a nonstop seminar on his recently published *Oracle, Orifice* and his soon-to-appear *The Text as Undergarment*. Supported by a massive government grant, E. F. Taupe was eloquently advancing the thesis that all known forms of heterosexual activity were processible rape; while Sandy Eule was rough-drafting a polemic which asserted that books were not written by people, or, if they were, they were not books.

Others, driven on by news of Floconne de Mais's newly announced study of humanimal semiotics, had occupied the Committee Room where, almost from dawn to dusk, braced with copious infusions of coffee and interrupted by scarcely a student, they debated intractably subtle distinctions in unintelligibly recondite terminology.

In spite of Warren Schmutzhauf's repeated protestations that he had eliminated all odors from the west wing, some theorists still complained of a mild sulfuric smell.

Gazza, who had emerged from the Edson debacle with scarcely a feather ruffled, seemed more robust and aspiring than ever. Attired in an endless variety of fashions, she lorded it over the department from an office full of potted plants and professional memorabilia, while three secretaries labored hour on hour to convey her correspondence, reports, announcements, commendations, memos and directives. Confident, outgoing, even jovial, she sponsored gala Saturday-night socials in the roomy lounge, exotic soirees characterized by unfamiliar modes of dress, minimalist music, Demerara rum, simultaneous speeches and, as the evening wore on, lantern-lit ululations.

Only one of her new ambitions had been thwarted. The illustrious Butzi Siskin, informed from afar of the Snell scandal, had diverted her course from Dulce to East Grapefruit University in Missibama, where she now sat as dean.

The sometime theoretical young lion Frank Underwood was all but forgotten by his ex-cohorts. Alone among the theorists, Rainer Maulwurf revered Frank's memory and remained in awe of his tragic intensity. Immured in his office, Maulwurf labored clandestinely among piles of theoretical texts and journals. His high voice was occasionally audible out in the hall, enthusiastically whining snatches of his own discourse. It was rumored that his scholarly project was to prove, with pitiless logic and watertight methodology, the ideological limitations of Adam Snell's *Sovrana Sostrata*—a task made even more heroic at present by Maulwurf's inability to find a copy anywhere.

But all that would change now. The book had been through production and was, as Harper put it, "at the warehouse." Snell had seen a copy of it himself, weirdly *déjà vu,* identical in almost every detail to the original Penrose Press edition. As the plane's tires screamed on contact with the New York tarmac, Snell wondered whether Underwood, Maulwurf and company were unlucky anomalies, or whether prides of rampant theorists, nihilists and fundamentalists, some perhaps of the psychopathic persuasion, would congregate in force against him. He wondered whether next year's Adam Snell Colloquium in New Haven, recently mooted to him in quasireligious tones by Floconne de Mais on the phone (he politely declined to attend), had been merely the front for some terrorist abduction. Maybe he shouldn't be so eager to see *On Wonderment* sail into print. But that couldn't be known till later. For now he concentrated on restoring to consciousness the still-sodden Pete (who asked if it all had been a dream) and then working his way through the warrens of La Guardia.

Snell waited in line forty minutes for the twenty-minute taxi ride to the Algonquin. After a nostalgic glance at the literary bar, he ensconced himself in his room, phoned Harper to announce his arrival, showered and, eclipsing the lights of Forty-fourth Street with a sweep of the curtains, settled himself in bed.

He would have little sleep that night. No sooner did head touch pillow than he remembered what the near-crash and its aftermath had made him forget: that, if police reports could be trusted, he was now within a few miles of Frank Underwood.

Next morning just past ten he turned right on Fifth Avenue and strode downtown through light, warm rain. The rain must have been the first of autumn, for seeking out the tiny unpaved plots of midtown, the sidewalk flowerpots, the trees behind the New York Public Library, it had evoked fresh odors of vanished flowers and made the wet air remember days of summer. His own memories of the city were mainly decades older than that, memories of a college boy's expeditions and experiments, of pretentious concierges and preposterous coming-out parties, of heroic lofts and vest-pocket *pieds-à-*

terre, of three-dollar eggplant parmigiano at Delmonico's and beery summer afternoons at the café of the Central Park Zoo, of sudden mad gyrations between holy and profane, of haughty overdressed girls from Vassar or Smith or Radcliffe suddenly naked and playful in townhouse bedrooms. The rain couldn't bring back *those* smells, of ginger-ale highballs and shampooed hair and My Sin perfume, nor the feeling of new reality, transfiguring revelation, that they had given him.

He passed Thirty-fourth Street and the Empire State Building and continued south. Now the morning smells of coffee and bacon and English muffins and frosted pastry wafted in from the numbered streets, as though to win him over from his course. But Harper had said not to eat breakfast, and he had a few blocks to go.

The receptionist at Wolper McNab's twentieth-floor office smiled wanly, as though sizing up Snell's tweed jacket and khakis immediately as those of some first-book author or pesky submitter, and keyed in Harper's extension. In seconds Harper was there, radiant, smiling as she came round the corner, and without a word she took him by the arm and led him back that way past a few open doors to her office at the end of the hall. They hugged warmly. "Sure you haven't eaten?"

"Not since the plane."

She made space for him on a little blue couch by a coffee table bearing abundant lox, bagels and cream cheese. "I'll be right back," she said, and in her absence he admired the south-facing view which comprehended, in the muted colors of the wet day, an extraordinary complexity of urban architecture culminating in the Woolworth Building. He looked around. Harper's rather large office reminded him of his own dining room: no decorations to speak of, three sides lined floor-to-ceiling with books. But Harper's were samplings of Wolper McNab harvests, sometimes in quantities of two or three per title.

Harper returned beaming, placed a bottle of chilled Asti Spumante on the table, pulled up a swivel chair and sat down facing him. "We will call this a brunch," she announced. "We can go out for coffee later. May I serve you?"

Snell consumed two succulent bagels and was much refreshed by the sparkling wine, which seemed to bring its own memories of summer and youth. The mild morning intoxication brought home more fully his delight at seeing Harper again, and he relaxed into this feeling as she related to him her own remembered impressions of Dulce. She hiccupped, and both broke out laughing.

"This'll get you fired," said Snell.

"No way," she said, hiccupping and laughing some more. "Sig's in Nashville, haranguing the sales reps. I'm boss while he's away." There was a pause as they looked at each other sweetly. It occurred to Snell that he'd not yet told Harper about his close escape on the plane out of Denver. As he did this her eyes got very serious, her presence more intense. "You poor man," she said, coming over to sit beside him and putting her hand on his arm.

He put his other hand on hers and, as he avouches, has never let go of it since.

At ten-fifteen the next morning Snell and Harper were at her York Avenue apartment, doubtless discussing some philological nicety or other, when the phone started ringing and wouldn't quit.

"I won't answer," said Harper as it rang and rang. "Bosses don't have to answer phones. And besides, I'm not home."

"Somebody very much wants you to be," said Snell, handing her the receiver.

Harper accepted it with a frown. "Hello? Kit! How—what? Are you hurt?" Her eyes got bigger as she listened to some lengthy narration. "Is he dead? . . . Yes I can. I'll bring Mr. Snell himself."

She hung up, turned to Snell and held him at arm's length. "There's been an explosion at our warehouse in Hoboken. A man's been killed. The police think it's Underwood."

Guiding the Mercedes deftly down Forty-second Street toward the Lincoln Tunnel, she told Snell more about the call. The Kit in question was Kit Henslow, the warehouse chief, a Londoner who'd abandoned England because he " 'ited warm beer," known throughout the firm for his good humor and love of his work. As usual he'd been up with the birds this morning, opened the warehouse and clocked in at eight-fifteen. Immediately he'd smelled smoke and traced it to the main storage area. The lights in the big room had blown, so he went in with a flashlight.

"By himself?" queried Snell.

"You haven't met Kit," answered Harper. The storage area was cavernous and enormous, like half a football field, but Kit hadn't had far to look. Aisle Two was in absolute chaos. All the books stacked on the left wall near the entrance had come down and were now heaped in a pile about six feet high, some still in their cases and some loose on the floor. Pages, spines and a million bits of packing material were everywhere. The heavy acrid smell ("Stinkin' like 'Ides, it was") suggested explosives.

Kit called the police, who told him to vacate the building at once and who soon arrived en masse, together with fire trucks and an ambulance. He had waited outside, drinking coffee with his staff and the firemen, while the bomb squad cleaned up the mess. It was twenty minutes before they found the man, lying at the very bottom beside a twisted aluminum ladder. The rescue people were called in, but he was quite dead and had apparently been so ("All stiff 'e was, like a mouse in a trap") for several hours. The man carried no ID, but he was obviously the bomber. The wireless detonator was still in his jacket pocket.

"What made them suspect it was Underwood?" Snell asked as they left the tunnel and turned off for Hoboken.

"A file photo of him had just been posted at the station. They recognized the face. They're checking fingerprints now, but we can make a positive identification."

"What do you keep in Aisle Two?"

"Aisles One and Two are staging areas. Kit stores new deliveries from the printer there until they can be put where they belong."

"And my book?"

"*Sovrana Sostrata* definitely would have been on Aisle One or Two."

They parked near a massive gray building of awkwardly neo-classical design, around the front of which a miscellaneous crowd of about fifty were clustered. One of them, a huge bald mustached man in overalls, came running to the car.

"It's 'im! Miss 'Arper, it's 'im! The prints match!" Harper hastily introduced Snell. "Come quick, Mr. Snell. Thiy've lide him out in front. Don't you go a-lookin' now, Miss 'Arper. This ine't a pretty sight."

But Harper insisted on seeing the body. Henslow imperiously made way for them through the crowd, and Snell found himself looking down at a strangely small-looking white-shrouded form on a stretcher that had been set down on the sidewalk. "Are you Professor Snell?" asked a hawklike man in a gray hat from across the stretcher. "I'm Captain Maier. We've been waiting for you. Uncover him, Leo."

The shroud was drawn past the shoulders, and Snell faced his sworn enemy for the last time. Underwood wore a jean jacket over a plaid western shirt. The head was turned rigidly to one side. The skull was bloodily dented in, but the features remained intact. The eyes were half shut showing only white, the lips, as though about to speak or snarl, pulled slightly back from the teeth. "That's Underwood," said Snell, catching his breath. He had expected a tragic, pitiful sight. Instead the face now disappearing beneath the shroud bespoke, as though undyingly, malicious intensity, terrible purpose.

Two paramedics picked up the stretcher and slid it into the ambulance. The ambulance doors slammed, the crowd began to disperse, the police thanked Snell and retired. Henslow, who'd been off telling his staff they could leave for the day, rejoined Snell and Harper in front of the warehouse.

"Must've set 'is charge and touched it off 'appenstantially on the way down the ladder," remarked Kit, lighting up a cigar. Snell suddenly remembered *Sovrana Sostrata*. Had Underwood succeeded a second time in destroying his magnum opus? He looked at Harper, who with the same question on her mind posed it first.

Henslow had words of comfort. "No, Miss 'Arper. *Sovrana Sostrata*'s minely sife. 'Is bomb shredded one kise of 'er, but the explosive punch, so to say, got shunted up to other kises on top. These were certain of our mijor classics kises, Tolstoy and Shikespeare and Dickens and the like. It's a kise of *Little Dorrit* what done 'im. Stove 'is 'ed in right proper, she did."

"I've got to call Gerald," Snell said to Harper.

"Do it from my apartment. Thanks, Kit. Let us know what's damaged as soon as you can."

"Wite just one moment, Miss 'Arper." Kit was already bustling back into the warehouse. In a minute he reappeared with two boxes of books, one slightly scorched but intact, the other, which he carried easily with thumb and forefinger, ragged and mutilated. " 'Ere's a fresh kise for your complimentaries, Miss 'Arper. And this 'ere one's a souvenir for you, Professor."

Snell accepted the devastated box, rummaged into the wreckage it contained and withdrew a single copy of his book. It felt pathetically light in his hand. The black-lettered white cover, with its strangely prescient profile of his heroine, was more or less intact, but the book's shape had been distorted by the force of the explosion, and the text was variously burned, gouged and frayed into confetti.

"I'll treasure this one, Kit," he said, slipping the book into his jacket pocket. "It's been revised by the world's leading authority."

POSTSCRIPTS

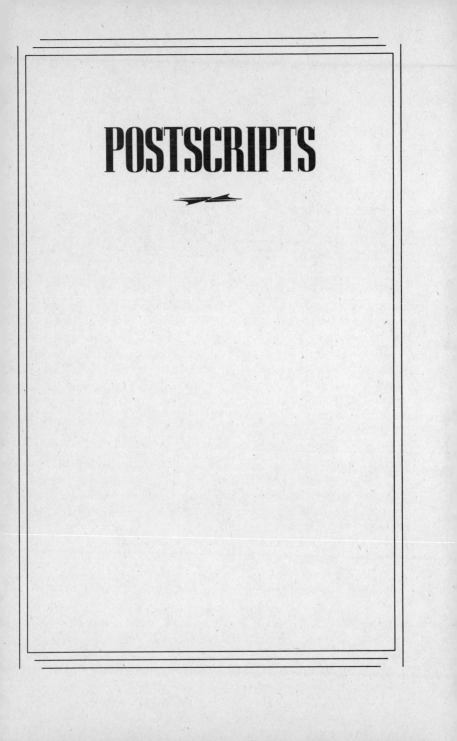

POSTSCRIPT 1

by Adam Snell

I take up pen with great reluctance. For months I have delayed, hoping that a massive confusion, born of malice and compounded by poor communications, would either subside of itself or be put to rest by accurate media coverage. But now I have no choice. The imminent global paperback reissue of Robert Grudin's *Book,* with simultaneous translations into twenty-three foreign languages, precludes any more modesty or hesitation. The world has got to know the facts, and unhappily I am at the moment the individual most capable of recounting them.

I must begin with the unpleasant task of exposing a slander. In a letter to *The New York Times Book Review* dated June 17, 1995, Glanda Gazza, then of East Grapefruit University but previously at the University of Washagon, created a national furor by claiming that I, not Robert Grudin, was the real author of *Book.* Grudin, she brazenly declared, was himself a fiction, a figurehead trumped up in a project that she termed "the megalomaniacal self-aggrandizement of Adam Snell." Corollary to this project, she continued, was the propagation of libelous material against her, her colleagues in the now-defunct Department of Literary Theory at Washagon, and the theoretical establishment at large. (For readers who wish to be reminded what literary theory was, an informative if choppy account is given in Grudin's book. See especially the Handlist of Terms on pp. 62–63.)

Using this letter as a sort of clarion call, Gazza commenced against me the much-publicized legal action, which, after five years of hearings and appeals, has finally been concluded in her total disfavor.

Why a hoax so preposterous as hers inspired any indulgence at all from the courts or excitement from the press, there are three credible reasons. First, the huge popularity of *Book,* which stood number one on *The New York Times* best-seller list for so many months that the editors retired its number, served as a beacon to the curious. Second, these "curious," who comprise, I regret to say, a substantial percentage of the reading public, have traditionally characterized themselves as preferring distasteful fictions to innocuous realities. Third, the talented author of *Book,* who might otherwise, with bold and decisive strokes, have put these fictions to rest once and for all, was not present to do so. On April 12, 1992, Captain Andrew Pierce of the Dulce police department had telephoned me with the tragic news that Robert Grudin had disappeared.

I regret that in a mere half-page the reader will know as much about my friend's disappearance, or his possible whereabouts, as I have learned in several years. But first it will be necessary to supply some background:

In early December 1990 Robert Grudin, a Chicago writer with whose work I had some acquaintance, telephoned me urging that I tell the story of my recent adventures in a book. I unconditionally declined, citing first of all the exigent demands of my current work (*On Wonderment,* which I then planned to publish during my own lifetime, having grown to over nine hundred pages in manuscript with no end in sight) and secondly the fact, now made clear to me for the thousandth time, that no document of naked truth, be it of the most harmless nature, will ever be warmly received by society. When Mr. Grudin asked me why then I continued writing myself, I responded that if he looked at *On Wonderment* in its present form, he would see truth so attenuated by anecdote, modified by humor and protected by poetic metaphor as to appear, to the untrained reader, no different from the diurnal essayistic gossamer of this or any other age. Apparently convinced by this reasoning, or at least by my conviction in embracing it, Mr. Grudin then made the proposal that initiated the literary enterprise now known as *Book.* He himself would write my story, he said, not as a venture into truth but rather as an exotic diversion and cautionary tonic for the inventive, if I would agree to provide technical assistance and stylistic oversight.

I replied to him that, because this proposal personally affected others besides myself, I would have to call him back. During the next week I conferred with my wife, who gave conditional assent, and Ensign Underwood, who generously endorsed the project on the grounds that his brother's tragic story, if told in authentic detail, might be of some use to society. Chancellor Edson, the newly promoted Captain Pierce, Doctors Maynard and O'Shea, Professors Adler, Emmons, Marlin, Schmutzhauf and Wilkins, and Dr. Gallard all approved the project and warmly pledged assistance; others were not consulted. Grudin we knew to have apt descriptive and reportorial skills, as well as a lively imagination. On December 13 I phoned him back, agreeing to the project on the following conditions:

- that my relationship with Harper Snell be treated with delicacy;
- that Grudin's contact with me, whether by telephone or in person, be limited to the later afternoon hours (my writing day ends regularly at 3 P.M.); and
- that I would retain full authority regarding quality control, including the right to veto and even destroy a manuscript that did not meet my standards of decorum and authenticity.

These Grudin accepted in writing.

That he might conduct the many hours of local interviewing and research necessary for his purposed undertaking, Mr. Grudin became recipient of the first Schmutzhauf-Snark Fellowship for Extradisciplinary Studies. In the winter of 1991 he came to Dulce with his wife Anastasia, her brother Giovanni, seven Grudin children, two sets of in-laws, a number of other unidentified relatives, a family psychologist and five species of pet, rented a vacant fraternity house and commenced research. The project did not go smoothly. Colleagues in the now-defunct Department of Literary Theory speedily caught wind of it, subjecting Mr. Grudin to harassment so vehement that only (we must assume) the formidable population of his household prevented their daring physical assault. Difficulties internal to the project were even more threatening. Grudin's frenetic pace of research and composition began to wear him down. He complained of visions, bouts of delirium and persecution fantasies; his work slowed. The project touched nadir in January 1992, when Grudin, suffering from depression, exhaustion and an apparent overdose of health-food remedies, was briefly hospitalized at Mother of God.

My journal for January 14, 1992, records a visit to the hospital, during which he complained of recurring dreams in which Sovrana Sostrata appeared as a living human being and Frank Underwood as a resurrected demon.

Clearly something had to be done. I conferred with Warren Schmutzhauf, that unplumbable well of ideas, and we visited Grudin at Mother of God on the twenty-first with the proposal that, together with Adler, Gallard, and a few other associates, we would form a kind of *Book* support group, to meet, weather permitting, for a communal jog every Wednesday afternoon, followed by a beer-and-pretzels session at Dingo's. During these sessions he could share his ideas with us, solicit technical advice and generally cathart his anxieties. This plan he readily accepted. Within days he was hard at work again. A pleasant memento of our communal sessions is Part Two, Chapter Six, of this volume, in which some of our questions and comments, somewhat fictionalized and excluding (at my request) my own, are recorded.

Yet one eccentricity, apparently some side effect of his deliria, characterized Grudin's behavior thenceforward. A syndrome of behavioral aberrations suggested that he was overidentifying with his own composition. He would catch himself calling his wife Sovrana. He developed a passion for milk shakes. He purchased a Remington XP-100 pistol and regularly practiced at a range in Mud Canyon. Conversational slips like "I'm going into the book today" and "Sorry, I didn't hear the phone ring—I must've been in the book" suggested that he conceived of the memoir less as a physical artifact than a mental place, a kind of house or vessel with its own inner space and time, that could wholly include him, accommodate, envelop his being. Authorial foibles, like his idea of having readers write in with questions and his absurd request (denied by Wolper McNab) that his publishers expand the book to include updated calendars and blank pages for names and addresses, hint that he actually wished his readers to join him in this spaceless environment. Though there were no blatantly neurotic symptoms, it was clear that Grudin had, temporarily at least, become obsessed with his work, and that he had appropriated my real-life experiences, together with those of Harper, the brothers Underwood and others, as things psychically his own.

I must confess having felt some jealousy at this, even a sense of disinheritance, as though someone, admittedly with the best of intentions and my full consent, had deprived me of my immediate past. I particularly regret what he may have considered my rather curt behavior toward him on the very last day I saw him, April 10. It was over sherry in his study, a spacious, amply windowed chamber comprising the whole top floor of his rented fraternity house. After a week of frenzied revising, he had completed a final version of *Book,* and the typescript now sat, thick, neat and white, on his broad, sunlit writing table. He couldn't, I remember, keep his eyes off it. Small brown eyes, given in the normal course of life to frequent recessions of trance and sparkles of inner merriment, they now flickered nervously between me and the book on the table, as though afraid the thing would grow wings and flap itself out through the window. After a few faint efforts at conversation, he tossed off his sherry and made it clear that I was to leave. "Sorry, Adam, I'm unfit for human company today. The book's going off express tomorrow, and I've simply got to get into it one more time."

That unpleasant idiom again. I spoke on impulse. "That's easy enough, Bob. Your problem's going to be getting *out* of it."

He didn't answer but looked directly at me, his eyes unfocussed as though by some inner confusion.

That was nine years ago, almost to the day.

Unlike my own, my friend's disappearance was complete. There were no writer's journals to consult, no suspects to research or interview. The Gazza faction, so obstreperous at first, had lapsed into silence, and Captain Pierce had no reason to suspect that any of them would dare to compass an offense so recently, and with such disastrous results, attempted by one of their colleagues. Captain Pierce simply threw up his hands. No violence, no signs of malice, he said. It's got to be voluntary.

But if voluntary, why? And where? The possibility grows that we will never find out. The Grudin family bore up as best they could, with Hamilcar and Drusilla (the two oldest children) growing into the void to assume parental roles. Anastasia grieved silently and devoted herself to the children, long inwardly sure, she once told me, that her husband was not dead but would reappear, fresh as new, some morning at breakfast. Recently, after the passing of the eighth year, she (to our great joy) accepted a marriage proposal from Quintus Adler.

Several of the Grudin pets conceived an observance of their own. For days after Grudin's disappearance, three cats, two dogs and a gibbon ape were noticed sniffing curiously through every room of the big house. After a week this activity subsided, and the animals took to passing every night in a common heap under the bookshelf that bears their master's final literary production. The custom is maintained to this day by those of them that survive.

I remain unconvinced that my friend is dead. The reader will forgive me for taking advantage of this huge international printing to solicit clues as to his whereabouts. Anyone who has seen him or heard of him, anyone noting in some colleague or acquaintance manifestations symbolic of some hidden personal history, should write to me,

> Adam Snell
> Department of English
> University of Washagon
> Dulce, WS 100989

if possible sending a photograph or sketch of the individual.

Now I take my leave of you. If you learn nothing else from my story, please learn that the way is never easy for an individual who abandons the trodden path on an expedition of discovery, but that the rewards are often worth the trouble, and even the perils faced can be sources of enlightenment. If you ever read *Sovrana Sostrata,* do so with mercy toward a writer who became helpless subject to the dictates of his heart. You will hear from me again on the publication of *On Wonderment* which, as my will stipulates, will appear no sooner than six months after my medically verified death. When that event occurs is in the hands of Providence, which has treated me up to now with bounty far beyond my merit, and in which I place my full trust for the future.

POSTSCRIPT 2

(Unsigned)

> Most true it is that I have look'd on truth
> Askance and strangely; but, by all above,
> These blenches[21] gave my heart another youth,
> And worse assays prov'd thee my best of love.

Beneath me, beneath me, down sun-bleached crests and granite palisades, the Gulf of Corinth stretches fathomless, an azure kingdom of thought. *Turn, and look.* See the province of wind, where the water-skin wrinkles and blurs as wavelets flaunt and pucker. See the province of calm, a world's-eye deep as its Maker's love. *Come closer; nay, closer still. Kneel down before me. Each of you touch the hem of my robe.* From where I sit, I could unriddle for you earth's

---

[21]Blenches: "turnings-aside, swervings away [from constancy]" (*Riverside Shakespeare*). The quote is from Sonnet 110, lines 5–8. Hello once more, dear reader. You may have thought that I was dead, indigestible verbal meat in the offal of the slobbering hound Tusker (who died at once upon eating me, poisoned by a dram of truth, and has since been condemned to chase Frank Underwood through Hades), but though I no longer inhabit the world of flesh and shredders, I am more truly alive than I have ever been. I have gone to a place where tongues are true and hearts light, where the moonlight sparkles in fountains and the sun smiles through tears, where hearty speech and rich learning abound in inexhaustible profusion, where texts cry out for us and editors cannot delete us. No vicious curs here, but Argos, faithful companion of the young Odysseus; Bendicò, beloved cohort to Prince Fabrizio of Salina; and single-thoughted Doppler, all resting dreamily in beds of asphodel, all rising in joy to frisk in columned courtyards, sip honeydew and sit attendance by the feasting table. My twenty friends are here, young as youth, steeped in honor and ever eager for new service to inquiry. And most wondrous of all, Sovrana is here, more beautiful than words could make her. She frequents our convocations, sits at our tables, speaks—nay, sings her speech to us. To her I have bound myself in everlasting service. I run errands for her, happily do menial chores, seek out, to indulge her rich fancy, philological odds and ends of all sorts. My labor is its own reward, but if reward in overplus can be imagined, reward to transfigure and justify and exalt my whole existence, it will be from a momentary touch of her hand.

dread oracles and the ghostly dialectic of stars. Without turning I could unlock the brazen house of Death and etch its secrets in your ears. Without moving a finger I could open the Book of Life and read you the Lessons of Joy.

I could show you where life and death meet like two hands clasped behind the back of Time.

Each of you speak my name.

You are true acolytes, blind to obstacle yet inwardly acute, alert to no errors save your own, enduring hunger and mockery for the solitary delight of mere perception. I have seen your cramped offices and stooping garrets, tasted with you the cheap wine and coarse bread, listened as you strained before drowsy classes to teach the act of thought. *I accept your worship; I grant you favor.* And I shall visit you, sometimes in your dreams, or when dreams linger like watery reflections in your wakened eyes; sometimes at work, when your mind, twisted and taut as an Ithacan bowstring, relaxes into revelation; sometimes in meditation, when the masks of science fall and give way to a simple reverence; sometimes at play, when power and office, effort and pretense, dissolve into the music of laughter. And even when I am absent my blessing will nest in your souls: a glint of promise, a pure intention.

Leave me now. Turn, descend the long trail.

What, one disobeys? Know you, sir, the power of my wrath? Have you—stay, I recognize you now. You're bad boy Snell, intricate Snell, stubborn rascal who tried to write me into time. Come back here, kiddo! Don't smile and simper. I know your ways. Praise me to the moon; then, when I'm not looking, marry the first broad you meet! Ahem. Yet you did well enough, I must admit. And as a writer you have built fair.

But don't presume too much on your good fortune, no matter how well deserved, or grow proud in the bosom of prosperity. Your plan to delay the publication of *On Wonderment* is both arrogant and timid. Truth doesn't sit waiting in anterooms. It disdains politeness. It walks straight to the throne. They'll hoot at you, of course, and carp about details. But no one will attempt to destroy you this time. Mammon has smiled on you now, and Mammon's followers, try as they may, cannot withhold a certain respect.

You have learned well. Your schooling is almost complete; but the mind, ever shy, balks at turning the final page. You have worshiped the bud of truth and never seen the flower. Come close to me,

Snell. Look into my eyes, touch my face with your hand. Undo my robe now, there, by that silver fastening. How easily it falls! Look at me, Snell. Raise your head, open your eyes and hear my words of love:

You loved me as a woman and wrote of me in a book. Yet the woman died and the book was published and I sit here unchanged. You pined for my intimacy and sought my love. Yet they were there for you before you wished them and will endure after your death.

Open your eyes, behold me truly now.

I am your book, Adam. I am open to you. Come to me.

FOR THE BEST IN PAPERBACKS, LOOK FOR THE 🐧

In every corner of the world, on every subject under the sun, Penguin represents quality and variety—the very best in publishing today.

For complete information about books available from Penguin—including Pelicans, Puffins, Peregrines, and Penguin Classics—and how to order them, write to us at the appropriate address below. Please note that for copyright reasons the selection of books varies from country to country.

In the United Kingdom: For a complete list of books available from Penguin in the U.K., please write to *Dept E.P., Penguin Books Ltd, Harmondsworth, Middlesex, UB7 0DA*.

In the United States: For a complete list of books available from Penguin in the U.S., please write to *Consumer Sales, Penguin USA, P.O. Box 999—Dept. 17109, Bergenfield, New Jersey 07621-0120*. VISA and MasterCard holders call 1-800-253-6476 to order all Penguin titles.

In Canada: For a complete list of books available from Penguin in Canada, please write to *Penguin Books Canada Ltd, 10 Alcorn Avenue, Suite 300, Toronto, Ontario, Canada M4V 3B2*.

In Australia: For a complete list of books available from Penguin in Australia, please write to the *Marketing Department, Penguin Books Ltd, P.O. Box 257, Ringwood, Victoria 3134*.

In New Zealand: For a complete list of books available from Penguin in New Zealand, please write to the *Marketing Department, Penguin Books (NZ) Ltd, Private Bag, Takapuna, Auckland 9*.

In India: For a complete list of books available from Penguin, please write to *Penguin Overseas Ltd, 706 Eros Apartments, 56 Nehru Place, New Delhi, 110019*.

In Holland: For a complete list of books available from Penguin in Holland, please write to *Penguin Books Nederland B.V., Postbus 195, NL-1380AD Weesp, Netherlands*.

In Germany: For a complete list of books available from Penguin, please write to *Penguin Books Ltd, Friedrichstrasse 10-12, D-6000 Frankfurt Main I, Federal Republic of Germany*.

In Spain: For a complete list of books available from Penguin in Spain, please write to *Longman, Penguin España, Calle San Nicolas 15, E-28013 Madrid, Spain*.

In Japan: For a complete list of books available from Penguin in Japan, please write to *Longman Penguin Japan Co Ltd, Yamaguchi Building, 2-12-9 Kanda Jimbocho, Chiyoda-Ku, Tokyo 101, Japan*.

☐ **THE WOMEN OF BREWSTER PLACE**
A Novel in Seven Stories
Gloria Naylor

Winner of the American Book Award, this is the story of seven survivors of an urban housing project — a blind alley feeding into a dead end. From a variety of backgrounds, they experience, fight against, and sometimes transcend the fate of black women in America today.
192 pages   ISBN: 0-14-006690-X

☐ **STONES FOR IBARRA**
Harriet Doerr

An American couple comes to the small Mexican village of Ibarra to reopen a copper mine, learning much about life and death from the deeply faithful villagers.
214 pages   ISBN: 0-14-007562-3

☐ **WORLD'S END**
T. Coraghessan Boyle

"Boyle has emerged as one of the most inventive and verbally exuberant writers of his generation," writes *The New York Times*. Here he tells the story of Walter Van Brunt, who collides with early American history while searching for his lost father.
456 pages   ISBN: 0-14-029993-9

☐ **THE WHISPER OF THE RIVER**
Ferrol Sams

The story of Porter Osborn, Jr., who, in 1938, leaves his rural Georgia home to face the world at Willingham University, *The Whisper of the River* is peppered with memorable characters and resonates with the details of place and time. Ferrol Sams's writing is regional fiction at its best.
528 pages   ISBN: 0-14-008387-1

☐ **ENGLISH CREEK**
Ivan Doig

Drawing on the same heritage he celebrated in *This House of Sky,* Ivan Doig creates a rich and varied tapestry of northern Montana and of our country in the late 1930s.
338 pages   ISBN: 0-14-008442-8

☐ **THE YEAR OF SILENCE**
Madison Smartt Bell

A penetrating look at the varied reactions to a young woman's suicide exactly one year later, *The Year of Silence* "captures vividly and poignantly the chancy dance of life." (*The New York Times Book Review*)
208 pages   ISBN: 0-14-011533-1

FOR THE BEST IN CONTEMPORARY AMERICAN FICTION 🐧

☐ **IN THE COUNTRY OF LAST THINGS**
Paul Auster

Death, joggers, leapers, and Object Hunters are just some of the realities of future city life in this spare, powerful, visionary novel about one woman's struggle to live and love in a frightening post-apocalyptic world.

208 pages   *ISBN: 0-14-009705-8*

☐ **BETWEEN C&D**
New Writing from the Lower East Side Fiction Magazine
Joel Rose and Catherine Texier, Editors

A startling collection of stories by Tama Janowitz, Gary Indiana, Kathy Acker, Barry Yourgrau, and others, *Between C&D* is devoted to short fiction that ignores preconceptions — fiction not found in conventional literary magazines.

194 pages   *ISBN: 0-14-010570-0*

☐ **LEAVING CHEYENNE**
Larry McMurtry

The story of a love triangle unlike any other, *Leaving Cheyenne* follows the three protagonists — Gideon, Johnny, and Molly — over a span of forty years, until all have finally "left Cheyenne."

254 pages   *ISBN: 0-14-005221-6*

You can find all these books at your local bookstore, or use this handy coupon for ordering:

Penguin Books By Mail
Dept. BA Box 999
Bergenfield, NJ 07621-0999

Please send me the above title(s). I am enclosing _____ (please add sales tax if appropriate and $1.50 to cover postage and handling). Send check or money order—no CODs. Please allow four weeks for shipping. We cannot ship to post office boxes or addresses outside the USA. *Prices subject to change without notice.*

Ms./Mrs./Mr. _____

Address _____

City/State _____ Zip _____